The Elements of

BOAT STRENGTH

for Builders, Designers, and Owners

▼

DAVE GERR

INTERNATIONAL MARINE / McGRAW-HILL

Camden, Maine • New York • San Francisco • Washington, D.C. • Auckland
Bogotá • Caracas • Lisbon • London • Madrid • Mexico City • Milan
Montreal • New Delhi • San Juan • Singapore • Sydney • Tokyo • Toronto

Also by Dave Gerr

Propeller Handbook
The Nature of Boats: Insights and Esoterica
for the Nautically Obsessed

To Honor and Clare, who prove
that the future must be bright.

International Marine
A Division of The McGraw·Hill Companies

10

Copyright © 2000 International Marine
All rights reserved. The publisher takes no responsibility for the use of any of the materials or methods described in this book, nor for the products thereof. The name "International Marine" and the International Marine logo are trademarks of The McGraw-Hill Companies. Printed in the United States of America.

Library of Congress Cataloging-in-Publication Data
Gerr, Dave.
    The elements of boat strength : for builders, designers, and owners / Dave Gerr.
      p. cm.
    Includes bibliographical references and index.
    ISBN 0-07-023159-1 (alk paper)
    1. Boatbuilding.   2. Boats and boating—Maintenance and repair.   I. Title.
VM321.G44 1999
623.8'17—dc21   99-28949
                            CIP

Questions regarding the content of this book should be addressed to
    International Marine
    P.O. Box 220
    Camden, ME 04843
    www.internationalmarine.com

Questions regarding the ordering of this book should be addressed to
    The McGraw-Hill Companies
    Customer Service Department
    P.O. Box 547
    Blacklick, OH 43004
    Retail customers: 1-800-262-4729
    Bookstores: 1-800-722-4726

This book is printed on 60# Finch smooth
Printed by Quebecor, Fairfield, PA
Drawings, charts, and photographs by Dave
    Gerr, unless otherwise noted
Design by Faith Hague
Production by Janet Robbins
Edited by Jonathan Eaton, Alex Barnett,
    Constance Burt, and Pamela Benner

NOTE: Although every effort has been made to present rules and procedures that will produce strong, safe, and long-lasting hulls, the builder uses the information in this book at his or her own risk. The author and International Marine make no representations as to the suitability of these rules and procedures for determining the scantlings of any vessel. If a builder needs any further information regarding the use of a scantling rule or engineering boat structures, he or she is urged to consult a qualified naval architect or marine engineer. The author welcomes information regarding any suggestions, corrections of errors or omissions, and other improvements readers may suggest.

CONTENTS

FORMULAS, TABLES, AND CHARTS

ACKNOWLEDGMENTS

*T*his book, like any other, is the result of many solitary hours of hard work. No book, however, could be successful without outside aid. Indeed, many individuals and companies provided assistance to me throughout my writing and in my office's ongoing design work, which needed completion at the same time. Without their help, *The Elements of Boat Strength* simply could not have been finished.

In particular, Jon Eaton, at International Marine, was an unflagging source of support and guidance, and a pillar of patience throughout this all-consuming project. Pat Kearns, of the American Boat & Yacht Council (ABYC), provided far more assistance than I think she ever realized. And the ABYC itself has proven, time and time again, to be the most invaluable resource for technical information—perhaps the finest association in the industry.

Captain Bill Brogdon undertook the Herculean task of checking each and every formula, as well as reading through the entire manuscript. His corrections, suggestions, insights, and additions were invaluable and mightily appreciated.

My ever-trusty staff of design engineers kept work flowing through the office while I was—more often than I had planned—otherwise occupied with writing and research. Alan Salisch and Mark Kunz, your efforts made a tremendous difference.

Kanter Yachts, Covey Island Boatworks, Kortchmar & Willner, Cape Dory/Newport Shipyards, Westbourne Custom Yachts, American Dream Makers, North River Boatworks, Hills Marine, and Sutherland Boat and Coach all have built some of my designs, and were generous in sharing know-how and experiences—a source of much lore and insight. The Lund Boat Company, Derecktor Shipyards, Topper Hermanson Boats, and Treworgy Yachts each took time from their busy schedule to provide valuable photographs and information. Paul Fleury and Michael Charters selflessly shared their electrical know-how.

And then there are the many friends and clients who have kept me going and shared their experiences so generously: Spyros Garbis, Chris Wentz, Herb Gliick, Frank MacLear, Carol and Gene Montgomery, Paul and Anne Cohen, David Raskin, Paul and Linda Bremer, Tom Reinertson and Arlah Alley, and Sam and Judy Haigh—just a few of the many wonderful individuals who have helped make my work so rewarding.

INTRODUCTION

This book was not written for specialists looking for the latest arcane developments in structural engineering; rather, it was written for the average boatbuilder (amateur or professional), mechanic, marine surveyor, serious yachtsman, and naval architect. *The Elements of Boat Strength* is intended to be an easy-to-use reference for calculating reliable, practical, and solid scantlings for boats of differing types and service. (*Scantlings* are the sizes, shapes, materials, and weights of the structural components of a boat.)

It is necessary to take the time to make sense of a few tables and graphs; however, all the calculations in this book can be done by anyone with a basic understanding of high-school math and every formula can be solved using an inexpensive, student-grade scientific calculator.

Boats are packed with odd, complex, and interesting structures and assemblies. To make things plain, I've included many photos—so many that they've spilled over into a photo gallery, which begins on page 332.

Why *The Elements of Boat Strength?*

As I write this, I'm working on a case in which a production boat's hull flexed so much in ordinary weather that one of its windows literally blew out underway. I've seen vessels that had engine mounts cracked from inadequate engine beds and a transmission that split open at sea due to improper engineering and installation. There was the aluminum charter boat with 80 percent of its underwater welds burned away by corrosion, and the aluminum ocean-racer with its hull stove in in just 30 knots of wind and 6-foot (2 m) seas. I've seen hulls with gallons of water in their foam or balsa cores, and vessels whose keels fell off. Boats have sunk because bulkheads popped loose or masts snapped or chainplates ripped out or steel plates rusted to nothing.

This is the reason for *The Elements of Boat Strength*—the need for well-engineered and well-built boats. Boats carry sailors to sea. Their first, last, and most important job is to take their crew out and bring them back safely, come what may. If your vessel's structure isn't up to snuff—sooner or later—a day of reckoning will come. With luck, this day will be merely expensive and inconvenient. Without luck, lives may be lost. The procedures and recommendations in *The Elements of Boat Strength* will help ensure that your next boat is up to its most important job . . . without needing luck at all.

Boat-Structure Calculations and Practices

The construction of boats—until the last 150 years or so, almost always wooden boats—dates back to the ancient Phoenicians and beyond. The ensuing three or four millennia of cut-and-try, experiment-and-discard, test-and-retest have gradually taught us how to build vessels that will hold together . . . most of the time. It wasn't, however, until the last 150 or so years that the art of building boats strong enough—but no stronger than needed—was formalized. Indeed, there are two standard methods for determining the scantlings of a vessel: The first method—and by far the oldest—is rule-of-thumb; the second is engineering analysis. Rule-of-thumb is considerably quicker and easier to apply; however, simple rule-of-thumb can be unreliable and limiting—especially when you stray from the norm or when you use new or different materials.

Scantling Rules

The most reliable and most practical rules-of-thumb are formalized "scantling rules." These rules are based on engineering analysis cross-checked against a database of successful vessels. The results are then condensed and simplified for quick application using easily determined factors. This is the subject of this book. Such rules establish the required construction materials and dimensions based on a few easily obtainable numbers, such as length overall, displacement, and boat speed. Scantling rules have been one of the principal methods of specifying boat construction for well over a hundred years. They have been used by classification societies, such as the American Bureau of Shipping (ABS) and Lloyds, and by many of the finest designers and builders, such as Herreshoff and Nevins. Because of their ease of use—as compared with a detailed engineering analysis—many builders and designers prefer to work with scantling rules. It is important to keep in mind, however, that scantling rules work *only* for the specific type and size of boat intended by the initial rulemaker.

The scantling rules in this book were developed by the author and are intended to cover all monohull vessels between 10 and 120 feet (3 and 37 m) in length overall, power and sail, displacement and planing, up to about 45 knots top speed. For larger and smaller vessels, for multihulls, and for higher speed, builders must do a more detailed engineering analysis.

Determining Scantlings by Engineering Analysis

Engineering analysis—although considerably more time-consuming than scantling rules—frees the builder to use unusual combinations of materials; to push the performance envelope; to employ unique structural solutions, unusual hull forms or deck structures, and experimental fittings and gear; and to design any specific component of a boat sensibly and with reasonable certainty. Engineering boat structures is a relatively modern approach (compared to rule-of-thumb and scantling rules). The concept of systematic, detailed engineering of a boat structure is not much over 150 years old. In most cases, smaller craft—under 100 feet (30 m) or so—have been built by rule-of-thumb almost exclusively until shortly after World War II. Nevertheless, if you're involved in cutting-edge boatbuilding, you should gain a basic understanding of engineering, thus acquiring the tools to solve the unusual construction questions that you are sure to encounter.

I'm pleased to offer this book, with its easy-to-use scantling rules and detailed discussions of materials and building techniques for the most common standard forms of fiberglass, wood, aluminum, and steel construction. Throughout the book are worked examples to make the processes clear and straightforward. The appendices contain reference material such as bolt-strength tables, unit-conversion tables, and the like.

Alternate Building Methods

I wouldn't even begin to claim that the methods and approaches in *The Elements of Boat Strength* are the only means to build strong, safe boats. I wouldn't even claim that these methods are necessarily the best methods. Indeed, there are so many ingenious and clever alternatives for creating objects as complex and wonderful as boats that no single book could hope to include even a small fraction of them. You should, however, find that the scantlings given here will produce safe, sound, cost-effective vessels. I would even claim that—if the methods given are followed carefully and with common sense—the result will be a superior boat.

Decimal Exponents

Decimal exponents are used extensively throughout this book. If you "don't like math," decimal exponents can seem a little technical. Don't let them put you off, however. Decimal exponents are easy to master; it takes just a few moments. For instance, in

Formula-, Table-, and Chart- Numbering System

The formulas and tables in this book are numbered sequentially together, for each chapter. For example, Formula 4-2 is the second formula in the fourth chapter. Table 4-9 follows Formula 4-8, even though there is no Table 4-8. In almost all cases, the charts (or graphs) are associated with a specific formula. Thus, Chart 4-3 is a graphic representation of Formula 4-3. All such charts have the same number as their formula. Of course, not every formula has a corresponding chart; Formula 4-2 does not, for instance. Accordingly, there will be gaps in the numbering for either formulas, charts, or tables taken separately. Taken as a whole, they run in order in each chapter. This should help you locate specific items. For example, if you're searching for Chart 4-10, and happen to flip open to Formula 4-16, you simply page back through the formula and table numbers until you reach Chart 4-10 (and its related formula) in sequence.

Formula 9-1 for plank thickness (Plank Thickness, in. $= 0.74 \times Sn^{0.4}$), 0.4 is the decimal exponent.

It is quite easy to solve this on a pocket scientific calculator (an inexpensive one from any local stationery store or Radio Shack); but it is important to understand what decimal exponents are

$X^{0.5}$ *is the same as* $X^{1/2}$ *is the same as* $\sqrt{X}$ *or* $\sqrt[2]{X}$ *, the square root of X*

$X^{0.334}$ *is the same as* $X^{1/3}$ *is the same as* $\sqrt[3]{X}$ *, the cube root of X*

and so on.

You can see that a decimal is just another way of writing a fraction and that it makes no difference whether we use a decimal or a fraction as the exponent. (The decimal, of course, is easier to enter in a calculator.)

You also can see that a decimal or fractional exponent is the same as taking the root of a number, and the root is always the same as the inverse (or reciprocal) of the decimal. Thus, raising a number to the 0.5 power is the same as taking the square root of that number. (The inverse or reciprocal of 0.5 = 1 ÷ 0.5 = 2, and $\sqrt{X}$ is the same as $\sqrt[2]{X}$.) Raising a number to the 0.334 power is the same as taking the cube root of that number. (The reciprocal of 0.334 = 1 ÷ 0.334 = 3, giving $\sqrt[3]{X}$.)

The nice thing about decimal exponents is that they allow quick manipulation of formulas with exponential relationships that don't happen to fall exactly on even powers or roots, such as square or cube roots. In the case of Formula 9-1, the data showed that plank thickness did not vary as the square root of the scantling number (Sn), but as the Sn to the 0.4 power. This could be rewritten a number of ways:

$$Sn^{0.4} \text{ is the same as } Sn^{4/10} \text{ is the same as } \sqrt[10]{Sn^4}$$

Not only is the 0.4 exponent easier to enter into a calculator, it is also easier to write by hand or to type. Try it yourself. Take your calculator and punch in the number for the Sn. Then, hit the exponentiation key (usually the X^y key). Now enter the exponent and finally press the equal key. That's it, there's your answer. For example, if you raise an Sn of 2.5 to the 0.4 power, the answer would be 1.44; an Sn of 8.7 raised to the 0.4 power would equal 2.37.

ONE

Scantling Rules and the Scantling Number

The principal reference point for all the scantling rules in *The Elements of Boat Strength* is the scantling number (Sn). To determine the dimensions, weights, and shapes of structural components for a boat, it is first necessary to determine the Sn for the vessel being considered. The system laid out here has been designed so that the Sn is the same for all the rules (for each material), for any given boat, so that the resulting Sn value is numerically the same whether calculated in English or metric units. Only length, beam, and depth of hull are required for the basic Sn calculation.

FORMULA 1-1

The Scantling Number (Sn)

$Sn = LOA$ (ft.) $\times$ Beam (ft.) $\times$ Depth of Hull (ft.) $\div 1,000$ (English)

$Sn = LOA$ (m) $\times$ Beam (m) $\times$ Depth of Hull (m) $\div 28.32$ (Metric)

Where

LOA = Length overall of the hull proper, not including bow pulpits, false stems on clipper bows, rails, stern platforms, boomkins, and bowsprits

Beam = Beam overall of the hull proper, not including rub strips, guards, and rails

Depth of Hull = Depth of hull at midships from the sheer down to the top of the keel inside the boat; depth of hull is not draft

NOTE: Midships is at exactly half the waterline length, not half the LOA.

Example:

If our new vessel, *Fish 'n Squish*, had the following dimensions,

LOA	40.00 ft.	12.19 m
WL	37.20 ft.	11.34 m
Beam	12.56 ft.	3.83 m
Depth of Hull	5.91 ft.	1.80 m

it would have an Sn of 2.97.

40 ft. LOA $\times$ 12.56 ft. Beam $\times$ 5.91 ft. Depth of Hull $\div$ 1,000 = 2.969; use 2.97

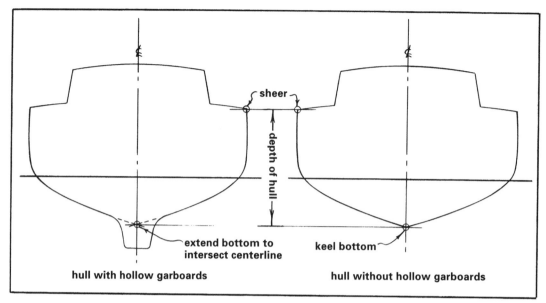

Determining depth of hull at midships

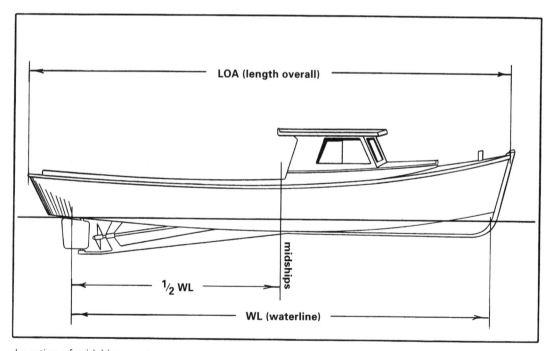

Location of midships

*12.19 m LOA × 3.83 m Beam × 1.80 m
Depth of Hull ÷ 28.3 = 2.969; use 2.97*

Adjusting for Long Overhangs

When the LOA divided by Waterline Length (WL) is greater than 108 percent, find the corrected LOA to use in the Sn calculation:

FORMULA 1-2
Long-Overhang Correction for Formula 1-1

$$Corrected\ LOA = (LOA + WL) \div 2$$

Adjusting for Hollow Garboards and/or a Deep Sump

In vessels with pronounced hollow garboards and/or a deep sump, the depth-of-hull measurement will be proportionately too large. For such craft, a sketch of the midships section should be made, and the hull bottom—port and starboard—should be extended down and in to intersect the centerline. Take the depth-of-hull measurement from sheer down to this intersection.

Adjusting for Pronounced Flare

As with depth of hull, vessels that have pronounced flare amidships (i.e., outward slope to their topsides) will have large beams overall in proportion to their volume. This too will generate an excessively large Sn. When beam overall is more than 1.12 percent of beam on the waterline, find the corrected beam to use in the Sn calculation.

FORMULA 1-3
Pronounced-Flare Correction for Formula 1-1

$$Corrected\ Beam = (Beam\ Overall + Beam\ Waterline) \div 2$$

NOTE: When a vessel has extreme tumblehome (i.e., the opposite of flare), use the maximum beam overall without any correction.

Additional Adjustment Factors

The Sn is the starting point for entering and using the rules that follow. Speed, type of service, and displacement-length (D/L) ratio will be used in specific instances (in the following rules) to adjust the scantling results. The Sn itself, however, applies consistently to all standard hull forms because it approximates total hull volume, which is closely linked to displacement, and required power for a given speed—the two principal factors determining the loads on a vessel. Because the Sn is closely tied to true weight or displacement, no adjustment for displacement is necessary for vessels with D/L ratios between 275 and 100. This range covers the majority of ordinary craft. Adjustments for higher or lower D/L ratios are covered in each specific rule as they apply.

Scantling Rules Apply to Standard Construction Methods and Materials

The scantling rules that follow are intended for use with normal or standard construction methods and materials. High-modulus materials (e.g., carbon fiber, Spectra, and Kevlar) are not generally covered; nor are what are currently somewhat exotic techniques such as prepreg laminates, glued rather than welded aluminum, and foam-cored cold-molded wood. If you wish to build with such materials and methods, you must do a detailed engineering analysis.

Types of Vessels Covered by *The Elements of Boat Strength*'s Scantling Rules

It is critical to note again that the scantling rules in this book were developed by the author, to cover only

- standard monohull vessels (i.e., power and sail, displacement and planing)
- vessels between 10 and 120 feet (3 and 37 m) length overall
- vessels with a maximum speed of 45 knots

To determine scantlings for larger or smaller vessels, for multihulls, and for higher-speed craft, builders must do a detailed engineering analysis or consult a qualified naval architect or marine engineer.

TWO

Fiberglass Construction Materials and Methods

*I*t is necessary to understand fiberglass itself before we describe the scantling-rule calculation for fiberglass boats: what is fiberglass? What are its constituents? How was it developed? How is it fabricated and handled? What special considerations must be accounted for in its design and construction?

History and Development of Fiberglass Construction

Modern fiberglass boat construction is based on an ancient principle: adding just 2 percent of a fiber-like impurity to something like clay or plaster of Paris will dramatically increase its strength—especially its resistance to cracking on impact or in bending. This is why, for instance, you can't make bricks without straw—at least not strong, usable bricks. The more fiber you add in proportion to the binder (the fiber-to-binder ratio or fiber content), the stronger the combination—the composite. As you can see, the first "composite material" application is

several thousand years old. Of course, if you try to combine much more than 2 percent fiber (straw or whatever), things get too stiff to mix or work properly. Instead, you have to add the binder to the fiber rather than the other way around.

PAPER "HIGH-TECH" COMPOSITES

Papier-mâché, for example, is nothing more than this, and it's another "high-tech" composite that has been with us for three or more millennia. The ancient Egyptians used it to make sarcophagi (i.e., highly molded and brightly painted coffins); eighteenth-century Europeans utilized it to make jewelry boxes and furniture; and during World War II, it was even employed—in a big way, believe it or not—to make airplane fuel tanks! Papier-mâché has its drawbacks—it's not especially strong; it's not at all fire-resistant; and, worst of all, it's unable to stand up to moisture. As long as it is kept well painted or varnished and in a reasonably dry environment, fine; get it wet, though, and it's finished.

BAKE-A-LITE?

Strangely, it was largely the pressures of the newfangled electronics industry that encouraged improved composites. The old insulators—gutta-percha, waxed paper, shellac, and ceramics (which had been adequate for the ordinary telegraph-line voltages)—weren't up to the job as we began using higher currents. The Belgian chemist Leo Baekeland found in 1906 that reacting phenol and formaldehyde would produce a reasonably tough and somewhat water-resistant resin. It wasn't until many months later that he realized that adding fibers (in this case, in powdered form) to his brittle resin would generate superior strength. The result was Bakelite, the first "modern" high-tech composite and the beginning of our contemporary plastics revolution. Between the two world wars, many household appliances and a vast amount of electric equipment were fitted or equipped with Bakelite handles, knobs, cases, and insulators.

ASBESTOS, ANYONE?

From here on, it was a regular, ongoing process to increase strength, stiffness, and weather resistance in these new, highly moldable composite wonder goos. All sorts of binder/chemical combinations were tried along with all manner of fibers—everything from wood pulp to asbestos. Indeed, asbestos-phenolic composites seemed to have all the answers at the end of World War II. Known largely as Durestos, this material was tough, strong, and quite stiff, rivaling even modern laminates in some respects. Back then, no one was much concerned with asbestos health risks, so I guess we can consider ourselves lucky that Durestos didn't gain wide acceptance. Think of the multimillion-dollar

Plug for deck and hull for the author's 72-foot (21.9 m) charter schooner design.

Durestos cleanups that would be underway today if it had!

Modern Fiberglass Construction

Today, we've settled on fiberglass fibers (nothing more than modern-day straw) in polyester resins (modern-day clay) as the most suitable and cost-effective combination for building large, waterproof, composite structures—boats. The process most builders use is almost precisely identical to the application of papier-mâché, employed by the ancient Egyptians. For ancient papier-mâché sarcophagi, a hollow female mold was made from clay or plaster of Paris. It was coated with a mold-release agent (the Egyptians used soap or linseed oil) so the layup wouldn't stick. Alternating layers of paste or glue and paper then were laid in and pressed tightly down until the desired thickness was built up.

The majority of modern production hulls are built up exactly this way. If you were building a new boat, *Glass Slipper,* you would build a hollow female mold (the shape of the hull), which then is coated with a mold-release agent (today, a wax). Next, alternating layers of polyester resin and fiberglass cloth (of varying styles and weights) are laid in until the desired thickness is reached. Maybe "modern" technology isn't quite as modern as we think it is!

HAND LAYUP, VACUUM-BAGGING, OR CHOPPER GUN

What was described previously is commonly known as *hand layup*. It is the most widely used and one of the most successful methods of forming a hull. There are, however, two standard alternatives. The first is really a hand-layup enhancement: the entire hand-layup process on *Glass Slipper* is performed as described, but—after the layup and before the resin cures—a vacuum bag (really a sheet of plastic) is taped in place over the fiberglass in the hollow female mold. Some of the air is sucked out by a pump, causing the outside air to press down evenly on the entire plastic sheet—and thus the laminate—with great force. The result is extremely dense, strong, even layups—considerably stronger than hand layups. This is because vacuum-bagged layups have more glass in proportion to the resin. (Remember, the more fiber you use—if properly applied—the stronger the laminate.)

Atmospheric pressure, by the way, is about 14.7 pounds per square inch (psi) (101 kPa). Using *Glass Slipper*'s builder's trusty vacuum pump, if pressure were reduced by just 25 percent to 11 psi (76 kPa), the resulting force on and through the vacuum bag would be 3.7 psi (25.5 kPa). Doesn't sound like much? Well, 3.7 psi equals 533 pounds per square foot (25.5 kPa equals 2,600 kg/m^2). And if *Glass Slipper* were an average 28-footer (8.5 m), it would have about 480 square feet (44.6 m^2) of hull surface. Net result: 255,800 pounds (115,900 kg) total pressure—about equal to a 115-ton hydraulic press! (In practice, pressures of 7 to 9 psi [48 to 62 kPa] are common.)

At the other end of the spectrum is the chopper-gun layup (see photo on p. 332). With a special gun, the builder blows small, short glass fibers mixed with liquid resin onto the surface of the mold. This is then rolled down by hand. (The short fibers are called *chopped fibers*; hence the name *chopper gun*.) Because the fibers are short, run in random direction, and laid down without precise thickness control, a chopper-gun-layup *Glass Slipper* hull is less dense and less strong than a hand-laid-up hull, and far less strong than one that is vacuum-bagged. But chopper-gun layup is very quick and low cost.

We know chopper-gun hulls are cheap. Does this mean they are bad? It doesn't, but—as always—you get what you pay for. Clearly, chopper-gun layups have to be thicker and thus heavier for the same approximate strength. Even so, they don't quite reach the reserve of strength and longevity that a good hand-laid-up hull has. Still, if cutting-edge performance is not a major factor and getting boats out on the water inexpensively is, a properly engineered chopper-gun hull can fill the bill.

ADVANTAGES AND DISADVANTAGES OF THE THREE STANDARD METHODS

Knowing all this, we can assess the pros and cons of the three standard laminating methods. Generally, hand layup is the industry standard. A properly hand-laid-up hull has a smooth, even surface inside and out, and has constant thickness throughout each specific region of the hull. The mechanical properties of the hull will be more than adequate for the majority of average vessels.

Vacuum-bagged laminates are denser, with less resin in proportion to the glass-fiber reinforcement. Such laminates have higher mechanical properties for the same thickness. Although not required for sound hulls, designers and builders can reduce weight or increase performance (or both) by using vacuum-bagging. The vacuum-bagging procedure can add construction costs (often less than expected), and skins on sandwich construction may become too thin for safety on smaller craft or high-speed vessels.

Chopper-gun layups are low cost and—because they have the highest resin content per weight—are the weakest, or have the lowest mechanical properties. Chopper-gun layups are suited to mass production of hulls where weight and performance are not critical. Chopper-gun layups can also be used effectively to fabricate internal and secondary components on otherwise hand-laid-up hulls. Of course, these same parts would be lighter if hand-laid-up or vacuum-bagged, but the cost savings in production applications may be well worth this compromise.

Considerations in Sandwich Fiberglass Construction

Contrary to some common conceptions, fiberglass is neither particularly strong for its weight nor particularly stiff—indeed, fiberglass is rather bendy. To compensate, these days many boats are laid up using *sandwich construction*. Such vessels have cores of end-grain balsa; closed-cell foam; plastic honeycomb or plastic-impregnated paper honeycomb; or, in areas of high loads, plywood or solid wood, with thin fiberglass skins inside and out. This is excellent construction practice if properly engineered and properly fabricated. It increases stiffness without adding weight and—as a bonus—adds built-in insulation.

PROPER CORE INSTALLATION

While on the subject of cores, it is important to note that any of the closed-cell foams from major manufacturers is acceptable. End-grain balsa core is also extremely good. Indeed, it currently provides the highest stiffness for the lowest cost of any core. It is critical that the balsa core be presaturated with resin before layup. If it isn't, when the first layer of fiberglass mat is applied against the new *Glass Slipper*'s core, the dry balsa will wick away the resin and ultimately lead to a core-bond failure. This is a really big—frequently uncorrectable—problem.

GETTING GOOD CORE-TO-LAMINATE BOND

The proper core-installation procedure is to lay up the outside skin (inside the female mold), then lay down a wet, resin-rich layer of chopped-strand mat, and squish down the precoated (or presaturated) core onto the still-wet, resin-soggy mat.

Because hulls have compound curvature, almost all cores (balsa and foam) come in sheets cut with *kerfs* (i.e., slits or notches) into numerous little squares, which in turn are bonded to a thin, flexible (usually thin, light fiberglass) binder sheet. The kerfs are necessary for the core sheet to bend and mold into the hull shape. When installed, however, the kerfs also spread open, leaving small voids running along the core. It is *critical* that the kerfs be filled with as much resin as possible. For both balsa and foam, the best procedure is to drape the core sheets over the corner of an upturned barrel, for example. This spreads the kerfs so the builder can spray (hot-coat) the core with resin with maximum penetration into the open cuts (i.e., the kerfs).

Prepared and precoated like this, the core must be rolled down hard by hand while both the core and soggy mat are still wet. The purpose of the resin-rich squishy mat in conjunction with the precoated core is to ensure a good bond between the skin laminate and the core, and to squish as much resin up into the core's kerfs as possible. Properly done, this procedure will produce a very sound, long-lasting hull.

Some companies manufacture special core-bond putties to be used in place of the wet mat. These putties are applied or troweled onto the hull and the precoated core is again rolled down hard on it. Next, a vibrator is used on top of the core to help further press the core down on the putty and to work as much putty up into the core kerfs as possible. Core-bond putties can be used instead of the resin-rich mat, as and when specified by the core manufacturer. Correctly applied, such putties are excellent, but the builder absolutely must use either resin-rich mat or a proper dedicated core-bond putty between the core and the skin laminates to ensure a proper bond. You cannot use ordinary Bondo or some home-brewed putty for core-bonding.

In a female mold, the core kerfs are almost always laid down (facing outward); however, the builder must still use either resin-rich mat or putty between the core and the inside skins as well. It cannot be overemphasized how critical careful attention to detail in bonding and installing cores is to a successful hull.

The best method of bonding a core to a hull is to vacuum-bag it—even if the rest of the laminate is not vacuum-bagged. Most builders report virtually no additional labor in vacuum-bagging cores. At the same time, vacuum-bagging presses the core down onto the skins with the maximum pressure attainable and also sucks up resin to fill all the kerfs nearly 100 percent with resin.

PEA-SOUP CORE FAILURES

Virtually the opposite of high-quality hand-layup, fiber-reinforced plastic (FRP) with foam core, or presaturated balsa core, is inexpensive chopper-gun boats with balsa cores. Frequently, these are installed in, say, their transoms as stiffening for the outboard mount.

Again, the only way to get a good bond between the fiberglass layers and the balsa core is to press down hard—hand-rolling fabric styles or vacuum-bagging. Chopper-gun spraying, even after rolling, applies less reliable and predictable pressure. What's worse, such boats—built in small shops—are often constructed on a lean budget and tight schedule. The builder will be tempted to skimp on (or even ignore totally) presaturating the core.

With the engine-mount fastening gear and the continuous engine and prop vibrations, it is not a question of *if* the transom and core will fail, but rather *when*. I've seen boats in the shop for repairs with such construction. When the transoms were taken apart—often you could peel them open with your fingertips—the rotten balsa inside resembled congealed, decaying pea soup. It is this kind of third- or fourth-rate construction that has given balsa a questionable reputation in some circles, which is totally undeserved. Balsa is one of the best cores when installed correctly. (The proper chopper-gun transom core, by the way, is marine plywood carefully presaturated with three coats of polyester resin *before* it's laid in and sprayed up or chopped over.)

WATER-FILLED CORES

Similarly, I've seen boats that were hand-laid-up with foam cores using ordinary auto-body Bondo as core putty, with no mat and no core presaturation or hot-coating. One of these vessels, a 34-foot (10.4 m) fishing boat, leaked through an improperly bedded spray strip. Water was forced, under pressure, so effectively through the screw holes and into all the open channels left by the unfilled kerfs that nearly the entire hull shell—from keel to sheer—was filled with water (see photo on p. 332). When this boat was hauled out of the water, water literally shot out of holes drilled in the bottom. One hole alone filled a 1-gallon (3.8 l) coffee can three-quarters full in just a few minutes. This was a new boat and it was never fully reparable. This would not have happened with proper core-bonding procedures.

AVOID EXCESS RESIN

Although the mat layers between the cores and the skins should be resin-rich and squishy, this is the *only* place a layup should be soggy. The *sole* way to get a strong, light layup is to use just enough resin to get a thorough wet-out and a good bond—*not one whit more*. Again, the more fiber (i.e., fiberglass) used in proportion to the binder (i.e., resin), the stronger the laminate. Any additional resin actually reduces strength. Strangely, some builders don't know this. Whether you're designing or building, it is vital to keep this principle in mind.

Components of Traditional Fiberglass Laminates

Since fiberglass was introduced for hull construction in the late 1940s and early 1950s, there have been just three "standard" fiber-

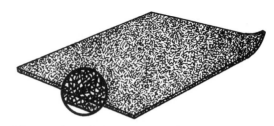

Mat consists of short chopped fibers running in all directions. Squashed together (usually in a binder), these fibers generate relatively low strength. (Courtesy Brunswick Technologies, Inc.)

glass materials, all commonly composed of E-glass (ordinary, electrical-, or construction-grade fiberglass).

CHOPPED-STRAND MAT

Chopped-strand mat (CSM)—frequently known simply as *mat*—is literally that: strands of glass fibers are chopped into short pieces (about 1/2 inch to 2 inches [12 to 50 mm] long) and mashed together with a temporary binder called a *seizing*. The result is a mat-like material. Because the mat's fibers are short and run every which way, it is not particularly strong. However, it is fairly easy to wet-out, and—because it is soft, thick, bulky, and somewhat sponge-like when wet—it is good for bonding to layers of other types of glass and cores. For this reason, the most common way to lay up a hull is with alternating layers of mat and woven roving.

WOVEN ROVING

Woven roving is a heavy, coarse fabric literally woven from bundles of glass fibers. Because the fibers run for long lengths in two specific directions (at right angles to each other), woven roving forms a strong reinforcement. In fact, an all-roving laminate can be nearly twice as strong, for the same weight, as the

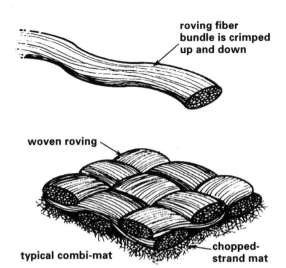

roving fiber
bundle is crimped
up and down

woven roving

typical combi-mat

chopped-
strand mat

Woven roving is much stronger than mat because the fiber bundles are aligned in neat rows
at right angles to each other. The crimping of the
roving bundles does weaken them some, and
the small gaps made by the thick bundle's weave
makes for a higher resin content than with a
uni-di (see p. 20). Nevertheless, roving and is
the "standard" layup reinforcement, and is excellent for most ordinary vessels. (Courtesy Brunswick
Technologies, Inc.)

standard combined-roving-mat laminate. It
takes great skill and attention to detail, however, to produce a high-quality, all-roving
layup. Without soft, spongy mat between the
roving layers, it is difficult to make the comparatively hard, flat plies of roving stick to
each other reliably. Because the combined-
roving-mat layup has proved adequate for ordinary boats, few builders go to this extra
expense.

FIBERGLASS CLOTH

True fiberglass cloth is also quite strong. It is
used almost exclusively in small boats and for
finish work, though, because it is fairly expensive. Unlike woven roving, glass cloth has
a very fine weave, not dissimilar to the fiber-

glass, fireproof curtains you can buy in department stores. Glass cloth is often used as
a surface layer to smooth out the roughness of
mat and woven roving. For instance, a simple
single layer of glass cloth on the inside of the
hull makes a nice smooth finish. Accordingly,
lightweight fiberglass cloth is sometimes
termed *finishing cloth*.

STANDARD POLYESTER RESIN

The most common resin for fiberglass construction is ortho-polyester resin. (Fiberglass
is also known as FRP for *fiber-reinforced plastic* or GRP for *glass-reinforced plastic*.) The
liquid polyester is mixed with a catalyst and
an accelerator to produce a chemical reaction
chemists call *polymerization*. Boatbuilders—
being practical—just call it *curing*. This
means that the molecules in the plastic inter-
lock with each other to form a very rigid unit.
Ideally, the whole hull (or at least its plastic
part) is just one long-chain (i.e., interlinked)
molecule. If you visualize this giant "molecule" wrapped around all that glass reinforcement, you get an idea of why glass boats work
so well.

MEKP: THE CATALYST

Although there are a number of catalysts
available, the most frequently used is methyl
ethyl ketone reacted with hydrogen peroxide,
or MEKP. MEKP is tricky stuff. It is highly
corrosive and, if it touches your skin, you better wash pretty darn quick. Even more excit-
ing, MEKP is rather volatile—yes, it can
explode. In fact, if the accelerator used to
speed up the curing process were to come in
direct contact with the MEKP, an explosion
and certainly a fire could result. Accordingly,
most polyester resins used in boatbuilding
come with an accelerator already mixed in.

THE STANDARD FIBERGLASS LAYUP

During the past 40 years or so, the standard, plain-vanilla hull layup has become alternating layers of woven roving and CSM. As with the core, the mat between roving layers produces better adhesion between layers (a better interlaminar bond); however, except at the core, the mat shouldn't be any wetter than absolutely necessary. Most frequently, builders will purchase this combination already stitched together: a woven roving with a mat stitched or glued to it. Such fabrics are often referred to as *fab-mat*, *bi-ply*, or *combi-mat*. They save labor in construction by allowing the builder to apply the two layers as one.

The fiber-to-binder ratio is called the *glass-to-resin ratio* or *glass content*, and for a standard hand-layup using alternating layers of woven roving and CSM, it is about 35 percent by weight. For an all-mat layup, the glass content is about 28 percent by weight; for an all-woven-roving layup, the glass content or ratio is about 40 percent by weight. Again, it is important to note that the higher the glass content (the glass-to-resin ratio), the higher the laminate's mechanical properties (i.e., the greater its strength).

Plywood Bottom Framing

The internal structure/framing described in chapter 5 is not the only method of reinforcing the interior of a hull; it would be impossible to cover all possible approaches. One fairly common alternative, however, is to install a framework of longitudinal and transverse plywood panels across the hull bottom. These plywood bottom stiffeners and frames are sprayed with several coats of resin. Then they are tabbed in place to the bottom of the hull, and both the tabbing and ply are usu-

ally sprayed with a finish coat of gelcoat. This method is proven and works. It is common on many smaller-production powerboats.

I prefer cored framing (described in chapter 5) because its wider form spreads loads and reduces stress concentrations. Furthermore, there is no partially exposed plywood (i.e., not covered all around with FRP laminate) in the bilge, where small scratches and cracks can permit water penetration and potential long-term degradation. The plywood bottom-framing method is not covered in detail in this scantling rule; however, the method itself is basically safe and workable.

PLYWOOD FLOORS

For plywood floors—as opposed to the cored floors recommended in Formulas 5-7 and 5-8—you can use plywood that totals 1.15 times the thickness of the recommended cored-floor laminate, both sides, but not less than $1/2$ inch (12 mm); see photo on p. 332. A 0.32-inch laminate would be 0.64-inch both sides, and 0.64-inch × 1.15 = 0.74; use $3/4$-inch (8.1 mm laminate would be 16.2 mm × 1.15 = 18.6 mm; use 20 mm). These ply floors should otherwise be shaped and proportioned as described in Formulas 5-7 and 5-8. The ply floors should be tabbed in place with tabbing exactly as for bulkheads (see Formula 5-5); however, the ply floor tabbing should be 10 percent thicker.

PLYWOOD ENGINE BEDS AND BOTTOM STRINGERS

For solid plywood engine beds and bottom stringers, find the core thickness from Formula 5-1 and multiply it by 0.75. Determine the height of the cores from Formula 5-1 and increase it by 10 percent. The tabbing should be 1.3 times heavier than for the bulkhead tabbing found in Formula 5-5.

THREE

Fiberglass Design Considerations, Modern Laminates, and One-Off Construction Methods

Fiberglass Design Considerations

AVOIDING HARD SPOTS

Because fiberglass is quite flexible or bendy and most fiberglass layups are also fairly thin, they can flex repeatedly, especially at hard spots, tight bends, machinery mounts, and bolt and fastening holes. Thus, it is vitally important that large backing plates are employed to spread out loads; large extended tabbing/bonding areas are used to fasten stringers, bulkheads, and other attachments; and all transitions in laminate thickness are gradually tapered throughout.

It is also critical that all corners in the laminate and in secondary bonds be made with a radius or fillet. Fiberglass laminates do not work well with hard, sharp corners. The builder must use foam or balsa fillets or putty-grout fillets to round over any layup making a sharp inside turn. This is equally true for a transom corner, a stem, tabbing a bulkhead or stringer in place, or bonding in machinery or tank flats.

CORE TAPERING

Because the skins of cored fiberglass laminates are even thinner than solid laminates, spreading loads and avoiding hard spots is—if anything—more important. Indeed, the U.S. Coast Guard and the American Bureau of Shipping (ABS) *require* that the transition from a cored area of the hull to a solid, uncored area be done gradually with an angle or slope in the core.

THE NOT-SO-SECONDARY "SECONDARY BOND"

On properly manufactured fiberglass craft, the hull is laid up in one continuous process, with no more than 16 hours (fewer is better) between applying layers.

FORMULA 3-1

Time between Laminate-Layer Application

A still better rule is that no more than twice the resin's gel time should be permitted between the application of

(continued)

If this is done, all of the layers (more or less) cure together to form a single unit locked together in a *primary bond*. Of course, bulkheads, stiffeners, and interior structure have to be added later—after the hull proper has fully cured. The tabbing that attaches such items to the inside of the hull makes a *secondary bond*, which is never as strong as any primary bond. (There is little significant chemical cross-linking.)

Clearly, this is unavoidable. Happily, it is also perfectly okay; however, the builder must take proper steps to get a good secondary bond. The area to be bonded must be ground slightly (i.e., roughed up to produce a good "tooth" to which to glue), vacuumed clean, and then wiped down and rendered oil-free with acetone or styrene. (Styrene is preferable when bonding to laminates that are more than three months old; it softens the old resin more for better secondary adhesion.) Only then can the tabbing/bonding be wet-out, rolled, and pressed down. Most builders use ordinary polyester resin for all laminating, including critical secondary bonds. Again—if done with care—this is fine; however, a few of the finest builders use vinylester resin for all structural secondary bonds. Vinylester yields still stronger, longer-lasting secondary bonds.

What if these basic secondary bonding steps aren't taken? The photograph on page 333 shows a boat that came to one of my builder's shops for repairs. This vessel literally had started to come apart in a storm. The bulkhead/stiffener panel, shown in the photograph, pulled out when it was yanked on with one hand. Not only had this builder neglected to prep for good secondary bond, but—as you can see—he also didn't use foam spacers or even fillets to ease the radius at the corner of the tabbing.

AVOIDING NAKED WOOD

Solid-wood or solid-plywood cores are frequently used in fiberglass hulls. Also, wood cleats and panels are almost always found in the interior, whether for supporting machinery or joinerwork. For structural woodwork (as opposed to interior cabinetry), there must be no bare wood in the boat—period! Every single piece of wood simply must be sealed (see photo on p. 333). If it isn't, not only can it rot, but worse still, it also will expand and contract from the constant moisture changes found on any boat. In time—sometimes an amazingly short time—this will cause the wood to split and to separate from the FRP structure—bad news, indeed. Usually, wood that is otherwise exposed but is in contact with the glass structure should be coated liberally with resin and sprayed with gelcoat. Unless you've got a good eye, it can even be hard to spot timber that has been so treated. If the wood is not partially laminated or structurally fastened to the glass structure, it's okay to set it in marine bedding compound and seal it with Cuprinol, or to paint it—but coat it with something, coat it all around, and coat it well.

GELCOAT AND AVOIDING PRINT-THROUGH

Print-through is the term used to describe a smooth-finished surface that has been marred by the weave of the underlying fiberglass reinforcement, showing as distinct ridges. The usual layup procedure is to wax the inside of the female mold, then spray it evenly with a gelcoat 20 to 30 mils (i.e., 20 to 30 thousandths of an inch) thick (0.5 to 0.76 mm).

(A gelcoat more than 30 mils [0.75 mm] thick is prone to crack; less than 20 mils [0.5 mm] thick is too thin for adequate coverage and surface quality.) *Gelcoat* is high-quality resin pigmented to the color desired for the surface finish. The gelcoat is allowed to reach partial cure (about three to four hours, depending on the resin system). Next, a layer of mat is laid down on the partially cured gelcoat; this is known as the *skin coat*.

For most vessels more than 25 to 30 feet (7.5 to 9 m), the skin coat is from 1- to $1^1/_2$-oz./sq. yd. (305 to 457 g/m^2) mat. For boats less than 25 feet (7.5 m), the skin coat is usually $^3/_4$- to 1-oz. mat (228 to 305 g/m^2). The mat skin coat is allowed to cure (usually overnight), then the remainder of the structural laminate is applied. Again, on vessels more than 30 feet (9 m) or so, this next layer is usually another 1- to $1^1/_2$-oz. (305 to 457 g/m^2) mat; on vessels less than 25 feet (7.5 m), the next layer is usually $^3/_4$-oz. (228 g/m^2) mat. The purpose of the mat is to eliminate the print-through—that is, showing the rough weave or the structural reinforcing cloth behind it (usually roving). Mat accomplishes this because it is soft and squishy, and has a high resin content (or low glass content—same thing).

Most builders will try for a total of 2 oz. (610 g/m^2) of mat (or a little more) between the gelcoat and the balance of the structural laminate ($^3/_4$ to 1 oz. [228 to 305 g/m^2] on vessels less than 25 feet [7.5 m]). This is necessary but unfortunate because—as discussed previously—the mat is relatively heavy and weak. However, you must allow for this mat skin on most average design laminates. Another factor to keep in mind is that the finer the weave of the structural cloth, the less it will print-through. Thus, some of the light stitch-mat styles (discussed later in this chapter) can use somewhat less mat in the skin coat. Alternately, if most of the laminate is standard 24-15 fab-mat (i.e., 24-oz. [813.6 g/m^2] roving plus 1.5-oz. [457 g/m^2] mat), you could make the layer immediately under the skin coat of 14-oz. (474.6 g/m^2) roving. This too would help reduce print-through.

When the resin cures, it generates heat. This is a natural product of the *exothermic* chemical reaction, which means that it gives off heat. Many builders refer to the heat as *exotherm*. The greater the heat or exotherm during cure, the more the laminate will shrink when it cools down after cure. This shrinkage aggravates print-through. Accordingly, print-through also can be reduced by using the slowest-cure resin mixture practically permissible; by keeping the internal layup skins thinner; and by keeping the entire shop cool to reduce temperature overall. All this is a truly delicate balancing act, and it is critical that the resin manufacturer be consulted regarding the best procedure for the exact resin system and formulation to use.

RESIN MIXING AND STORAGE

Although the fiberglass-cloth reinforcement has essentially unlimited shelf life, the resins used are quite volatile chemical mixtures. I am frequently astonished by how little care some builders give to storing and preparing their resin. Keep track of the ages of your resin drums, and don't try to use them after they're too old—you'll be sorry if you do. All resins must be stored in a cool environment, out of direct sunlight. The drums must be kept sealed airtight and watertight, and even condensation in partly used but resealed drums must be kept to a minimum. Also—most important—the resins must be stirred in their storage drums *before* distribution and use. Many an inexplicable laminating failure has been a result of ignoring these simple precautions.

Modern Laminates: Fibers and Resins

In the past 15 years or so, new, more advanced fabric styles and materials and new resins have become more common. These new approaches give the designer and builder the opportunity to produce stronger, stiffer, lighter hulls. Usually, though, such laminates cost more—sometimes significantly more.

As we discussed previously, traditional or standard fiberglass is available in CSM, woven roving, and cloth. All these are of E-glass—standard marine- or construction-grade fibers. S2-glass or S-glass is identical in chemical composition to E-glass, but it is aircraft-grade fiberglass. The individual fibers are spun finer and are of higher purity with fewer defects. This dramatically improves the strength of individual fibers and, thus, the resulting laminate.

Similarly Kevlar, Spectra, and carbon fiber can be used in place of E-glass. These fibers can have anywhere from 3 to 10 times the strength and stiffness of ordinary E-glass, giving much stronger laminates. All these modern fibers have higher stiffness as well as higher strength characteristics. Stiffness is measured in a unit known as the *modulus* (modulus of elasticity), so these fibers are often referred to as *high-modulus* fibers or *high-modulus* reinforcement.

MODERN FABRIC STYLES: UNI-DI, BI-AXIAL, AND STITCH-MAT

Uni-Di Fabric Styles

Another way to increase the mechanical properties of a laminate is to remove kinks or bends in the individual fibers and to align the fibers in the direction needed for strength. To do this, the builder applies layers of fibers all running in the same direction. These fibers are held together in a cloth roll with a very light stitching and/or some binder or seizing. This fabric style is called *uni-directional*, or *uni-di*. Because the fibers are not bent by being woven in and out, over and around each other, they are stronger even than woven roving (which is composed of woven bundles of fibers). The fibers all lay in the same direction, so they have maximum strength in that one direction. Additionally, the neatly aligned fibers pack together very closely and wet-out easily. This means that they will have a very low resin or binder content in proportion to their weight. (They will have a high glass-to-resin ratio.) Pure, vacuum-bagged, uni-di laminates will have glass contents as high as 55 to 60 percent—under the very best conditions, as high as 65 to 70 percent.

Directional fabric has all the bundles of fibers aligned neatly, running in the same direction. There is no crimping and few gaps to hold resin. (Courtesy Brunswick Technologies, Inc.)

Bi-Axial Fabric Styles

Unfortunately, there are two practical problems with using pure uni-di fabric styles. The first and most obvious is that strength only runs in one direction. To counteract this, the builder has to apply uni-di styles in multiple layers running at opposing angles. The first layer will be laid on at, for example, 45 degrees to the fore-n-aft line, then the second layer will be laid on, crossing the first at 45 degrees to the fore-n-aft line, like double-diagonal planking. This is known as ±45 degrees, +45 degrees, −45 degrees, or simply 45,45. Alternately, the layers could run transversely and straight fore-n-aft. This is 0 degrees, 90 degrees, or 0,90.

Just as with *combi-mat* or *fab-mat* (i.e., CSM stitched to woven roving), glass suppliers make fabric styles that combine uni-di layers for the builder. Again, this allows the builder to apply two layers as one. These fabric styles are commonly known as *bi-axial* (even when they are 0,90). There are even *tri-axial* and *quadra-axial* styles. A tri-axial might have three uni-di layers: +45, −45, and 0 degrees, all prestitched together in a single roll of cloth. By combining +45,−45 bi-ax with 0,90 bi-ax styles, the builder can generate even strength in all directions; however, although stronger than woven roving, this isn't as strong as the pure uni-di along its one-strength direction.

Stitch-Mat Fabric Styles

The second problem with uni-di fabric styles is that there is no mat

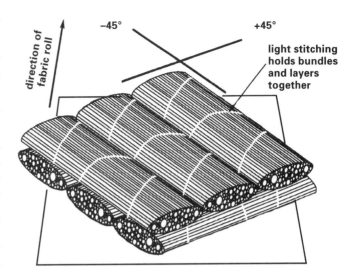

Plus/minus 45-degree bi-axial fabric style, in both diagonal directions across the fabric roll. If a mat were stitched to one side of this fabric, it would be a plus/minus 45-degree stitch-mat. (Courtesy Brunswick Technologies, Inc.)

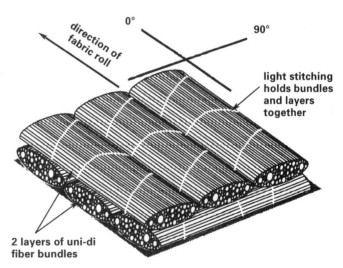

0,90 bi-axial fabric style has strength along the length of the fabric roll and across the roll. If a mat were stitched to one side of this fabric, it would be a 0,90 stitch-mat. (Courtesy Brunswick Technologies, Inc.)

between the layers to ensure a good interlaminar bond. If great attention to detail is used and if the hull or component is vacuum-bagged in a high-elongation, gap-filling resin system, this can work. For most applications, however, some mat is desirable. This, again, is a delicate balance. First, mat is comparatively weak and heavy, so you want to use as little as possible. Second, many mat products are not compatible with high-strength resin systems. To solve this difficulty, glass manufacturers make fabric styles that are bi-axial with a light or thin layer of mat stitched to it. These are known as *stitch-mat* styles. A typical stitch-mat is Hexcel Knytex DBM1708. This is a +45,−45 bi-axial (the "DB"), built from two layers of 8.5-oz./sq. yd. uni-di (totalling 17 oz./sq. yd.—the "17"), with a single layer of $^3/_4$-oz./sq. ft. (0.75-oz.) mat stitched to it. (The "08" is for the 0.75-oz. mat, rounded off.) In metric units, this is two bi-ax uni-di layers 288.1 g/m^2, with a 25.4 g/m^2 mat. Additionally, this mat is specifically made without the chemical binder or seizing that can be incompatible with high-strength resin systems.

Stitch-mat reinforcements are available in a wide variety of styles, both 0,90 and +45,−45, and with differing thicknesses and weights of mat. This is an excellent way to make the best use of higher-strength fabrics and resin systems without excessive labor. Applying a stitch-mat is like applying three layers at once: two uni-di and one mat.

Even with ordinary E-glass, stitch-mat bi-axial fabric styles can offer a substantial increase in strength. The flexural strength of DBM1708, for instance, is 63,000 psi (434 mPa), while a standard E-glass fab-mat (mat/roving) layup has a flexural strength of just 30,000 psi (206 mPa).

ALTERNATE RESIN SYSTEMS

Polyester Resin

There is little point in using any of the modern fabric styles or high-modulus materials with standard orthophthalic-polyester resins. This is the plain-vanilla resin that has remained the industry standard for years. Its drawback is that it tends to be rather brittle; it cracks under high load rather than stretching, giving, and then returning to its original shape. Ortho-polyester resin elongates about 2 percent of its length before cracking, with tensile strength of 9,400 psi (65 mPa). This means that when the thinner high-modulus fibers and modern fabric styles flex in ortho-polyester, the resin cracks before the fibers develop their full usable strength.

The next step up in resin systems is isophthalic-polyester. Isos have somewhat better elongation and much better resistance to chemical attack—blistering or degradation by oil or pollutants. Isos elongate 2.5 percent before cracking and have roughly the same tensile strength of ortho resins. A vacuum-bagged E-glass iso-polyester laminate using bi-axial stitch-mat fabric styles will generate a fairly strong hull—stronger than the standard mat/roving layup. The increase in cost over a mat/roving ortho-polyester layup is modest.

Vinylester Resin

To make full use of the greater strength of the modern fabric styles and high-modulus fibers, you need to utilize a high-strength, high-elongation resin system. The two commonly used in boatbuilding are vinylester resins and epoxy resins. Vinylesters have much greater elongation than any of the polyester resins—they stretch farther before cracking and breaking. On average, vinylesters elongate fully 5 percent before cracking, with a tensile strength of 11,800 psi (82 mPa).

This means that laminates using vinylesters are much tougher than polyester laminates. It also means that interlaminar bonds (the bonds between layers and to the core) are stronger, because it is harder to peel the layers apart. Imagine the cured resin stretching like taffy and springing back if you try to peel the layers apart. This is known as having high *peel strength*. Vinylesters, furthermore, have even higher resistance to chemical attack and to blistering than do any of the polyesters.

Another nice feature of vinylester is that it is compatible with standard mat chemical binders and with standard polyester shop equipment and methods. Builders used to polyesters have little difficulty switching to vinylesters, or switching back and forth between the two. Furthermore, vinylester has the unique property of forming a good bond to polyester; polyester, in turn, will bond well to it. This also makes for great flexibility in the production shop. In most cases, a vinylester-resin system using bi-axial stitch-mat fabric styles with either E-glass or high-modulus reinforcement fabric will produce about as strong a laminate as reasonable, practical, and necessary.

Epoxy Resin

The resin system still stronger than vinylester is epoxy. Epoxy resin not only fills relatively large gaps (helping to avoid small-void defects in fabrication), but it also is both stronger and has even higher elongation than vinylester. Elongation is usually more than 5 percent, and tensile strength is 12,500 psi (86 mPa). Epoxy has still higher resistance to chemical attack and blistering than vinyl-

ester's already high resistance. Because of its gap-filling and very high elongation, epoxy has the highest peel strength of any ordinary resin system. Accordingly, epoxy layups can be made successfully without using mat at all (an epoxy-compatible mat or core-bond putty must be used to bond to cores). When the mat is eliminated completely, the highest glass or fiber content is possible and, thus, the highest mechanical properties. A carefully vacuum-bagged bi-axial S-glass epoxy laminate, for instance, can have a flexural strength of nearly 85,000 psi (586 mPa). This is as strong as stainless steel, although the S-glass epoxy laminate weighs just one-fifth as much and will never corrode. Laminates like this are quite expensive, both in materials and in skilled labor and design. Application equipment and methods are not readily compatible with polyester. Epoxies are usually best suited to and most practical for the cutting edge in racing performance and military or rescue-craft applications.

One-Off FRP Construction Methods

All of the foregoing discussion is based on the standard production-shop method of fiberglass construction in a female mold. For one-off or limited-run production, or for special components like tanks, other methods may be used. These methods dramatically reduce the labor involved in building the female mold in the first place; however, they usually require considerable additional labor in finishing the exterior surface.

All the basic materials, considerations, and approaches described previously still apply, but one-off methods do not use gelcoat because there is no prepared smooth-finished

Close-up view of Baltek's DuraKore showing how it fits together to form a complex curved form. (Courtesy Baltek Corporation)

Thirty-six-foot (10.9 m) fishing-boat hull under construction at "Pettegrow" using Baltek's DuraKore strip technique. (Courtesy Baltek Corporation)

exterior surface. Instead, the builder has to engage in the painstaking, time-consuming process of fairing the surface by repeatedly filling and sanding—using ever finer grits and filling smaller and smaller voids—until the desired surface quality is obtained. The exterior is then painted for the final finish surface.

The most common methods of one-off FRP construction are foam core over a disposable wooden male-skeleton mold; foam core or solid FRP over a male mold or plug; Baltek DuraKore, a proprietary balsa-core strip-plank process; and C-Flex, a proprietary solid (single-skin) FRP process. Refer to chapter 6 for foam-core construction and to standard books on fiberglass boatbuilding and/or the manufacturers for detailed descriptions. For DuraKore, refer also to *Boatbuilding with Baltek DuraKore,* by David Brown, and to *The Baltek DuraKore Scantling Handbook,* by the author.

C-FLEX ONE-OFF METHOD

Seemann Fiberglass, Inc.'s C-Flex consists of bundles of thin fiberglass rods bound together into "planks" with a light, transverse fiberglass weaving holding the rods in place. These planks can be bent around a male mold to form a fair substrate for a solid-glass (single-skin) FRP hull. To use C-Flex, you can use the standard scantling rule given in chapter 4, and simply replace the interior portion of the laminate with the equivalent thickness of C-Flex. Currently, C-Flex is available in two thicknesses:

| C-Flex | CF-39 | 0.080 in. | 2.03 mm |
| C-Flex | CF-65 | 0.125 in. | 3.17 mm |

The thinner C-Flex is suited to smaller boats with closer mold-station spacings. It is also critical that a very slow-cure, low-shrink

The Westbourne-44 high-speed Express Cruiser designed by the author. Constructed entirely of Baltek DuraKore and balsa-core panels, this boat came in under its predicted weight and has a top speed of 36 knots. (Courtesy Bob Grieser)

resin be used with the C-Flex to avoid shrinkage distortion. This is commonly called a *casting resin*. Consult with the manufacturer for details before building a C-Flex hull.

Mass-Production Tooling

FIBERGLASS TOOLING/MOLDS

Mass-production fiberglass boats have an additional structural element—the tooling or molds. Although it can be helpful to have hull and deck molds fairly light to keep them manageable, neither lightness nor great strength is important—low cost and ease of construction are. Almost all molds are made up entirely of mat layups braced with external core and stiffeners. The following is a good guide to standard practice:

Small components and canoes:
8 layers $1^1/_2$-oz. (457 g/m^2) mat
Boats 20 to 50 feet (6 to 15 m):
12 layers $1^1/_2$-oz. (457 g/m^2) mat

Boats more than 50 feet (15 m):
16 to 18 layers $1^1/_2$-oz. (457 g/m^2) mat

Where tight bends and creases are molded in, the buildup can be made from an equivalent layup of $^3/_4$-oz. (228 g/m^2) mat.

EXTERNAL STIFFENING OR PIPING

External stiffeners often were made of steel pipes welded and bolted into a framework surrounding the outside of the hull or deck mold. These pipes were then tabbed onto the mold exterior. Properly configured, the entire mold and pipe framework would be supported on two pivots—one at the bow and one at the stern—which permits rotating the tooling so all layup can be down-handed work. Because of this practice, mold-stiffening is sometimes generically termed *piping*.

Although pipe-mold stiffening works, I don't care for it. The piping rusts and cor-

Another use for core. Here it stiffens the Gerr 34 hull mold. This is a lighter and easier-to-handle structure than a solid-glass mold reinforced with piping.

rodes when the tooling is stored outside. Also, the coefficient of expansion for metal is very different than for fiberglass, which leads to distortion and separation of the piping's tabbing over time.

TABBED-ON PLYWOOD STIFFENING
Instead of pipe stiffening, I recommend tabbing on external plywood stiffening webs. These webs can be of low-grade exterior B-B or B-C ply, and of about the same thickness as the bulkheads that would be installed inside the hull, but not less than $1/2$ inch (12 mm). The depth of the ply stiffener webs should be 12 times the thickness or more. Tabbing is of all mat, roughly similar in weight and in tabbing run out to that used for bulkheads of the same thickness; however, only rudimentary corner-filleting is required. A good rule-of-thumb is to arrange and space the ply stiffening so there is no panel on the mold that is more than 12 feet (3.6 m) unsupported fore-n-aft and no more than 5 feet (1.5 m) unsupported *athwartships* (i.e., along the girth or transverse surface of the mold).

For longevity, all the plywood and other wood-reinforcing used on the mold should be sprayed/sealed with three coats of gelcoat or resin.

BALSA-CORE MOLD STIFFENING
I recommend installing balsa core under the outer two or three layers of mat, over most of the central 70 to 80 percent of the mold—extending it farther fore-n-aft can't hurt. The core should be roughly the thickness of the core to be used on the hull topsides. Install the core first and the ply web stiffeners over it.

PLYWOOD TURNING RINGS
A nice trick is to make transverse turning rings of plywood that double as part of the web stiffeners. These rings rest on pipes set in a ply-and-timber frame secured on rollers on the shop floor. They are an efficient and inexpensive way to rotate the tooling. The ply-turning rings should be located about 20 percent aft of the bow and forward of the stern. Molds more than 50 feet (15 m) should have a third midships turning ring, and more than 75 feet (22 m) should have two rings equi-spaced between the end rings. Turning-ring ply thickness should be twice the standard bulkhead thickness for the hull, and fore-n-aft webs should be tabbed to both sides of the rings and onto the hull for a considerable length to hold the turning rings rigid. The circular perimeter of the rings should be banded with steel or aluminum strapping. This strapping forms the metal "tire" that bears on the rotating pipes in the timber frame. A little grease makes rotation a surprisingly easy operation even for large tooling. Ropes should be set up to turn the mold and to hold it set at the desired working angle.

FOUR

Fiberglass Scantling Rule: Basic Solid-Glass Hull Shell

*H*aving explored the fundamentals of FRP construction, we can now determine the scantlings for a fiberglass vessel. The following rule will permit calculation of complete scantlings for most ordinary types of fiberglass boats with solid-glass (uncored) hulls, also known as *solid* or *single-skin construction*.

Materials

There are four basic materials used in this rule:

1. fiberglass or other reinforcing cloth or fiber
2. low-density core: usually foam or balsa
3. resin system: polyester, vinylester, or epoxy
4. high-density core, solid wood: timber block, laminated wood, or plywood

FIBERGLASS

As discussed in chapter 3, fiberglass comes in a wide array of styles. The basic FRP rule applies to the most common layup of alternating layers of woven roving and CSM. Hand-laid-up in polyester resin, this laminate has an average density of 96 lb./cu. ft. (1,538 kg/m^3). Average glass (or fiber) content is 35 percent by weight.

FOAM OR BALSA CORE

For sandwich construction, either closed-cell foam cores or end-grain balsa cores may be used. Take great care to bed, bond, and presaturate or coat all cores with resin, as described in the previous chapter. Standard structural foam cores are about 5.5 lb./cu. ft. (88 kg/m^3) density, while standard balsa is 6.5 lb./cu. ft. (104 kg/m^3). (Other densities are available for special applications.)

Although there are significant differences between the mechanical properties of foam and balsa cores, this rule treats them as being roughly the same. Keep in mind, however, that balsa cores are generally the stiffest, with the highest sheer strength. A slightly thinner laminate will give a stiffer hull than with standard foams. A highly elastic foam, on the other hand, will require somewhat thicker skins for the same stiffness, but will deflect farther without cracking or breaking.

RESIN SYSTEM

The basic rule assumes standard ortho- or iso-polyester resin, formulated for marine structural applications. It is the resin system that actually holds the boat together; follow the manufacturer's recommendations and instructions rigorously.

SOLID WOOD

Wood cores and reinforcement are used—in some form or another—on the majority of fiberglass vessels. All wood, without exception, must be presealed with resin before applying the fiberglass laminate. All wood that is not covered with laminate must be sealed with a minimum of three coats of resin. Plywood is frequently used as core for engine beds, transoms, and high-load hardware attachments. All plywood *must* be fabricated from a glue rated waterproof (not simply water-resistant) by boil test (see chapter 12). The ideal plywood is rated marine grade; however, ordinary exterior grade is usually acceptable for core construction.

Solid-timber core should be from softwoods such as fir, pine, or larch. Hardwoods—like oak or locust—have greater expansion rates with changes in moisture and are thus more likely to split away from the fiberglass structure.

Wherever wood cores are penetrated by fasteners, great care must be taken to seal the edges with resin and/or a marine bedding compound.

Standard Solid (Single-Skin) Fiberglass Scantlings (Roving/Mat/Polyester)

FORMULA 4-1

Calculating Basic Shell Thickness

FRP shell thickness (lower topsides), inches = $0.25 \times \sqrt[3]{Sn}$

FRP shell thickness (lower topsides), mm = $6.35 \times \sqrt[3]{Sn}$

Where

Sn = Scantling Number

This lower-topsides shell thickness is the "basic thickness" for this rule. Other areas of the laminate are based on this basic thickness.

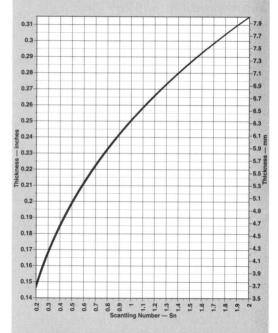

Solid-Glass Hull Thickness (Lower Topsides): Small Boats

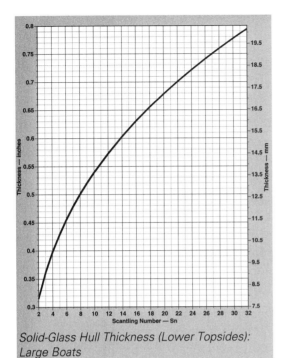

Solid-Glass Hull Thickness (Lower Topsides): Large Boats

Example:

Let's return to our example boat, *Fish 'n Squish,* from chapter 1, which had the following characteristics:

LOA	40.00 ft.	12.19 m
WL	37.20 ft.	11.34 m
Beam	12.56 ft.	3.83 m
Depth of hull	5.91 ft.	1.80 m

This gave an Sn of 2.97 (see Formula 1-1). Accordingly, the solid fiberglass thickness for the boat's lower topsides would be 0.36 inch (9.2 mm).

$$0.25 \times \sqrt[3]{2.97\ Sn} = 0.36\ in.$$

$$6.35 \times \sqrt[3]{2.97\ Sn} = 9.19\ mm$$

This is the thickness for the lower topsides only. Other regions on the hull and deck are determined as follows.

FORMULA 4-2

Hull-Regions Laminate Thickness

Hull bottom extends from bottom laminate height (BLH) (see Formula 4-3) and down: multiply lower topsides thickness by 1.15

Lower topsides extends from BLH up to half the distance to the sheer: no thickness adjustment

Upper topsides extends from half the distance up the sheer to the sheer: multiply lower topsides thickness by 0.85

Keel Region: multiply lower topsides thickness by 1.5

Deck and Cabin: same thickness as upper topsides

FORMULA 4-3

Bottom Laminate Height

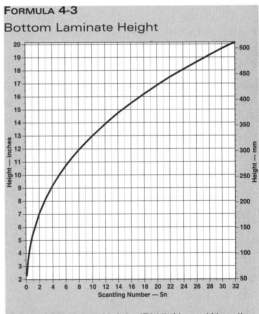

Bottom Laminate Height (BLH) Above Waterline

The height above the design waterline (DWL) at which the topsides laminate starts is derived from

(continued)

$BLH\ in. = 5.4 \times Sn^{0.38}$ *(English)*

$BLH\ cm = 13.71 \times Sn^{0.38}$ *(Metric)*

This height can be constant from bow to stern; however, for higher-speed craft, workboats, and serious cruising boats, the BLH height should be increased evenly from midships forward to the stem, so that—at the stem—the BLH is twice the formula height above. This provides additional impact resistance at the forefoot.

Example:

For *Fish 'n Squish,* the bottom laminate should extend from 8 inches (20 cm) above the DWL down to the keel.

$$5.4 \times Sn\ 2.97^{0.38} = 8.12\ in.;\ use\ 8\ in.$$

$$13.71 \times Sn\ 2.97^{0.38} = 20.7\ cm;\ use\ 20\ cm$$

Adjusting Laminate Thickness at Hull Bottom for Boat Speed

The previous thicknesses are suitable for both the bottom and topsides of vessels with a top speed of 10 knots or less. This same thickness should be used on the topsides of higher-speed craft, but the bottom thickness (from the BLH down) should be adjusted as follows.

FORMULA 4-4

Speed-Adjusted Bottom-Laminate Thickness

Increase laminate thickness 1 percent for every knot over 10 knots.

Example:

Our 40-foot (12.19 m) *Fish 'n Squish's* Sn is 2.97; thus, its under-10-knot bottom thickness should be 0.41 inch (10.5 mm) (i.e., 15 percent greater than the upper topsides). If, however, *Fish 'n Squish* were a 25-knot planing hull, then

25 knots – 10 knots = 15,
or increase thickness 15 percent

0.41 in. × 1.15 = 0.47 in.

10.5 mm × 1.15 = 12.1 mm

Adjusting Laminate Thickness for Heavy Displacement

The basic scantling rule assumes the vessel has D/L ratios between 100 and 275 or less. For D/L ratios outside this range, make the following adjustments. Heavy-displacement boats—with D/L ratios greater than 275—place additional strain on their hulls. All the laminate thicknesses should be adjusted as follows.

FORMULA 4-5

Heavy-Displacement Laminate Increase

Percent increase of laminate thickness for heavy displacement = 0.89 + (D/L Ratio ÷ 2,500)

Where

D/L Ratio = Displacement-Length Ratio

D/L Ratio = Tons ÷ (0.01 × WL ft.)³ (English)

D/L Ratio = (Mtons ÷ 1,267) ÷ (WL m ÷ 328)³ (Metric)

Tons = full-loaded displacement, in long tons of 2,240 lbs.

Mtons = full-loaded displacement, in metric tons of 1,000 kg (2,204 lbs.)

WL = Waterline length, in feet or meters

Example:

Up to now, our *Fish 'n Squish* has had an average D/L ratio under 275. If, however, *Fish 'n Squish,* with a waterline of 37.2 feet (11.34

m), had a displacement of 18 long tons (18.28 metric tons), the D/L ratio would be 349. This would increase the boat's laminate thicknesses as follows:

Increase = 0.89 + (349 D/L Ratio ÷ 2,500) = 1.029; use 3 percent thicker

Vessels with D/L ratios under 100 also require an increase in skin thickness over the standard rule. This is because their hulls are either long and slender or wide and shallow, and thus are subjected to proportionately higher bending or slamming loads. For craft with D/L ratios under 100, increase the laminate thickness as follows.

FORMULA 4-6

Light-Displacement Laminate Increase

Increase of laminate thickness for light displacement = 1.13 – (D/L ratio ÷ 770)

Example:

If *Fish 'n Squish*, with a waterline of 37.2 feet (11.34 m), had a displacement of 3.5 long tons (3.56 metric tons), the D/L ratio would be 68. This would increase the laminate thickness as follows:

Increase = 1.13 – (68 D/L ratio ÷ 770) = 1.04; use 4 percent thicker

Combining Speed Adjustment and Displacement Adjustment for Hull-Bottom Laminate Thickness

On larger heavy workboats (e.g., an offshore crewboat), both the speed and displacement adjustments might apply. First, find the increase for displacement and apply that to all the laminates.

Next, find the increase for the speed and multiply the displacement-adjusted bottom-laminate thickness by that to get the final bottom thickness.

Weight of Dry Glass Cloth (Alternating Roving–Mat Laminate) for Required Thickness

Refer to manufacturer's style sheets for laminate thickness per layer; however, the following formula gives close estimates for layups of alternating layers of woven roving and CSM.

FORMULA 4-7

Chopped-Strand Mat Weight vs. Thickness

(English)

NOTE: Mat is usually specified in oz./sq. ft., not the more customary oz./sq. yd.

Weight of Dry Mat (oz./sq. ft.) = Laminate Thickness (in.) × 31.25

Laminate Thickness (in.) = Weight of Dry Mat (oz./sq. ft.) ÷ 31.25

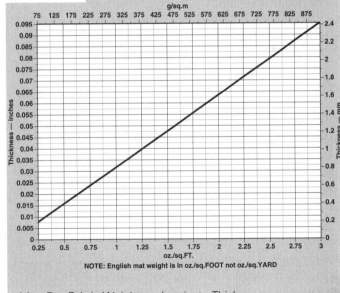

NOTE: English mat weight is in oz./sq.FOOT not oz./sq.YARD

Mat: Dry Fabric Weight vs. Laminate Thickness

(continued)

Density of Finished Layup, with Resin = 85 lb./cu. ft.

Glass Content of Finished Layup with Resin, by Weight = 28 percent

(Metric)

Weight of Dry Mat (g/m²) = Laminate Thickness (mm) × 375.3

Laminate Thickness (mm) = Weight of Dry Mat (g/m²) ÷ 375.3

Density of Finished Layup, with Resin = 1,360 kg/m³

Glass Content of Finished Layup with Resin, by Weight = 28 percent

FORMULA 4-8

Woven Roving and Bi-Axial Uni-Di Weight vs. Thickness

(English)

Weight of Dry Roving (oz./sq. yd.) = Laminate Thickness (in.) × 580

Laminate Thickness (in.) = Weight of Dry Roving (oz./sq. yd.) ÷ 580

Density of Finished Layup, with Resin = 99 lb./cu. ft.

Glass Content of Finished Layup with Resin, by Weight = 38 percent

(Metric)

Weight of Dry Roving (g/m²) = Laminate Thickness (mm) × 774

Laminate Thickness (mm) = Weight of Dry Roving (g/m²) ÷ 774

Density of Finished Layup, with Resin = 1,585 kg/m³

Glass Content of Finished Layup with Resin, by Weight = 38 percent

NOTE: For bi-axial styles, this formula is less accurate; consult manufacturer's data whenever possible.

You can use these formulas to determine the laminate specification, or you can refer to the following table. The table is drawn up for stock cloth weights.

Remember that laminate thicknesses are not exact numbers. The actual thickness obtained will vary up or down by ±8 percent. This variation is caused by differing shop procedures, different application styles among workers, how easy or difficult it is to get at and press down on the part being laminated, and many similar factors. Use the thicknesses and specifications given here for calculating laminates, but keep the limits of real-world accuracy in mind.

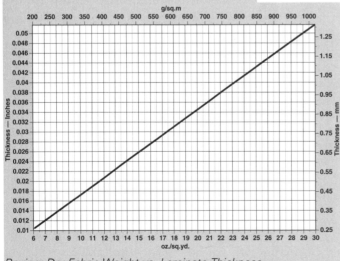

Roving: Dry Fabric Weight vs. Laminate Thickness

TABLE 4-9 Fabric Weight vs. Thickness Table

Fabric Weight, oz./sq. ft. (g/m²)	Thickness, in. (mm)
Mat Weight vs. Thickness	
0.75 (228.75)	0.024 (0.61)
1.00 (305.00)	0.032 (0.81)
1.50 (457.50)	0.048 (1.22)
2.00 (610.00)	0.064 (1.63)
Roving Weight Thickness	
14 (475)	0.024 (0.61)
16 (542)	0.028 (0.70)
18 (610)	0.031 (0.79)
24 (814)	0.041 (1.05)

NOTE: Two of the most common combi-mat styles are as follows:

- 24-15 Combi-Mat = 24 oz./sq. yd. (814 g/m²) woven roving with 1.5 oz./sq. ft. (457 g/m²) chopped-strand mat; 0.089 in. (2.26 mm) thick
- 18-10 Combi-Mat = 18 oz./sq. yd. (610 g/m²) woven roving with 1.0 oz./sq. ft. (305 g/m²) chopped-strand mat; 0.063 in. (1.60 mm) thick

FORMULA 4-10

To Convert from Oz./Sq. Yd. to g/m², and Vice Versa

(Conversion for most fabric styles)

Multiply oz./sq. yd. by 33.9 to get g/m².

Divide g/m² by 33.9 to get oz./sq. yd.

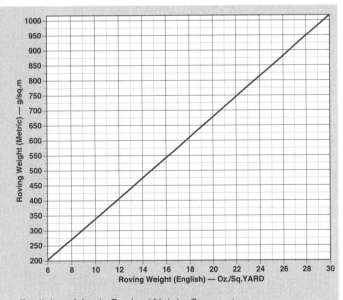

English-to-Metric Roving-Weight Conversion

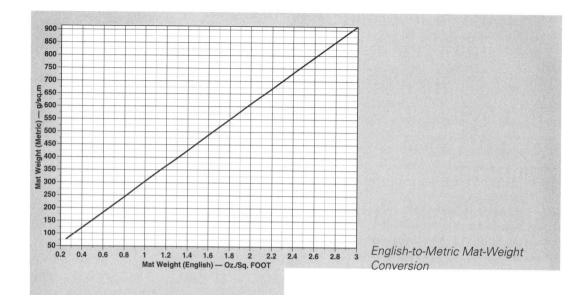

English-to-Metric Mat-Weight Conversion

To Convert from Oz./Sq. Ft. to g/m², and Vice Versa

(Conversion for standard English chopped-strand mat)

Multiply oz./sq. ft. by 305 to get g/m².

Divide g/m² by 305 to get oz./sq. ft.

Example:

We found that *Fish 'n Squish*'s lower topsides require a 0.36-inch-thick (9.2 mm) laminate. You can calculate the thickness of any combination of roving and mat weights from the tables or formulas, but assuming a standard 24-15 combi-mat, we find that four layers of 24-15 combi-mat (i.e., four layers 24-oz. roving, four layers 1.5-oz. mat) are required (0.36 in. ÷ 0.089 in. 24-15 = 4.04 layers; 9.2 mm ÷ 2.26 mm 24-15 = 4.07 layers).

FORMULA 4-12

Additional Laminate on Keel and Stem

To protect from grounding, impact, and hauling damage, and to provide added longitudinal strength, the rule increases the thickness of the laminate on the keel and stem over the above outside bottom laminate. The keel and stem region should have a laminate 1.5 times that of the bottom laminate, after the adjustments to thickness for speed and displacement. The additional laminate should extend transversely to protect the projecting portions of the keel and skeg, or for 8 percent of the beam, whichever is greater.

FORMULA 4-13

Additional Laminate on High-Stress Areas

High-speed planing powerboats should increase the laminate above the propellers on the hull-bottom underside to 1.1 times the thickness of the standard hull-bottom layup. The area of additional thickness should run from the struts aft to the transom, and should extend for a width of 2 times the propeller diameter, centered over the propeller shaft.

Deck-Hardware Areas

Sailboats should increase the laminate thickness at the chainplates and under and around the mast step by 1.25 times the surrounding or local laminate— usually the upper topsides and deck layup. This increase should be at least 3 times the width of the chainplate attachment, and 1.5 times the length.

All vessels should increase the laminate thickness at high-load hardware (e.g., bollard, mooring and docking cleats, davit bases, and winches) by 1.25 times the surrounding or local laminate— usually the upper topsides and deck layup. The buildup should extend around the base of the hardware and be at least 2 times the hardware footprint in all directions.

FORMULA 4-14
Adjusting Thickness for Type of Service

Racing boats and light trailerable day boats can use just 95 percent of the glass or laminate thickness given previously. Workboats such as patrol and pilot boats, fishing vessels, passenger vessels, and charter boats should increase all laminate and core thicknesses by 5 to 10 percent.

Working through a Full Laminate Specification

Using our example boat, *Fish 'n Squish*, we can now work through a complete hull- and deck-laminate specification. We will assume that *Fish 'n Squish* has a standard D/L ratio between 100 and 275, and—for the moment—that it's a 25-knot planing vessel, for yacht use. Using the dimensions given previously, we found that *Fish 'n Squish* has an Sn

of 2.97, which gives a basic or lower topsides laminate thickness of 0.36 inch (9.2 mm).

FIND THICKNESS

Deck: 0.36 in. × 0.85 = 0.30 in.

Deck: 9.2 mm × 0.85 = 7.82 mm

Upper Topsides: same as deck

Lower Topsides: 0.36 in. (9.2 mm)

Hull Bottom: 25 knots is 15 knots over 10 knots; increase bottom thickness 15 percent

Hull Bottom: 0.36 in. × 1.15 × 1.15 (for knots over 10 knots) = 0.47 in.

Hull Bottom: 9.2 mm × 1.15 × 1.15 (for knots over 10 knots) = 12.16 mm

Keel and Stem: 0.36 in. × 1.5 × 1.15 × 1.15 (for knots over 10 knots) = 0.71 in.

Keel and Stem: 9.2 mm × 1.5 × 1.15 × 1.15 (for knots over 10 knots) = 18.24 mm

Hull-Bottom High-Stress Areas: 1.10 × 0.47 in. = 0.52 in.

Hull-Bottom High-Stress Areas: 1.10 × 12.16 mm = 13.37 mm

Deck-Hardware-Mounting Areas: 1.25 × 0.30 in. = 0.375 in.

Deck-Hardware-Mounting Areas: 1.25 × 7.82 mm = 9.77 mm

SPECIFY LAMINATE (ENGLISH)
Use 24-15 combi-mat 0.089-inch thick for the majority of laminate.

Deck: 0.30 in. ÷ 0.089 in./layer = 3.37 layers 24-15 combi-mat

3 layers 24-15 combi-mat: 0.267 in.

1 layer 1.5-oz. mat: 0.048 in.

Deck Laminate Total Thickness: 0.315 in.

Upper Topsides: same as deck

Lower Topsides: 0.36 in. ÷ 0.089 in./layer = 4.04 layers 24-15 combi-mat

NOTE: A 1.5-oz.-mat skin coat is needed under the gelcoat, with a total of 2 oz. (or a little more) between the gelcoat and the roving, so add a layer of 1.5-oz. mat outside.

4 layers 24-15 combi-mat: 0.356 in.

1 layer 1.5-oz. mat: 0.048 in.

Lower Topsides Laminate Total Thickness: 0.404 in.

Hull Bottom: 0.47 in. ÷ 0.089 in./layer = 5.28 layers

5 layers 24-15 combi-mat: 0.445 in.

1 layer 1.5-oz. mat: 0.048 in.

Hull-Bottom Total Thickness: 0.493 in.

Keel and Stem: 0.71 in. ÷ 0.089 in./layer = 7.97 layers

8 layers 24-15 combi-mat: 0.712 in.

1 layer 1.5-oz. mat: 0.048 in.

Keel and Stem Region Total Thickness: 0.760 in.

Hull-Bottom High-Stress Areas: 0.52 in. ÷ 0.089 in./layer = 5.8 layers

Add 1 layer 24-15 combi-mat over propellers and at struts.

Deck-Hardware-Mounting Areas: 0.375 in. ÷ 0.089 in./layer = 4.2 layers

Add 1 layer 24-15 combi-mat plus 1 layer 1.5-oz. mat at chainplates, mooring cleats, etc.

SPECIFY LAMINATE (METRIC)

Use 24-15 combi-mat (814 g/m² roving plus 457 g/m² mat; 1,271 g/m² total) 2.26 mm thick for the majority of laminate.

Deck: 7.82 mm ÷ 2.26 mm/layer = 3.4 layers 24-15 combi-mat

3 layers 24-15 (1,271 g/m²) combi-mat: 6.78 mm

1 layer 457 g/m² mat: 1.22 mm

Deck Laminate Total Thickness: 8.00 mm

Upper Topsides: same as deck

Lower Topsides: 9.2 mm ÷ 2.26 mm/layer = 4.04 layers 24-15 combi-mat

NOTE: A 457 g/m² mat skin coat is needed under the gelcoat, with a total of 610 g/m² (or a little more) between the gelcoat and the roving, so add a layer of 457 g/m² mat outside.

4 layers 24-15 (1,271 g/m²) combi-mat: 9.04 mm

1 layer 457 g/m² mat: 1.22 mm

Lower Topsides Laminate Total Thickness: 10.26 mm

Hull Bottom: 12.16 mm ÷ 2.26 mm/layer = 5.38 layers

5 layers 24-15 (1,271 g/m²) combi-mat: 11.30 mm

1 layer 457 g/m² mat: 1.22 mm

Hull-Bottom Total Thickness: 12.52 mm

Keel and Stem: 18.24 mm ÷ 2.26 mm/layer = 8.0 layers

8 layers 24-15 (1,271 g/m²) combi-mat: 18.08 mm

1 layer 457 g/m² mat: 1.22 mm

Keel and Stem Region Total Thickness: 19.30 mm

Hull-Bottom High-Stress Areas: 13.37 mm ÷ 2.26 mm/layer = 5.9 layers

Add 1 layer 24-15 (1,271 g/m²) combi-mat over propellers and at struts.

Deck-Hardware-Mounting Areas: 9.77 mm ÷ 2.26 mm/layer = 4.3 layers

Add 1 layer 24-15 (1,271 g/m²) combi-mat plus 1 layer 1.5-oz. (457 g/m²) mat at chainplates, mooring cleats, etc.

NOTE: All the laminates have been arranged with 3 oz. (915 g/m²) of mat outside, under the gelcoat. In a female mold, the gelcoat is sprayed on, followed by the skin coat of 1.5-oz. (457 g/m²) mat, then the first layer of 24-15 (1,271 g/m²) combi-mat, with the mat down—facing out. This is to eliminate print-through (see chapter 3).

NOTE: Wherever we've spec'd combi-mat, we could also use a layer of roving and a layer of mat of the indicated individual weights. This will yield precisely the same thickness and strength; it's simply more labor.

COMMENTS ON THE LAMINATE SPECIFICATION

The laminate specified previously contains a number of features that are helpful but not required. First, by specifying the entire hull laminate out of all the same fabric styles and weights (i.e., 24-15 combi-mat and a 1.5-oz. mat; 814 g/m² roving stitched to 457 g/m² mat, and a 457 g/m² mat), there is minimum waste and the maximum fabric quantities can be ordered for the best pricing. Second, the construction/layup process is most straightforward: the gelcoat and skin coat are applied, followed by three layers of 24-15 combi-mat on the entire hull. A fourth layer is run inside (from halfway up the topsides down) to form the lower-topsides thickness. A fifth layer is run from the BLH down, forming the hull bottom. Finally, two additional layers are added inside at the keel region. All layers go on mat down, so a layer of mat bonds each ply of combi-mat to the exposed (i.e., upturned) roving below.

Try to produce uniform laminates of this pattern whenever practical. There are other considerations, however, that may make this less convenient or desirable. Smaller, lighter hulls may be too thin for this approach. You can, perhaps, try to do the same with a lighter combi-mat, for example an "18-10" (i.e., 18-oz. roving plus 1.0-oz. mat; 610 g/m² roving plus 305 g/m² mat). Some weights and styles may not be obtainable, or sticking with one style throughout may cause some specific region (e.g., the deck or topsides) to be either too light or too heavy. In these cases, it's usually best to adjust the laminate by changing the inner layers to a different fabric style.

Another consideration is lowering the number of layers at thick sections of the hull shell to reduce labor. In these areas, it might be worth going to, perhaps, a 24-20 combi-mat.

FORMULA 4-15

Shell Laminate Overlaps

The rolls of fiberglass should be laid on with overlaps for continuous strength in each layer, as follows:

Each Overlap = 2 in. (5 cm)

Overlap Stagger = 4 in. (10 cm) or more

If butting some plies is unavoidable, the overlap stagger must be at least 8 inches (20 cm).

Weight of Laminate

The weights of fabric—in oz./sq. yd. or g/m²—to which we are referring are the weights of the dry glass cloth, as specified by the manufacturer. For structural calculations and stability calculations, you need the weight of the finished laminate with resin, in pounds per square foot or in kilograms per square meter. This is a fairly simple matter; if you know the density of the material, multiply by the thickness. Our standard mat/roving layup is 96 lb./cu. ft. (1,538 kg/m³). For more accuracy, however, you can refer to Table 4-16.

Example:

Take the lower topsides of our *Fish 'n Squish.* The laminate we called for was 0.404-in.-thick (10.26 mm) mat/roving combination. Multiply 0.404-in. thick × 8.00 lb./sq. ft. 1-in. thick = 3.23 lb./sq. ft. (10.26 mm thick × 1.53 kg/m² 1 mm thick = 15.67 kg/m²). Use the same approach for each region of the laminate.

You can also determine the weight of dry glass and resin required. Because the laminate is 35 percent glass by weight, just multiply the laminate weight by 35 percent to get the dry-glass content, and by 65 percent to get the resin content (or as appropriate for the lami-nate). For *Fish 'n Squish*'s lower topsides, this would be 1.13 pounds of dry glass cloth for each square foot and 2.1 pounds of resin for each square foot for the lower topsides (or 5.48 kg of dry glass cloth for each square meter and 10.19 kg of resin for each square meter for the lower topsides).

Multiplying these values out for the entire hull structure gives you purchase quantities. (Be sure to add in a wastage allowance.) For an even more detailed purchase breakdown, subdivide each laminate section into its respective thickness of mat, combi-mat, and roving only. Then, determine weights and quantity for each fabric style and its resin, per square foot or per square meter.

Alternative for Building Bulk in Laminate

The bottom and keel laminate we called for on *Fish 'n Squish* is fairly thick. The boat's bottom, for instance, is five layers of 24-15 (1,271 g/m²) combi-mat, 0.493 inch (12.52 mm) thick. An alternative to laying down five layers of combi-mat would be to replace the combi-mat in the center of the laminate (where the fibers are stressed the least) with a bulk material. These are mat-like products available under various trade names such as

---

TABLE 4-16 Hand-Layup Polyester Laminate Densities (Weights)

	Glass Content by Weight	Density, lb./cu. ft. (kg/m³)	lb./sq. ft. (kg/m²), 1-in. (1 mm) thick
Mat only	28%	85 (1,360)	7.08 (1.36)
Mat/Roving	35%	96 (1,538)	8.00 (1.53)
Roving only	38%	99 (1,585)	8.25 (1.58)

CoreMat and Tiger Core. They are usually manufactured in dry thicknesses ranging from 1.5 to 10 mm (0.059 to 0.39 inch). After wet-out and roll-down, these finish to between 1 and 9 mm (0.039 and 0.35 inch).

For *Fish 'n Squish*'s hull bottom, we could replace the interior three layers of 24-15 with a single layer of 9 mm (0.35 inch) bulk-mat, with a finish of about 8 mm (0.31 inch). This would leave a single layer of 24-15 to make essentially inside and outside skins over a bulk-mat core, plus the external-mat skin coat. The advantage is that the labor of applying the three interior 24-15 layers has been reduced to one layer—not insignificant. Our new bulk-mat hull bottom would finish 13.74 mm (0.54 inch) thick—an increase of 9 percent in thickness.

All-mat laminates (which also can be used for bulking) and materials like bulk-mat are not as strong as mat/roving laminates. This drawback to bulk-mat (or to mat-laminate bulking) is largely overcome by using it in the laminate interior, where the fibers do the least work. Another drawback, however, can't be easily overcome. Bulk-mat laminates are relatively brittle. When they are loaded heavily enough to flex, they have a greater tendency to crack.

FORMULA 4-17

Bulk-Mat Laminates

For this reason, bulk-mat or all-mat-bulked laminates should total at least 5 percent thicker than the equivalent mat/roving laminate. Furthermore, no more than 70 percent of the laminate, at the center, should be of bulk-mat or mat-bulk, and the inner and outer skins (of mat/roving) should be a minimum of 0.90 and 1.0 inch (22.8 and 25.4 mm) thick, respectively.

We're just skirting these limits with the bulk-mat laminate we spec'd previously. Bulk-mat or all-mat-bulk is workable and safe. It is an excellent way to reduce labor cost and production time. In the final analysis—for really rugged use—the standard mat/roving laminate originally specified has slightly greater resistance to severe impact damage. The mat/roving laminate can take greater deflection (thus absorbing more energy) before failure.

Some builders use bulk-mat under the skin coat to further reduce the chance of print-through. I don't recommend this application because the external bulk-mat is brittle and subject to extensive cracking on sharp impact.

Bulk-mat is, however, a superb material for laminating up interior, trim, and detail components quickly, especially when weight is not critical. Intelligent use of bulk-mat to fabricate components such as instrument panels, bridge moldings, deck boxes, fish wells, and trim moldings is a very economical way to make relatively stiff FRP parts quickly.

FIVE

Fiberglass: Internal Structure

Longitudinals

The hull shell we specified in chapter 4 is only part of the picture. The shell requires internal structure for adequate strength. The principal components of this internal structure are engine beds, longitudinal stringers, bulkheads and/or ring frames, and floors.

Longitudinal Stringers

FORMULA 5-1

Number of Longitudinal Hull Stringers

For single-skin (solid FRP) hulls, this rule requires five continuous longitudinal stringers on each side of the hull inside (10 stringers total). The underside of the deck requires similarly spaced stringers as well.

Working up one side of the hull, two stringers—usually engine beds—are located roughly equidistant between the keel and the chine (or the turn of the bilge). One stringer is either a stringer proper at the turn of the bilge or is the reinforced chine itself. Two additional stringers are located roughly equidistant between the sheer and the chine (or the turn of the bilge). Without this stringer system, the solid FRP hull shell will be too bendy.

ENGINE BEDS/STRINGERS

Engine beds/stringers are the principal fore-n-aft (longitudinal) members in most FRP hull bottoms. They should run continuously and unbroken over the bottom inside for nearly the full length of the vessel. Single-engine craft will have two engine beds and twin-engine craft will have four (two for each engine). On single-engine planing vessels, it is recommended that four "engine beds" still be used. The outer beds act simply as longitudinal stringers about midway between the inner engine bed and the chine (or the turn of the bilge).

Engine beds are foam or balsa cores cut to shape—with vertical sides and the top (upper) corners well rounded—and covered with an FRP laminate that runs off onto the hull bottom on both sides of the stringer. This runout is usually referred to as *tabbing*. At the engine mounts, the top third of the core—at the engine-mount-bolt area—must be solid wood. Engine-bed/stringer dimensions should be as follows (see also chapter 2).

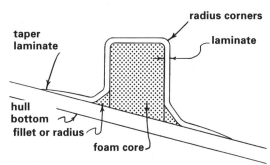

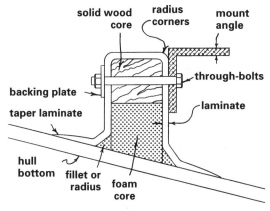

Engine-bed stringers not at engines

Engine-bed stringers at engines

FORMULA 5-2

Engine-Bed/Stringer Dimensions

Height and width of engine-bed/stringer core (foam or balsa core), not at the engines:

in. = 3.1 × $Sn^{0.3}$ (English)
mm = 78.7 × $Sn^{0.3}$ (Metric)

Height of cores at the engines = 1.5 × the width, with roughly the top third of solid wood

Where

Sn = Scantling Number

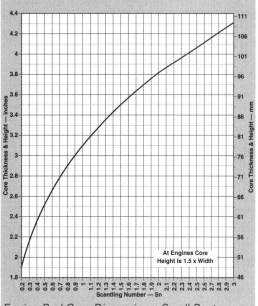

Engine-Bed Core Dimensions: Small Boats

(continued)

Engine-bed/stringer laminate thickness, not at engine mounts:

(English)

in. $= 0.18 \times Sn^{0.4} \times$ *% increase for speed* $\times$ *% increase for displacement*

(Metric)

mm $= 4.6 \times Sn^{0.4} \times$ *% increase for speed* $\times$ *% increase for displacement*

Laminate thickness at engine mounts = $1.4 \times$ *laminate not at the engine mounts*

Laminate tabbing runoff = $10 \times$ *laminate thickness, on both sides of the engine bed/stringer*

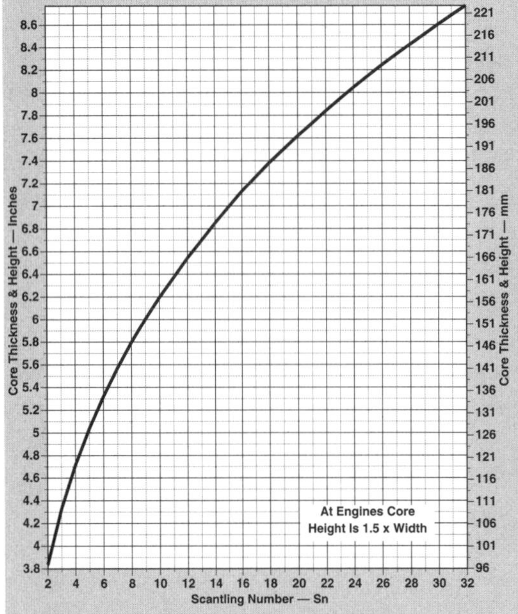

Engine-Bed Core Dimensions: Large Boats

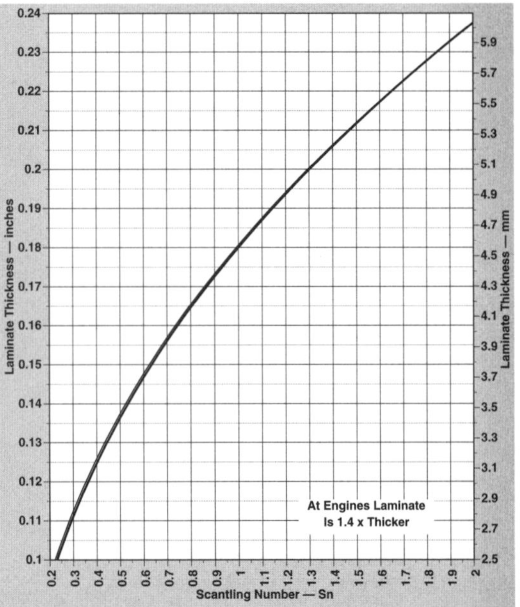

Engine-Bed Laminate Thickness: Small Boats

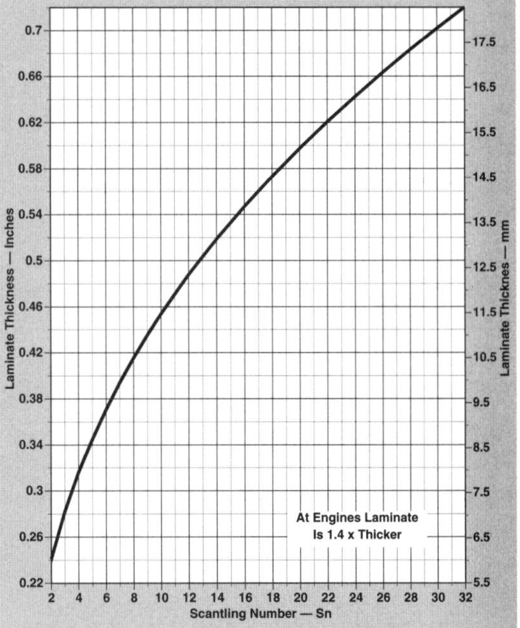

Engine-Bed Laminate Thickness: Large Boats

Example:

Our 40-foot (12.19 m) *Fish 'n Squish*, with an Sn of 2.97, would require foam or balsa cores 4.3 inches thick and 4.3 inches high (109 × 109 mm) not at the engine mounts; and 4.3 inches wide and 6.45 inches high (109 × 164 mm) at the engine mounts.

Adding the 15 percent increase for the boat's 25-knot speed, the laminate should be 0.32 inch (8.1 mm) thick, not at the engines, and 0.45 inch (11.3 mm) thick at the engines. A layer of 1.5-oz. mat plus three layers of 24-15 combi-mat (457 g/m^2 mat plus 814 g/m^2 roving) will generate this away from the engine mounts.

Five layers of 24-15 combi-mat would be sufficient at the engine mounts. It is best to use a layer of 1.5-oz. (457 g/m^2) mat against the core. This makes for better adhesion to the core, so you should add another layer of 1.5-oz. (457 g/m^2) mat to the engine beds at the engine mounts.

The laminate should be tabbed onto the hull for 3.2 inches (81 mm) and, at the engine mounts, 4.5 inches (113 mm) on either side of the engine beds/stringers.

The engine beds can be higher and/or wider than called for previously if necessary to mount the engine properly, but never lower or thinner. In all cases, there must be a foam or balsa fillet strip or a putty fillet in the corners of the stringer where it meets the hull. The laminate must run smoothly over this fillet onto the hull inside to ensure proper strength.

NOTE: Some builders have installed hollow- or partially hollow-core engine beds/stringers. They reason that the core is really just a former and does no work, so they can save weight. Although many fine craft are constructed this way, hollow stringers worry me, because any small cracks or leaks into the hollow stringer will turn it into a rather long water tank. Not only could this add considerable weight, but—should it freeze—it also will burst open the stringer and destroy its strength. It is accurate, however, that the core is a nonstructural former. You can use any low-cost foam that is convenient, as long as it is compatible with the resin and cannot absorb water. (Solid-wood core at the engine mounts is *always* required.)

FORMULA 5-3

Longitudinals or Hull and Deck Stringers

Hull stringers are determined as follows:

Stringer Core Width, in. = $3.12 \times Sn^{0.28}$ (English)

Stringer Core Width, mm = $79.2 \times Sn^{0.28}$ (Metric)

Stringer Core Height = half core width

Stringer Laminate Thickness, in. = $0.17 \times Sn^{0.38}$ (English)

Stringer Laminate Thickness, mm = $4.32 \times Sn^{0.38}$ (Metric)

Stringer Laminate Tabbing Runout on Hull: $10 \times$ laminate thickness, on both sides of the stringer

Deck Stringer Spacing: no greater than the maximum distance—center to center—of the widest separation between the hull stringers on the upper topsides, or 32 inches (80 cm), whichever is less

(continued)

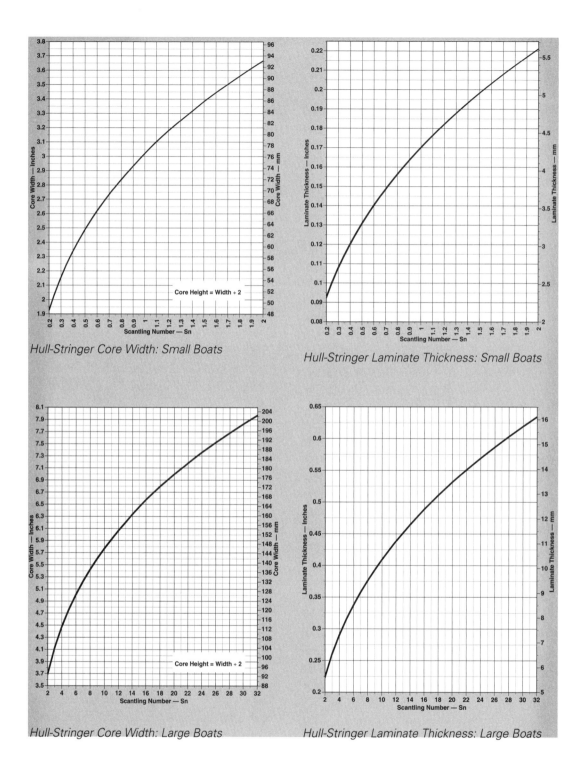

Hull-Stringer Core Width: Small Boats

Hull-Stringer Laminate Thickness: Small Boats

Hull-Stringer Core Width: Large Boats

Hull-Stringer Laminate Thickness: Large Boats

The stringer cores should be roughly trapezoidal in section, with their sides angled in at 15 to 20 degrees from the base (against the inside of the hull). The top (inside) corners of the core must be well rounded off to allow the laminate to drape over it properly.

Example:

Fish 'n Squish, with an Sn of 2.97, would require hull stringers with cores 4.25 inches wide and 2.25 inches high (108 mm wide and 54 mm high). The laminate thickness should be 0.25 inch (6.5 mm). This could be made of three layers of 24-15 combi-mat, totalling 0.267 inch (6.7 mm). The tabbing should extend 2.67 inches (6.7 cm) onto the hull.

FORMULA 5-4
Chine Reinforcing

On hard-chine craft, the corner of the chine itself forms a stiffening member. This eliminates the need for the bilge stringer; however, chine reinforcing should be added longitudinally along the inside of the chine, as follows:

Chine Reinforcing Thickness = 35 percent of the hull-bottom thickness

Chine Reinforcing Width = 70 times the reinforcing laminate thickness

Example:

We found that *Fish 'n Squish* would have a hull-bottom thickness of 0.493 inch (12.52 mm). Accordingly, the chine reinforcing would be 0.17 inch (4.38 mm) thick, and it should be 11.9 (use 12) inches wide—6 inches along the bottom, and 6 inches up the topsides (310 mm; that is, 155 mm along the bottom and 155 mm along the topsides).

As with all tabbing and reinforcing, the chine reinforcement should be tapered away from maximum thickness at the chine to just one or two layers of cloth at the edges.

Transverse Members

BULKHEADS AND RING FRAMES

Bulkheads and/or ring frames provide most of the transverse strength in FRP hulls. Bulkheads must be tabbed into the hull along both front and back faces and around their entire perimeter (see photo on p. 334). Bulkheads should be—very roughly—evenly spaced; strive to make them closest together between Stations 2 and 6, where slamming and rigging loads are maximum on both powerboats and sailboats (see photo on p. 333).

NOTE: Where bulkheads will intrude on the interior, ring frames can be substituted (discussed later in this chapter). Standard bulkheads are slightly stiffer than ring frames, however, so use as many true bulkheads as practical.

On sailboats, there should be ideally two bulkheads at the mast—one in front of the mast step and one aft. At least one bulkhead/ring frame at the mast is required. There must also be at least one bulkhead/ring frame at or near the shroud chainplates.

The tabbing that holds the bulkhead in place may be of combi-mat, but it is best made of a bi-axial-style stitch-mat, which more efficiently transmits the loads into the hull. The light mat on the stitch-mat provides a more reliable bond between layers and to the hull and bulkhead than bi-ax alone.

FORMULA 5-5

Bulkheads—Number, Thickness, and Tabbing

Minimum Number of Bulkheads and/or Ring Frames: $0.5 \times$ Scantling $LOA^{0.7}$ (English)

(continued)

Minimum Number of Bulkheads and/or Ring Frames: $1.15 \times$ Scantling $LOA^{0.7}$ (Metric)

NOTE: Use the scantling length overall, not the Sn.

For Workboats: Increase the number of bulkheads or ring frames by at least one.

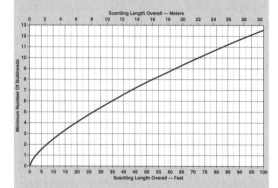

Minimum Number of Bulkheads

Minimum Bulkhead Thickness (for Solid Plywood): in. $= 0.45 \times Sn^{0.3}$ (English)

Minimum Bulkhead Thickness (for Solid Plywood): mm $= 11.43 \times Sn^{0.3}$ (Metric)

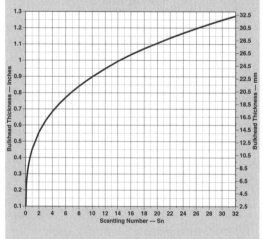

Bulkhead Thickness

Minimum Cored-Bulkhead Thickness: $1.1 \times$ minimum solid-plywood thickness

Weight of Bi-Axial Glass Tabbing, oz./sq. yd. $= 22 \times Sn^{0.3}$ (English)

Weight of Bi-Axial Glass Tabbing, $g/m^2 = 746 \times Sn^{0.3}$ (Metric)

Tabbing Runout on Hull and on Bulkhead, in. $= 0.6 \times (oz./sq. yd.)^{0.56}$ (English)

Tabbing Runout on Hull and on Bulkhead, mm $= 2.1 \times (g/m^2)^{0.56}$ (Metric)

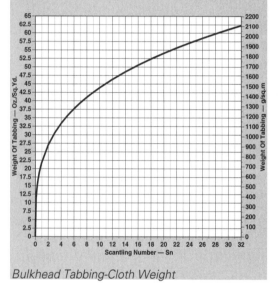

Bulkhead Tabbing-Cloth Weight

Example:

Our trusty *Fish 'n Squish* doesn't have extreme overhangs, so its scantling length overall is simply 40 feet (12.19 m). It would require

  6.6 (use 7) bulkheads minimum (if a workboat, add 1 for 8 bulkheads minimum).

  0.62-in.; use ⁵/₈-in. solid-ply bulkheads, or

  15.8 mm; use 15 mm solid-ply bulkheads, or

0.68-in.; use $^5/_8$- or $^3/_4$-in. balsa-cored or foam-cored bulkheads, or

17.4 mm; use 18 mm balsa-cored or foam-cored bulkheads

30.4-oz./sq. yd. tabbing, use two layers Hexcel/Knytex DBM1708 (35.5 oz./sq. yd.)

1,030 g/m² tabbing, use two layers Hexcel/Knytex DBM1708 (1,204 g/m²)

4.3-in. tabbing run out onto the hull and the bulkhead

109 mm tabbing run out onto the hull and the bulkhead

Alternately, 24-15 combi-mat of approximately this weight can be used, but will not be quite as strong. Do not use mat only for tabbing.

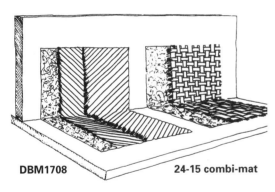

DBM1708   **24-15 combi-mat**

Plus/minus 45-degree bi-axial stitch-mat is superior to 24-15 combi-mat for tabbing in bulkheads and panels. It has a higher proportion of roving to mat and the fibers are better aligned to take torsional loads. Plus/minus 45 bi-axials are not superior for laying up stringers. Here, combi-mat or 0,90 stitch mat places 50 percent of the fibers along the working axis. Plus/minus 45 bi-axial would have all the fibers working at an angle (along the bias), which is weaker.
(Courtesy Hexcel/Knytex)

NOTE: DBM1708 is a bi-axial style E-glass with 0.75-oz. (228 g/m²) mat attached (thus the final "08," a rounding of 0.75). The "17" stands for 17-oz./sq. yd. bi-ax fabric—an 8.5-oz. layer running diagonally one way, and a second 8.5-oz. layer running diagonally across the first layer (576 g/m² bi-ax fabric of two 288 g/m² diagonal layers).

In all cases, there must be a putty fillet or a foam or balsa fillet strip in the corner of the bulkhead where it meets the hull. The fillet should be formed to approximately a 2-inch (50 mm) radius.

Bulkheads thinner than $^5/_8$ inch (15 mm) are somewhat bendy and can be inconvenient to work with; accordingly, many builders use $^5/_8$-inch (15 mm) or thicker bulkheads even on smaller hulls. The alternative is to install either temporary or permanent cleats on thinner bulkheads to help hold them rigid until they are fully tabbed in place.

WATERTIGHT/COLLISION BULKHEADS

Use Formula 9-29 for watertight bulkheads. Except when the bulkheads are to be tabbed into the hull, use tabbing 1.3 times heavier than for standard bulkheads (above); tabbing runouts 1.1 times longer on both the bulkheads and on the hull. Stiffeners should end about 2 to 3 inches (50 to 75 mm) inboard from the tabbing on the bulkhead.

FORMULA 5-6

Bulkhead Backing Strip

Where the bulkhead contacts the hull, it leaves a hard spot. This can cause the bulkhead line to form a crease, clearly visible from outside, and it can cause stress concentrations that weaken the hull. Before installing the bulkhead or

(continued)

ELASTOMETRIC FOAM SPACERS AT BULKHEAD-TO-HULL JOINT

The U.S. Coast Guard requires a trapezoidal foam spacer between the edge of the bulkhead and the inside of the hull shell on FRP vessels intended for passenger-carrying as Subchapter-T boats (see photo on p. 334). The purpose of the spacer is, again, to avoid hard spots on the hull and to distribute the loads over the width of the tabbing. You must install the spacers to comply with the Code of Federal Regulations and obtain certification.

RING FRAMES IN PLACE OF BULKHEADS

More bulkheads are better than fewer bulkheads. If possible, it is best to use one or two additional bulkheads over the minimum specified previously. Frequently, even using the minimum number of bulkheads is difficult or inconvenient, however, because the bulkheads would interfere with the machinery, tanks, or accommodations. Where a bulkhead can't be used, a ring frame can be substituted (see photo on p. 334). The ring frame should be exactly the same dimensions and construction as the engine beds/stringers, not at the engine mounts, but—of course—running transversely.

FLOORS

Floors provide additional transverse strength at the hull-bottom inside. They spread the loads of ballast-keel bolts and the mast step.

In cored-FRP construction, floors are principally used on sailboats; however, high-speed planing craft (more than 30 knots) should have at least one floor midway between each bulkhead, between Stations 1 and 6, where slamming loads are highest. Floors should be foam- or balsa-cored FRP, similar to the engine beds/stringers.

FORMULA 5-7

Floors for Powerboats

Fore-n-aft Thickness of Floor Core (Foam or Balsa):

$in. = 3.1 \times Sn^{0.3}$ *(English)*

$mm = 78.7 \times Sn^{0.3}$ *(Metric)*

Minimum Height of Floor Cores = 2.5 × the fore-n-aft thickness

Where

Sn = Scantling Number

(See also chapter 2)

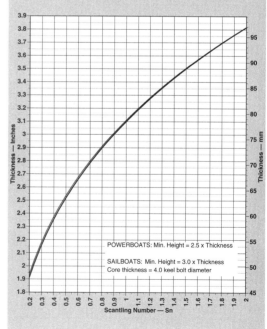

Floor-Core Thickness: Small Boats

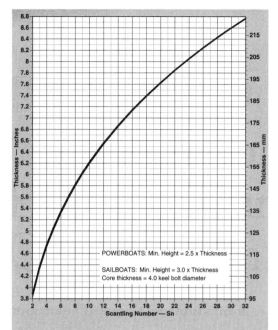

Floor-Core Thickness: Large Boats

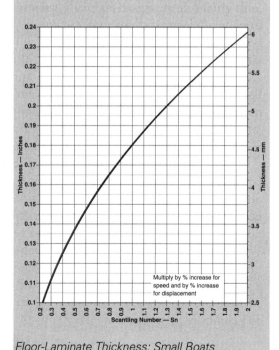

Floor-Laminate Thickness: Small Boats

Powerboat Floor-Laminate Thickness

in. = 0.18 × Sn$^{0.4}$ × % increase for speed × % increase for displacement (English)

mm = 4.6 × Sn$^{0.4}$ × % increase for speed × % increase for displacement (Metric)

Laminate Tabbing Runout: fore-n-aft core thickness, on both sides of the floors

Floor-Laminate Thickness: Large Boats

Example:

Our 40-foot (12.19 m) *Fish 'n Squish*, with an Sn of 2.97, would require foam or balsa cores 4.3 inches thick, fore-n-aft, and 10.75 inches high (109 × 273 mm). The tabbing runout would be 4.3 inches (109 mm).

Once again, adding the 15 percent increase for the boat's 25-knot speed, the floor laminate should be 0.32 inch (8.1 mm) thick. As with the engine beds, a layer of 1.5-oz. mat plus three layers of 24-15 combi-mat (457 g/m^2 mat plus 814 g/m^2 roving) will accomplish this. Use a layer of 1.5-oz. (457 g/m²) mat against the core for best drape and adhesion.

In both cases, the laminate should be tabbed onto the hull for 4.3 inches (109 mm) on either side of the engine beds/stringers, and the same distance transversely on the end of the floors athwartships.

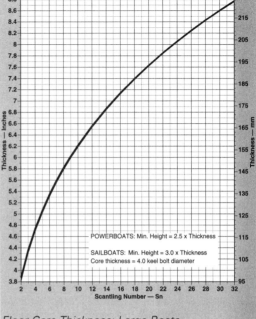

Floor-Core Thickness: Large Boats

FORMULA 5-8

Floors for Sailboats: Cores

Floor-Core Thickness: same as for powerboats or 4 × keel-bolt diameter, whichever is larger

Minimum Floor Height: = 3 × wood core thickness

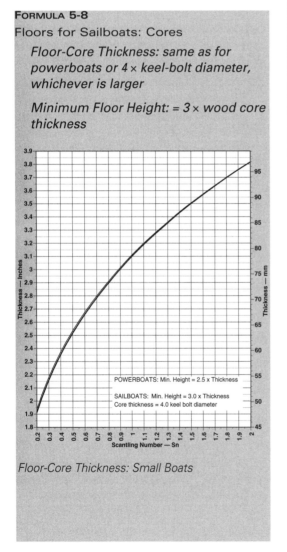

Floor-Core Thickness: Small Boats

Cores for floors with keel bolts and floors at the mast step should be solid wood sawn and/or laminated to shape (not plywood, and not foam or balsa core). Special care must be taken to seal the wood with at least three coats of resin before installation, and then to reseal the keel bolt and any other fastening holes with resin after boring. Finally, great care must be taken to seal and bed the keel bolts in marine bedding compound, inside and out.

The top corners of the floors must be well rounded-off for proper drape of the fiberglass without hard spots, and a foam, balsa, or putty-grout fillet must run along the floor joint at the hull.

Floors at keel bolts and mast steps take very large loads; their laminate needs to be quite heavy.

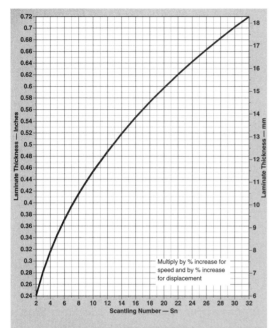

Floor-Laminate Thickness: Large Boats

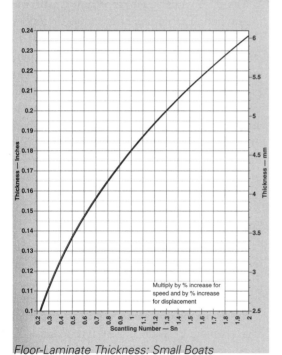

Floor-Laminate Thickness: Small Boats

FORMULA 5-9

Sailboat Floor-Laminate Thickness and Maximum Spacing

Floor-Laminate Thickness = same as powerboat floor laminate

Laminate Tabbing Runout = 12 × laminate thickness

Maximum Floor Spacing at Ballast Keel, in. = 16 × $Sn^{0.2}$, on center (English)

Maximum Floor Spacing at Ballast Keel, mm = 406 × $Sn^{0.2}$, on center or centered on each keel bolt (Metric)

Minimum Number of Floors at Mast Step = 3 × $Sn^{0.2}$

Where

Sn = Scantling Number

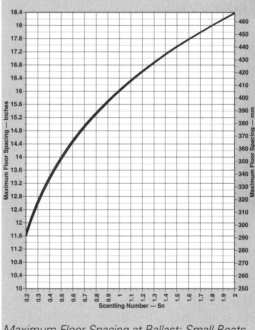

Maximum Floor Spacing at Ballast: Small Boats

(continued)

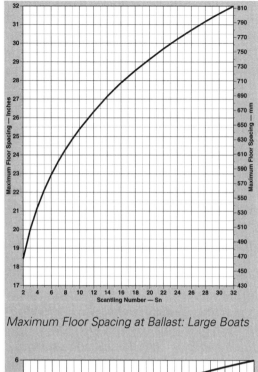

Maximum Floor Spacing at Ballast: Large Boats

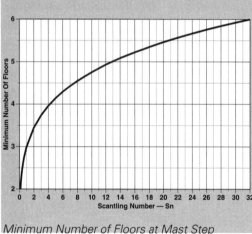

Minimum Number of Floors at Mast Step

Example:

If our *Fish 'n Squish* is a 40-foot (12.19 m) sloop with an Sn of 2.97, we would find

Minimum Wood-Core Floor Thickness = 4.29; use 4.25 in.

Minimum Wood-Core Floor Thickness = 108.9; use 110 mm

Minimum Wood-Core Height = 12.87; use 13 in.

Minimum Wood-Core Height = 326.7; use 325 mm

Laminate Thickness = 0.28 in.

Laminate Thickness = 7.1 mm

Laminate Tabbing Runout on Hull = 3.34; use 3.5 in.

Laminate Tabbing Runout on Hull = 85.2; use 90 mm

Maximum Floor Spacing at Ballast Keel = 19.9 (use 20 in.) on center

Maximum Floor Spacing at Ballast Keel = 532 (use 530 mm) on center

Minimum Number of Floors at Mast Step = 3.73; use four floors

NOTE: The mast step should land on, be notched over, and be fastened to the floors. Floors must extend at least 30 percent of beam-overall athwartships (a span of 30 percent of beam or more); a 40 to 45 percent span is better where possible. On the inside of hulls without hollow garboards, the minimum heights given will usually automatically create floors of sufficient athwartships span. With hollow garboards or on very steep deadrise hulls, it may be necessary to increase floor height to get sufficient athwartships span.

If this intrudes too much on the interior arrangement or machinery, the floor height amidships can be limited to the minimum given previously and the floor extended athwartships with a laminated "half-frame" top of solid laminated timber, the same width as the floor and the same height as the floor width (square in section). This laminated half-frame floor top is screwed and glued to the top of the standard floor core. It is run athwart-ships up the hull-bottom inside until the required span is reached. The laminated "partial-frame" floor top should be tapered away at the ends, port and starboard, by reducing the number of laminations in steps. The entire standard floor core plus the laminated half-frame floor top forms the complete solid-wood core, and it is then entirely glassed over with the recommended floor laminate.

Additional Structures

HULL-TO-DECK JOINT

The hull-to-deck joint is critical, yet there are so many variations of hull construction, boat type, construction method, and desired finished appearance that it is difficult to give a comprehensive rule. The following discussion will serve as a general guide.

There are three common hull-to-deck joint configurations: out-turned flange, in-turned flange, and shoebox. Each works well structurally.

Out-Turned Flange Hull-to-Deck Joint

My personal preference is for the out-turned flange because it is easier to assemble with good quality control. The topsides are turned outboard to form a flat shelf at the sheer, and the deck is extended outboard to form a matching flange above. During assembly, the deck can be rested on the hull and maneuvered around until you get a proper fit. The parts are then clamped in place, marked, and drilled for the vertical through-bolt fasteners. If you lay up excess flange width (which you should), it's not difficult to get a good fit, and the excess is now trimmed back to the finished flange-width dimension. Then the deck is lifted off, bedding compound is ap-plied, and the whole is reassembled and bolted together permanently.

All the bolts are easy to install, tighten securely, and inspect—a great advantage, in addition to the ease of overall fit. The whole is finished off with a vinyl, aluminum, or wooden molding/rubstrip. This not only hides the joint, but also acts as a very effective chafe guard. Some surveyors have developed a poor opinion of the out-turned flange joint because they have inspected cheaply made vessels with improper scantlings and machine-screw fastenings rather than proper through-bolts. Correctly fabricated, I believe the out-turned flange, however, is the most rugged and the easiest to build. Proper construction requires through-bolts, never pop rivets or machine screws. Heavy FRP flanges and rugged, rigid vinyl or wood molding cover caps are also a must.

In-Turned Flange Hull-to-Deck Joint

The in-turned flange is common on sailboats in particular, but can be found on all types of vessels. In this case, the hull-side laminate is turned in, not out, at the sheer. The deck simply rests on this in-turned shelf, as with the out-turned shelf of the out-turned flange. Fitting and installation are roughly the same for both in-turned and out-turned flanges; however, the vertical bolts are not as readily accessible inside the hull for easy assembly and checking as they are with the out-turned flange. Another drawback is that—for fabrication—the in-turned flange requires that a removable shelf be built onto the hull mold. This complicates not only initial tooling, but also the layup of every hull and the process of pulling the hull from the mold each time. Again, the exterior of the joint is covered and protected by a rubstrip.

Some people believe that the in-turned flange presents a sleeker appearance than the out-turned flange, but this depends on how the flange-covering rubstrip is treated in each case, overall styling considerations, and personal taste.

Shoebox Hull-to-Deck Joint

The shoebox hull-to-deck joint is similar to its namesake. The topsides are bent in slightly to vertical with a slight knuckle so it forms a flange exactly straight up and down at the joint (i.e., the upper inch or two [25 to 50 mm]). The deck is fabricated with a flange turned down roughly at right angles to the deck (parallel to the vertical topsides above the knuckle). Then the deck is lowered onto the hull, with the down-turned deck flange surrounding the outside of the hull topsides at the knuckle.

There are many successful hulls with the shoebox hull-to-deck joint, but I don't understand its popularity. On most larger craft, by the time some of the interior machinery, tanks, and rough joinerwork have been installed (usually before the deck is attached), it is totally impossible to reach some portions of the interior to fasten through-bolts. In all these areas, then, sheet-metal screws or the like must be used; this forms a weak joint. Furthermore, the fit between the down-turned deck flange and the vertical topsides, above the knuckle, must be quite precise. Not only does this present initial tooling problems, but it also can add alignment and fitting time during assembly. Where—in the final event—the gap turns out too large, the builder has no choice but to fill with putty-grout on a vertical surface; again, bad practice.

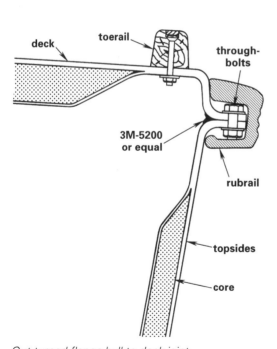

Out-turned flange hull-to-deck joint

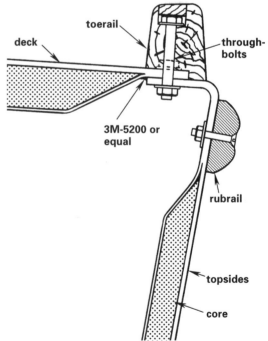

In-turned flange hull-to-deck joint

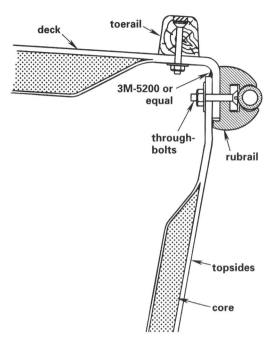

Shoebox hull-to-deck joint

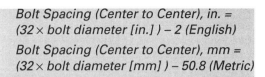

Bolt Spacing (Center to Center), in. =
(32 × bolt diameter [in.]) – 2 (English)

Bolt Spacing (Center to Center), mm =
(32 × bolt diameter [mm]) – 50.8 (Metric)

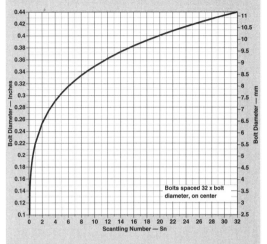

Hull-to-Deck-Joint Bolt Diameter

Flange Width, in. = 23 × (bolt diameter, in.)$^{2.25}$ (English)

Flange Width, mm = 0.4 × (bolt diameter, mm)$^{2.25}$ (Metric)

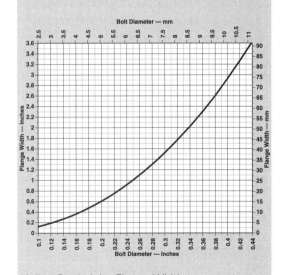

Hull-to-Deck-Joint Flange Width

All types of hull-to-deck joints must be carefully bedded for watertightness and additional strength. You can use a soggy, resin-rich mat strip, 1.5 to 2 oz./sq. ft. (457 to 610 g/m^2), laid between the two flanges. Alternately, you can use an adhesive sealant, such as 3M-5200. Both methods work, but I believe the adhesive sealant to be somewhat longer-lasting and—being more elastic—less likely to leak in the event of local damage.

The following formula gives the required through-bolt and flange dimensions for each of the three hull-to-deck joints.

FORMULA 5-10

Hull-to-Deck Joint

Bolt Diameter, in. = 0.22 × Sn$^{0.20}$
(English)

Bolt Diameter, mm = 5.58 × Sn$^{0.20}$
(Metric)

Example:

For our trusty *Fish 'n Squish* with an Sn of 2.97, we would find

Bolt Diameter = 0.27; use 0.25-in. diameter

Bolt Diameter = 6.9; use 7 mm diameter

Bolt Spacing = 6 in.

Bolt Spacing = 174; use 170 mm

Flange Width = 1.016; use slightly over 1 in. (e.g., 1¹⁄₁₆ in.)

Flange Width = 31.8; use 32 to 35 mm

HULL-TO-DECK-JOINT BONDING ANGLE

The conventional interior treatment for the hull-to-deck joint is to finish it with a molded-in-place fiberglass bonding angle. This angle is made by laminating fiberglass strips inside the hull-to-deck joint. Although this is the standard method, I've come to believe that this bonding angle is not required. For instance, one of my designs is a 34-foot, FRP, 20,000-pound (9,090 kg), twin-diesel Sportfisherman. A number of these vessels have been in hard service for several years. They routinely cruise at 25 knots in Force 5-plus conditions, and not infrequently run at 33 knots in such weather. These craft have the out-turned flange hull-to-deck joint and have no internal bonding angle. None of these vessels has shown the slightest sign of weakness, flexing, or leaking at the hull-to-deck joint. Additionally, installing the bonding angle is often awkward and time-consuming. Nevertheless, the bonding angle is considered standard practice. You may also be required to install it if building to a classification-society rule. If you plan to use

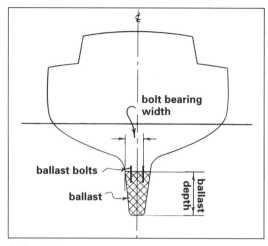

Ballast bolts

a bonding angle, it should be sized using the following formula.

FORMULA 5-11

Bonding Angle

Bonding-Angle Laminate Thickness = 0.7 × upper-topsides laminate thickness

Bonding-Angle Width = 16 × bonding-angle laminate thickness

FORMULA 5-12

Keel-Ballast Bolts

To find the diameter of the keel-ballast bolts,

Load per Bolt, in Pounds or Kilograms = (S.F. 8 × ballast depth × ballast weight) ÷ (2 × bolt-bearing width × number of bolts on one side)

Where

Ballast Depth = distance from hull bottom, or keel-bolt attachment level, to the underside of the ballast, in. or mm

Where

S.F. 8 = a safety factor of 8

Ballast Weight = total weight of ballast, pounds or kilograms

Bolt-Bearing Width = average distance from one row of ballast bolts to the opposite side of the top edge of the ballast keel. (If the keel has a single row of bolts down the centerline—not recommended—all bolts are used, NOT half on one side.)

NOTE: Neglect all bolts on the centerline for keels fastened with most bolts running down two sides of the ballast.

Refer to the bolt-tensile-strength table in appendix 3 to find the bolt diameter.

Example:

Our reliable old *Fish 'n Squish* is a 40-foot (12.19 m) cutter with 8,300 pounds (18,290 kg) of ballast. The bottom of the ballast keel is 45.6 inches (1,158 mm) below the keel-bolts attachment point, and the average bolt-bearing width is 10.5 inches (267 mm). The boat has 18 ballast bolts. Two bolts on the centerline are neglected, leaving 16—8 on each side. Then

Load per Bolt, lb. = S.F. 8 × 45.6-in. ballast depth × 8,300 lb. ÷ 2 × 10.5 in.-bolt width × 8 bolts = 18,020 lb. per bolt

Load per Bolt, lb. = S.F. 8 × 1,158 mm ballast depth × 3,765 kg ÷ 2 × 267 mm bolt width × 8 bolts = 8,165 kg per bolt

Referring to the bolt-breaking-strength table, we would fit *Fish 'n Squish* with $^3/_4$-inch-diameter (20 mm) silicon bronze bolts, with an ultimate tensile strength of 20,068 pounds (9,100 kg) or higher.

The floor's wood core must be at least four times the bolt diameter or 3 inches (80

mm). Accordingly, the 4.25-inch (110 mm) floor thickness found previously is acceptable.

FORMULA 5-13
Keel-Bolt Backing Plates

Backing plates must be placed under each keel-bolt nut, on top of the floors. The backing plates should be equal to the floor's core width in diameter and one-third the thickness of the keel-bolt diameter. Usually, the backing plates are simply square, the same width as the floor width. Even better is a continuous plate on top of the floor from the port-to-starboard keel bolt.

Stainless-steel bolts should have either stainless or mild-steel backing plates; bronze bolts must use bronze backing plates. (Mild-steel backing plates should be hot-dip galvanized and/or well painted all around with an epoxy-based paint.) The use of stainless-steel keel bolts should be avoided whenever possible. Stainless-steel can suffer from severe pitting corrosion over time. For this reason, Type 302 or 304 alloys are not acceptable for any keel bolts; only 316L ("L" for low carbon) and Aquamet 22 (also known as Nitronic 50) have sufficient resistance to pitting. Neither is as resistant as bronze. If stainless-steel bolts are used, aluminum backing plates can be used; however, they should be 1.5 times thicker than the thicknesses given for steel and bronze. Monel is also an excellent keel-bolt material. Use either bronze or Monel backing plates with Monel bolts.

Example:

For *Fish 'n Squish's* $^3/_4$-inch-diameter keel bolts, the backing plate should be $^1/_4$ inch thick and 3 inches in diameter. For *Fish 'n*

Squish's 20 mm diameter keel bolts, the backing plate should be 6.6; use 8 mm thickness and 80 mm diameter.

The best procedure would be to use a single plate 3 inches (80 mm) wide, fore-n-aft, and running athwartships continuously under both keel bolts in the floor.

FORMULA 5-14
Laminate at Chainplates

There are several methods of attaching chainplates to the hull. They may be attached to bulkheads, internal knees, special framing, or tie-rods. The common "traditional" method, however, is to bolt the chainplates to the hull topsides. Where this is done, the topsides laminate must be increased as follows:

Chainplate-Region Topsides Laminate = 1.3 × topsides laminate thickness

Fore-n-Aft Length of Chainplate Region = beam overall at chainplates

Height of Chainplate Region = from sheer down to lowest chainplate bolt, plus a distance equal to 20 times the lowest bolt diameter down beyond the lowest bolt

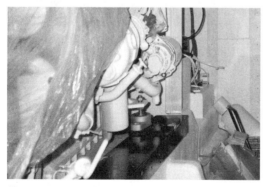

Proper steel engine mounts. These angles have been placed on top of the beds. They impart tremendous rigidity to the structure.

Improper engine mounts. These plywood mounts impart no rigidity. They aren't even sealed. It's only a matter of time before they soften or split, causing vibration, misalignment, or worse.

As we saw in Formulas 5-1 and 5-2, the engine beds are critical structures. Continuous, unbroken longitudinal strength is vital. In addition, the engine itself must be fastened to the beds with great strength and rigidity. The engine mounts must be bolted to a steel or aluminum angle. This angle must be through-bolted to the wood-core portion of the engine bed with a metal backing strip on the opposite side.

Most commonly, the angle is bolted to the side of the engine bed, with the flange projecting out from the side to accept the engine mounts. The angle can be installed with the flange facing up or down, as required. Alternately, the angle can be placed on top of the engine bed, and flush against one side. The engine mounts are then bolted to a weldment on top of the angle, or through-bolted down into a transverse insert bar, and run across the wood core, port to starboard, which is drilled and tapped to receive the mount bolts. The top-mounted angle should not only be bolted through the side of the engine bed, but also lag-bolted from the top down into the wood core. The lag bolts should be roughly centered between each pair of transverse through-bolts.

Engine Mounts

The engine-mount angles should extend at least 1.3 times the length of the distance between the engine-mount centers, with the engine roughly centered on the angles.

Use five transverse through-bolts in each bed. Use four lag bolts, in addition to transverse bolts, through the top (if angle is placed on top of bed).

Bolt Diameter (Lag and Transverse), in. = engine weight, lb. ÷ 4,000 (English)

or

Bolt Diameter (Lag and Transverse), in. = 0.012 × hp$^{0.66}$ (English)

Use whichever is larger.

Bolt Diameter (Lag and Transverse), mm = engine weight, kg ÷ 70 (Metric)

Bolt Diameter (Lag and Transverse), mm = 0.37 × kw$^{0.66}$ (Metric)

Use whichever is larger.

Steel angles should be 0.75 times the bolt-diameter thickness. Aluminum angles should equal the bolt diameter in thickness. Both flanges should be at least 10 percent wider than the maximum width of the engine mount's base plate.

Angles that are bolted to the side of the engine beds, with bolts 0.5 inch (12.5 mm) or more in diameter, require two tripping brackets. The brackets should be welded in place approximately 4 inches (100 mm) forward of the aft engine mount and 4 inches (100 mm) aft of the forward engine mount. The tripping brackets should be the same thickness as the angle.

Backing-Strip Length = angle length

Backing-Strip Width = 0.8 × height of angle

Backing-Strip Thickness = 0.6 × angle thickness, but not less than $\frac{3}{16}$-in. (5 mm) steel or $\frac{1}{4}$-in. (6 mm) aluminum

Insert-Bar (if used) Thickness = bolt diameter

Insert-Bar (if used) Width = 3 to 4 times bolt diameter

NOTE: Like all penetrations into a wood core, great care must be taken to seal the slot for the insert bar with resin and to bed the bar very well in marine bedding compound.

SIX

Fiberglass Sandwich or Cored Construction

*A*s discussed in chapter 2, fiberglass is neither a particularly strong nor stiff material. Again, contrary to common belief, solid FRP structures tend to be somewhat heavy when built for adequate stiffness. The best way to reduce weight while increasing stiffness and—to some degree, reducing internal-structure complexity—is to employ *sandwich construction*. It is, however, absolutely vital that you follow the core-installation and bedding procedures outlined in chapter 2. Double-check these procedures with your core and resin manufacturers to get their specific installation/bedding recommendations. Don't let potential core problems scare you away from sandwich construction. Cored hulls and decks are rugged, safe, reliable, and long-lasting. In fact, they are my preference for most FRP structures, including hull bottoms. You simply must take proper care during construction.

WHY CORES WORK

Fundamentally, the way to make a structure stiffer is to make it thicker. Of course, you can't just double the thickness as you would double the weight—too heavy. Instead, use a core material (for this rule, foam or balsa). This way, you have an FRP outer shell and an FRP inner shell bonded (glued) to a tough but very light sandwich material in between. The increase in stiffness is huge. If you had,

An assortment of standard core products: end-grain balsa, rigid panels, and kerfed Contour-kore; pre-manufactured fillet strips and Ribkore; DuraKore strips and center-bottom Baltekmat bulk. (Courtesy Baltek Corporation)

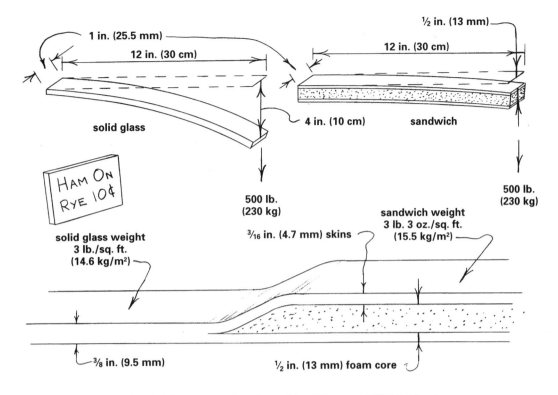

Sandwich anatomy: bending with a 500-pound (230 kg) load

for example, a $^3/_8$-inch-thick (9.5 mm) strip of ordinary solid glass about 1 inch (25.5 mm) wide and a foot (30 cm) long, you would find that a 500-pound (230 kg) load hung on one end would bend it about 4 inches (10 cm). If you took that same strip and slit it in half to make two layers $^3/_{16}$ inch (4.7 mm) thick and 1 inch (25.5 mm) wide, you would have the beginnings of a sandwich-construction hull laminate.

If you add a core—for example, a $^1/_2$ inch (13 mm) of closed-cell foam or end-grain balsa—between the two layers and glue it in place firmly, you would have a much different story. The same 500-pound (230 kg) weight would deflect it barely a $^1/_2$ inch (13 mm)—an eightfold increase in stiffness. Note that you've increased thickness from $^3/_8$ inch (9.5 mm) to $^7/_8$ inch (22.5 mm)—230 percent thicker. In return, you got an 800 percent increase in stiffness, but with only the slight additional weight of the core in between. This is the principle of cored or sandwich construction. Indeed, the increase in stiffness is so marked that you can decrease the total thickness of the fiberglass—the two (i.e., inner plus outer) FRP skins—to less than that of the entire solid-hull laminate. Weight savings are substantial.

Sandwich Hull Shell

Formula 6-1
Sandwich Fiberglass Scantlings

To determine the scantlings for cored or sandwich FRP construction—using the standard layup of alternating layers of mat and woven roving, in polyester resin—calculate the solid-hull-shell thickness as described in chapter 4, then proceed as follows:

Basic Hull-Core Thickness = 2.2 × solid FRP thickness at lower topsides, for entire hull—bottom and topsides—except on planing hulls, where the bottom core is thicker

Planing Hull-Bottom Thickness = 2.2 × solid FRP thickness of hull bottom

Deck-Core Thickness = 1.5 × basic hull-core thickness

Total FRP Laminate Thickness = 0.70 × the solid FRP thickness

For most boats more than 20 feet (6 m), the following is recommended:

Outer-Skin Laminate = 0.40 × the solid FRP thickness

Inner-Skin Laminate = 0.30 × the solid FRP thickness

The additional thickness outside adds abrasion and impact resistance where it is needed most. On small vessels, convenient and practical laminate styles may force you to use roughly the same thickness both inside and out. This is acceptable although not quite as tough as having the thicker outer skin. Sometimes having equal thicknesses in and out is referred to as having a "balanced" laminate or having "balanced" skins.

Formula 6-2
Core Density

For vessels with Sns under 3.0, all the cores should be closed-cell foam, 5.5-lb./cu. ft. (88 kg/m³) density, or end-grain balsa, 6.5-lb./cu. ft. (104 kg/m³) density—or slightly greater. For the bottoms and topsides of boats with Sns more than 3.0, and in the bottoms of all craft with top speeds more than 25 knots, the core density is to be closed-cell foam, 8.0-lb./cu. ft. (128 kg/m³) density, or end-grain balsa, 9.5-lb./cu. ft. (152 kg/m³) density—or slightly greater. (The deck cores can be the lighter density.) This is because both sheer and compressive strength of the core is directly proportional to its density. Higher-density cores are required to handle these greater loads and the bigger panel sizes in larger and/or faster hull laminates. Deck cores on workboats and charter vessels, for example, with Sns more than 3.0 are to be closed-cell foam, 8.0-lb./cu. ft. (128 kg/m³) density, or end-grain balsa, 9.5-lb./cu. ft. (152 kg/m³) density—or slightly greater. Higher-density cores can always be used in place of the minimum required lower density; however, they are more expensive.

ALTERNATE CORES AND DENSITIES

There are types of cores other than closed-cell foam and end-grain balsa; plastic-impregnated paper-honeycomb, all-plastic honeycomb, and aluminum-honeycomb cores (some filled with foam, some open-cell) are the most common. Each is excellent and has specific advantages; however, they are not covered in this rule. Both closed-cell foam and end-grain balsa are available in other densities besides the two "standards" mentioned previously. The higher densities are useful on larger, faster boats and in areas of very high loading, such as at the attachments for cranes, hoists, and windlasses. The lower densities can be used for internal-framing cores like stringers. This rule does not cover application of these other densities, except as mentioned for internal stiffeners in chapter 5.

Example:

Let's return to our salty, 25-knot *Fish 'n Squish*: 40 feet (12.19 m) LOA, beam 12.56 feet, Sn 2.97. We found its solid FRP hull shell in chapter 4. Using this, we can apply Formulas 6-1 and 6-2 to find the sandwich fiberglass scantlings as follows.

Find Laminate and Core Thickness (English)

Outer Deck: solid glass was 0.30 in. × 0.40 = 0.12 in.

Inner Deck: solid glass was 0.30 in. × 0.30 = 0.09 in.

Deck Core: basic core thickness = 0.75 in. × 1.5 = 1.12 in.; use 1.25-in. core

Upper Topsides: laminate same as deck

Upper-Topsides Core: basic core thickness = 0.75-in. core

Outer Lower Topsides: solid glass was 0.36 in. × 0.40 = 0.14 in.

Inner Lower Topsides: solid glass was 0.36 in. × 0.30 = 0.11 in.

Basic Core Thickness: Lower Topsides Core = solid glass was 0.36 in. × 2.2 = 0.79; use 0.75-in. core. (NOTE: On a displacement hull, the 0.75-in. basic core thickness would be used for the bottom core as well.)

Core Density: Sn less than 3.0; use 5.5-lb./cu. ft. foam or 6.5-lb./cu. ft. balsa

Outer Hull Bottom: solid glass was 0.47 in. × 0.40 = 0.19 in.

Inner Hull Bottom: solid glass was 0.47 in. × 0.30 = 0.14 in.

Planing Hull-Bottom Core: solid glass was 0.47 in. × 2.2 = 1.03 in.; use 1-in. core

Planing Bottom-Core Density: 8-lb./cu. ft. foam or 9.5-lb./cu. ft. balsa

Keel and Stem: 0.71-in. solid glass, *DO NOT USE CORE*

Outer Hull-Bottom High-Stress Areas: solid glass was 0.52 in. × 0.40 = 0.21 in.

Inner Hull-Bottom High-Stress Areas: solid glass was 0.52 in. × 0.30 = 0.15 in.

Deck-Hardware-Mounting Areas: See Formula 6-3.

Find Laminate and Core Thickness (Metric)

Outer Deck: solid glass was 7.82 mm × 0.40 = 3.13 mm

Inner Deck: solid glass was 7.82 mm × 0.30 = 2.34 mm

Deck Core: Basic Core Thickness = 20 mm × 1.5 = 30 mm core

Upper Topsides: laminate same as deck

Upper-Topsides Core, Basic Core Thickness: 20 mm core

Outer Lower Topsides: solid glass was 9.2 mm × 0.40 = 3.68 mm

Inner Lower Topsides: solid glass was 9.2 mm × 0.30 = 2.76 mm

Basic Core Thickness: Lower Topsides Core = solid glass was 9.2 mm × 2.2 = 20.24; use

20 mm core (NOTE: On a displacement hull, the 20 mm basic core thickness would be used for the bottom core as well.)

Core Density: Sn less than 3.0; use 88 kg/m³ foam or 104 kg/m³ balsa

Outer Hull Bottom: solid glass was 12.16 mm × 0.40 = 4.86 mm

Inner Hull Bottom: solid glass was 12.16 mm × 0.30 = 3.65 mm

Planing Hull-Bottom Core: solid glass was 12.16 mm × 2.2 = 26.75; use 25 mm core

Planing Bottom-Core Density = 128 kg/m³ foam or 152 kg/m³ balsa

Keel and Stem = 18.24 mm solid glass, DO NOT USE CORE

Outer Hull-Bottom High-Stress Areas: solid glass was 13.37 mm × 0.40 = 5.35 mm

Inner Hull-Bottom High-Stress Areas: solid glass was 13.37 mm × 0.30 = 4.0 mm

Deck-Hardware-Mounting Areas: see Formulas 6-2 through 6-5

Specify Laminate (English)

(Refer to Formulas 4-7 and 4-8 and Table 4-9, or manufacturer's data sheets.) One of the difficulties with sandwich construction—particularly acute for vessels 50 feet and less—is that the inner and outer skins are too thin to use multiple layers of 24-15 combi-mat and still include sufficient mat to avoid print-through and for core bedding. This will cause the actual laminate to be thicker than required by the rule. Instead, we can use 18-10 combi-mat, 0.063 inch thick (i.e., 18-oz./sq. yd. roving stitched to 1.0-oz./sq. ft. mat) for the majority of the laminate (see photo on p. 335).

Deck Outer Skin: 0.12 in. ÷ 0.063 in./layer = 1.9 layers 18-10 combi-mat

1 Layer 0.75-oz. Mat	0.024 in.
2 Layers 18-10 Combi-Mat	0.126 in.
1 Layer 1.5-oz. Mat (Skin Coat)	0.048 in.
Outer Deck-Laminate Thickness	0.222 in.

Deck Inner Skin: 0.09 in. ÷ 0.063 in./layer = 1.4 layers 18-10 combi-mat

1 Layer 18-10 Combi-Mat	0.063 in.
1 Layer 1.0-oz. Mat	0.032 in.
Inner Deck-Laminate Thickness	0.095 in.
Total Laminate Thickness	0.320 in.

Deck Core: 5.5-lb. foam or 6.5-lb. balsa	1.250 in.
Total Deck Thickness	1.570 in.

Upper-Topsides Outer Skin: 0.12 in. ÷ 0.063 in./layer = 1.9 layers 18-10 combi-mat

1 Layer 0.75-oz. Mat	0.024 in.
2 Layers 18-10 Combi-Mat	0.126 in.
1 Layer 1.5-oz. Mat (Skin Coat)	0.048 in.
Upper-Topsides Outer-Laminate Thickness	0.198 in.

Upper-Topsides Inner Skin: 0.09 in. ÷ 0.063 in./layer = 1.4 layers 18-10 combi-mat

1 Layer 18-10 Combi-Mat	0.063 in.
1 Layer 1.0-oz. Mat	0.032 in.
Upper-Topsides Inner-Laminate Thickness	0.095 in.
Total Laminate Thickness	0.290 in.

Upper-Topsides Core: 5.5 lb./ft.³ foam or 6.5 lb./ft.³ balsa	0.75 in.
Total Upper-Topsides Thickness	1.04 in.

Lower-Topsides Outer Skin: 0.14 in. ÷ 0.063 in./layer = 2.2 layers 18-10 combi-mat

1 Layer 0.75-oz. Mat	0.024 in.
2 Layers 18-10 Combi-Mat	0.126 in.
1 Layer 1.5-oz. Mat (Skin Coat)	0.048 in.
Lower-Topsides Outer Laminate	
Thickness	0.198 in.

Lower-Topsides Inner Skin: 0.09 in. ÷ 0.063 in./layer = 1.4 layers 18-10 combi-mat

1 Layer 18-10 Combi-Mat	0.063 in.
1 Layer 1.0-oz. Mat	0.032 in.
Lower-Topsides Inner-Laminate	
Thickness	0.095 in.
Total Laminate Thickness	0.290 in.
Lower-Topsides Core: 5.5 lb./ft.^{3}	
foam or 6.5 lb./ft.^{3} balsa	0.75 in.
Total Lower-Topsides Thickness	1.04 in.

(NOTE: The upper and lower topsides are the same in this case because the thickness of the necessary mat skin coat increases the laminate thickness over the rule requirements.)

Hull-Bottom Outer Skin: 0.19 in. ÷ 0.063 in./layer = 3.0 layers 18-10 combi-mat

1 Layer 0.75-oz. Mat	0.024 in.
3 Layers 18-10 Combi-Mat	0.189 in.
1 Layer 1.5-oz. Mat (Skin Coat)	0.048 in.
Hull-Bottom Outer-Laminate	
Thickness	0.261 in.

Hull-Bottom Inner Skin: 0.11 in. ÷ 0.063 in./layer = 1.74 layers 18-10 combi-mat

2 Layers 18-10 Combi-Mat	0.126 in.
1 Layer 1.0-oz. Mat	0.032 in.
Hull-Bottom Inner-Laminate	
Thickness	0.158 in.
Total Laminate Thickness	0.42 in.

Hull-Bottom Core: 8.0 lb./ft.^{3} foam	
or 9.5 lb./ft.^{3} balsa	1.00 in.
Total Hull-Bottom Thickness	1.42 in.

Solid-Glass Keel and Stem (see Formula 6-10): 0.71-in. thick – 0.395 in. sandwich hull-bottom FRP laminate = 0.315 in., and 0.315 ÷ 0.089 in./ply (24-15 combi-mat) = 3.54 layers

1 Layer 0.75-oz. Mat	0.024 in.
(outer laminate)	
3 Layers 18-10 Combi-Mat	0.189 in.
1 Layer 1.5-oz. Mat (Skin Coat)	0.048 in.
2 Layers 18-10 Combi-Mat	0.126 in.
(inner laminate)	
1 Layer 1.0-oz. Mat	0.032 in.
1 Layer 18-10 Combi-Mat	0.063 in.
(added buildup)	
3 Layers 24-15 Combi-Mat	0.267 in.
Total Keel and Stem Thickness	0.75 in.

Hull-Bottom High-Stress Areas: Use same as standard hull bottom; standard hull bottom is thicker than required by rule, and is as thick as required by rule for high-stress areas.

Specify Laminate (Metric)

(Refer to Formulas 4-7 and 4-8 and Table 4-9, or the manufacturer's data sheets.) One of the difficulties with sandwich construction—particularly acute for vessels 15 m and under—is that the inner and outer skins are too thin to use multiple layers of 24-15 combi-mat (814 g/m^2 roving by 457 g/m^2 mat; 1,271 g/m^2 total) and still include sufficient mat to avoid print-through and for core bedding. This will cause the actual laminate to be thicker than required by the rule. Instead, we can use 18-10 combi-mat, 1.6 mm thick (610 g/m² roving stitched to 305 g/m² mat; 915 g/m² total) for the majority of the laminate.

Deck Outer Skin: 3.13 mm ÷ 1.6 mm/layer = 1.9 layers 18-10 combi-mat

1 Layer 228 g/m² Mat	0.61 mm
2 Layers 18-10 (915 g/m²) Combi-Mat	3.20 mm
1 Layer 457 g/m² Mat (Skin Coat)	1.22 mm
Outer Deck-Laminate Thickness	5.03 mm

Deck Inner Skin: 2.34 mm ÷ 1.6 mm/layer = 1.4 layers 18-10 combi-mat

1 Layer 18-10 (915 g/m²) Combi-mat	1.60 mm
1 Layer 305 g/m² Mat	0.81 mm
Inner Deck-Laminate Thickness	2.41 mm
Total Laminate Thickness	7.44 mm
Deck Core: 88 kg/m³ foam, or 104 kg/m³ balsa	30.00 mm
Total Deck Thickness	37.44 mm

Upper-Topsides Outer Skin: 3.13 mm ÷ 1.6 mm/layer = 1.9 layers 18-10 combi-mat

1 Layer 228 g/m² Mat	0.61 mm
2 Layers 18-10 (915 g/m²) Combi-Mat	3.20 mm
1 Layer 457 g/m² Mat (Skin Coat)	1.22 mm
Upper-Topsides Outer-Laminate Thickness	5.03 mm

Upper-Topsides Inner Skin: 2.34 mm ÷ 1.6 mm/layer = 1.4 layers 18-10 combi-mat

1 Layer 18-10 (915 g/m²) Combi-Mat	1.60 mm
1 Layer 305 g/m² Mat	0.81 mm

Upper-Topsides Inner-Laminate Thickness 2.41 mm

Total Laminate Thickness	7.44 mm
Upper-Topsides Core: 88 kg/m³ foam or 104 kg/m³ balsa	20.00 mm
Total Upper Topsides Thickness	27.44 mm

Lower-Topsides Outer Skin: 3.68 mm ÷ 1.6 mm/layer = 2.2 layers 18-10 combi-mat

1 Layer 228 g/m² Mat	0.61 mm
2 Layers 18-10 (915 g/m²) Combi-Mat	3.20 mm
1 Layer 457 g/m² Mat (Skin Coat)	1.22 mm
Lower-Topsides Outer-Laminate Thickness	5.03 mm

Lower-Topsides Inner Skin: 2.76 mm ÷ 1.6 mm/layer = 1.4 layers 18-10 combi-mat

1 Layer 18-10 (915 g/m²) Combi-Mat	1.60 mm
1 Layer 305 g/m² Mat	0.81 mm
Lower-Topsides Inner-Laminate Thickness	2.41 mm
Total Laminate Thickness	7.44 mm
Lower-Topsides Core: 88 kg/m³ foam or 104 kg/m³ balsa	20.00 mm
Total Lower Topsides Thickness	27.44 mm

(NOTE: The upper and lower topsides are the same in this case because the thickness of the necessary mat skin-coat increases the laminate thickness over the rule requirements.)

Hull-Bottom Outer Skin: 4.86 mm ÷ 1.6 mm/layer = 3.0 layers 18-10 combi-mat

1 Layer 228 g/m² Mat	0.61 mm
3 Layers 18-10 (915 g/m²) Combi-Mat	4.80 mm

1 Layer (457 g/m²) Mat (Skin Coat) 1.22 mm
Hull-Bottom Outer Laminate
Thickness: 6.63 mm

*Hull-Bottom Inner Skin: 3.65 mm ÷
1.6 mm/layer = 1.74 layers 18-10 combi-mat*

2 Layers 18-10 (915 g/m²)
Combi-Mat   3.20 mm
1 Layer (305 g/m²) Mat   0.81 mm
Hull-Bottom Inner-Laminate
Thickness: 4.01 mm
Total Laminate Thickness   10.64 mm

Hull-Bottom Core: 128 kg/m³
foam or 152 kg/m³ balsa   25.00 mm
Total Hull-Bottom Thickness   35.64 mm

*Solid-Glass Keel and Stem (see Formula
6-10): 18.24 mm thick – 10.03 mm Sandwich
Hull-Bottom FRP Laminate = 8.21 mm, and
8.21 ÷ 2.26 mm/ply (24-15, 1,271 g/m²
combi-mat) = 3.6 layers*

1 Layer 228 g/m² Mat   0.61 mm
                              (outer laminate)
3 Layers 18-10 (915 g/m²)
Combi-Mat   4.80 mm
1 Layer 457 g/m² Mat
(Skin Coat)   1.22 mm
2 Layers 18-10 (915 g/m²)
Combi-Mat   3.20 mm
                              (inner laminate)
1 Layer 305 g/m² Mat   0.81 mm
1 Layer 18-10 (915 g/m²)
Combi-Mat   1.60 mm
                              (added buildup)
3 Layers 24-15 (1,271 g/m²)
Combi-Mat   6.78 mm
Total Keel and Stem Thickness   19.02 mm

Hull-Bottom High-Stress Areas: Use same
as standard hull bottom; standard hull
bottom is thicker than required by rule and
is as thick as required by rule for high-stress areas.

COMMENTS ON THE LAMINATE SPECIFICATION

In all cases, the necessary skin-coat and core-bedding mat increased the practically necessary laminate thicknesses beyond that required by the rule—a common difficulty with the thin laminates in sandwich construction. The 1.5-oz. (457 g/m²) mat skin coat is laid in the mold first, followed by the 18-10 (915 g/m²) combi-mat, mat down (facing out). The 0.75-oz. (228 g/m²) mat is applied on top of that, under the core as bedding, followed by the core itself.

You could elect instead to apply the 0.75-oz. (228 g/m²) mat on top of the skin coat followed by the 18-10 (915 g/m²) combi-mat, mat up. In this case, there would

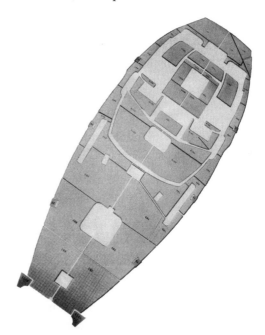

Complete deck-core kit for a 34-foot sailboat.
(Courtesy Divinycell/Barracuda Technologies)

be additional mat on the surface to prevent print-through, and the upturned mat face of the combi-mat would be laid on wet as the core bedding. It is slightly stronger to have the roving closer to the outside (farther from the core center), however. And, the 1.5-oz. (457 g/m^2) mat skin plus the 1.0-oz. (305 g/m^2) mat on the 18-10 yields 2.5 oz. (762 g/m^2) total, which should be enough to prevent print-through with the finer weave of the 18-oz. (610 g/m^2) roving—as opposed to 24-oz. (814 g/m^2).

On the inner skin, the 18-10 (915 g/m^2) combi-mat could have been applied directly to the inside of the core, mat down. In this laminate for our *Fish 'n Squish,* however, the additional 1.0-oz. (305 g/m^2) mat was added to build up the required inner-skin thickness. Again, the 1.0-oz. (305 g/m^2) mat is placed against the core so the roving will be farther out from the core center, which is slightly stronger.

Although the laminate we've come up with is somewhat thicker than required by rule, it has a higher proportion of mat in it than the nearly balanced roving-mat the rule assumes. Because mat is weaker than roving, the extra thickness is not much overkill.

Always keep in mind the principle that there should be a fresh, wet mat layer between each layer of roving and against both faces of the core to ensure proper interlaminar bonds.

OPTIONS FOR REDUCING EXCESS LAMINATE THICKNESS

There are many fabric styles, and—as long as you follow the basic rules for skin coat and interlaminar mat—you can use any combination or style of fabric to bring the individual skin thickness closer to the minimum spec'd by the rule. Finer styles give you more flexibility—a 14-07 combi-mat, for instance (475 g/m^2 roving times 228 g/m^2).

The best fabric styles for light, thin sandwich laminates are the knitted stitch mats such as Brunswick's 1603—a 0,90 bi-axial with two layers of 8-oz. uni-di, stitched to a 0.25-oz. mat. Alternately, you could use Knytex's 1208—a 45,45 bi-axial with two layers of 6-oz. uni-di, stitched to a 0.75-oz. mat (1603 is 0,90 bi-ax with two layers of 271 g/m^2 uni-di, plus 76 g/m^2 mat; 1208 is 45,45 bi-ax with two layers of 203 g/m^2 uni-di, plus 228 g/m^2 mat).

The stitch-mat styles have a higher proportion of uni-di-to-mat than most woven-roving combi-mats and are thus stronger. The uni-di bi-ax is also less prone to print-through than the coarser-weave rovings. Furthermore, the fabrics themselves are thinner, giving you more flexibility in adjusting skin thickness. Brunswick's 1603 totals just 0.035 inch (0.89 mm) thick; 1208 is 0.045 inch (1.14 mm) thick. The drawback is that bi-axial stitch-mat fabric styles are somewhat more expensive.

Sandwich Construction Details

DECK-HARDWARE-MOUNTING AREAS

Sandwich cores have low compression strength. They can't transmit the loads from high-strength deck fittings, such as cleats, chocks, sail track, and winches, from the inner to the outer skins. The three standard methods for transmitting these compressive loads are solid-plywood core (or very high-density foam), stainless-steel or aluminum compression tubes (sleeves around the fastener through-bolt), and epoxy annuluses.

Solid-Plywood Cores

Solid plywood has extremely high compression strength compared to standard low-density foam or balsa cores. In the region around the deck hardware, solid plywood is installed instead of the normal core. Care must be taken to presaturate the ply with resin, seal all fastener holes, and bed the fittings well or water can get at the ply core, causing decay.

FORMULA 6-3
Solid-Plywood-Core Dimensions

Solid-Plywood-Core Thickness: Same thickness as the standard core

Solid-Plywood-Core Dimensions: Extend at least 1.1 times the footprint of the mounted hardware in all directions

Solid-plywood cores can be practically installed only in advance. If the deck-hardware layout is known, ply cores are a reliable method and—if the solid-ply areas are made a little oversize—they make locating fittings fairly easy. Numerous solid-plywood cores can add significant weight, however.

Some manufacturers make very high-density foam cores for use in place of solid plywood for this application. These high-density foams save weight over the plywood and cannot rot. Consult your core supplier for information on its products.

Compression Tubes

Where plywood cores aren't used, you can simply drill a slightly oversize hole and install a compression tube between the underside of the hardware and the backing plate, under the deck. This frees you to install deck hardware at any location; however, it requires careful fitting of the tube length to ensure a tight, snug, watertight joint.

Epoxy Annuluses

A recommended alternative to metal compression tubes is epoxy annuluses. These are simply compression tubes formed of poured-in-place epoxy grout.

FORMULA 6-4
Epoxy-Annulus Diameter

Epoxy Annulus = 2.0 × bolt diameter

Locate the deck hardware and mark the fastener holes. Drill holes two times the bolt diameter. Fill the holes with high-density, high-strength epoxy grout. Back the underside of the holes with plastic that doesn't stick to epoxy, held in place with duct tape until cure. After the epoxy has hardened, remove the plastic and tape; relocate the fastener; rebore for the correct through-bolt size (through the center of the epoxy annuluses); and fasten the hardware permanently in place.

Any grout protrusions can be knocked off quickly with a disk sander, and any small surface gaps can be filled with a dab of grout filler. The advantage of the epoxy annulus is that it can be inserted anywhere without pre-planing. The fit is easy, and added weight is virtually nil.

Some builders find it quicker to "pot" the through-bolt and the curing epoxy grout in place in one step. They use the backing plate and the hardware base to retain the epoxy. This too is acceptable as long as the grout can be kept from running out.

DECK-HARDWARE BACKING PLATES

In all cases, the deck hardware requires a backing plate under the deck. Backing plates are usually aluminum, even for bronze hardware. Well above the waterline, with the backing plates inside and out of the weather, galvanic corrosion is not a problem.

Lightly loaded hardware, such as an awning cleat and flagpole socket, does not require a backing plate, but large washers must be used under the nuts inside.

DECK-HARDWARE-MOUNTING PRECAUTIONS

Never fasten any hardware to a cored deck or exterior with screws. You absolutely must use through-bolts every time, for every fitting.

Take great care to bed all hardware with a marine bedding compound. It is vital to keep water from seeping into the core. Even small amounts of water (which do little harm at first) can freeze. The frozen water bursts open the core and laminate slightly, which leads to more water penetration. The result is a self-perpetuating destructive cycle. Bed well, bed everything, bed carefully.

SOLID GLASS (NO CORE) AT HIGHLY LOADED HULL PENETRATIONS

Where there are holes or fasteners through the hull carrying large loads or substantial running gear, the core must be locally removed and replaced with a solid-glass laminate that equals the standard solid-glass hull laminate at high-stress areas or at the chainplates (see Formulas 4-13 and 5-14).

The principal items requiring core removal are as follows:

- Ballast-bolt region in the hull bottom, if the bolts do not run through the floors as recommended
- Penetrations for rudder ports
- Penetrations for shaft logs and stern tubes
- Strut bases and their mounting bolts
- All chainplate bolts and attachments
- Towing eyes and hoisting rings

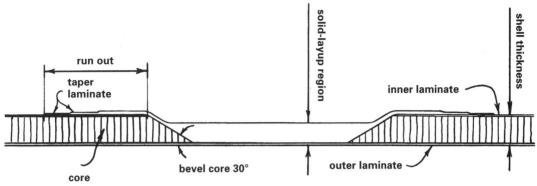

Solid glass at highly loaded hull penetrations

- Trim tabs
- Steering-gear mountings and fastener penetrations
- Around installation cutouts for surface-propeller drives and for jet drives. NOTE: Additional solid-plywood cores or similar reinforcing is also required for propulsion units; follow the manufacturer's recommendations.

In these areas, the core is not installed. Surrounding core edges are carefully beveled back to approximately a 30-degree slope. The required additional inner laminate is run down off the core onto the inside of the outer laminate and built up until the specified thickness is achieved.

FORMULA 6-8

Solid-Glass-Region Specifications

Tabbing (On Top of the Remaining Inside Core, Around the Removed-Core Area): 10 × the thickness of the added inside laminate or 6 in. (15 cm), whichever is greater

Tabbing Thickness: 30 percent of the interior solid-glass layup used to build up the total required solid-glass thickness

Tabbing should taper away gradually, to just one or two layers of glass at its outermost edge.

INTERNAL STRUCTURE: NO DECK OR TOPSIDES STRINGERS

One of the nice things about cored FRP construction is that the required internal structure is simpler. No deck or hull-topsides longitudinal stringers are required. This can represent considerable time savings, both when building the hull and in installing bulkheads and joinerwork later. Engine beds/stringers, bulkheads, ring frames, and floors are all required exactly as determined in chapter 5, however.

Chine Reinforcement

Hard-chine planing craft should have chine reinforcement installed as described in Formula 5-4. This can be done by applying the additional laminate required to the inside only of the cored chine structure. Preferably, I recommend that the core be stopped some distance back from the chine, and the chine region be made of a solid-glass laminate in the thickness specified in Formula 5-4.

Improper strut mounting. This simple plywood pad is badly deteriorated. There was no backing plate—only washers—which repeatedly compressed into the ply, causing loose struts and vibration.

Proper strut mounting through solid-glass bottom-laminate region with heavy backing plate.

Hard chines take concentrated abrasion abuse. Solid-glass laminate is superior in this one regard. Installing it along the chine adds only little weight, but increases toughness where needed. Furthermore, most builders find it is easier to lay up solid-glass corners.

Solid-Glass Keel and Stem (Use No Core)

For the same reason that chines are recommended to be solid glass, the keel and stem region must be solid glass. The keel and stem take the most continuous and severe impact and abrasion abuse.

The solid-glass-keel region can decrease in width toward the stem, but not to less than 6 inches (15 cm).

Internal Ballast

Where internal ballast is fitted in a sailboat (instead of external bolted-on ballast), the hull must be all solid glass (no core).

Tapering of Core at Transition from Solid Glass to Cored Areas

As discussed in chapter 3, it is important to avoid hard spots in FRP construction. Accordingly, wherever there's a transition from a cored to a solid-glass region of the hull or deck, you must use a tapered core fillet to make a sloping, gradual change. (Again, these

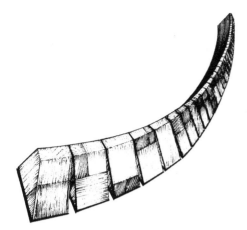

Typical premanufactured fillet strip, for tapering transition from cored to solid laminate. (Courtesy Baltek Corporation)

are required by ABS and U.S. Coast Guard requirements for Subchapter-T boats.) Most core manufacturers sell core fillet strips specifically designed for this use.

Alternately, you can make your own fillet strips by cutting pieces of standard core to shape. Still another option is to knock down the edge of the core with a grinder, but don't forget to presaturate the ground-off area with resin before continuing with the layup. Some builders leave the core untapered and trowel-in a fillet of putty grout. This is not recommended; not only is the grout heavier than the core fillets, but it is also brittle. If the structure is flexed by a heavy load, the putty fillets will crack; the core fillets would not. Cracked putty-grout fillets can work loose, causing stress concentrations and/or small leaks in the laminate.

FORMULA 6-12
Core-Fillet Angle
Ideal Core-Fillet Angle: between 18.5 and 30 degrees, or a slope between 3:1 and 1.76:1

This is the ideal fillet angle. Some off-the-shelf fillet strips have a steeper angle. These are generally adequate, but be leery of using angles steeper than 30 degrees.

Laminate Corners

There are two ways to make corners in laminates for transoms, chines, trunk-cabin to deck joints, and cockpit corners. One method involves making *butted-core corners*: Install the cores covering the entire interior, with each core (from either surface) butting tight to the other at the corners. The second method is to make *solid-glass corners*: Stop the cores back from the corner and simply run the inner laminate down off the core (over the fillet-strip edge), down onto the inside of the outer laminate (without core), and then up again onto the other core inside. Both methods are entirely acceptable and can be used interchangeably on the same hull.

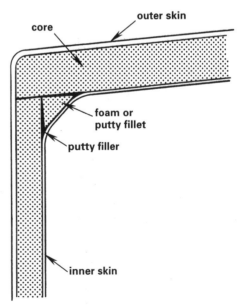

Butted-core corner

Butted-Core Corners

With butted cores, you must take great care to fill all gaps in the corner and between the cores with putty grout. You must also apply either a putty-grout fillet on the inside corner or a foam-core fillet, before applying the inside laminate. Although I use them whenever it seems convenient, butted cores usually require slightly more work. In addition, cores at sharp exterior corners are more easily subject to exposure from abrasion than solid glass.

Solid-Glass Corners

Solid-glass corners are usually slightly easier to fabricate than butted cores. The corners are thicker solid glass, so they are more resistant to abrasion and easier to repair if damaged. Also, using solid-glass corners throughout (in conjunction with the solid-glass keel) segregates the core into distinct regions. If there should ever be a core water-penetration problem, this isolates it to one region. Solid-glass corners are roughly the same as recommended in Formula 6-9.

> **FORMULA 6-13**
>
> Solid-Glass Corners
>
> *Distance Corner and Core: 4 to 8 × core thickness*

Hull-to-Deck Joint

Hull-to-deck joints for sandwich hulls and decks are fabricated exactly as for solid-glass hulls, as described in chapter 5. The core is stopped back from the hull to deck joint, on both the topsides and the deck, exactly as with a solid-glass corner. The core cut-back distance is the same as in Formula 6-13.

High-Modulus Laminates

Up to this point, we've stayed with industry-standard, plain-vanilla FRP laminates; all the reinforcing fibers employed have been ordinary E-glass, while all the resin has been polyester. Chapter 3 discussed the advantages of high-modulus fiber reinforcement combined with vinylester or epoxy-resin systems. For most common applications, these high-modulus laminates offer only a modest advantage with single-skin construction. In sandwich construction, however, such laminates come into their own. They offer greater strength with thinner (and thus lighter) skins, and they are available in light fabric styles that offer more flexibility in specifying sandwich layups. The following rules can be used to determine a high-modulus-reinforcement cored hull and deck structure.

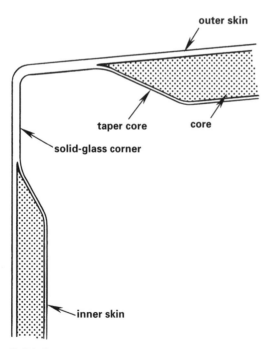

Solid-glass corner

Note that Kevlar is not only costly, but is also difficult to work with. It requires special cutting techniques and equipment, and it's more difficult to wet-out evenly and consistently than most other types of reinforcement.

S-GLASS OUTER SKIN, KEVLAR INNER SKIN

The highest strength to lightest weight will be achieved by using S-glass exterior and Kevlar interior laminates that are vacuum-bagged.

FIBER ORIENTATION AND STITCH-MAT STYLES

Standard mat/roving laminates have roughly the same strength in all directions. Whatever the resin system, the +45,−45 and 0,90 bi-axial fabric styles have maximum strength only along their two respective axes. The strength on the diagonal (along the "bias") is lower. Accordingly, you should try to alternate +45,−45 and 0,90 styles. This produces a finished laminate with close to uniform strength in all directions.

GRAPHITE AND CARBON FIBER

This rule does not cover graphite or carbon-fiber reinforcements (really the same material—carbon—but graphite is, by convention, purer and somewhat stronger). Although carbon-fiber laminates have very high stiffness properties, they also have quite low elongation (i.e., they don't stretch much before they break). This makes carbon-fiber laminates brittle and subject to sudden, violent failure. Carbon/graphite laminates and reinforcement can offer real advantages at the cutting edge of design and construction. These laminates must, however, be carefully engineered and, again, are *not* covered in this rule.

FORMULA 6-17

The Hammer Puncture Test

Sandwich laminates, whether standard E-glass/polyester or S-glass/ Kevlar/ vinylester, all share one real problem: the thin skins are subject to puncture. It's easy to forget this and to play games with thin skins that seem otherwise strong enough. You must not do this. Always keep puncture resistance in mind. Small, light pleasure craft and high-performance racing vessels can skirt the edges of safety here—as long as the designer, the builder, and the boat's future crew are fully aware of the trade-offs. For all other boats, the bottom laminate—at least up to the bottom-laminate height (see Formula 4-2)—must be able to withstand the following puncture test. If it fails, you must increase skin thickness.

Make a sample of the bottom laminate panel you've specified. Use an ordinary carpenter's curved claw hammer, between 20 and 24 ounces (including handle) and from 12 to 13 inches long (0.57 to 0.68 kg and 304 to 330 mm). An average man (145 to 180 pounds [66 to 82 kg]) should be able to strike the outer skin of the panel fairly hard, repeatedly, with the round (nail-driving) end and see no penetration, no crushing of the core, and no delamination. (Surface marring/denting and crushing of the outer layers of glass is normal and acceptable.) The hammer should then be turned over—clawside down. With the sharp claw, strike the panel (in a previously untested area) with moderate force (less than fairly hard, but not lightly—a firm strike). The claw should not penetrate more than $1/16$ inch (1.6 mm) into the core. The skin should show no delamination from the core around the impact area. The inner skin and the core directly below the penetration must be unaffected. Laminates for workboats and for serious voyaging cruisers should allow no penetration into the core at all.

NOTE: Small boats with Sns under 1.0 will have outer-bottom laminate thicknesses of roughly 0.10 inch (2.5 mm) or less. Skins much thinner will usually not pass the hammer test. Here, you're squarely up against the puncture limits of sandwich construction. You must make the decision for each boat whether the type of craft and intended service can tolerate lower puncture resistance safely, or if you should pay the weight and cost penalty of additional thickness to the outer-bottom skin.

Weight of Sandwich Laminate

The weights of hand-laid-up sandwich laminates can be determined by referring to Table 4-16 and the method described in chapter 4. For vacuum-bagged layups and bi-axial style fabrics, and for standard balsa and sandwich cores, refer to the following tables.

TABLE 6-18 Vacuum-Bagged Laminate Densities (Weights)

Material	Glass Content by Weight	Density, lb./cu. ft. (kg/m³)	lb./sq. ft.. (kg/m²), 1-in. (1 mm) thick
Stitch-mat with balanced mat/bi-ply like CDM1815	40%	101 (1,618)	8.42 (1.62)
Stitch-mat with light mat like CM1603	45%	107 (1,714)	8.92 (1.71)
All bi-ply with no mat* like DB120	50%	112 (1,794)	9.33 (1.78)

*Must be used with epoxy resin only; vacuum-bagging strongly recommended.

TABLE 6-19 Standard Core Densities (Weights)

Material	Density, lb./sq. ft. (kg/m²)	lb./cu. ft. (kg/m³), 1-in. (1 mm) thick
Closed-cell foam	5.5 (88)	0.46 (0.088)
Closed-cell foam	8.0 (128)	0.66 (0.128)
Balsa	6.5 (104)	0.54 (0.104)
Balsa	9.5 (152)	0.78 (0.152)

FORMULA 6-20

Laminate Density (Weight) vs. Glass Content

You can estimate the density of any laminate from its glass content by weight:

lb./cu. ft. = 57.97 + 108.3 × percent of glass content, by weight (English)

kg/m³ = 917.3 + 1,754.4 × percent of glass content, by weight (Metric)

Or, you can estimate the glass content of a sample by measuring its specific gravity, as follows (see also appendix 4):

Percent of Glass Content, by Weight = (lb./sq. ft. – 57.97) ÷ 108.3 (English)

Percent of Glass Content, by Weight = (kg/m³ – 917.30 ÷ 1,754.4 (Metric)

Example:

If you made a sample of your proposed laminate and measured its specific gravity as 1.57, then its density is (1.57 × 62.4 lb./cu. ft.) or 97.9 lb./cu. ft. (1,570 kg/m³).

(97.9 lb./cu. ft. – 57.97) ÷ 108.3 = 0.368; use 37 percent glass content, by weight

(1,570 kg/m³ – 917.3) ÷ 1,754.4 = 0.372; use 37 percent glass content, by weight

SEVEN

Wood Construction Materials and Methods

*T*raditional wood construction—known as *plank-on-frame* or *carvel plank*—is the underpinning of almost every other method of boatbuilding. We'll use traditional plank-on-frame construction as the starting point for other more modern variants of wooden-boat construction. Before we can delve into the details of a plank-on-frame scantling rule, however, we have to know what this construction is. We also have to understand what that deceptively simple and common material, wood, is: what makes it up, how best to employ it, and how it's formed and fastened.

History and Development of Plank-on-Frame Construction

For more than 4,000 years, boats were fashioned of wood and virtually nothing else. Metal hulls are barely 150 years old; fiberglass goes back a mere 50 years or so. By comparison, we know the ancient Phoenicians and Egyptians were systematically building sizable vessels of wood in 2000 B.C. We can be

sure that boats were being formed from hollow logs or from logs lashed together for thousands of years before that. Indeed, the hollow-log boat or dugout canoe can be quite a handsome and sophisticated vessel. Even today, indigenous peoples around the world are still fabricating such craft using the same methods that were almost certainly employed during the Stone Age. As recently as 1992, a client stopped by my office with photos he had taken a few weeks before of an outrigger dugout canoe under construction in Micronesia. This boat was beautifully finished off, carefully crafted, and proven capable of long ocean passages.

LOG BOATS

If it will serve, it's still hard to improve on a log canoe. Log canoes are solid, can't leak, and—if large trees are available—can be sizable. Of course, here you run into one of the log boat's drawbacks. You can't very well make a 90-footer (27 m) with a 22-foot (6.7 m) beam from a single tree. Even if you

A log canoe starts with a single felled tree hewn to shape with hatchet and adz. It's been done just this way for more than 5,000 years. (Courtesy Stephen J. Winter)

The log canoe body takes shape. After that massive trunk is shaved down to this form, it's not so big. The builder is hewing the bow piece separately, which will be sewn in place. (Courtesy Stephen J. Winter)

The Polynesian outrigger log canoe finished, before paint or rig. If you look closely at the bow, you can make out the two lashings that hold this separate piece in place. (Courtesy Stephen J. Winter)

A log canoe's first sail. (Courtesy Stephen J. Winter)

could find a large enough tree for a 40-footer (12 m), think of the waste of lumber and the limitations of shape. Modern planked-up hulls are—I believe—a direct logical outgrowth of the log canoe and the centuries of effort that have gone into overcoming its limitations. You can only make a log boat substantially larger if you take a second log, split it in half, shape it properly, and add it to the top of the sheer running full length. This is, in fact, just how the Chesapeake log canoes (still being raced today) evolved. Originally, these craft were based on ordinary American Indian dugout canoes. As the European settlers required larger vessels, they added second, third, and even fourth logs to build up the sides and to extend the length along the stem. Fifty- and sixty-footers (15 to 18 m) were fashioned this way, with individual logs fastened to each other along their edges with iron drift bolts or wooden dowels.

ANCIENT BOATS

The amazing thing is that this closely approximates the construction technique employed in ancient Greek vessels around 1000 and 1500 B.C. These craft were fashioned—in principle—exactly as the Chesapeake log canoes of today. The greatest difference in construction is that square tenons were used at the joints between logs (planks) rather than iron pins or dowels. As these ancient boats grew larger, they added internal framing as well to further strengthen the structure. Of course, the larger Chesapeake log canoes do much the same.

PLANK-ON-FRAME

All this works and—obviously—has worked for 4,000 years. Still, the drawbacks are obvious too: Boats built up from several carved-out logs need quite large trees, they're labor-intensive, there's considerable waste of timber that is simply hacked or chiseled away and burned, the larger boats need internal stiffening anyway. From here, it's easy to see how "modern" *plank-on-frame* or *carvel* construction came into being. The original single log—of the multilog boat—shrank in proportion to become the keel-stem-sternpost/backbone, the stiffening structure became regular frames or ribs, and the side logs became straightforward planks.

CARVEL AND CLINKER

This describes the standard plank-on-frame or carvel plank hull to a tee. Certainly, all manner of vessels have been constructed in exactly this fashion for at least 2000 years. There are essentially two main variants of the plank-fastened-to-frame method of hull construc-

tion. These depend on the approach taken to the planking itself. The most common now is smooth or carvel plank. Here, planks are neatly fitted over the frames (also called *ribs*) so that each plank butts smooth, tight, and even to its neighboring planks or to the keel. The alternative—and a most successful one, at that—is *lapstrake* or *clinker-built* hulls. In these craft, the planks are fastened to the frames shingle-fashion, overlapping and fastened to the plank below by a small percentage of the plank width. Both lapstrake and smooth plank-on-frame (carvel) construction work excellently and are employed regularly all over the world today. Smooth-plank, however, is the most common method and virtually the standard for most yachts longer than 20 feet (6 m). We will examine smooth-plank construction in detail in the following chapter (see photo on p. 337).

FIRST FASTENINGS

Another interesting consideration in traditional wooden-boat construction is the method of fastening used throughout the structure. We take metal fastenings for granted today; they're cheap and plentiful. This was not the case just 300 years ago, and was much less so the farther back you go. As a result, boats were fastened together with wooden dowels, mortise-and-tenon joints, and even sewn. Some of the most rugged and seaworthy vessels ever built had sewn planks and partially sewn framing. The fabled Viking ships were clinker-built, often with planks sewn to each other along the plank laps and sewn to the frames. Cord of carefully prepared animal sinew lasted well in this application. These oceangoing vessels were very light and flexible. They bent and gave in response to the forces imposed on them and so could take incredible punishment.

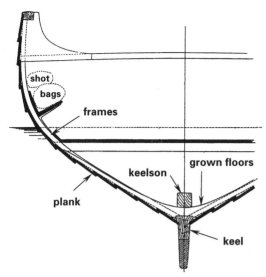

Typical lapstrake construction

Square-cut galvanized-iron boat nail. (Courtesy Tremont Nail Company)

NAILS FROM TREES

Nevertheless, sinew lashings and stitching need attention and renewal; they're also finicky and labor-intensive. Combine this with the gradually developing preference for smooth-planked boats (in larger sizes especially) and you can see how we arrived at what we would consider today more conventional fasteners. These were dowels hammered into holes of just the right diameter. Such dowels were largely employed to fasten planks to frames, but also could be used in most places metal screws and bolts are used today. Such dowel fastenings were called *trunnels* (literally, *tree nails*). After being driven home, a small wedge was hammered into a slot in the trunnel's top, locking it in place. Once the wood structure had swelled with water, these trunnels could only be removed by boring them out. The fact is that trunnels don't corrode and are inexpensive. If you want to take the time and learn how to use them, they make quite excellent fasteners to this day.

IRON SPIKES AND NAILS

For larger timbers (in larger boats particularly), iron spikes called *drifts* or *drift bolts* were preferred and are still used frequently in the built-up keel/backbone structure. With the advent of mass-produced galvanized-iron nails, trunnels were gradually replaced for planking. These old-fashioned, square-cut, hot-dip galvanized-iron boat nails still make strong, reasonably long-lasting fasteners. As far as I know, they are only available now from Tremont Nail Company in Wareham, Massachusetts.

BRONZE SCREWS

Today, almost all wooden boats are fastened with bronze (or Monel) wood screws, bronze keel bolts, and bronze strapping. Bronze, with its extremely high corrosion resistance in the marine environment, was always the fastener of choice whenever enough of it could be acquired inexpensively. It was, however, Captain Nat Herreshoff who invented the bronze wood screw as we know it today and first employed it for fastening planks to frames, as well as for fastening other structural components in the hull.

COPPER RIVETS, CLENCH NAILS, AND BOLTS

The alternative to the bronze (or Monel) wood screw (and to the trunnel) was the copper rivet. These are still used by some traditional builders, but they are not as long-

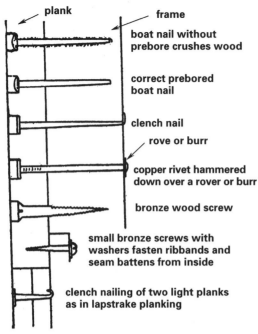

plank

frame

boat nail without
prebore crushes wood

correct prebored
boat nail

clench nail

rove or burr

copper rivet hammered
down over a rover or burr

bronze wood screw

small bronze screws with
washers fasten ribbands and
seam battens from inside

clench nailing of two light planks
as in lapstrake planking

Plank fasteners

lasting as bronze wood screws. This is because as the wood in the plank and frame swells, it stretches the rivet slightly and/or compresses the wood under the rivet's heads. Consequently, when the wood dries out and shrinks again, the rivet is a little loose. Repeated cycles exacerbate the situation. Furthermore, the softer copper required for proper heading of the rivet and the somewhat more slender diameter (compared to bronze screws) are less effective at restraining the plank from sliding on the frame (resisting shear)—one of the plank fastener's chief functions. Accordingly, the rule we use here generally applies to bronze wood screws as fasteners. (Copper rivets do make one of the best fastenings for plank laps in clinker construction.)

Another alternative is clench nails. These are similar to rivets but, rather than

headed over a rivet ring, the clench nail is simply long enough to project through the inside of the frame or plank. The projecting inside end is bent over and hammered flat down inside, making it act much like a rivet. Again, this method is acceptable but suffers from all the drawbacks of copper rivets (although also excellent for fastening clinker plank laps).

Some builders advocate through-bolts for plank fastening. These too suffer from the wood expansion/contraction problems experienced by rivets and clench nails. Such bolts are the same diameter as bronze screws and are usually made of bronze. Accordingly, they're just as strong in shear. Although bronze through-bolts are workable for fastening planks to frames, I don't see any great advantages that would justify the extra work required to fit them.

ANNULAR-RING BOAT NAILS

There is a modern alternative to the bronze or Monel wood screw: the *annular-ring* (or *barbed-ring*) bronze or Monel boat nail. Often sold under trade names like Anchorfast or Gripfast, annular-ring boat nails are nearly as strong and long-lasting as bronze or Monel wood screws. The boat nail is usually somewhat less expensive and somewhat quicker and easier to install. We examine these as alternate fastenings.

Wood, the Wonder Material

Wood is a high-tech composite material. The fact that it was invented by nature and not humans, and that it's been around several hundred million years longer than we have, doesn't alter the fact that it's one of the strongest and most tenacious materials known—period. Stronger in tension and in bending than even high-tensile steel, wood is also just plain tougher than steel; pound for pound, it will absorb more energy or abuse before failure than even the best steels. A structure built of good-quality, dry, straight-grained wood will be lighter and stiffer than the same structure fabricated from nearly any other material—even including most modern, manmade, high-tech composite laminates like Kevlar/epoxy and carbon-fiber/epoxy. (The best carbon composites can exceed wood in strength in stiffness, pound for pound, but at considerably higher cost.)

AS STRONG AS SUGAR

Wood's secret is its internal structure. It is formed of fairly regularly aligned tubules of cellulose—literally, cells made up of sugar. (The suffix -ose means sugar.) These cellulose-fiber tubules account for about half of the wood by weight. They are formed of a linear polymer of high molecular weight in quite long chains, all of ordinary sugars. The individual cells are joined in fibers (usually averaging about $1/25$ inch [1 mm] long) held together with *lignin*, a tough resin-like binder that acts, in many ways, not unlike manmade resin in FRP construction. Lignin constitutes about one quarter to one third of the weight of wood. Interestingly, a large portion of the cellulose in wood is crystallized, which is what gives wood's polymers their high molecular weight. This also makes wood surprisingly water-resistant because the crystals do not absorb water.

The aligned tubule/fiber structure of wood is what makes it so light and stiff—it's a uni-directional composite. Most boatbuilding woods have densities between 24 and 44 lb./cu. ft. (384 to 706 kg/m³). On average,

this is half as dense as water. By comparison, steel is about 500 lb./cu. ft. (8,000 kg/m³), and even the relatively light metal, aluminum, is 168 lb./cu. ft. (2,690 kg/m³). Yet wood's individual fibers are nearly as strong as steel in tension, and are stronger than aluminum. What's more, the fibers in wood are arranged in patterns that resist crack propagation during high-load conditions. The hollow cellular structure of wood creates creases rather than cracks when local cell walls buckle. What's more, the individual tubules (bound in lignin) form crack-stoppers, which resist the spread of cracks during high stresses. Generally, compression creases in wood (rather than the cracks formed in metal or many manmade laminates) run a short way in from the surface and stop, which tends to be self-stabilizing. If more load is applied, new creases form, and often previous creases are not enlarged or extended. The result is that wood is exceptionally tough for its weight. It can absorb far more energy, pound for pound, before fracturing than metal or laminates.

STRUCTURE OF WOOD
The Outer Layer

The larger structure in wood is created by the way trees grow. In a mature tree, the outer bark is a layer of somewhat corky dead cells that protect the trunk from abrasion and that form an insulating layer. Just inside of the outer bark is—not surprisingly—the inner bark, which carries the nutrients prepared by the leaves to the living parts of the tree. Then, inside this layer is the *cambium*, a microscopic layer that gives birth to new cells in the bark and in the timber that form the majority of the core of a tree. Every year, as new cells form in the cambium, a new layer of wood, called an *annual ring*, is formed. The tree trunk grows outward, forming successive layers each year (or each growing season).

The Core

The core of the trunk is made of what we generally think of as ordinary wood. It too, however, is subdivided. The outermost layer (under the bark and cambium) is the *sapwood*. In fully grown softwood trees, this layer is roughly 1.5 inches thick. In hardwoods, however, the sapwood can encompass as much as 50 percent or more of the trunk's diameter. The sapwood is a mixture of dead and living cells that form tubes that store nutrients and transport sap. The *heartwood* is the balance of the core of the trunk. It's composed almost entirely of dead cells. Every year a new layer of sapwood gradually becomes heartwood, while a new layer of sapwood is born under the cambium. Broadly speaking, the sapwood and heartwood have the same physical strength. The problem with sapwood is that the living cells and the sap they contain are more prone to decay in moist environments, such as on boats.

INSULATING QUALITIES

Yet another advantage of wood's hollow-tubule structure and consequent low density is that it is an excellent insulator. Wood does not transmit heat or—of course—electricity. Wood, in and of itself, is also a fairly good insulator of sound. Metal, laminates, and even water transmit sound's compression waves far faster and with less energy loss. Thin, hard, dry membranes of any substance, however, can make excellent sounding boards. Wood is so good for this purpose that it is the material of choice in nearly all musical instruments. In modern, monocoque laminated hulls, this sounding-board effect can cause noise difficulties. Additional sound-deadening insulation may be required in some areas, such as on the hull-bottom inside, over the propeller.

WOOD TYPES

Trees are subdivided into two major groups of species: *hardwoods* and *softwoods*. These names can be deceptive because some softwoods—such as Douglas fir and yellow pine—are physically harder than some hardwoods, such as basswood and cottonwood. In spite of this paradox, both the difference between and the definition of hardwood and softwood are precise.

Hardwoods

Hardwoods are trees that lose their leaves once a year in the fall—they are *deciduous*. Their leaves are generally broad and flat. Most hardwoods are *deliquescent*; that is, they have pronounced branching and forking in their trunks and main branches. This makes hardwoods excellent for finding and getting out natural crooks and bent timbers with the grain running along the curve for maximum strength. The botanical term for hardwood is *angiosperm*.

Softwoods

By contrast, softwoods are cone-bearing trees (*coniferous*) with needle- or scale-like leaves. Almost all softwoods keep their leaves throughout the year, with a few exceptions, such as the larch (also known as hackmatack or tamarack). Most softwoods are highly *excurrent*, which means that they grow with tall, straight, single trunks with minimal branching and forking. Even the main branches that support the smaller branches and leaves are proportionately thinner than main branches on hardwoods. Softwood-tree branches also project out from the trunk at sharper angles. Softwoods are generally poor sources for natural crooks, but their long straight trunks are excellent for spars, long planks, and long framing timbers, such as clamps and bilge stringers. The botanical term for softwood is *gymnosperm*.

Proper Structural Use of Wood

SLASH-SAWN TIMBER

Because of the annual-ring structure of uncut timber, cut boards and timbers behave very differently depending on how they're sawn. The wood grain you see in a plank is essentially the run of the wood-fiber tubules along the annual rings. If a log is placed in a sawmill and simply cut lengthwise from end to end in successive slices, the majority of the resulting plank will have hooked or curved grain. Such timber is called *slash-sawn* or *plain-sawn*. Slash-sawn lumber—although inexpensive—is inferior in strength because the grain does not run straight along its length. Worse still, slash-sawn lumber has an unavoidable tendency to cup and warp with changes in moisture content. Slash-sawn lumber should be used as little as possible (best not at all) in traditional wooden-boat construction. You can recognize it easily because of the clear hooked or swirled appearance of the grain on the face of the board.

RIFT-SAWN TIMBER

If care is taken with the cutting sequence and the rotation of the log as it is run through the sawmill, most of the lumber can be cut so that the grain runs fairly even and straight along its length. Essentially, this lumber is cut so that the resulting boards are

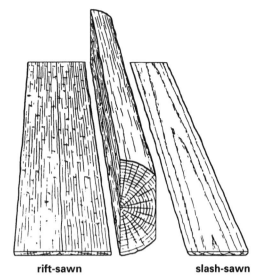

rift-sawn　　　　　**slash-sawn**

Rift- and slash-sawn boards

at roughly right angles to the center of the trunk (i.e., to the *pith*). Such lumber is called *rift-sawn* or *quarter-sawn* (from one of the standard methods of cutting up the log in quarters). This is proper boatbuilding lumber. You can recognize it easily because the grain will run fairly straight along the surface of the board. Not only is rift-sawn lumber stronger because of its straight grain, but it also has much less tendency to cup or warp. Swelling and contraction with changes in moisture content generally occur at approximate right angles to the board faces. Rift-sawn lumber is so useful that it goes under other names as well as quarter-sawn; the most common are *edge-grain*, *vertical-grain*, and *vertical-cut*.

TANGENTIAL AND RADIAL GRAIN DIRECTION

Even in a rift-sawn board, the orientation of the grain is critical. The *fiber direction* essentially runs along the length of the board, corresponding to up and down on the tree. The *radial direction* is the direction across the grain in the plank: if you returned the plank to the place in the log that it came from, the direction across the grain would point radially either directly in or directly out from the log's center. The *tangential direction* in the board runs with the grain across the tree—more or less tangent to the average of the annual rings in that board. Again, if you put the board back into the log that it came from, the tangential direction would be at right angles to the radial line and roughly along the annual rings.

There are three important things to keep in mind about the tangential and radial directions in a rift-sawn board. First, the board will swell and contract more in the tangential direction than in the radial direction. In most average woods, the change will be approximately twice as much in the tangential direction. Second, fasteners hold better when driven in at right angles to the tangential direction, or along the radial-axis direction. Third, the board will be considerably stiffer when the load is applied in the radial direction.

Considering these factors explains why steam-bent (and laminated) frames should be installed so that the radial direction of the frame stock's grain is at right angles to the hull. This makes it easier to bend the frame to begin with; it allows the frame to flex and give more before breaking; and the plank fasteners hold best driven in at right angles to the tangential direction as well. By the same token, planks are installed so the radial direction faces inboard and outboard and the tangential direction runs along the surface of the hull. Again, this ensures strong fastening as well as a tighter caulked joint between planks when the wood swells more in the tangential direction, squeezing the planks together.

NO FASTENING INTO ENDGRAIN

Of course, you can and will fasten into both sides or all sides of some framing in a hull. This is fine as long as you keep in mind the difference between the tangential and radial directions in each component. What you can never do is fasten into endgrain—into the end of a plank in the same direction as the grain/fibers. Not only would such fastenings have virtually no strength, but they will also accelerate water penetration into the timber, weakening it and creating rot pockets.

WOOD GRAIN IN THE REAL WORLD

Of course, wood is a natural material; it's not geometrically regular. Many boards, even though carefully rift-sawn, will have some hook or angle in the grain; sometimes in large timbers, straight edge-grain will actually be appar-

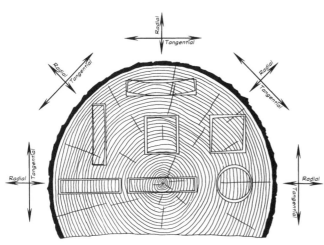

Warpage and shrinkage in boards sawn in different ways

correct
grain running roughly
along sawn timber

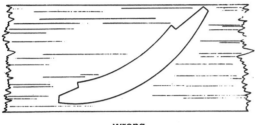

wrong
grain running across
sawn timber

Grain in sawn timbers

ent on two adjacent sides. Large timbers, such as keels in larger boats, will essentially be hewn from a substantial cross section of a single log. Such timbers can't properly be classified as either rift- or slash-sawn. The important thing is to try and use relatively clear straight-grained wood throughout, ideally from lumber that shows minimal hook in the board's surface and in which you can generally determine the radial and tangential directions.

UNI-DIRECTIONAL WOOD

It's also critical to remember that wood is a true uni-directional material. All significant strength runs along the grain. Strength across the grain is—as a rule—merely between 2 and 4 percent of the strength along the grain. Even a relatively small angle in the wood grain, relative to the board it's in, will result in reduction in strength. For example, if you had a rift-sawn Douglas-fir board with an average grain angle of 4 degrees, the effective strength of the board would be 9,500 psi (65.5 mPa) in bending.

Grain angles of 4 and 5 degrees are quite common, and have notably less strength. You can see that it is important to employ the straightest-grain lumber practical (increasingly difficult in the current lumber economy), and to make allowances for the decrease in strength due to grain angle.

SMALLER TIMBERS LAST LONGER

It's a curious thing, but it seems clear to most people that larger, heavier framing members would be stronger and last longer than thinner lighter ones. This is, however (more often than not), incorrect when applied to boat structures. A 12.5-inch-square (300 mm) keel timber may well be physically stronger (in the absolute sense) than an 8-inch-square (200 mm) keel timber. Unfortunately, larger timbers usually have more defects (both from their sheer volume to contain such defects and because of their necessarily longer and more uneven drying/seasoning process). Additionally—and most important—timbers swell and contract in direct proportion to their dimensions.

Broadly speaking, timbers swell and contract about 1.2 percent of their radial dimension and 2.4 percent of their tangential dimension, cycling between 15 and 10 percent moisture content. Thus, the dry 12.5-inch (300 mm) keel timber will swell radially to 12.8 inches (307 mm); the 8-inch timber will swell to just 8.2 inches (205 mm). The larger changes in dimension (in larger timbers) inflict greater distorting loads on the structure as a whole. Furthermore, repeated swelling-shrinkage cycles open cracks in the timber itself and between other members fastened to that timber. This causes loose fastenings (structural weakness), and opens potential rot pockets. Wherever there are knots or sharp changes in grain direction, swelling-shrinkage-cycle crack creation within the timber is further aggravated.

For this reason, it's important to use the smallest timbers that are strong enough to stand up to the required loads. Larger structural members—although seemingly stronger in the short term—will actually weaken the structure over the long haul. Such unnecessarily heavy timbers will also accelerate decay.

WINTER-CUT LUMBER

Even considerations as subtle as the time of year a tree is cut affect longevity. Lumber that is felled in the winter or late fall has less sap in it than lumber felled at other times of the year. This means that there are fewer potential microorganisms in the wood (when it's cut) to promote decay. Furthermore, the relative humidity in cold weather is lower, which promotes faster drying in weather that's too chilly for much fungal action to begin. These factors make winter-cut wood less prone to decay and superior for boat construction.

MOISTURE CONTENT, SEASONING, AND STRENGTH

All wood in the atmosphere contains some small amount of water. This is measured as *moisture content*. Moisture content is taken as a percentage of weight of water relative to the weight of the wood bone dry—with no water at all. ("Bone dry" can only be achieved by heating in an oven.) For structural use, wood should be dried to well below 20-percent moisture content. The ideal average is 12 percent, the moisture-content standard for testing the properties of wood samples. The drying, also known as *seasoning*, can't be permitted to take place too quickly. If it does, the lumber dries unevenly, causing it to check, split, warp, and crack.

Essentially, as green fresh-cut lumber dries, all the free water in the cell cavities evaporates first. Only when this stage is reached does the water bound in the cell walls themselves just begin to dry out. This stage—the *fiber saturation point*—is around 30 percent moisture content. It is important to use timber that has been gradually and carefully dried or seasoned below the saturation point, to well under 20 percent moisture content. Not only does low moisture content reduce the chance of decay, but drier timber is also stronger than moisture-laden timber.

Although well-seasoned timber in a dry environment has a moisture content of about 12 percent (to a low of about 6 or 8 percent in extremely dry conditions), wood in traditional plank-on-frame boats has a moisture content of about 15 percent. This is a fair average for well-painted wood in the underwater planking and framing of a hull. At 15 percent moisture content, strength in bending is roughly reduced to about 65 percent of strength at 12 percent moisture content. Strength in compression is reduced to about 78 percent of strength at 12 percent moisture content.

KILN-DRYING AND BOG SEASONING

Kiln-dried lumber is perfectly acceptable, but only if the kiln-drying has been done gradually and at relatively low temperatures, under properly controlled conditions. Air-dried lumber usually takes longer to dry (to season) than kiln-dried; consequently, air-dried lumber develops fewer checks and cracks. If you can get it, air-dried lumber seasoned slowly is superior; but again—in the current lumber economy—such timber is difficult and expensive to obtain.

Interestingly, some of the finest boat lumber is from logs that have been "pickled" in the bottom of swamps and bogs. These logs—aged in the swamp for years—have all their natural sap and fluids leached out. When they're dredged up, sawn, and air-dried, the result is timber that is as strong, hard, and rot-resistant as it's possible to get.

THE BEST LUMBER SPECIFICATIONS

The best lumber you can use in a boat is clear (knot-free), straight-grained (no swirls or bends), rift-sawn, winter-cut, air-dried heart-wood. Some hardwoods obtained to these specifications—like white oak and hickory—are so hard and tough that they will literally bend heavy iron spikes driven into them with sledges. There was a time when a sizable industry revolved around harvesting and seasoning such timbers. Today, however, wood like this is nearly impossible to locate. Usually, if you want this degree of quality in your lumber, you have to go and get it out yourself, which means finding and selecting the best trees; paying the property owners for permission to cut and transport the felled trees (cut in late fall or winter); arranging for a good sawmill to rift-saw the logs to your specifications (and making allowance for the smaller size of these boards after drying-shrinkage); and finding a proper location to air-dry your lumber for the required months or years. All this can be a satisfying undertaking, but is not generally commercially realistic. In practice, you'll simply have to compromise on the best commercially available lumber you can locate. Today, ideal boat lumber is a dream; you simply have to make do with what you can find.

HAND-HEWN TIMBERS LAST LONGER

Another factor that has changed over the years is that timbers hand-hewn with chisel, axe, and adze are less prone to decay than sawn timbers. In the old days, most large timbers were only roughly sawn to size and then trimmed to shape by craftsmen with well-sharpened hand tools. The power saws and grinders used today chew up the woodgrain at the cut, leaving the mangled tubules and cell edges much more prone to fungal attack. Again, except in rare instances where old-time shipwrights can be employed, this is not a practical approach for most modern builders.

DECAY AND BORERS

Because wood is basically sugar, it makes quite a delectable treat for numerous forms of life. The most common of these are the varied fungal growths that live off the wood, digesting it as they grow. Such decay is generally (and inexplicably) termed *dry rot*, even though there's nothing dry about it. (It can only occur in wood with a fairly high moisture content—generally more than 20 percent; at the same time, it can't occur in wood wholly submerged in salt water, which is poisonous to fungus.) The other common form of attack is from marine borers, such as teredo worms, and other boring insects, such as carpenter ants and termites.

A third, less well-known form of attack is a byproduct of galvanic action. If, for instance, too much zinc is installed on a bond-

Decay caused by stray current at a through-hull fitting.

ing system, it can raise the negative potential of any attached metal hardware to more than 400 millivolts. This overprotection produces ions in seawater that can manufacture alkaline byproducts that destroy the lignin holding wood fibers together. It is sometimes termed *alkali rot*. Most often, it shows up as a whitish or yellowish, foamy, soapy gunk around metal fittings.

PRESERVATIVES AND SEALERS
Extensive use of preservatives in traditional boat construction is not common. Among other things, most preservatives contain toxic chemicals that are subject to government regulation. Nevertheless, the U.S. Navy and several production builders found—during and immediately after World War II—that preservatives can effectively reduce decay. Lumber that has been pressure-treated with preservative gives the best results here; however, painted-on preservatives are still useful. Copper-based formulations are most common. Copper-naphthenate solutions such as Cuprinol seem to offer the best trade-off between price, effectiveness, and ease of application. These preservatives accept most paints without discoloration or adhesion problems.

Kerosene and Linseed Oil
A moderately effective traditional preservative is one or two coats of painted kerosene. This is slightly toxic to fungal growth and helps seal the wood to moisture. Large timbers also can be coated with a couple of coats of boiled (not raw) linseed oil. Probably the best treatment is a coat or two of kerosene followed by a brushed-on coat of a 50/50 mixture of kerosene and boiled linseed oil, finished with a coat of boiled linseed oil only. This procedure seems to drive some of the remaining moisture out of the wood, kill some remaining fungal spores, and slow down water penetration and evaporation, thereby slowing changes in moisture content. The greatest benefit is to reduce swelling and contraction in larger timbers, thus reducing cracks and checks. Such cracks—as we've seen—weaken the timber and form vulnerable points for fungal attack. Some builders, for the same reason, paint all the large backbone timbers (e.g., keel, stem, and horn timber) and floor timbers with red lead as well.

The old standby for coating, protecting, and treating unpainted wood on deck, in the cabin, and wherever other coatings were not used is (by volume) equal parts turpentine, linseed oil, and carnauba wax (also known as Brazil wax). Mix the ingredients thoroughly and shake well before every application. Simply rub this into the wood with a soft cloth and, after an hour or two, wipe off any excess. Repeat as necessary to saturate thoroughly. Larger timbers can be painted with a brush and then rubbed down.

BEDDING JOINTS: LUTING

The mating or *faying* surfaces of all bolted joints in timbers (and between structural members) must be sealed and bedded. This was formerly referred to as *luting*, and was traditionally done using red- or white-lead paint, hot tar, marine glue, or—most commonly—a luting mixture. Luting mixture was created from one-part oil-based bedding putty and half-part white lead (by volume). This was stirred together with a few drops of boiled linseed oil until it had about the same consistency as soft butter or very heavy cream. Finally, a small amount of turpentine or a sprinkling of red lead was stirred in (just enough to turn the mixture a faint pink). Instead of traditional luting compound, today I would recommend using a highly elastic adhesive-sealant marine bedding compound, such as 3M-5200.

Care should be taken to seal the heels (i.e., exposed endgrain) of all framing everywhere. Red lead alone works, but brushing on a few coats of kerosene/linseed-oil mixture before the red lead is even better.

Seams and joints in cabin, cockpit, and other deck structures were usually bedded on white lead or additionally on cotton caulking strands saturated with white lead. Again, for permanent structures, I recommend 3M-

Luting a deadwood timber before installation. 3M-5200 is my preferred modern method. Traditional luting mixture can be used. Another traditional method is Irish felt bedded in roofing cement (tar). Luting is also sometimes termed "gacking up." (Courtesy Kortchmar & Willner)

5200 today. If the item is to be unbolted and removed occasionally, use one of the polysulfide, nonadhesive polyurethanes or other non-adhesive sealants.

MODERN SEALANTS AND CAULKING COMPOUNDS

These days, sealants and caulking compounds abound. Most of the common brands work well, but there are differences—different types, different purposes. Boat Life-Caulk is a polysulfide-based sealant that will cure under paint or water. It gets fairly tacky in about two days and cures totally in about five. Sikaflex is a polyurethane—No. 231 is primarily a bedding compound with low adhesive properties; No. 420 is primarily an adhesive; No. 241 is both a sealant and an adhesive. All the Sikaflexes cure under paint or water. 3M-5200 is also an adhesive sealant and it, too, cures under water. Although not truly a glue, it has the highest adhesive properties of the sealants—so high, in fact, that (with bolts pulled for removal) 12,000-pound

(5,400 kg) keels have been temporarily held in place by 3M-5200 alone! This is the drawback to 5200: heaven help you if you have to remove a fitting bedded in it!

Woolsey's Dolphinite is the flip side of the coin. Dolphinite won't cure under paint or water, it's not a good adhesive, and it never really cures at all (it is always soft or tacky). It is, however, a fine bedding and sealant with the great plus that you can remove the fittings you used it on fairly easily. All these products are suited for use under water as well as on deck. Silicone sealants won't cure under paint or water and they're *not* intended or suitable for *any* underwater work. They are good, however, for sealing ports, edgings, deck hardware, and the like.

INTERIOR PAINTING?

One of the great controversies in traditional boat construction is whether to paint the hull interior. Some builders and many reference sources strongly advise that you leave the interior of planking and frames unpainted, except for a possible coat of kerosene and/or boiled linseed oil. Other builders and references advocate painting every surface in the interior as well as the exterior. I don't know which school of thought is correct. I have personally owned two plank-on-frame hulls (both more than 20 years old) that had been painted inside; they showed no more evidence of rot than unpainted hulls of similar age. I suspect it is not too important one way or the other, as long as good building practice has been followed throughout, and as long as the interior wood has been otherwise coated with preservative or with kerosene and boiled linseed oil.

SALTING

Salt water is unfriendly to dry rot. Wood submerged in salt water will not rot, although it can be attacked by borers. With this in mind, many traditional craft (e.g., coasting schooners, wooden tugs, and heavy yachts) were fitted with *salt boxes* or *salt bags*. These receptacles were sited at strategic locations along the inside of the hull with the intention that they provide a continual salt-water drip, thus discouraging decay. Although salting has adherents, I don't believe it is markedly effective, and it can cause problems with electrical systems and metal fittings. I don't recommend it.

VENTILATION

Finally, it is important to consider ventilation of the structure when building any wooden boat. Where air can pass freely, the moisture content of wood will remain under 15 percent and rot has great difficulty taking hold. The most common locations for so-called dry rot are under the corners of the sheer, behind the clamp, under and behind the coach roof and cockpit carlins, and in the under-deck corners of stems and transom knees. All these locations are fairly high up and under the deck. The heat of the sun warms the wood, while condensation (freshwater) collects in cracks and crevices. If air can't circulate, this warm, moist, freshwater environment is heaven for fungus. During construction, you must take every step possible to promote free circulation of air in these areas and to build in avenues for collected water to drain away into the bilge.

EIGHT

Wood Design Considerations

*A*ll traditional plank-on-frame construction has fundamentally the same structure. A keel forms the backbone of the hull. This backbone curves up forward to form a *stem*, and projects up aft in a *sternpost*. The sternpost is the simplest form of aft-end backbone extension. On a deep-keel boat, where the hull sweeps aft in a longer run to a transom, the sternpost runs roughly vertically up from the keel, for a relatively short distance, to a *horn timber*, which in turn runs horizontally aft to the transom. The transom itself is fastened to the horn timber with a *transom knee*.

Keel and Backbone

PLANK KEELS
Keels come in a wide variety; the possibilities are as endless as the hull forms they serve. Small boats may have simple plank keels, literally from a single plank. Quite large powerboats can have relatively thin flat keels, built up from multiple timbers. These too are called plank keels (because they resemble a flat plank, even though they are built up from several). Even fair-sized sailboats can have plank keels, either penetrated with a centerboard case or with a ballast keel and deadwood bolted to its bottom.

DEEP KEELS AND KEELSONS
Deep keels are commonly found on larger, heavy-displacement workboats, as well as other vessels. These keels are considerably deeper in cross section than they are wide and also are usually built up of several timbers. Still larger displacement vessels usually have an additional keel/backbone member called the *keelson*. This is a longitudinal member running along the keel, bolted down on top of the floors and into the keel. The keelson is used on heavy boats with Sns of 9 or higher.

DEADWOOD
Where the keel projects far down into the water, below the body of the hull, it is built up to great depth with numerous timbers called the *deadwood*. The deadwood is usually

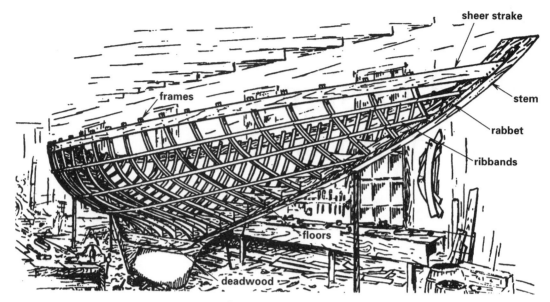

Bow view of framing

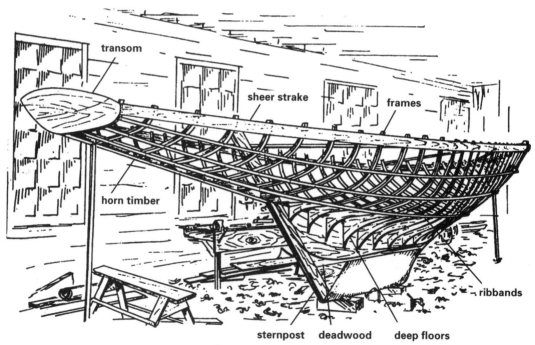

Stern view of framing

roughly the same thickness as the rest of the keel, unless it is a separate component bolted onto the bottom of a wide-plank keel.

RABBETS AND KEEL BATTENS

Deep keels are usually rabbeted to take the *garboard strake* (i.e., the planks running along the keel), as is the stem. Alternately, it is common practice to make up the keel of two pieces: the lower external piece is called the *keel*, the upper internal piece is called the *keel batten*. (Sometimes—and confusingly—this is also referred to as the *keelson*, the *keel apron*, or the *hog* or *hog timber.*) In this case, the keel batten and the keel, as a unit, together form the keel proper. Plank keels are usually fabricated this way, with a keel and keel batten. The keel batten may well be a larger and heavier timber, with a cross-sectional area greater than the external keel in this construction.

LAMINATED KEELS

Large keel timbers (and large timbers in general) are a problem because of the substantial dimensional changes with variations in moisture content. Although some classification societies' scantling rules call for very heavy timbers in the keel, I believe this is counterproductive. An excellent way to avoid the problem of swelling in large timbers, however, is to laminate the keel from smaller stock using epoxy glue. Then coat and seal the entire keel structure with epoxy. The individual smaller timbers generate fewer dimensional changes; they are

easier to work with and are less expensive to obtain; any size and shape required can be built up; and coating with epoxy holds the moisture content almost perfectly stable—thus, there is no expansion or contraction problem. Laminated keels should not be made of oak, which contains acids that don't bond as well to epoxy as some other woods. Yellow pine and Douglas fir are excellent for laminated keels and stems.

THIN TIMBERS FOR EPOXY LAMINATIONS

It is important not to epoxy-laminate large timbers from individual layers that are too thick themselves. Such larger timbers—even saturated with epoxy—will swell and shrink enough to cause structural and glue-bond

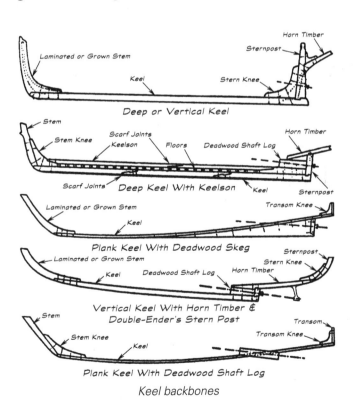

Keel backbones

problems. Generally, you should not laminate wood thicker than 2$^{1}/_{2}$ inches (60 mm). The most stable structure and the longest life will be achieved if lumber no thicker than 1$^{1}/_{2}$ inches (38 mm) is used.

HEAVY KEEL TIMBERS ADD LITTLE STRENGTH

It is important to keep in mind that a large heavy keel, in and of itself, does not add any great strength or rigidity to the hull as a whole. The strength and stiffness of the entire hull is generated by the rough box-section girder, which is formed by *the entire hull as a unit*. The deck, sheer clamp and shelf, planking, bilge stringers, and keel all work in concert. Doubling or tripling the cross-sectional area of a keel adds no more strength to the structure as a whole than, say, arbitrarily doubling or tripling the deck thickness or the plank. Avoid the common tendency to use massive keel timbers.

LEAD BALLAST STRUCTURAL KEELS

Another option for large keels in sailboats with lead outside ballast is to form part of the keel/backbone structure out of a long, shallow lead keel-ballast casting. No wooden keel structure at all is required in this area. Fore and aft of the ballast keel, the wood keel and deadwood can be fastened and scarfed to the lead keel just as if it were timber. These structural ballast keels should be cast from lead with about 2 percent antimony content. This is stronger than a solid-oak keel of the same dimension, without any of timber's dimensional instability. The lead can be carved and machined for the plank rabbet and drilled and taped for floor bolts. This is an exceptionally strong and long-lasting arrangement.

The Stem

The stem almost always has a pronounced curve to it, often approaching a 90-degree bend at the forefoot. There are several ways to build up such a timber.

NATURAL CROOK STEMS

In small craft, the traditional method is to find a grown natural crook that would approximate the desired stem shape in size and curvature. The stem is then hewn from the crook as a single piece. Somewhat larger hulls can have their stems fashioned from two or three natural crooks sawn to shape and bolted together.

BUILT-UP STEMS

Natural crooks are difficult to locate (more so with every passing year, it seems). Accordingly, most medium- to large-sized boats have built-up stems fabricated from several sawn timbers; usually two or three timbers are sufficient. If two timbers are used, the lower stem timber with the maximum bend is called the *stem knee* or *anchor stock*. When three timbers are used, the lowest and aftermost timber is called the *gripe*. The next timber up (usually with the maximum curvature) is the *stem knee*. In all cases, the uppermost timber is termed the *stem*, even though all these timbers together form the stem proper.

These timbers are notched together with carved hook joints or locking keys and are carefully through-bolted. Bolt diameter, key, and nib size should be proportioned approximately the same as for scarfed timbers of similar dimensions (see chapter 10). All are trimmed and dressed to the exact cross-sectional shape of the stem, which frequently varies along its length. For these built-up stems, be sure to cut each individual timber so the woodgrain runs along the majority of its length, not across it.

LAMINATED STEMS

Built-up stems are excellent but require heavy and labor-intensive construction. My preference is for laminated stems, made using epoxy glue and coated with epoxy. Traditionally, such laminated stems were built up with the laminations running longitudinally athwartships (like a laminated frame rotated to face the bow). Theoretically, this is the correct and strongest method. Such laminating jobs are time-consuming, however. A jig has to be formed, numerous clamps prepared, and the whole procedure requires several hands and much wood.

Alternative Laminated Stems

I have had very good results using stems that were laminated up from layers running fore-n-aft, made approximately like a sawn frame that has been rotated around to face forward, only with more layers. These fore-n-aft laminated stems are fashioned from three to six layers each, sawn to shape, with butts well staggered. The advantage here is that sawing the flat plank stock to shape is quick, simple work. The clamping job is also easier, with most of the clamping pressure coming from annular-ring boat nails and bronze screws that are left in place, unless they interfere with finishing off the timber. The folks at Covey Island Boatworks introduced me to this stem construction. Although theoretically weaker than standard horizontally laminated stems, I have found these fore-n-aft laminated stems to be more than strong enough.

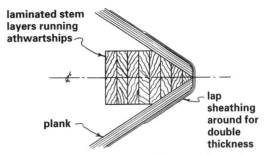

Traditional stem of a plywood boat with exterior hull sheathing

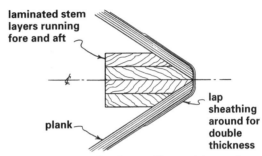

Alternate stem of a plywood boat with exterior hull sheathing

Frames and Floors

FLOORS

Frames are fastened to the keel, stem, horn timber, and sternpost with floors. First, floors are cut from fairly heavy plank and are bolted down into the top of the keel. The floors are then fastened fore-n-aft into the frames. Floors also can be bolted down centered on top of the frames. Such floors are screw-fastened into the frames from above, as well as bolted to the top of the keel. On vessels with hollow garboards, floors may be quite deep, especially in the run—at the deadwood, sternpost, and horn timber. These floors are often notched around the backbone timbers, and may fasten into the sides of the sternpost and deadwood. Floors like this are often made in two sections. The lower section is really three separate, roughly triangular pieces, each fastened into the side sternpost or horn timber. The upper section is a crosspiece like a normal floor or frame across the bottom. It runs from port to starboard and is fastened to the frames. This upper crosspiece is sometimes referred to as the *strongback*.

Floors can also be made of metal, see pages 172–74.

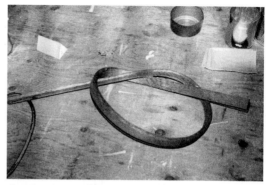

Steamed-oak frames can literally be twisted in knots. (Courtesy North River Boatworks)

STEAM-BENT FRAMES

Steam-bent frames are generally superior for round-bilge hulls. This is because the grain in the frame runs smoothly and evenly in the direction of the frame throughout its length. (Laminated frames are nearly as strong and resilient as steam-bent frames, but they require more labor.) By contrast, the grain in sawn frames almost always runs at off angles to the direction of the frame itself. As a consequence, sawn frames in round-bilge hulls are only about half as strong as steam-bent or laminated frames.

Large Steam-Bent Frames

Steam-bent frames more than 2 inches (50 mm) thick athwartships are quite difficult to bend, however. The common solution is to split the frame athwartships and to bend it in place in two sections. For example, a 3-by-3-inch (76 × 76 mm) frame would be bent in two layers 3 inches (76 mm) fore-n-aft and $1^1/2$ inches thick (38 mm) athwartships. It is not necessary to glue the two layers together; they are simply clamped in place to the ribbands and screwed together, just enough to hold them when the clamps are removed. The

regular plank-fastening screws are long enough to pass through both frame layers, thus ensuring that the double frame acts as a unit.

Some people worry about rot occurring between the two layers of a steam-bent frame. However, this does not seem to be a problem. I have inspected several vessels more than 50 feet (15 m) long that were built with split-bent frames. These boats were all more than 30 years old and, although they had rot in several locations, the one place there wasn't any was between the split frame halves!

Steam-Bent Frame Bevels

Another advantage to steam-bent frames is that they can be twisted against the ribbands at the same time they are bent in place. This means steam-bent frames can be cut square all around and still take the correct bevel automatically during the bending process (if the bevel is not too severe). Such twisted-in-place bent frames make an angle where they meet the floors, which are flat and run square athwartships. Accordingly, the floors are beveled and/or shimmed out where they meet these frames to make a tight fit.

SAWN FRAMES IN BOW AND STERN OF ROUND-BILGE HULLS

There are places where sawn frames make sense and can save labor in round-bilge hulls. In the bow, where the hull is roughly vee-shaped, the frames are nearly straight. Here, sawn frames can be cut so the grain runs close to lengthwise along the frame. Ideally, you would get these frames from boards with grain that had a natural sweep similar to the desired curvature. Such frames are almost as strong as steam-bent frames. At the same time, up in the bow, the bevel is most severe and it may not be possible to bend it in here. Sawn frames can be cut and then dressed to the exact bevel, making a better fit and still mating the floors at right angles. Similarly, at the transom in hulls with pronounced reverse curve (particularly on hulls with wine-glass transoms), sawn frames can be gotten out more easily than bent frames. In this application, though, the sawn frames are weaker than bent frames would be. Still, it is nearly impossible to bend in frames near the transom on a hull with tight hollow garboards, deep deadwood, and tumblehome in the upper portion of the transom. Sawn frames may be the only practical solution (and a perfectly acceptable one). Usually, single-sawn frames are used.

Sawn Frames on Round-Bilge Hulls

When sawn frames are used throughout on a round-bilge hull, they should be double the size—fore-n-aft—of bent frames and essentially made up of two frames side by side, with the butt joints in each sawn section or *futtock* well staggered. Such frames are called *double-sawn frames*. Very large heavy craft with Sns over 10 often use sawn frames of the same

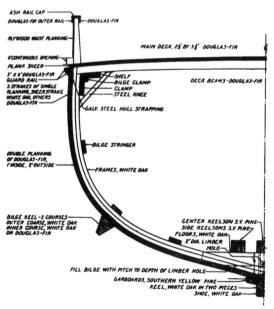

Section through steam-bent frame workboat

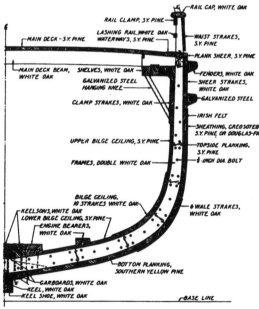

Section through double-sawn frame tug

doubled fore-n-aft dimension, but divided into three fore-n-aft layers or subframes (i.e., *triple-sawn frames*). With all the futtock butts well staggered, this is slightly stronger still, and the individual timbers are smaller and easier to handle during fashioning.

Sawn Frames on Hard-Chine Hulls

On hard-chine hulls, sawn frames work well all around. Compared to round-bilge hulls, hard-chine hulls have fairly straight frames from keel to chine and from chine to sheer. As a result, the grain in a sawn frame on hard-chine hulls runs fairly straight along its length. Hard-chine hulls almost always are built with sawn frames, although some hard-chine hulls can have pronounced curve in the forefoot and in the topsides at the bow. In these locations, it is occasionally sensible to use bent frames. In hard-chine hulls, the sawn frames need only have joints at the chine. Here, the bottom and topsides futtocks are joined with gussets. Frames like this are called *single-sawn frames*.

MORTISING FRAMES INTO THE KEEL

One of the oddest practices in wooden-boat construction is mortising the heels of frames into the keel. Mortising is exacting work and—if done at all—must be performed on both sides of the keel for each frame. The mystery is that some of the finest builders throughout history have followed this practice. All I can tell you is that it is always wrong! Never notch the keel for the heels of frames—ever! The drawbacks are numerous:

- The notches weaken the keel.
- The notches form pockets for fungal growth and decay to start.
- The notches create numerous small corners that can split during swell/contraction cycles.

- The notches add absolutely no strength to the frame or to its attachment to the keel.
- The construction of the notches interferes with proper drainage, through the limbers in the bilge.
- The notches consume substantial amounts of time in fabrication—wasted time.

The floors and the floors alone transmit the loads from the frames to the keel (and across the boat). Indeed, it is possible to cut the frames off completely above the keel, fastening them to the floors alone. This, in fact,

Garboard strake removed reveals frames notched into the keel—bad! Many rot pockets were found. Note the feeble little notches in each frame bottom. These were to form limbers but were quickly clogged.

is excellent construction practice. The frames can be cut off at a height of one frame siding (see chapter 9) above the keel. The limber can then be cut into the very outside corner of the floor, where it meets the garboard. This ensures the best possible drainage in the bilge.

Planking

Planking presents more options and varieties than any other portion of the hull structure, including single-carvel; double-carvel (usually called double-plank); strip-plank; lapstrake-, clinker-, or clench-plank; double-diagonal; Ashcroft; batten-seam; and herringbone-bottom. The scantling rule that follows primarily applies to carvel plank; however, adjustments are given for other planking methods.

CARVEL PLANK
Carvel plank is traditional single-plank-on-frame construction, with the planking made watertight by caulking and by the natural swelling of the planks themselves. The planks are laid on running fore-n-aft. This method requires moderate skill. Carvel plank is one of the easiest planking methods to repair because each plank can be unscrewed, removed, and replaced without disturbing other planks or the interior.

DOUBLE PLANK OR DOUBLE-CARVEL PLANK
Double plank is two layers of fore-n-aft carvel plank laid on so that the seams of the inside layer fall approximately in the middle of the plank on the outside layer. Double-plank construction requires high levels of skill because all the planks on both layers must fit very closely. The benefit is that double-plank

hulls tend to be tighter and smoother (to show fewer seams) than single plank. Traditionally, the two plank layers were laid on each other with a thick layer of shellac. This forms a somewhat flexible adhesive that is also reasonably water-resistant.

STRIP-PLANK
Strip-plank construction is strong and tight. It has almost no tendency to open up and leak when dried out. It is similar in principle to ordinary plank-on-frame, but individual planks are much narrower—square or almost square strips that are edge-nailed and glued to each other along their full length. Ordinary, traditional strip-plank construction requires less skill than any other planking method; however, the numerous edge-fastened strips are tedious and laborious to install. The solution is to arrange for a large, well-organized strip-plank crew. A team of seven (i.e., three on each side and one supervisor) can strip up a 40-footer (12 m) in just a few days. Modern wood-epoxy strip-plank construction is—by a slim margin—my construction method of choice for one-off hulls. It is even easier than

Stripping up a wood-epoxy strip-plank hull.
(Courtesy Alan Salisch)

traditional strip-planking and is dimensionally stable and exceptionally rot-resistant (nearly but not quite rot-impervious). Strip-planking is not as easy to repair as carvel planking, but it is easier than lapstrake and repairs usually can be made without disturbing the interior.

LAPSTRAKE (CLINKER- OR CLENCH-BUILT) PLANK

Lapstrake hulls are generally lighter than comparable hulls made single- or double-plank or strip-planked. The lapstrake seams have much less tendency than carvel plank to leak when the hull dries out and is subsequently relaunched. This combination of lightness and staying tight when dry made lapstrake the favorite choice for small launches (see photo on p. 338).

Lapstrake takes more skill than carvel plank. It takes great patience, especially to form the plank-lap joints as they run into the stem and sometimes into the transom or sternpost. Another drawback is that the wide planking stock required for larger hulls is nearly impossible to find today. For this reason, plywood lapstrake planking is used on

Lapstrake fishing vessels on the beach in Kittery, Maine. (Courtesy Alan Salisch)

some larger powerboat hulls. It is important, however, to keep in mind the lower longitudinal strength of plywood in this application.

DOUBLE-DIAGONAL PLANK

Double-diagonal plank is two layers of plank laid on the hull at roughly between 35 and 45 degrees to the fore-n-aft axis. In both traditional and cold-molded construction, it is one of the strongest constructions for its weight; however, it is labor-intensive and more difficult to repair than carvel. In traditional construction, double-diagonal planking requires great skill.

Cold-Molded Double- (or More) Diagonal Plank

The modern variant of double-diagonal plank is two *or more* layers of plank laid on at 35 to 45 degrees to the horizontal axis. If three or more layers are used, every third layer will run fore-n-aft. All the layers are glued together and coated with epoxy. This forms an exceptionally light, stiff, monocoque hull shell that is totally watertight. Although somewhat less skill is required to build cold-molded double-diagonal than traditional double-diagonal, it still requires considerable know-how and patience. When three or more layers are used, labor can be very time-consuming indeed. Unlike cold-molded strip-plank, multiple-diagonal planking does not lend itself as well to large planking crews working quickly.

ASHCROFT PLANK

Ashcroft plank is double-diagonal planking with both diagonal layers running the same way, but overlapped as in double-carvel planking. The planking starts at the keel and angles up and back to the sheer at roughly 40 degrees to vertical. This planking system had great popularity for a time in Great Britain, but I don't see any advantages to it with modern construction materials and methods.

BATTEN-SEAM PLANK

Batten-seam plank is ordinary carvel plank with small backing strips—the *battens*—running behind each seam. This helps reduce leaking in dried-out hulls on relaunching. Batten-seam plank is almost universally used on hard-chine hulls. The individual battens must be carefully lined up and notched into the frames so the planks can lie smooth and flush on top of them and the frames together. A fairly high level of skill is required. As with Ashcroft planking, batten-seam construction has been outdated by modern materials and methods. If the hull sections are suitable, plywood can be used. If not, then the hull can be planked in either ordinary carvel-plank or strip-plank.

PLYWOOD PLANK

Plywood plank is very attractive to the amateur. It offers rapid planking of large surfaces with minimum measuring and fitting. Plywood planking is neither a magic bullet nor a cure-all, however. Plywood cannot be made to take compound curvature. Accordingly, most traditional hulls *cannot* be planked up with sheet plywood. Hulls must be specifically designed (or specially modified in shape) to accept sheet plywood. The hull surface must be cylindrically or conically developed, which avoids compound curvature.

Furthermore, plywood is made up of layers of veneer with the grain running at right angles. This drastically increases plywood's strength across the grain because there is no true "across the grain." Unfortunately, only half the grain runs in any given direction,

which roughly halves the strength of plywood in the fore-n-aft direction. For instance, Douglas-fir plank has a tensile strength along its length (a modulus of rupture) of 12,200 psi (84 mPa); however, Douglas-fir plywood has a strength of just 5,570 psi (38.3 mPa).

When subject to repeated high strain (i.e., deflection) in a wet environment, internal defects—in the individual layers and between the layers—can cause local internal delamination, which is often undetectable from the outside. However, these defects substantially reduce the strength of the plywood planking. When highly loaded again, this region can fail dramatically. Accordingly—and contrary to common belief—plywood planking should not be made too much lighter than ordinary carvel planking would be on the same hull.

HERRINGBONE-BOTTOM PLANK

On hard-chine hulls, the bottom planking can be made of relatively heavy boards laid on diagonally, herringbone fashion, with the planks starting at the keel and angling back at about 45 to 55 degrees aft. Herringbone planking is usually nailed in place and is quick and easy to install. It will work with most hull surfaces, including those with compound curvature (unlike plywood). Herringbone bottoms are excellent for traditional hard-chine hulls. The topsides of such hulls are usually carvel-plank or strip-plank; however, they also can be lapstrake, which looks quite handsome and saves weight. On cold-molded hard-chine hulls, strip-planks on the bottom can be laid on herringbone fashion. This is sometimes easier and quicker than laying the strips on longitudinally along the bottom, and is just as strong. Some builders cross-plank V-bottom hulls with no angle—with the planks running square athwartships.

Decks

Decks and deck beams must be quite strong. Not only do they have to support the weight of crew and gear, but they also have to be able to withstand the weight of green water breaking aboard in rough weather. Even more important, the deck forms the upper portion of the hull-structure box-girder. If the deck is too weak, the entire hull will flex or pant.

LAID DECK

Traditional decks either were constructed of laid planks carefully caulked or were strip-planked, edge-nailed, and glued, often with caulking run into grooves in the upper third of the plank seams. Both of these systems were prone to leaks because the individual planks still shrink and expand repeatedly with changes in moisture—these changes are regular, pronounced, and frequent on decks. Decks can be exceptionally dry after just a few rain-free days at anchor in the hot sun. A day later, the same deck will be fully wetted with fresh water from a rainstorm. On the day after, the deck will be saturated with salt

A laid-pine deck. Each strake is edge-nailed to its neighbor and toe-nailed into the deck beam below. A bead of 3M-5200 is between each plank. (Courtesy Kortchmar & Willner)

water while driving hard to windward in rough seas.

CANVAS DECKS

The other traditional deck treatment was to plank up the deck normally—smooth carvel plank—but cover it with canvas laid in paint. This resulted in very clean, tight, waterproof decks, which were also quite light. (It is still the best non-skid deck surface.) The painted canvas expands and contracts with the expansion and contraction of the planks beneath it. Properly built, these decks will last for years without leaking.

PLYWOOD DECKS

Today, there is no better deck than marine plywood covered with a layer or two of glass cloth set in epoxy. Plywood decks are as light as canvas decks, are dimensionally far more stable, and also have diagonal (torsional) stiffness, which planked decks do not. Plywood decks are generally much quicker and easier to build and install than any traditional decking.

The layer of glass cloth is strongly recommended to protect and seal the grain of the surface veneer of the plywood. In the past, the fiberglass was often laid on in polyester resin. Although this can work if everything is done just right, polyester does not have the tenacity, elongation, and peel strength required to ensure a permanent watertight bond in such applications. Epoxy is the proper answer. If the plywood deck is also sealed and coated with epoxy on the underside and around all the edges, it will be virtually rot-proof, as well as highly stable dimensionally.

DECK BEAMS

For the same reason that the decks themselves must be strong, so must the deck beams. Deck beams are frequently heavier timbers than the frames. The deck beams must be securely fastened to the heads of the frames in traditional construction, and be well fastened to the shelf and/or clamp.

Shelf, Clamp, and Bilge Stringer

In addition to the keel, there are several other critical longitudinal members required for proper strength.

SHELF AND CLAMP

Up at the sheer—running along the inside of the frames, just under the deck beams—are the shelf and the clamp. These longitudinal members tie the frames together fore-n-aft at the sheer, and provide a strong foundation for the deck beams. The clamp is a longitudinal generally higher than it is wide athwartships. The shelf is usually roughly square, and is bolted to the inboard upper edge of the clamp. On small boats, sometimes only the clamp is used. Even on larger craft and on cold-molded hulls, the shelf can be dispensed with, but—in this case—the clamp must be made somewhat heavier, and is more difficult to fit unless laminated in place. The clamp and shelf, port and starboard, should be tied together at the stem with a large athwartships knee, called the *breasthook*. The breasthook is bolted to the inside face of the stem, and the clamp and shelf are screwed and bolted to the breasthook. Both the shelf and clamp should be tied similarly into the transom with *quarter knees*.

BILGE STRINGER

At the turn of the bilge, a longitudinal member called the *bilge stringer* is run inside of and fastened to the frames. The bilge stringers, port and starboard, also should be tied together and to the stem with a breasthook and to the transom with quarter knees.

Other Structural Components

In addition to the principal ones already discussed, numerous other structural components comprise a hull, including hanging and lodging knees, mast steps and partners, engine beds, butt blocks, diagonal strapping, caulking, cabin and cockpit structures, and ballast keels. These are discussed in detail in the scantling rules in the following chapters.

NINE

Plank-on-Frame Scantling Rule

*I*n the preceding chapters, we reviewed the principles behind and standard structures employed in traditional wooden-boat construction. In this chapter, we discuss the scantling rule that will enable you to calculate the scantlings for most ordinary plank-on-frame wooden boats.

Recommended Woods

The wood used for each specific application—floors, frames, plank, knees—is critical. Boatbuilding woods are discussed in detail in chapter 12. Wherever possible, you should attempt to use the woods recommended in that chapter for the uses labeled "excellent" or "good." Woods listed as "acceptable" will be just that. You can employ them as required, but they will not last as long as those rated excellent or good for that specific application.

Molded and Sided Dimensions

Before we delve into the plank-on-frame scantling rule, however, we need to establish more precise terminology for describing scantling dimensions. Up until now, we have referred to planks, frames, and keels as being "so thick," "so wide," "so high," or "so deep." This can be imprecise because it's not always clear which direction is the "width," "depth," or "height." The correct terms are *molded* and *sided* dimensions, or *molding* and *siding*.

The molded dimension of any piece is its dimension measured in from the outside toward the interior of the hull. Thus, for a keel timber, the molding is the vertical dimension (the up-and-down direction points into the interior). Conversely, for the sheer clamp, the molding is the horizontal dimension (the side-to-side direction points into the interior). The siding is the direction at right angles to the molded dimension that is *not* running along the length of the woodgrain. A deck beam's molding, for example, is the up-and-down direction; its siding is in the fore-n-aft direction. It's worth taking a moment to make sure you understand this nomenclature because it eliminates much potential confusion.

For instance, a bilge stringer could be described as 4 inches (100 mm) wide and 2 inches (50 mm) high. This is vague, though, because as the bilge stringer runs forward to the bow, it twists nearly 90 degrees. Amidships, the bilge stringer is roughly horizontal on the frames, but forward it will lie nearly vertical against them. Where the 2-inch (50 mm) dimension would be approximately vertical (high) amidships, it will be more or less horizontal (wide) near the stem. By contrast, if we described the stringer as sided 4 inches (100 mm) and molded 2 inches (50 mm), there would be no possibility for error. The molded 2-inch (50 mm) dimension would always be the dimension measured in or out from the interior. We use molded and sided dimensions almost exclusively throughout the wood scantling rule.

For constancy and convenience in comparing materials, we'll stay with our example boat, the trusty *Fish 'n Squish*. In honor of the boat's new wood construction, however, we are renaming it *Logger Bobber*.

Logger Bobber has the following characteristics:

LOA	40.00 ft.	12.19 m
WL	37.20 ft.	11.34 m
Beam	12.56 ft.	3.83 m
Depth of Hull	5.91 ft.	1.80 m

This gave an Sn of 2.97 (see Formula 1-1).

Plank, Frames, and Floors

FORMULA 9-1
Plank Thickness

(Refer also to Formula 9-34.)

Plank Thickness, in. = 0.74 × Sn$^{0.4}$
(English)

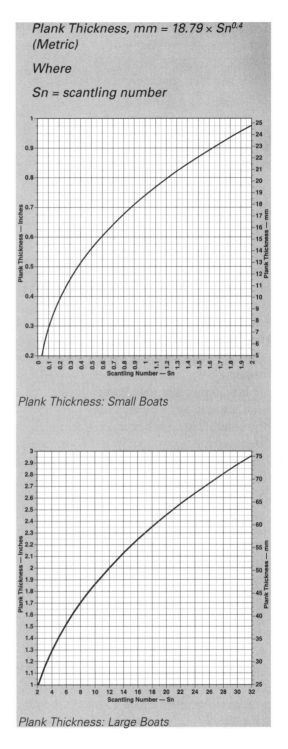

Plank Thickness, mm = 18.79 × Sn$^{0.4}$
(Metric)

Where

Sn = scantling number

Plank Thickness: Small Boats

Plank Thickness: Large Boats

- Increase the bottom-plank thickness only—from the chine or from the turn of the bilge down to the keel—by 1 percent for every knot over 25 knots.
- Increase the plank thickness (including speed-adjusted bottom plank) by 5 to 10 percent for hard-service workboats.
- Workboats and heavy offshore cruising boats will often increase the thickness of the garboard strake and the sheer strake by 10 percent over the neighboring planks.
- All boats can reduce plank thickness—from the BLH up—by 10 percent (see Formula 4-3).
- Light high-performance yachts can reduce plank thickness by 10 percent but at some cost in longevity.
- Strip-planking should be the same thickness as carvel-planking. The strips must be edge-nailed and glued along their entire length (see Formula 10-4).
- For sheet-plywood planking, calculate as before, then use the same thickness for the bottom plank and 90 percent of the thickness for the topsides plank. Note that plywood hulls are hard-chine, so use hard-chine frames and frame spacing.
- Lapstrake planks are 85 percent of the thickness for carvel planks.

For our *Logger Bobber*, this gives

$$Plank\ Thickness = 0.74 \times 2.97^{0.4} = 1.14;$$
$$use\ 1\tfrac{1}{8}\text{-}in.\ plank$$

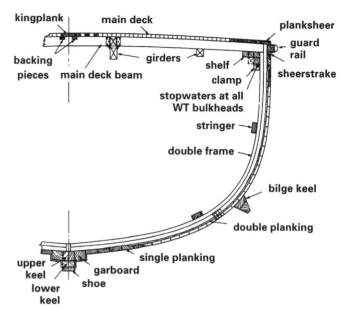

Section through heavy double-planked hull. Note extra-heavy garboards and single planking near keel and sheer. The large frames are bent double.

$$Plank\ Thickness = 18.79 \times 2.97^{0.4} = 29;$$
$$use\ 28\ mm\ plank$$

If *Logger Bobber* were a 30-knot boat, the bottom-plank thickness would be increased by 5 percent to 1.19 inches, say $1\tfrac{3}{16}$ inches (30.45 mm, say 30 mm). Old *Bobber*, however, runs at 20 knots, so we don't have to make any speed adjustment.

FORMULA 9-2

Frame Siding and Molding

Standard steam-bent frames are square in section—they have the same siding and molding.

Frame Siding and Molding, in. = 1.37 × $Sn^{0.36}$ (English)

Frame Siding and Molding, mm = 34.79 × $Sn^{0.36}$ (Metric)

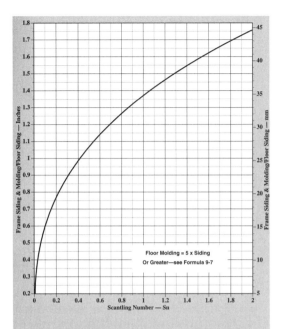

Frames and Floors: Small Boats

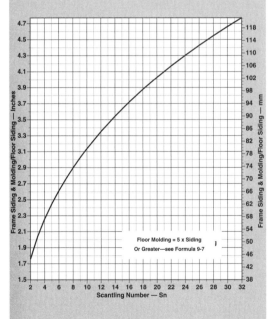

Frames and Floors: Large Boats

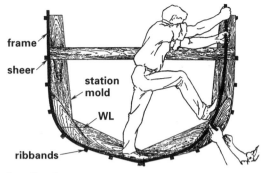

Bending frames

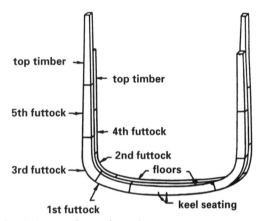

Double-sawn frame futtocks

- Double-sawn frames for round-bilge hulls should be twice the siding and the same molding as the single-bent frames.
- Single-sawn frames on hard-chine hulls should have the same siding as the square-bent frames, but the molding on the bottom futtock should be 3 times the siding. Molding on the topsides futtock should taper from 3 times the bent-frame siding at the chine to 1.3 times the bent-frame siding at the sheer.
- Gussets on hard-chine single-sawn frames are best made from marine plywood, through-bolted (or screwed and glued on

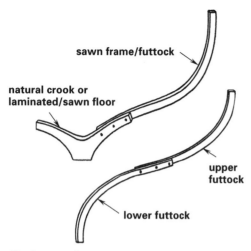

sawn frame/futtock

natural crook or
laminated/sawn floor

upper
futtock

lower futtock

Single-sawn frames

smaller craft) to both the front and back faces of the frame. Each gusset is sided one-third the frame siding, and extends for a distance of at least 3 times the frame molding along the side of the frame—measured both up and athwartships—from the inside of the plank at the chine (see photo on p. 338).

- An alternative to plywood gussets is simply to have the topsides futtock overlap the bottom futtock, bolting them together. This is somewhat quicker and easier than installing plywood gussets, but the joint is not quite as strong.
- Single-sawn frames used for ease of construction in the bow and stern of round-bilge hulls are sided and molded about the same as the standard bent frame; however, it is good practice to increase

the molding by 25 to 30 percent.
- On sailboats, it is recommended that the molding and siding of the frames immediately ahead and abaft of the partners be increased by 20 percent. This is a requirement on boats with Sns over 8.
- Lapstrake frames are molded slightly thinner, or 90 percent of the molding given previously, but use the same siding (see photo on p. 338).

Logger Bobber would require the following:

Bent Frames Sided and Molded, in. =
$$1.37 \times 2.97^{0.36} = 2.03 \text{ in.; use 2 in.}$$

Bent Frames Sided and Molded, mm =
$$34.79 \times 2.97^{0.36} = 51.48 \text{ mm.; use 50 mm}$$

If old *Bobber* were a hard-chine hull, its bottom-frame futtock would be molded 6

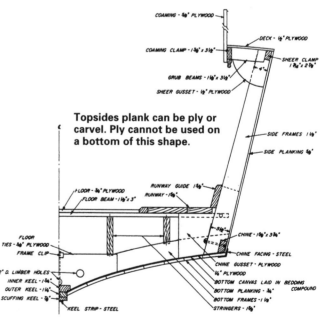

Topsides plank can be ply or carvel. Ply cannot be used on a bottom of this shape.

Section through a V-bottom workboat

inches (150 mm) and sided 2 inches (50 mm). Its topsides futtock would be sided 2 inches (50 mm), with molding tapering from 6 inches (150 mm) at the chine to 2.6, say $2^5/8$ inches (66 mm), at the sheer. Gussets would be $^5/8$-inch (15 mm) ply, extending a minimum of 18 inches (457 mm) along each futtock. (In the bow and stern, it is sometimes necessary to reduce the length of the gussets.)

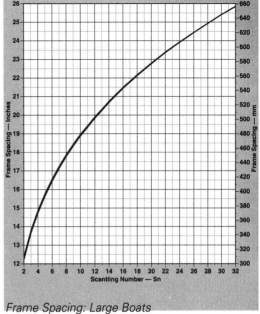

Frame Spacing: Large Boats

FORMULA 9-3

Frame Spacing

> *Bent-Frame Spacing, in. = 10.14 × Sn^{0.27}, center to center (English)*

> *Bent-Frame Spacing, mm = 257.5 × Sn^{0.27}, center to center (Metric)*

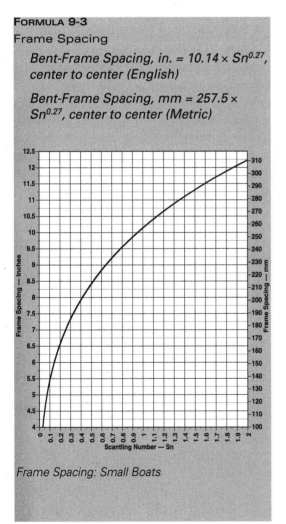

Frame Spacing: Small Boats

- Decrease frame spacing by 1 percent for every knot over 25 knots.
- Double-sawn frames on round-bilge hulls have the same spacing as standard bent frames.
- Single-sawn frames on hard-chine hulls are spaced 2.5 times farther apart than bent-frame spacing.
- No frame spacing on any hull is to exceed 36 inches (900 mm).
- Bent frames on lapstrake hulls are spaced closer, or 90 percent of the spacing given previously (see photo on p. 339).

Returning to *Logger Bobber*, we would use

> *Bent-Frame Spacing = 10.14 × 2.97^{0.27} = 13.6 in., center to center*

> *Bent-Frame Spacing = 257.5 × 2.97^{0.27} = 345.5 mm, center to center*

For a hard-chine *Bobber*, we would multiply by 2.5 to get 34-inch (864 mm) frame spacing.

Adjusting Frame Siding and Molding for Convenient Frame Spacing

Frames can be spaced farther apart or closer together, as convenient, by increasing or decreasing frame siding and molding 3.2 percent for each inch or millimeter of increase or decrease in frame spacing.

Say you wanted *Logger Bobber*'s bent frames to fall evenly on 16-inch centers (or O.C., for *on center*). This is an increase in spacing of 2.4 inches. Accordingly, we would increase *Bobber*'s frame siding and molding from 2 to $2^1/_{16}$ inches (2.4-inch increase × 0.032 = 0.077, and 2.03 inches + 0.077 = 2.10 inches; use $2^1/_{16}$ inches).

or

If we wanted to increase *Bobber*'s frame spacing to an even 400 mm, we would find a frame siding and molding increased to 54 mm from the original 51.48 mm (400 mm – 345.5 mm = 54.5 mm increase, and 54.5 mm × 0.032 = 1.74 mm, so 51.48 mm + 1.74 mm = 53.2 mm; use 54 mm).

If you wish to decrease the frame spacing, frame siding and molding is decreased in the same way.

FORMULA 9-5

Strip-Plank Frame Spacing

Because of the more rigid nature of edge-nailed and glued strip-plank, the frame spacing (including the associated floors) can be substantially increased.

Strip-Plank Frame Spacing = 4 × bent-frame spacing

- Frame spacing may exceed 36 inches (900 mm).
- Calculate frame spacing and frame size, including all adjustments for speed, per the previous formulas, then multiply the spacing by 4 to get the strip-plank spacing.
- Hard-chine hulls with sawn frames may increase frame spacing over the bent-frame spacing (not the sawn-frame spacing) by 4.6 times.

FORMULA 9-6

Flat (Non-Square) Frames

It is sometimes desirable to use frames that are not square in section. In this case, use the standard square-section frames from Formula 9-2, and adjust as follows.

For every percent of reduction in molding, increase the siding:

Percent Siding Increase = 1 ÷ percent molding reduction

Or, if you know the new larger siding you wish, decrease the molding:

Percent Molding Reduction = 1 ÷ percent siding increase

- Siding may not be greater than 1.7 times the molding.

Say we wanted to reduce *Logger Bobber*'s frame molding from 2 inches (50 mm) to just $1^5/_8$ inches (40 mm). This is a reduction of about 80 percent of the square-section molding. The new flat-frame siding would be

1 ÷ 0.80 Molding Reduction = 1.25 siding increase

so

1.25 × 2 in. = 2.50; use 2½-in. siding

1.25 × 50 mm = 62.5; use 62 mm siding

2.5-in. siding ÷ 1.625-in. molding = 1.53, less than 1.7, okay

or

62 mm siding ÷ 40 mm molding = 1.55, less than 1.7, okay

FORMULA 9-7

Sawn Floors

(Refer also to the charts in Formula 9-2 and to Formula 11-17.)

Floor Siding = square-section bent-frame siding

Heavy-Floor Siding = 1.3 × standard floor siding

Floor Molding = 5 × standard-floor siding, minimum

- Heavy floors are used under the mast steps and on planing hulls or on displacement workboats, with heavy slow-turning diesel engines, under the engine beds at and between the engine-mount bolts.
- Heavy floors also may be used at ballast-keel bolts.

Say we stick with the 16-inch O.C. frame spacing; this means that *Logger Bobber*'s floors will be $2^1/_{16}$ inches thick and $10^3/_8$ inches high, minimum. Or, for the 400 mm O.C. frames, the floors would be sided 54 mm and molded 270 mm, minimum. (Higher floors or floors with deeper molded dimensions are stronger, but usually take up too much interior room.) Note that as a practical matter, it is acceptable for a few widely scattered floors to have lower moldings. This is sometimes necessary to work in tanks, machinery, or accommodations. There should never be more

than two such low floors on adjacent frames, and no more than 10 percent of the floors in the hull should be lower than the ideal minimum given.

Where heavy floors are used, they would be sided $2^3/_4$ inches or 70 mm. The minimum height molding of the heavy floors is the same as that on the standard floors: $10^3/_8$ inches (270 mm).

FORMULA 9-8

Laminated (or Grown) Floors

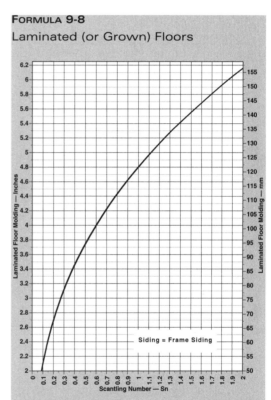

Laminated Floors: Small Boats

(Refer also to Formula 11-16.) Floors do not have to be bolted to the side of a frame. Instead, floors can be installed on top of the frame. Where this is done, the floor is bolted down into the floor and is screwed down into the top of the frame. If the frame itself runs from port

(continued)

to starboard on top of the keel, as a continuous member, the bolts into the keel will naturally pass through the frame as well.

Laminated Floor Siding = frame siding

Laminated Floor Molding, in. = 4.8 × Sn^{0.36} (English)

Laminated Floor Molding, mm = 122 × Sn^{0.36} (Metric)

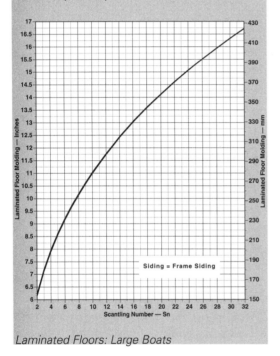

Laminated Floors: Large Boats

- Athwartships width of floor is to be 30 percent of the beam at that frame.
- Molding is to taper to 80 percent of frame siding at the port and starboard ends of the floors.
- An alternate composite metal-strap floor also can be used (see Formula 11-16).

If *Bobber* were to be built with laminated floors installed on top of its $2^{1}/_{6}$-inch-square frames (54 mm), we would use

Laminated Floor Siding = $2^{1}/_{6}$ in. (54 mm)

Laminated Floor Molding = $4.8 \times 2.97^{0.36}$ = 7.1; use 7 in.

Laminated Floor Molding = $122 \times 2.97^{0.36}$ = 180.5; use 180 mm

Molding tapers to $1^{3}/_{4}$ in. (44 mm) at ends

In the days when natural crooks were readily available, the laminated floors we described would have been hewn from these.

FORMULA 9-9
Limbers

Limber-Hole Radius = floor siding, but not less than $^{3}/_{4}$ in. (20 mm)

Limber holes in each floor, port and starboard, are vital to permit drainage of water to the lowest point in the bilge, where it can be pumped out efficiently. In the narrow bow near the stem and in the narrow bilge of a deep hollow-garboard hull, a single limber will be used on the centerline.

Keel/Backbone, Longitudinals, Web Frames, and Ceiling

FORMULA 9-10
Keel

Plank-Keel Molding, in. = $2.6 \times Sn^{0.4}$ (English)

Plank-Keel Molding, mm = $66 \times Sn^{0.4}$ (Metric)

Plank-Keel Siding = 1.75 × molding

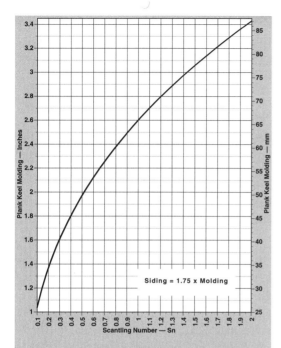

Plank Keels: Small Boats

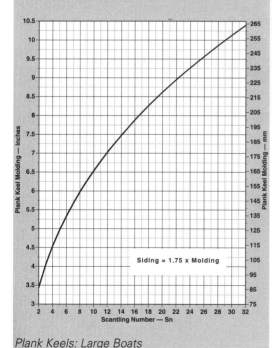

Plank Keels: Large Boats

Our *Logger Bobber* would use

Plank-Keel Molding = 2.6 × 2.97⁰·⁴ = 4 in.

$$\text{Plank-Keel Molding, mm} = 66 \times 2.97^{0.4}$$
$$= 102 \text{ mm; use } 100 \text{ mm}$$

Plank-Keel Siding = 7 in. (175 mm)

If *Bobber* were faster than 25 knots, you would add the suitable speed-adjusted increase for sided and molded dimensions. These dimensions are for the keel and keel batten combined—if this construction is used rather than a one-piece rabbeted keel. In this case, the keel batten might be approximately 2-inch (50 mm) siding by 8-inch (200 mm) molding and the keel 2-inch (50 mm) molding by 6-inch (150 mm) siding.

Keel shapes vary dramatically with hull type and construction method. The plank-keel dimensions from Formula 4-6 can be rotated 90 degrees to give minimum deep-keel dimensions. Usually, you'll find that hull shapes naturally tend to generate deep keels with somewhat fatter dimensions (i.e., wider moldings) than this rule indicates. This is acceptable and often unavoidable. Additionally, sailboats with external ballast often require considerably greater molding than indicated, especially if a deep-keel configuration is employed.

On most traditional hull forms, the keel is sided widest amidships and tapers away toward the ends, where it mates with the stem and the sternpost. This is not a requirement in any way, however, and the keel can have constant siding from stem to stern. Of course, *Logger Bobber*'s plank keel of 7-inch (175 mm) siding would be too wide at the stem for most normal 40-foot (12 m) hull forms; how-

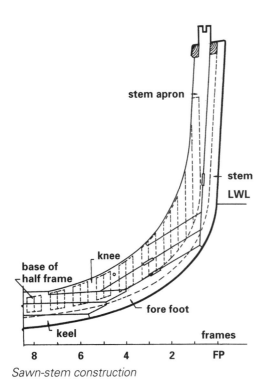

Sawn-stem construction

ever, the deep keel sided 4 inches (100 mm) could be kept at constant width from stem to sternpost on a 40-footer (12 m) like our trusty *Bobber*.

FORMULA 9-11

Stem and Sternpost

Stem and Sternpost Siding = plank-keel molding

Molding = 1.25 × the siding, or more

- *Increase siding and molding by 1 percent for every knot over 25 knots.*

Note that the keel siding will be greater than the stem and sternpost; however, the keel should taper down to the stem and sternpost formula siding (or close to it) at the stem and sternpost. Alternately, the stem and sternpost can be sided somewhat fatter to mate with the keel.

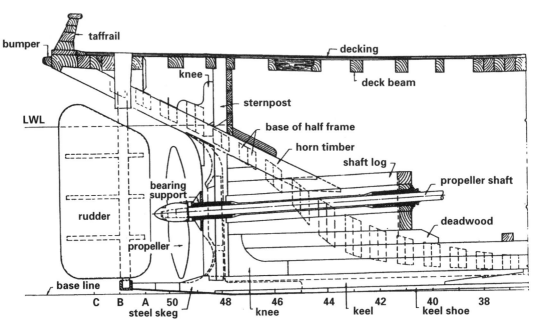

Deadwood, sternpost, horn-timber construction on harbor tug

Built-up stems usually have molding much greater than given here to allow for proper joints, keys, or hooks; long-enough faying surfaces; and proper through-bolting (refer to chapter 10). Stem siding must also be adjusted as necessary to mate with the keel. Laminated stems can come very close to the scantling dimensions. The sternpost may often be exactly as specified in the formula. Again, however, it must be adjusted in size and shape to mate with the keel and the deadwood.

FORMULA 9-12

Horn Timber

Horn-Timber Molding, in. = 1.85 × $Sn^{0.4}$ (English)

Horn-Timber Molding, mm = 47 × $Sn^{0.4}$ (Metric)

Siding = 1.2 × molding (or to mate with keel)

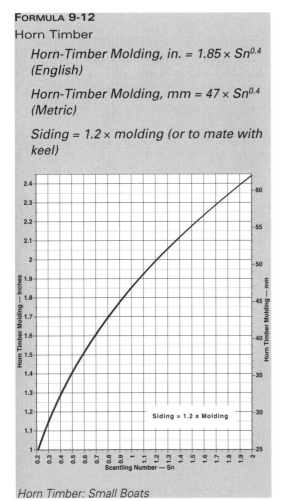

Horn Timber: Small Boats

Horn Timber: Large Boats

Logger Bobber's horn timber would be

Horn-Timber Molding = 1.85 × $2.97^{0.4}$ = 2.86 in.; use 2⅞ in.

Horn-Timber Molding = 47 × $2.97^{0.4}$ = 72.6; use 72 mm

Siding = 3.45 in. (86 mm)

FORMULA 9-13

Ceiling

Ceiling Thickness = 0.4 × plank thickness

Ceiling is a layer of "planking" fastened to the inside of the frames. Although it is common on many traditional designs, I recommend against installing structural ceiling except when unavoidable. Ceiling adds surprisingly little strength compared to its weight and cost. The other scantlings given in this chapter are sufficient without the additional strength of ceiling for most boats.

More important, the ceiling greatly reduces air circulation around the inside of the planks and frames, thereby promoting decay.

On yachts and light commercial craft, the ceiling's principal purpose is cosmetic. It makes a nice smooth-wall surface on the inside of the plank on the topsides, and it can help keep gear from rolling into the bilge water when a boat is heeled and driving hard. Ceiling also permits using joiner bulkheads that don't fall on the frames. Install the joiner ceiling sparingly, only in locations that it is required. If used for these purposes, I recommend that the ceiling be installed with $^1/_8$- to $^1/_4$-inch (3 to 6 mm) gaps between each ceiling plank; this greatly enhances ventilation. In many instances, ceiling like this can be screwed into the frames with oval-head screws set in finish rings. So installed, the ceiling planks can easily be removed and replaced for maintenance and repairs.

On cargo and fishing vessels, the ceiling protects the planking in the hold from being strained outward by the weight of the cargo or the catch. On such craft, ceiling must be used and should be installed tight without gaps. Such ceilings should have a gap of one strake left open, for full length under the clamp, for ventilation. The ceiling should end several frame bays short of the stem and of the transom, again to promote ventilation.

FORMULA 9-14

Belt Frames (Web Frames)

Belt Frames = 0.75 × frame siding and molding

When employed, belt frames are bent in and fastened down on top of the ceiling over a frame (fastened into the frame below) and are also bolted to the floor. Hanging knees attach the belt frame to the deck beam.

Belt or web frames are employed only on round-bilge hulls with extensive ceiling. Because this rule does not require ceiling, belt frames are seldom required in practice, except in heavy cargo and fishing vessels that have ceiling.

Belt frames are not required at all on vessels with Sns under 3. On vessels with Sns between 3 and 5, two belt frames are used—roughly one-third of the way aft of the bow and one-third of the way forward of the transom. On craft with Sns over 5, four belt frames are used—approximately one-quarter of the way aft of the bow to about one-quarter of the way forward of the transom. The purpose of the belt frames is to add strength at highly loaded areas, so they should be installed about athwartships from the mast, crane, main engine, and cargo hold.

FORMULA 9-15

Clamp and Bilge Stringer

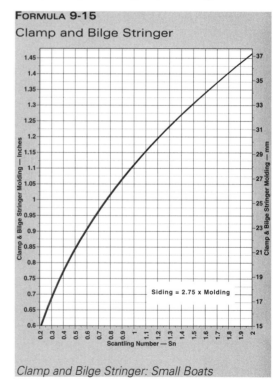

Clamp and Bilge Stringer: Small Boats

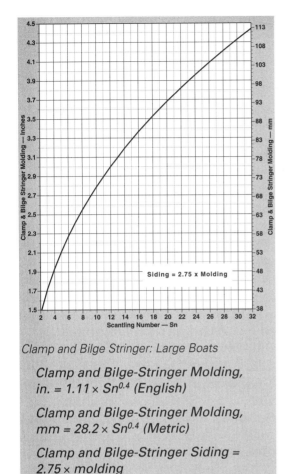

Clamp and Bilge Stringer: Large Boats

Clamp and Bilge-Stringer Molding, in. = 1.11 × Sn$^{0.4}$ (English)

Clamp and Bilge-Stringer Molding, mm = 28.2 × Sn$^{0.4}$ (Metric)

Clamp and Bilge-Stringer Siding = 2.75 × molding

(See photo on p. 339.)

- Both the clamp and the bilge stringer can taper in siding, at the bow and stern, to 60 percent of their maximum siding. The middle third of the clamp and bilge stringer should have maximum siding, with no taper. Such taper makes it easier to bend these members into place and saves some weight in the ends.
- Increase siding and molding by 1 percent for every knot over 25 knots.
- If no shelf is used, increase clamp molding by 30 percent.

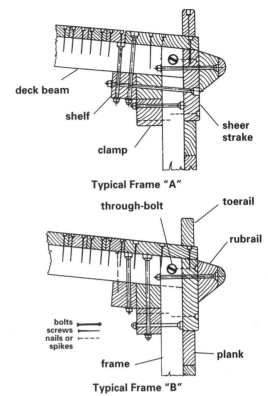

Sheer clamp and shelf, heavy boats

- Hard-chine boats do not use bilge stringers at the chine.
- Boats with Sns under 0.5 may omit the bilge stringer.

Our trusty old *Logger Bobber* would use the following:

Clamp and Bilge-Stringer Molding = 1.11 × 2.97$^{0.4}$ = 1.71; use 1¾ in.

Clamp and Bilge-Stringer Molding = 28.2 × 2.97$^{0.4}$ = 43.58; use 45 mm

Clamp and Bilge-Stringer Siding = 4 ⅞ in. (124 mm), tapering to 3 in. (75 mm)

If *Bobber* had no shelf, the clamp's molding would increase to 2¼ inches (57 mm).

edit, can you loose a line from this column?

Such heavy clamps are more difficult to bend in, especially in the bow where there is often combined edge-set and twist. In such cases, the heavy clamp should be laminated in place, from thinner stock.

The bilge stringer and clamp are screw-fastened to each frame, and should be fastened to each other and to the stem at the bow with a breasthook and to the transom with quarter knees, port and starboard. On vessels with Sns greater than 4, the clamp and bilge stringers are better through-bolted to the frames.

FORMULA 9-16
Strip-Plank Bilge Stringer

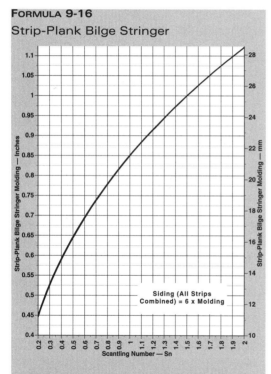

Strip-Plank Bilge Stringer: Small Boats

The bilge-stringer dimensions given by the previous formula are for standard traditional bilge stringers. Although these work well, they can produce a hard spot in the frames. I prefer to use a strip-plank bilge stringer. This is molded thinner and sided considerably wider than the standard bilge stringer. As a result, it makes less of a hard spot in each frame. It is like a narrow width of very heavy ceiling.

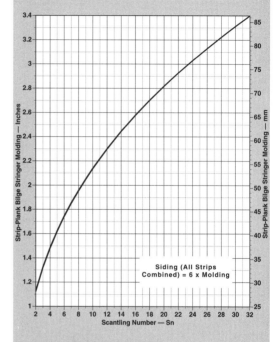

Strip-Plank Bilge Stringer: Large Boats

Strip-Plank Bilge Stringer:

Molding, in. $= 0.85 \times Sn^{0.4}$ (English)

Molding, mm $= 21.6 \times Sn^{0.4}$ (Metric)

Total Siding, All Bilge-Stringer Strip Planks Combined $= 6 \times$ molding

- Increase siding and molding by 1 percent for every knot over 25 knots.
- The bilge stringer can taper in siding, at the bow and stern, to 60 percent of its maximum total siding at midships. The middle third of the bilge stringer should have maximum siding, with no taper.

This would give *Bobber* a strip-plank bilge stringer of

$$Molding = 0.85 \times 2.97^{0.4} = 1.31 \text{ in.};$$
$$use \ 1\tfrac{3}{8} \ in.$$

$$Molding = 21.6 \times 2.97^{0.4} = 33.4 \ mm;$$
$$use \ 34 \ mm$$

Total Siding All Strip-Planks = approximately 8¼ in. (210 mm), tapering to 5 in. (125 mm)

The strip-plank bilge stringer is built up of strip planks edge-nailed together, inside the frames at the turn of the bilge. Every other strip is screw-fastened to a frame, alternating each frame. Strips are square to sided, approximately 1.2 times the molding.

FORMULA 9-17
Shelf

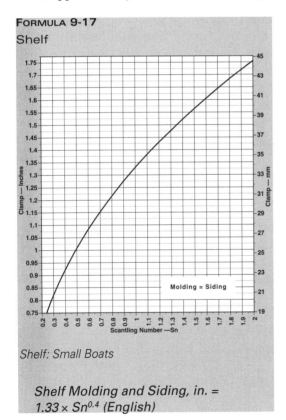

Shelf: Small Boats

Shelf Molding and Siding, in. = 1.33 × Sn⁰·⁴ (English)

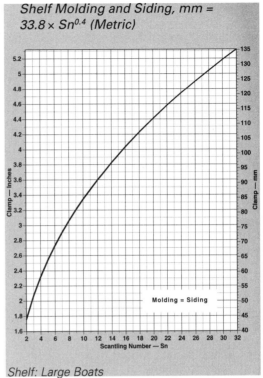

Shelf Molding and Siding, mm = 33.8 × Sn⁰·⁴ (Metric)

Shelf: Large Boats

Bobber would be fitted with

Shelf Molding and Siding, in. = 1.33 × 2.97⁰·⁴ = 2.05 in.; use 2 in.

Shelf Molding and Siding, mm = 33.8 × 2.97⁰·⁴ = 52.2 mm; use 50 mm

The shelf is through-bolted to the top inside of the clamp—flush with the clamp's top edge—to form a foundation for the deck beams. The through-bolts should run right through the frames. On vessels with Sns of 2.5 or less, it may be more practical to screw-fasten the shelf to the clamp only. Both the shelf and clamp together form the landing for the deck beams, and they must be beveled and smoothed off to match the varying angles the underside of the deck beams make, due to the deck crown.

FORMULA 9-18

Chine or Chine Log

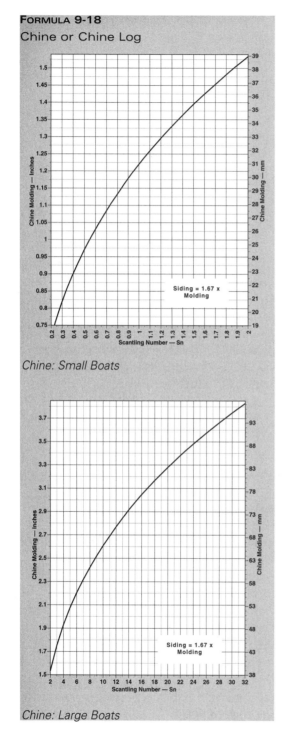

Chine: Small Boats

Chine: Large Boats

Chine Molding, in. = 1.22 × Sn^{0.33} (English)

$$Chine\ Molding,\ in. = 1.22 \times Sn^{0.33}$$
(English)

$$Chine\ Molding,\ mm = 31 \times Sn^{0.33}$$
(Metric)

$$Chine\ Siding = 1.67 \times molding$$

- Add 1 percent to siding and molding for every knot over 15 knots.

The chine forms a prominent projecting corner. Even on displacement hulls, it can take quite a beating. On planing boats, the chine needs to be exceptionally strong for impact and abrasion resistance. The chine or *chine log* can be formed from a single piece, beveled and rabbeted to mate with the plank, or it can be from two pieces—an interior chine or *chine batten*, and the external chine, called the *chine proper*. Like the keel batten, the chine batten is often a heavier timber than the outer chine. Because of abrasion considerations, if chine-batten construction is used, I recommend making the chine batten the full siding and molding specified for the chine, with the chine batten added on to fair out the plank intersection, as required.

On boats with herringbone-bottom planking, it is usual to run the bottom plank out along the underside of the chine log and the underside of the topsides plank. No rabbeting or outer chine is required. Similar construction is used on plywood hulls. Plywood chines should be glassed on the outside (glass cloth laid in epoxy). Often, planing plywood hulls have a shallow external chine and spray-knocker installed, which further protect the outside corner of the chine and help throw spray flat and wide.

Our 20-knot *Logger Bobber* would require

$$Chine\ Molding = 1.22 \times 2.97^{0.33} = 1.75\ in.$$

$$Chine\ Molding = 31 \times 2.97^{0.33} = 44.4\ mm$$

$$Chine\ Siding = 2.92\ in.\ (74.1\ mm)$$

Add 5 percent for 5 knots over 15 knots:

$$Chine\ Molding = 1.75\ in. \times 1.05 = 1.83;$$
$$use\ 1\frac{7}{8}\ in.$$

$$Chine\ Molding = 44.4\ mm \times 1.05 = 46.6;$$
$$use\ 47\ mm$$

$$Chine\ Siding = 3\frac{1}{8}\ in.\ (80\ mm)$$

Deck and Cabin

FORMULA 9-19
Deck

Laid-Deck-Plank Thickness = hull-topsides plank thickness

Canvas-Covered-Deck Plank Thickness = 0.9 × hull-topsides plank thickness

Plywood-Deck-Plank Thickness (FRP-Covered) = 0.75 × topsides-plank thickness

- *Plywood decks may be of a single layer scarfed together or joined with butt straps underneath. The best practice, however, is to make the deck of two layers of plywood with the butts well staggered.*

Returning to *Logger Bobber*, we find

Laid-Deck-Plank Thickness =
1⅛ in. (28 mm)

Canvas-Covered-Deck Plank Thickness =
1 in. (25 mm)

Plywood-Deck-Plank Thickness (FRP-Covered) = ⅞ in. (20 mm), better two layers
⁷⁄₁₆ in. (two layers 10 mm)

FORMULA 9-20
Deck Sheathing

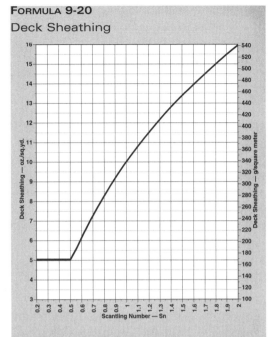

Deck Sheathing: Small Boats

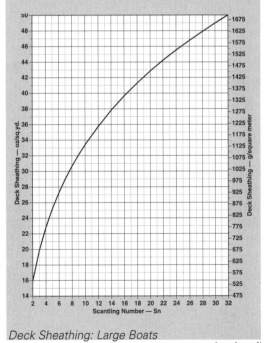

Deck Sheathing: Large Boats

(continued)

Plywood decks should be sheathed in fiberglass cloth laid in epoxy, as follows:

Deck-Sheathing Fabric Weight, oz./sq. yd. = (40 × Sn^{0.2}) – 30 (English)

Deck-Sheathing Fabric Weight, g/m² = (1,356 × Sn^{0.2}) – 1,017 (Metric)

- On small boats, glass cloth is used. Larger craft, with heavier deck sheathing, can use a bi-axial uni-di glass fabric style. This may be covered with finishing cloth if desired.
- On small boats, with Sns under 0.5, deck sheathing is optional but recommended. The minimum deck sheathing used should be 5 oz./sq. yd. (169 g/m²).
- Increase sheathing weight by 10 percent on workboats and offshore cruisers.
- 4 oz./sq. yd. (135 g/m²) of Dynel, Vectra, or Xynole polyester may be substituted for every 8 to 10 oz./sq. yd. (270 to 339 g/m²) of glass cloth.

Logger Bobber's ⁷/₈-inch (20 mm) plywood deck would be sheathed with

Deck-Sheathing Fabric Weight = (40 × 2.97^{0.2}) – 30 = 19.7; use 20 oz./sq. yd.

Deck-Sheathing Fabric Weight = (1,356 × 2.97^{0.2}) – 1,017 = 668; use 670 g/m²

FORMULA 9-21

Deck Beams and Carlins

Deck-Beam Molding, in. = 1.85 × Sn^{0.34} (English)

Deck-Beam Siding, in. = 0.92 × Sn^{0.4} (English)

Deck-Beam Molding, mm = 47 × Sn^{0.34} (Metric)

Deck-Beam Siding, mm = 23.3 × Sn^{0.4} (Metric)

Strong Deck-Beam Siding = 1.5 × standard deck-beam siding

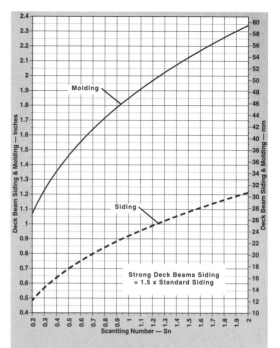

Deck Beams: Small Boats

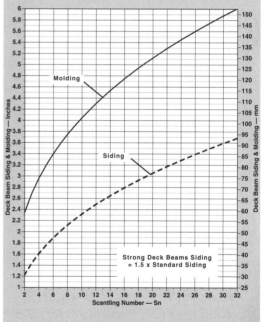

Deck Beams: Large Boats

- Strong deck beams are used at the fore-n-aft end of all major deck openings, such as at the fore-n-aft ends of the cabin and the cockpit, and at the frames immediately fore-n-aft of each mast.
- Deck carlins frame out the fore-n-aft sides of deck openings, such as along the cabin sides and the cockpit sides. Deck carlins are usually the same siding and molding as standard deck beams except at large removable hatch openings, such as cargo hatches and removable cockpits.

Our *Bobber* would be fitted with

Deck-Beam Molding = 1.85 × 2.97$^{0.34}$ = 2.67 in.; use 2⅝ in.

Deck-Beam Siding = 0.92 × 2.97$^{0.4}$ = 1.42 in.; use 1⁷⁄₁₆ in.

Deck-Beam Molding = 47 × 2.97$^{0.34}$ = 68.05 mm; use 68 mm

Deck-Beam Siding = 23.3 × 2.97$^{0.4}$ = 36.04 mm; use 36 mm

Strong Deck-Beam Siding = 2⅛ in. (54 mm)

Deck beams are fastened to the side of each frame. Where standard floors are used—through-bolted to the side of the frame—the deck beam is on the same side as the floor (above the floor). It is very important that each deck beam be through-bolted to the head of its frames, as well as down into the shelf and/or clamp. The bolt through the frame holds the frame heads from springing outward. On small boats, with Sns less than 1, the deck beams can be screw-fastened into the side of the frames.

FORMULA 9-22

Cabin Sides

Cabin-Side-Plank Thickness, in. = 1.1 × Sn$^{0.24}$ (English)

Cabin-Side-Plank Thickness, mm = 27.9 × Sn$^{0.24}$ (Metric)

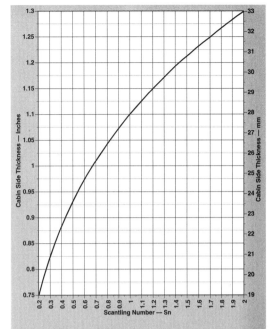

Cabin Sides: Small Boats

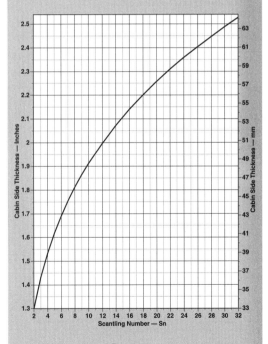

Cabin Sides: Large Boats

• Use 70 percent of plank thickness for plywood cabin sides.

Cabin sides were traditionally of planks edge-bolted together and notched into rabbeted cornerposts. Marine plywood is superior for this use, however. Single layers are acceptable, but double layers of plywood with the scarfs well staggered are better.

Bobber's cabin sides are as follows:

Cabin Sides (Plank) = 1.1 × 2.97$^{0.24}$ = 1.42 in.; use 1⅜ in.

Cabin Sides (Plank) = 27.9 × 2.97$^{0.24}$ = 36.2 mm; use 36 mm

Cabin Sides (Plywood) = 1 in. (25 mm); better: two layers ½-in. ply (two layers 12 mm ply)

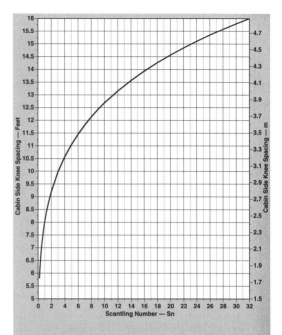

Cabin-Side Knee Spacing

FORMULA 9-23

Cabin-Side Reinforcement

Cabin sides form a weak point in hull construction. If a boat is knocked down in breaking seas (or if heavy seas break aboard), the cabin side can be stove open. This is dangerous and can lead to foundering. All offshore boats must have their cabin sides strongly reinforced, as follows:

Cabin-Side Braces (Hanging Knees) Spaced, ft. = 8 × Sn$^{0.2}$ (English)

Cabin-Side Braces (Hanging Knees) Spaced, m = 2.43 × Sn$^{0.2}$ (Metric)

Cabin-Side Braces (Hanging Knees) Siding, in. = 0.82 × Sn$^{0.36}$ (English)

Cabin-Side Braces (Hanging Knees) Siding, mm = 20.8 × Sn$^{0.36}$ (Metric)

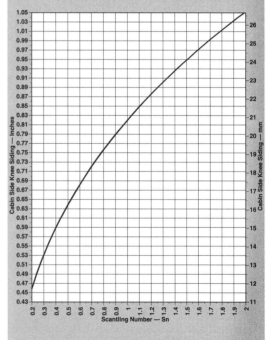

Cabin-Side Knee Siding: Small Boats

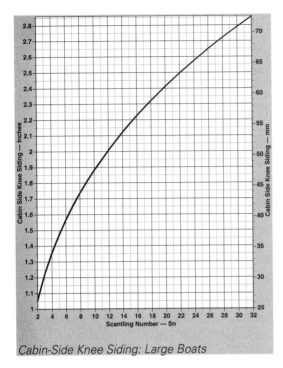

Cabin-Side Knee Siding: Large Boats

down through the cabin-deck carlin just fore-n-aft of each cabin corner.

For *Bobber*, we would install

Cabin-Side Braces (Hanging Knees)
Spacing = $8 \times 2.97^{0.2}$ = 9.9 ft.

Cabin-Side Braces (Hanging Knees)
Spacing = $2.43 \times 2.97^{0.2}$ = 3.0 m

Cabin-Side Braces (Hanging Knees)
Siding = $0.82 \times 2.97^{0.36}$ = 1.21; use $1\frac{1}{4}$ in.

Cabin-Side Braces (Hanging Knees)
Siding = $20.8 \times 2.97^{0.36}$ = 30.7; use 30 mm

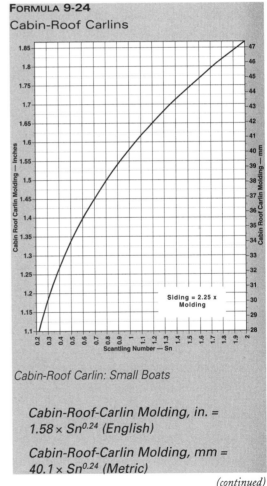

FORMULA 9-24
Cabin-Roof Carlins

Siding = 2.25 x Molding

Cabin-Roof Carlin: Small Boats

- Cabin hanging knees should extend at least 70 percent of the height of the cabin sides down from the underside of the roof beams. Extending all the way down to the cabin-deck carlin is better. The knees should extend approximately 14 times the cabin-roof thickness inboard from the roof carlin, or more.
- Bulkheads of the thickness recommended in Formula 5-5 may be used instead of hanging knees. Such bulkheads must be securely screwed and glued to the roof beams, as well as to cleats that fasten to the inside of the cabin sides.
- Tie rods should be installed just fore-n-aft of the cabin corners from the cabin carlin horizontally under the deck outboard to the shelf or clamp under the deck. Tie rods should also be installed vertically, bolted through the roof carlin, and run

Cabin-Roof-Carlin Molding, in. =
$1.58 \times Sn^{0.24}$ (English)

Cabin-Roof-Carlin Molding, mm =
$40.1 \times Sn^{0.24}$ (Metric)

(continued)

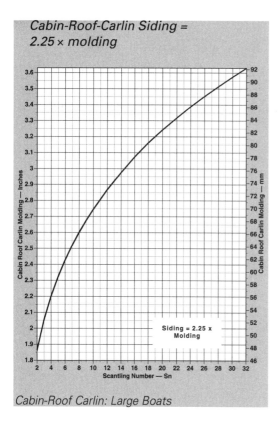

Cabin-Roof-Carlin Siding = 2.25 × molding

Siding = 2.25 x Molding

Cabin-Roof Carlin: Large Boats

The cabin-roof carlins form the support for the cabin-roof beams, and strengthen the upper corner of the cabin roof. Roof carlins are screwed and glued to the inside of the cabin side. On boats with Sns over 4, the roof carlins are better through-bolted to the cabin side.

Our example, *Logger Bobber*, would have carlins as follows:

$$Cabin\text{-}Roof\text{-}Carlin\ Molding = 1.58 \times 2.97^{0.24}$$
$$= 2.05\ in.;\ use\ 2\ in.$$

$$Cabin\text{-}Roof\text{-}Carlin\ Molding = 40.1 \times 2.97^{0.24}$$
$$= 52.07\ mm;\ use\ 50\ mm$$

$$Cabin\text{-}Roof\text{-}Carlin\ Siding = 4\tfrac{1}{2}\ in.\ (110\ mm)$$

The roof-carlin dimensions here are sided high and molded moderately thin. This can interfere with the top edge of cabin windows on some boats. When this occurs, you can reduce the carlin height (siding) by increasing the width (molding) proportionately. The cross-sectional area should be the same on the modified carlin as for the standard carlin given by the formula.

FORMULA 9-25

Cabin Roof and Roof Beams (Small Cabin Roofs) (Also Standard Cabin Soles)

It is important to keep weight high up to a minimum. Cabin roofs (also called coach roofs) should be built as light as possible. Additionally, the roof must be as thin as possible to maximize headroom in the accommodations. For cabin roofs with an athwartships span of 8 feet (2.4 m) or less, select the roof thickness and beam spacing from the following table.

TABLE 9-25A
Cabin-Roof Construction

Maximum Cabin-Roof Beam 8 ft. (2.4 m)

Roof Thickness		Beam Spacing O.C.	
Inches	mm	Inches	mm
¼	6	5.75	140
⅜	9	8.00	200
½	12	10.00	250
⅝	15	12.00	300

All with roof beams molded ¾ inch (20 mm), sided 2 inches (50).

Cabin roofs built to this table will support crew weight ruggedly, and will withstand severe weather.

- Cabin roofs are all to be of marine plywood. A single layer is adequate but double layers are superior.

- Cabin-roof beams may be steam-bent, but—if the cabin-roof crown is constant—it is usually best to make a jig and laminate them.
- The cabin roof should be covered with one layer of 10 to 12 oz./sq. yd. (339 to 407 g/m²) of glass cloth laid in epoxy.
- 4 oz./sq. yd. (135 g/m²) of Dynel, Vectra, or Xynole polyester may be substituted for every 8 to 10 oz./sq. yd. (270 to 339 g/m²) of glass cloth.
- Workboats and vessels with Sns over 4 should increase the roof-beam molding to 1 inch (25 mm). These craft should also use a total of 20 to 24 oz./sq. yd. (678 to 814 g/m²) of glass cloth laid in epoxy.

Cabin soles for most boats can be proportioned from the previous table, with the following notes:

- Height under the sole is not usually a problem, so the sole beams can be $1^3/8$ inches (35 mm) square, or alternately sided 1 inch (25 mm) and molded $1^3/4$ inches (45 mm).
- Because cabin soles are low in the boat, it is seldom worth going to great lengths to save small amounts of weight here.
- The standard cabin sole for small boats is $1/2$-inch (12 mm) ply covered with $1/4$-inch teak and holly-veneer ply.
- For almost all boats with Sns over 2, the standard sole is $3/4$-inch (18 mm) ply covered with $1/4$-inch (6 mm) teak and holly-veneer ply.
- For these 1-inch-thick (25 mm) soles, the sole beams should be approximately 2 inches (50 mm) square, or sided $1^1/2$ inches (38 mm) and molded $2^1/2$ inches (64 mm), from 16- to 18-inch centers (400 to 460 mm).

- If great added weight savings is required, substitute 1-inch (25 mm) balsa-cored panels for the $3/4$-inch (18 mm) ply.

FORMULA 9-26

Cabin Roof and Roof Beams (Large Cabin Roofs)

Cabin-Roof Thickness = ¾ in. (20 mm)

Cabin-Roof-Beam Spacing = 12 in. (300 mm) O.C.

Cabin-Roof-Beam Siding = 2 in. (50 mm)

Cabin-Roof-Beam Molding, in. = (Span, ft. ÷ 7.85) – 0.2 (English)

Cabin-Roof-Beam Molding, mm = (10.6 × Span, m) – 5 (Metric)

Where

Span = maximum beam of the cabin roof in feet or meters

Cabin-Roof Beams: Large Boats

- Cabin roofs are all to be of marine plywood. A single layer is adequate, but double layers are superior.
- The cabin roof should be covered with a total of 20 to 24 oz./sq. yd. (678 to 814 g/m²) of glass cloth laid in epoxy.
- 4 oz./sq. yd. (135 g/m²) of Dynel, Vectra, or Xynole polyester may be substituted for every 8 to 10 oz./sq. yd. (270 to 339 g/m²) of glass cloth.
- Workboats and vessels with Sns over 4 should increase the roof-beam molding by 10 percent. These craft should also use a total of 30 to 36 oz./sq. yd. (1,017 to 1,220 g/m²) of glass cloth laid in epoxy. Alternately, a bi-axial uni-di glass fabric style of this weight may be used, covered with finishing cloth or equivalent.

If *Logger Bobber* had a maximum cabin-roof beam of 9.8 feet (2.98 m), then its cabin-roof beams would be molded as follows:

Cabin-Roof-Beam Molding = (9.8 ft. ÷ 7.85)
− 0.2 = 1.04; use 1 in.

Cabin-Roof-Beam Molding = (10.6 × 2.98 m)
− 5 = 26.5; use 26 mm

Transom and Bulkheads

FORMULA 9-27
Transom

Transom-Plank Thickness (Planked Up)
= 1.2 × hull-topsides plank

Transom-Plank Thickness (Plywood) =
hull-topsides plank (Carvel plank)

Logger Bobber's transom is then

Planked Up = 1⅜ in. (33 mm)

Plywood = 1⅛ in. (28 mm)

(See photo on p. 339.)

FORMULA 9-28
Bulkheads

Bulkheads are not main structural members in traditional plank-on-frame hulls as they are in FRP and in some cold-molded and strip-plank construction methods. However, bulkheads can be used to increase strength and stiffness in the way of the masts and other highly loaded regions. This can be in addition to or sometimes instead of using hanging and lodging knees. Most bulkheads in plank-on-frame construction are simply interior partitions (joiner panels), dividing up the arrangement, engine spaces, forepeak and lazarette, and cargo holds. The exception is for bulkheads used to brace and stiffen the cabin sides; these are structural. For bulkhead thickness, use Formula 5-5.

FORMULA 9-29
Watertight/Collision Bulkheads

Watertight/collision bulkheads must be fastened to the face of a frame, with substantial filler blocks fastened as required to close any gaps at floors, futtocks, or gussets. At least one collision bulkhead in the bow is recommended for all vessels longer than 50 feet (15.2 m). As a general guide, this bulkhead should be neither less than 0.10 times nor more than 0.25 times the LOA aft of the bow. Where collision bulkheads are required by government agencies or classification societies, their requirements must be followed.

Watertight-Bulkhead Thickness =
standard topsides-plank thickness

Watertight-Bulkhead-Stiffener Siding =
standard frame siding for hull topsides

Watertight-Bulkhead Molding (fore-n-aft dimension) = 2 × standard frame siding for hull topsides

Watertight-Bulkhead-Stiffener Spacing = 2.5 × standard frame spacing

Watertight-Bulkhead-Stiffener Fastening = plank fastening

- Watertight bulkheads should be made of two layers of plywood glued and screwed (or Anchorfast-nailed) together.
- The stiffeners are screwed and glued to either face of the bulkhead, as convenient. The stiffeners may stop approximately 6 to 10 inches (150 to 250 mm) inboard from the plank. They need not be fastened to the frames, floor, or deck beams. Usually, stiffeners are installed running vertically.
- Where strong interior joinerwork, cleats and panels, or chain lockers are fastened to the watertight bulkhead, they can replace stiffeners in those locations.

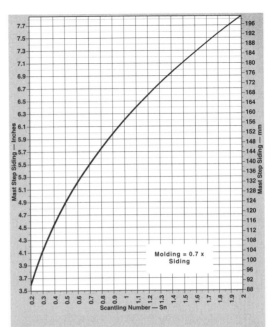

Mast Step: Small Boats

Mast Steps, Partners, and Engine Beds

FORMULA 9-30

Mast Step

Mast-Step Siding, in. = 6.2 × $Sn^{0.34}$ (English)

Mast-Step Siding, mm = 157.5 × $Sn^{0.34}$ (Metric)

Mast-Step Molding = 0.7 × siding

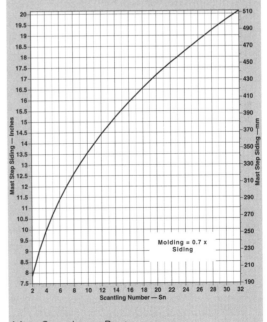

Mast Step: Large Boats

- The mainmast step must land on and be fastened to at least three floors—four or more floors are better.
- If a traditional wooden-mast heel is set into a mortise in the top of the step, the mast-step mortise must be provided with a drainhole.
- On schooners, both the mainmast and foremast steps should be approximately identical in size.
- On ketches and yawls, the siding and molding of the mizzenmast step may be reduced to 70 percent of the mainmast step. The mizzenmast step must land on and be fastened to at least two floors—three or more are better.
- Mast steps should be notched over each floor to keep them from sliding fore-n-aft. The notch cannot be deeper than 10 percent of the mast-step molding.
- The middle third of the step should be of constant molding. The fore-n-aft thirds should taper down to approximately 50 percent of the maximum molding.
- Mast steps must not make contact with the planking.

If *Logger Bobber* were a graceful yawl, it would be fitted with

Mainmast-Step Siding = $6.2 \times 2.97^{0.34}$ = 8.97 in.; use 9 in.

Mainmast-Step Siding = $157.5 \times 2.97^{0.34}$ = 228.04 mm; use 230 mm

Mainmast-Step Molding = 6¾ in. (160 mm)

Mizzenmast-Step Siding = 6¾ in.

Mizzenmast-Step Siding = 160 mm

Mizzenmast-Step Molding = 4½ in. (112 mm)

FORMULA 9-31

Mast Partners

Mast-Partners Molding = 0.8 × deck-beam molding

- The partners are solid-wood blocking, immediately under the deck, that fill the space between the strong deck beams just fore-n-aft of the mast.
- The partners are through-bolted fore-n-aft through each of these strong frames, fore-n-aft of the mast. Use two bolts port and two bolts starboard (four bolts total) on all boats with Sns of 2 or more. Vessels with Sns less than 2 may use just one bolt port and one bolt starboard (two total).
- The partners extend athwartships for 22 percent (or more) of the beam on deck at the mast step.
- On boats with Sns over 4, a tie rod should be installed athwartships under the deck, running from the mast partners outboard to the sheer clamp.

Logger Bobber's mast partners would be 2⅛ inches (54 mm) thick.

Mast partner installed. Note tie-rod/through-bolt port and starboard. (Courtesy Kortchmar & Willner)

Inboard engine beds end abruptly. This is poor practice. On this boat, the heavy diesels cracked all the frames near the engine bed's end in its first few years of life. Engine beds should extend as far fore-n-aft as possible and taper in molding toward their ends.

FORMULA 9-32

Engine Beds

Engine-Bed Siding, in. $= 3.1 \times Sn^{0.3}$
(English)

Engine-Bed Siding, mm $= 78.7 \times Sn^{0.3}$
(Metric)

Engine-Bed Molding $= 1.5 \times$ *siding, or more*

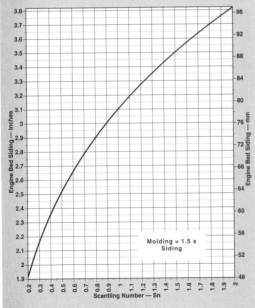

Engine Beds: Small Boats

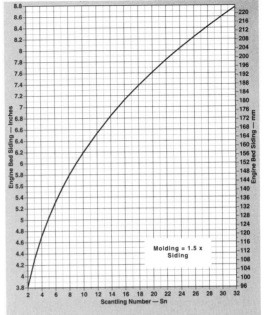

Engine Beds: Large Boats

- Increase both siding and molding by 1 percent for every knot over 15 knots.
- Engine beds may have deeper moldings than indicated, as required, to mount the engine, but not the lower molding.
- On displacement hulls, engine beds must extend at least two floors forward and two floors aft of the fore-n-aft engine-mount bolts—extending the bed six or more floors fore-n-aft is better.
- On displacement hulls—starting the distance of one engine-bed siding fore-n-aft of the fore-n-aft engine-mount bolts—the engine-bed molding should taper until the molding equals the siding at each end, fore-n-aft.
- On planing hulls, engine beds must extend at least six floors forward and six floors aft of the fore-n-aft engine-mount bolts. If the engine beds reach the transom before

six floors' distance, the engine bed will simply stop at the transom.

- On planing hulls, it is strongly recommended that the engine beds be extended for 50 to 60 percent of the hull bottom or more. If this is done, the engine-bed molding should continue to taper to 60 percent of siding at each end, fore-n-aft.
- Engine beds should be notched over and fastened to each floor to keep them from sliding fore-n-aft. The notches cannot be deeper than 10 percent of the engine-bed molding.
- Engine beds must not make contact with the planking.
- Engine beds are to have two cross braces—one just forward and one just aft of the fore-n-aft engine-mount bolts. The cross braces are to have the same siding and molding as the engine bed. Each cross brace is to be notched into the inside of the face of the engine bed, in a notch 10 percent of the bed's siding deep. Each cross brace is to be through-bolted from the outside face of each engine bed with two tie rods.

Assuming *Logger Bobber* were a 20-knot boat, the engine beds would be as follows:

Engine-Bed Siding = 3.1 × 2.97$^{0.3}$ = 4.29 in.

Engine-Bed Siding = 78.7 × 2.97$^{0.3}$ = 109.1 mm

Engine-Bed Molding = 6.43 in. (163.6 mm)

Increase scantling for speed:

20 knots – 15 knots = 5 knots, and 5 knots × 1 percent increase per knot over 15 knots = 5 percent increase

Engine-Bed Siding = 4.29 in. × 1.05 = 4½ in.

Engine-Bed Siding = 109.1 mm × 1.05 = 114 mm

Engine-Bed Molding = 6¾ in. (170 mm)

On the boat's 37.20-foot (11.34 m) waterline length, our 20-knot *Bobber* is planing. This means that the engine beds should extend at least six frames forward and six frames aft of the fore-n-aft engine-mount bolts. Better still would be to run the engine beds for as much of the length of *Logger Bobber*'s bottom as possible. In this case, the bed molding should taper down to 2³/₄ inches (68 mm) at the ends (60 percent of siding).

FORMULA 9-33
Engine Mounts

Engine mounts are the same as described in Formula 5-15.

FORMULA 9-34
Herringbone-Bottom Planking (Cross-Plank Bottom)

An alternative method for planking hard-chine hulls is to lay on the bottom plank athwartships rather than fore-n-aft. On flat-bottom boats, the plank is literally run exactly athwartships from chine to chine, usually continuous under the keel. On V-bottom hulls, the cross-planking is usually (although not always) installed at an angle raking aft and outboard from the centerline, at roughly 45 to 55 degrees. This looks vaguely like the bones in a fish, hence the name herringbone bottom.

Herringbone planking is usually simply nailed down over the keel and the chine. It is often installed with no caulking, with the planks just touching each other so that they take up and become watertight when wet. Indeed, some builders recommend leaving a space about equal to the thickness of a piece of ordinary writing paper between the planks of larger cross-plank boats, so that the swelling of the planks doesn't strain the bottom or the plank fasteners.

Herringbone-bottom (or straight cross-plank-bottom) structure should be sized as follows:

- Plank thickness should be 1.4 to 1.5 times the standard plank thickness (use 1.5 for workboats).
- Bottom frames are not usually used on vessels with Sns less than 3, and are often omitted on even larger craft. Vessels with Sns greater than 5 must use standard bottom framing and floors in addition to longitudinal bottom girders.
- The chine-log molding should be increased 10 percent. On workboats, increase molding 12 percent and siding 10 percent.
- Where the unsupported athwartships width or span from the outside face of the keel to the inboard edge of the chine log exceeds 4 feet (1.2 m), additional longitudinal hull-bottom girders must be installed inside the bottom plank—running straight fore-n-aft—to reduce the athwartships span between girders to 4 feet (1.2 m) or less. If bottom frames are used, their undersides are notched for the girder, which runs continuous just above the bottom plank. The girders must run the full length of the hull bottom and be fastened to the chine and transom.
- The bottom girder should be the same as the engine beds (see Formula 9-32), which they should double as. Accordingly, even small boats usually have bottom girders, which are fastened directly to the bottom plank.

Big-Boat Structural Members

Large offshore vessels and workboats often require additional structure in addition to that previously mentioned. The keel and keel batten are reinforced with a *keelson*, the deck is strengthened with longitudinal *deck girders*, and the hull itself may be further stiffened with added bilge stringers.

FORMULA 9-35
Keelson

Heavy workboats and offshore vessels with Sns larger than 15 should further reinforce their keel with an internal keelson. Yachts and high-speed vessels with diagonal hull-strapping need not fit a keelson unless their Sns are greater than 20.

The keelson is roughly a second internal keel bolted down through the top of the floors and into the keel below. In smaller sizes (for these large craft), the keelson may be from a single centerline timber. Larger craft, however, traditionally build up the keelson from several pieces: the *keelson proper* immediately above the keel on the centerline; *sister keelsons* bolted to either side of the keelson and down

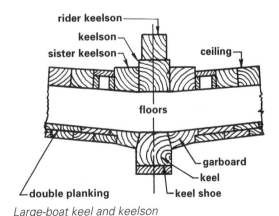

Large-boat keel and keelson

to the floors, and—on very large craft—a *rider keelson* bolted down on top of the centerline keelson. Building up the keelson structure from multiple pieces in this way keeps the timber dimensions smaller, which reduces problems with swelling and shrinkage.

Most boats under 90 feet (25 m) will not require a rider keelson. Also, in my opinion, it is better practice to laminate up a single centerline keelson from small stock than to hew and bolt together a keelson and sister keelsons. Whichever approach is used, the cross-sectional area of the keelson should equal approximately 80 percent of the cross-sectional area of the keel or of the keel and keel-batten combined.

Formula 9-36
Deck Girders

Large workboats that can experience substantial deck loads should install longitudinal deck girders running under and through-bolted to the deck beams. Vessels with Sns between 15 and 20 should install two girders about one-third and two-thirds of the way inboard from the maximum beam, and running straight fore-n-aft. Vessels with Sns over 20 should install four equi-spaced girders. Yachts with Sns under 20 do not require deck girders, nor do high-speed vessels (i.e., Sns less than 20) that have been diagonally strapped.

Deck girders should be molded the same as the heavy deck beams, and sided 1.1 times the siding of the heavy deck beams. The deck girders should be tied into the sheer clamp and shelf forward with knees or joining plates, and into the transom aft with knees. Where large cargo or fish-hold hatches are installed, it is best to adjust the girder spacing or the hatch dimensions so that the deck girders—running uninterrupted fore-n-aft—form the side structure of the hatch opening.

Formula 9-37
Multiple Bilge Stringers

Workboats and heavy offshore cruisers with Sns greater than 15 should further reinforce their hulls by adding additional bilge stringers (see Formula 9-15). Again, yachts and high-speed vessels that are diagonally strapped do not require these added stringers unless their Sns are greater than 20. A vessel like a tug or pilot boat that is expected to lie against other boats frequently would add a second bilge stringer midway up the topsides, between the standard bilge stringer and the sheer clamp. A vessel expected to take ground regularly should add a bilge stringer midway between the standard bilge stringer and the keel. Vessels with Sns greater than 20 should install both.

TEN

Fasteners, Straps, Knees, and Details

*T*raditional plank-on-frame wooden boats are only as strong as the fasteners that hold them together. Using the proper size and type of fastener and the correct joint is critical to a successful hull. In this chapter, we examine the standard fasteners and joints used throughout most wooden hulls.

Glue Joints

Glue was not traditionally used as a primary fastener on plank-on-frame boats; therefore, this section does not discuss glue joints in detail. However, Resorcinol waterproof glue was the standard for gluing plank scarfs and laminating timbers, such as laminated floors and stems. Although Resorcinol works well, modern two-part epoxy-adhesive systems are superior. Epoxy has exceptional gap-filling abilities and tremendous strength and elasticity. I recommend that epoxy be used for all structural gluing and laminating.

One important warning about epoxies, as well as other glues: They will not stick to anything with oil or grease (or any other petroleum-based product) contaminating the surface. Kerosene, regular motor oil, tallow, vegetable oil—all will destroy a glue's ability to form a reliable bond. Keep your joints oil-free. Similarly, some woods contain acids and/or oils that do not work well with some glues, particularly epoxy; oak and teak are two examples. Before making any glue joints or doing any laminating, read the glue manufacturer's literature carefully.

Scarf Joints

LONGITUDINAL JOINTS IN LARGE TIMBERS

The keel, stem, and other backbone timbers often must be made up of two or more lengths of timber joined together longitudinally. It's rare to find good clear stock sufficient to get out, for example, a 42-foot-long (12.8 m) keel in a single piece. The joints used to build up such longer timbers are called *scarf joints* (also spelled *scarph*). Scarf

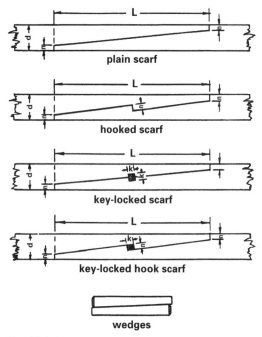

Scarf joints

joints allow you to connect two short timbers together end-to-end to form a long one, while transmitting most of the full strength of the timbers across the joint.

A sloped faying surface is made on each of the two timbers (in mirror image) so they can be mounted together and through-bolted over a substantial length. The standard rule is that the slope runs six times the depth of the timber. In large timbers, the sloped surfaces aren't allowed to run out to a feather edge; instead, they are cut off vertically or *nibbed* at the ends. The nibs are 25 percent of the depth of the timber high. Nibbed ends avoid feather edges where cracks can start, and they help keep the joint from sliding if the fastening-bolt holes elongate.

TYPES OF SCARF JOINTS

Because the two nibs together total half the depth of the timber, the actual faying surface is at a 12:1 slope. This simple joint is used for most construction; it is called the *plain scarf*. If additional resistance to sliding is required, a *hooked-scarf* joint or a *key-locked scarf* joint (sometimes called a *key scarf*) can be used, as shown. The key-locked hooked-scarf joint provides maximum resistance to sliding, with maximum longitudinal joint strength as well. Generally, the plain scarf will be adequate for smaller longitudinal members (e.g., clamps and stringers), while the key-locked scarf should be used in the principal keel timbers. The hooked scarf is as strong as the key-locked scarf, but harder to fashion. The key-locked hook scarf is only called for in large vessels that will experience extreme service loadings, such as minesweepers or harbor tugs.

SCARF KEYS AND HOOKS

The key is square and each side is 25 percent of the depth of the timber. If a hook is used, its height is 25 percent of the timber depth. In timbers under 6 inches (150 mm) deep, the key is usually fashioned from a single solid block. In deeper timbers, the key is made of two wedges, each with a 12:1 slope. The wedges are driven in from opposite sides after the joint has been bolted together. Any excess is cut off. A hard dense wood such as locust or oak should be used for keys. The fastening bolts should be snugged up again after driving in the key.

TIMBERS TO BE SCARFED

On vessels with Sns over 3, nibbed scarf joints should be used on other longitudinal members in addition to the keel, including the shelf, clamp, bilge stringer, and deck carlins.

SCARF-FASTENING BOLTS

The plain scarf should be fastened with bolts equally spaced along the length of the scarf in timbers. For timbers with cross-sectional areas less than 20 square inches (130 cm^2), use four bolts; between 20 and 100 square inches (130 and 650 cm^2), use five bolts; for more than 100 square inches (650 cm^2), use six bolts. The end bolts should be 25 percent of the timber depth in from the nib. The bolt diameter should be as shown in the following formula.

FORMULA 10-1

Scarf-Bolt Diameter and
Keel/Deadwood-Bolt Diameter

Bolt Diameter (in.) = (sq. in.)$^{0.4}$ ÷ 12

Bolt Diameter (mm) = 0.88 × (cm^2)$^{0.4}$

Where

sq. in. = timber sectional area, in square inches

cm^2 = timber sectional area, in square centimeters

Scarf-Bolt Diameter

- Bolt diameter must not exceed 25 percent of the timber thickness measured at right angles to the bolt axis.
- Hooked- or keyed-scarf joints on timbers between 20 and 100 square inches (130 and 650 cm^2) use only four through-bolts.
- Hooked or keyed scarfs are seldom called for on timbers less than 20 sq. in. (130 cm^2).
- The bolt line should be staggered (not in line) on all but the narrowest timbers. Bolts must be at least four diameters in from the side of the timber.
- Heavy washers are required under the heads and nuts of all bolts.

Keel/backbone bolts for fastening the stem, horn timber, and deadwood should be sized using either this formula or Formula 10-6, whichever gives the larger diameter (as long as the bolt diameter is not larger than 30 percent of the keel siding). Generally, the joints between backbone components should be fashioned to be similar to keyed- or hooked-scarf joints for timbers of the dimensions being joined. Where practical, through-bolts are best; however, drift bolts work excellently for fastening keel timbers. Drift bolts are fashioned from a rod that is hammered to a slight conical point at the leading end and to a mushroom head at the driving end. A hole slightly smaller than the drift diameter is bored in the timbers to be joined and the drift bolt is hammered home with a large washer under the mushroom head. Drift bolts should be driven in at slightly opposing angles to each other; this locks the backbone timbers from sliding. Drift bolts used to be of hot-dip galvanized wrought iron. Today hot-dip galvanized mild steel is the common substitute. Bronze is good but doesn't rust to lock in place as tightly. Some builders use a

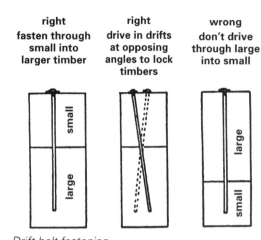

right
fasten through small into larger timber

right
drive in drifts at opposing angles to lock timbers

wrong
don't drive through large into small

Drift-bolt fastening

chisel to nick "barbs" into the sides of bronze drifts to increase holding power.

SCARF JOINTS IN PLANKS AND SMALLER TIMBERS

Smaller planks must also frequently be joined end to end to get sufficient length. Hull planks can be joined with butt blocks, but it's even better to scarf the planks into a single length. Ideally, plank scarfs are cut to a 12:1 slope just as in large timber scarfs. Because the planks are much thinner, however, no nibs are used. Glued scarfs are run out to a feather edge. These plank scarfs are glued together with no other mechanical fasteners. A well-made glued scarf joint, with a 12:1 slope, will have 90 percent of the strength of a continuous board without a joint.

Bilge stringers, clamps, shelves, and deck beams on small craft with Sns of 2 or less should also be made with the glued 12:1 plank scarf, without nibs.

Scarfs in planking should be separated fore-n-aft by at least three frame bays and vertically by a minimum of six strakes. Al-

Driving in a drift bolt to fasten deadwood and sternpost. The timbers are sealed with red lead.
(Courtesy Kortchmar & Willner)

though 8:1 scarfs can be used, they are weaker; however, they are standard for scarfing plywood plank and other plywood panels.

Hull Fasteners

FASTENER MATERIAL

Metal fasteners are best made from the following metals, in order of preference:

1. Monel
2. Silicon bronze, phosphor, or aluminum bronze

3. Aquamet 22 or Nitronic 50
   (chrome/moly stainless-steel alloys)
4. Stainless steel, Type 316L or 316
5. Stainless steel, Type 304 or 302
6. Galvanized mild steel (hot-dip galvanized only)
7. Brass screws—do not use

Monel is the best material for any marine fastening; it has high strength and very high corrosion resistance. Silicon bronze (occasionally phosphor or aluminum bronzes are available) is excellent for fastening. These bronzes have high corrosion resistance and high strength. They are not quite as strong as Monel; however, bronze is *the* standard marine-fastening alloy. Aquamet 22 and similar chrome/moly stainless-steel alloys are customarily used for propeller-shafting and rod-rigging. These alloys have exceptionally high tensile strength and corrosion resistance; they make ideal tie rods and bolts. Chrome/moly stainless is somewhat more prone to pitting corrosion than bronze or Monel, however.

All other stainless steels are subject to potentially severe pitting-corrosion attack when immersed in salt water, without free-oxygen (exactly the conditions of keel bolts and such). Thus, these stainless steels are less reliable than bronze, Monel, or chrome/moly stainless (in that order). Use stainless-steel fasteners under water only as a second choice. Stainless, however, makes fine internal bolts and tie rods. Type 316L ("L" for low carbon) is the most resistant to pitting corrosion and thus the first choice among stainless, followed by standard 316. The 302 and 304 stainless (even in low-carbon alloy) are still more liable to pitting attack than 316, and should not be used under water at all.

Galvanized mild-steel bolts have been employed for years. They are tolerable if you are willing to accept their shorter life expectancy and rust weeps. Only true *hot-dip* galvanized fasteners should be used.

Brass, with its high zinc content, has no place as a structural fastener on any boat. Brass is weaker than bronze or stainless steels, and it is also eminently prone to extreme brittle failure through corrosion called *dezincification*. Brass is, however, ideal for interior joinerwork.

FORMULA 10-2

Plank Fasteners

Plank-Fastener Diameter, in. = 0.09 + (plank thickness, in. ÷ 7.2) (English)

Plank-Fastener Diameter, mm = 2.29 + (plank thickness, mm ÷ 7.2) (Metric)

Screw Length = 2 × plank thickness

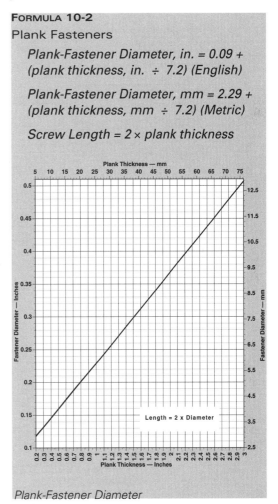

Plank-Fastener Diameter

TABLE 10-3 American Screw Gauge Screw Dimensions

No.	Shank Diameter, in. (mm)	Shank, Diameter, Nearest Fraction, in.	Head Diameter, in. (mm)
0	0.060 (1.52)	1/16	0.109 (2.78)
1	0.073 (1.85)	5/64−	0.141 (3.57)
2	0.086 (2.18)	5/64+	0.172 (4.37)
3	0.099 (2.51)	3/32	0.138 (3.51)
4	0.112 (2.84)	7/64	0.219 (5.56)
5	0.125 (3.18)	1/8	0.250 (6.35)
6	0.138 (3.51)	9/64	0.281 (7.14)
7	0.151 (3.84)	5/32−	0.297 (7.54)
8	0.164 (4.17)	5/32+	0.328 (8.33)
9	0.177 (4.50)	11/64	0.359 (9.13)
10	0.190 (4.83)	3/16	0.375 (9.53)
11	0.203 (5.16)	13/64	0.406 (10.32)
12	0.216 (5.49)	7/32	0.438 (11.11)
14	0.242 (6.15)	15/64	0.484 (12.30)
16	0.268 (6.81)	17/64	0.531 (13.49)
18	0.294 (7.47)	19/64	0.594 (15.08)
20	0.320 (8.13)	21/64	0.656 (16.67)
24	0.372 (9.45)	3/8	0.750 (19.05)

NOTE: Sizes in bold are usually special order items, not in regular stock.

In returning to our example boat, *Logger Bobber*, we found that it would require 1⅛-inch (28 mm) plank. Accordingly, *Bobber's* plank screws should be as follows:

0.09 + (1.125 in. ÷ 7.2) = 0.24-in. diameter; use No. 14 wood screws (0.242-in. diameter)

2.29 + (28 mm ÷ 7.2) = 6.17 mm diameter; use 6 mm wood screws

Screw Length = 2¼ in. (56 mm)

- Use three fasteners in each frame for wide planks and two fasteners per plank for narrow planks.
- On strip-planking, every other plank is fastened to the frame, alternating each frame bay.
- Annular-ring boat nails (i.e., silicon bronze or Monel) can be used instead of screws. The nails should be sized using Formula 10-12 and Tables 13A and 13B.
- In all planks over ⅝ inch (16 mm) thick, the screws should be counter-bored and bunged.
- Copper rivets, clench nails, and galvanized boat nails are not covered by this formula.

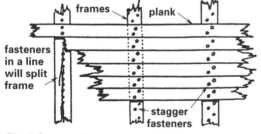

Plank-fastener layout

FORMULA 10-4
Butt Blocks

Where planks are too short to run the full length of the hull (which is common), the short planks are joined from a single long strake. This can be done with scarf joints or butt blocks.

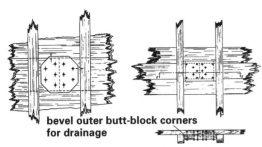

**bevel outer butt-block corners
for drainage**

**bolts shown are for large vessels; most boats use
wood screws**

Two butt-block arrangements

*Planks can never be butted at a frame.
A full butt block must be installed
between frames. Butt blocks should be
sized as follows:*

*Butt-Block Molding (Thickness) = plank
thickness*

*Butt-Block Height = 1.125 × plank height
at the butt block*

*Butt-Block Width (Fore-n-Aft) = 12 ×
plank height at the butt block*

*Butt-Block-Fastener Diameter = plank-
fastener diameter*

*Butt-Block-Fastener Length = 1.5 × plank
thickness (See photo on p. 339.)*

- Butt blocks must be screw-fastened, not nailed.
- Use five fasteners in each plank end, 10 total for each butt block.
- Planks less than 5 inches (127 mm) wide can use four fasteners; planks less than 3.5 inches (89 mm) wide can use just three fasteners.
- Counter-sink, counter-bore, and bung on all planks more than $5/8$ inch (16 mm) thick.

- Planks over 9 inches (228 mm) must use six fasteners.

FORMULA 10-5

Strip-Plank Edge Nails

Nail Diameter, in. = (plank thickness, in.)$^{0.34}$ ÷ 10.3 (English)

Nail Diameter, mm = 0.2 + 0.8 × (plank thickness, mm)$^{0.34}$ (Metric)

Nail Length = 1.75 × plank-siding minimum to 2.25 × plank-siding maximum

Nail Spacing = approximately 6 × plank thickness

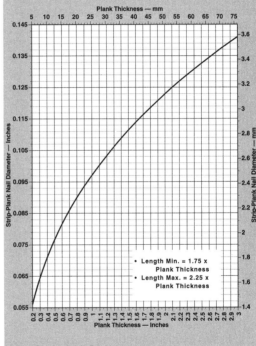

Strip-Plank-Nail Diameter

- Bronze or Monel annular-ring boat nails are preferred; stainless-steel nails are acceptable; and galvanized boat nails can be used, but may weep rust and begin to fail after 10 years or so.

- Nail spacing can be as much as 10 to 12 times plank thickness where there is little curvature, and should be as close as 4 times plank thickness where the hull is highly curved.
- Nails are staggered. For example, if the spacing is 6 inches, then the centers of the edge nails on the plank above will be offset 3 inches fore-n-aft from the plank below it.
- The planks must be edge-glued as well as nailed, although a high-strength adhesive sealant like 3M-5200 may be used instead of glue.

Say we strip-planked *Logger Bobber* with $1^1/_8$-inch-thick (28 mm) plank. The average plank siding would be about 1.2 times the thickness or $1^3/_8$ inches (34 mm). Accordingly, we would use the following:

$$Nail\ Diameter = (1.125\ in.)^{0.34} \div 10.3 = 0.10\text{-}in.\ diameter$$

$$Nail\ Diameter = 0.2 + 0.8 \times (28\ mm)^{0.34} = 2.67\ mm\ diameter$$

$$Nail\ Length = 1.75\ to\ 2.25 \times 1^3/_8\ in. = 2^3/_8\ to\ 3\ in.$$

$$Nail\ Length = 1.75\ to\ 2.25 \times 34\ mm = 60\ to\ 77\ mm$$

$$Nail\ Spacing = approximately\ 7\ in.\ (180\ mm)$$

FORMULA 10-6

Floor-to-Frame Fasteners

Fastener Diameter, in. = $0.24 \times Sn^{0.36}$ (English)

Fastener Diameter, mm = $6.1 \times Sn^{0.36}$ (Metric)

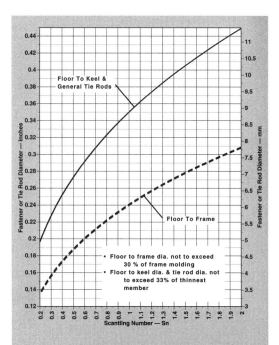

Floor Fasteners and General Tie Rods: Small Boats

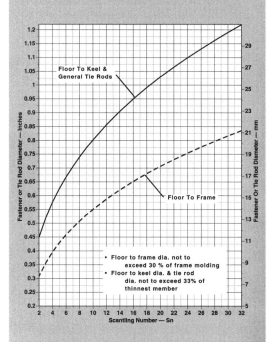

Floor Fasteners and General Tie Rods: Large Boats

- Vessels with Sns higher than 2 should use through-bolts.
- Vessels with Sns of 2 or less can use wood screws.
- Fastener diameter must not exceed 30 percent of frame molding.
- Washers must be used under the heads and nuts of all bolts.

Reliable old *Logger Bobber*'s floors should be fastened with the following:

$$Fastener\ Diameter = 0.24 \times 2.97^{0.36} = 0.36;\ use\ {}^{3}/_{8}\text{-}in.\ diameter$$

$$Fastener\ Diameter = 6.1 \times 2.97^{0.36} = 9.02;\ use\ 9\ mm\ diameter$$

$$0.375\text{-}in.\text{-}Diameter\ Bolt \div 2.125\text{-}in.\ frame\ siding = 17\ percent;\ okay$$

$$9\ mm\ diameter\ bolt \div 54\ mm\ frame\ siding = 17\ percent;\ okay$$

FORMULA 10-7

Floor-to-Keel Fasteners and General Tie Rods

The bolts fastening the floors down to the keel and the general tie rods used in places such as the mast partners and cabin sides are generally the same diameter.

Fastener Diameter, in. = 0.35 × Sn$^{0.36}$ (English)

Fastener Diameter, mm = 8.9 × Sn$^{0.36}$ (Metric)

- Bolt diameter may not be larger than 33 percent of the floor siding.
- Two bolts should be used in each floor (i.e., one port and one starboard). At the bow near the stem and at the narrow deadwood aft, a single bolt on the center-line may be used where this is unavoidable.
- For general tie-rod use, the bolt diameter may not be larger than 33 percent of the thickness of the thinnest member it penetrates.
- Where diameter exceeds 33 percent, reduce diameter until a 33 percent ratio is achieved.
- Heavy washers must be used under the heads and nuts of all bolts.

Logger Bobber's floors would be fastened with the following:

$$Fastener\ Diameter = 0.35 \times 2.97^{0.36} = 0.52;\ use\ {}^{1}/_{2}\ in.\ diameter$$

$$Fastener\ Diameter = 8.9 \times 2.97^{0.36} = 13.16;\ use\ 12\ mm\ diameter$$

$$0.5\text{-}in.\text{-}Diameter\ Bolt \div 2.125\text{-}in.\ floor\ siding = 23\ percent;\ okay$$

$$12\ mm\ Diameter\ Bolt \div 54\ mm\ floor\ siding = 22\ percent;\ okay$$

Most of the other structural tie rods at the mast, engine beds, cabins, and sides should be of this same diameter.

MAST-STEP TIE RODS

On sailboats with keel-stepped masts, the compression load on the mast is trying to drive the mast step through the bottom of the boat. This forces the keel down, which in turn pulls down the frames attached to the floors. In response, this pulls the frames together, which pinches the deck together athwartships. Finally, this causes the deck to bulge up at the centerline. To counteract these forces, a tie rod should be installed from the partners vertically down through the mast step. The tie rod can be installed just forward or just aft of the mast at the partners. It is surprising to me how many boats I see without a mast-step tie rod. I inspected one such vessel in which the plywood deck had lifted a full $^{1}/_{4}$ inch (7 mm) off the deck beams at the centerline near the mainmast. This boat was just 20 feet (6 m); even small vessels should be fitted with a mast-step tie rod.

Of course, when a mast is stepped on deck, the resulting forces are very different and a mast-step tie rod is not appropriate.

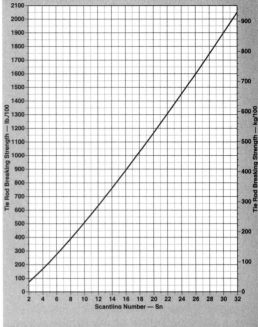

Mast-Step Tie-Rod Breaking Strength: Large Boats

FORMULA 10-8

Mast-Step Tie Rods

Tie-Rod Breaking Strength, lb. = 3,200 × $Sn^{1.2}$ (English)

Tie-Rod Breaking Strength, kg = 1,450 × $Sn^{1.2}$ (Metric)

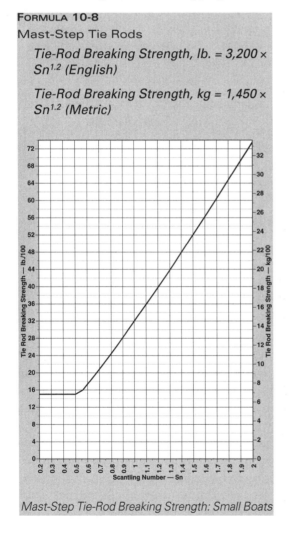

Mast-Step Tie-Rod Breaking Strength: Small Boats

- The minimum breaking strength for small boats with Sns less than 0.55 should be 1,500 lb. (680 kg), which equals the breaking strength of $^{1}/_{8}$-in.-diameter (3 mm) 1 × 19 stainless-steel rigging wire. Anything lighter will be to liable to damage from being stepped on and knocked about.
- Find the breaking strength and then refer to the bolt-tensile-strength table to find the diameter (see appendix 3).
- Mizzenmast tie rods can be 70 percent of the mainmast tie-rod diameter.
- Foremast tie rods on schooners should be the same diameter as the mainmast tie rod.
- The tie rod may best be made from 1 × 19 wire with a turnbuckle for tensioning. The 1 × 19 wire should have the same tensile strength as the tie rod.

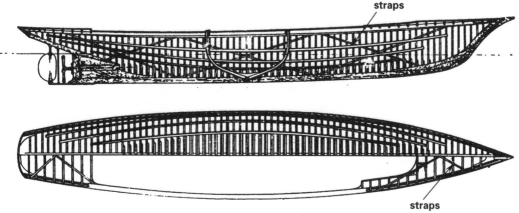

Diagonal strapping

- On larger boats, two tie rods can be used—one forward and one aft of the mast, at the partners. The combined breaking strength of the two tie rods should equal the strength of a standard single tie rod.

If *Logger Bobber* were a cutter, its mast-step tie rod would be

Tie-Rod Breaking Strength = 3,200 × 2.97$^{1.2}$
= 11,816 lb.

Tie-Rod Breaking Strength = 1,450 × 2.97$^{1.2}$
= 5,354 kg

Diameter in Silicon Bronze
(from the Bolt-Strength Table) = ⁹⁄₁₆ in.

Diameter in Silicon Bronze
(from the Bolt-Strength Table) = 16 mm

FORMULA 10-9
Keel-Ballast Bolts
  Use Formulas 5-12 and 5-13.

- Ballast bolts must pass through the center of the floors.
- The floors must be sided at least four times the ballast-bolt diameter.

DIAGONAL STRAPPING

One of the reasons the frigate *U.S.S. Constitution* was so strong, could carry such heavy cannon for her size, and has survived as long as she has is her diagonal bracing. The use of diagonal bracing was fairly new in the late eighteenth century, and it put *Old Ironsides'* designer, Joshua Humphreys, at the cutting edge of marine technology. It also meant that Yankee know-how—and the strength of live oak—gave so substantial an advantage that the *Constitution* never lost a battle. It's indicative of how little diagonal bracing is understood, however, that over a hundred years later—when the *Constitution* was rebuilt—these diagonals were left out. It wasn't until the 1997 restoration that the missing members were refitted and the *Constitution* was again fit to sail.

The fact is that traditional plank-on-frame construction is quite strong and efficient, with one exception: Plank-on-frame hulls are not torsionally stiff; they can wrack or twist. In the broadest sense, the stem twists clockwise, the transom twists counterclockwise. This lack of torsional stiffness can also lead to *hogging*, where the bow and stern droop. The fix: Diagonal braces or strapping—ruggedly screwed and through-bolted to the plank and frames—distributes torsional loads into the structure giving the necessary torsional strength. Humphreys used wood diagonals on *Old Ironsides*; the modern standard—as far as I know, pioneered by Captain Nat Herreshoff—is bronze strapping.

It is astonishing to me just how few plank-on-frame boats are built with diagonal strapping. It's not particularly difficult or costly, and it will add years to the life of any plank-on-frame boat. Diagonal straps should be proportioned as follows.

Width (Siding), in. = $1.65 \times Sn^{0.4}$ (English)

Width (Siding), mm = $41.9 \times Sn^{0.4}$ (Metric)

Thickness (Molding) = width ÷ 22

Fastener Diameter = width (siding) ÷ 14 (but not less than ⅛ in. [3.2 mm])

Fastener Spacing = width (siding) ÷ 2.5 (along both edges of strap)

Fastener in from Edge = 3.5 × fastener diameter

Fastener Length = 0.75 × plank thickness

- Small boats and inshore boats don't require diagonal strapping; however, all boats with an Sn greater than 2.5 will benefit markedly from diagonal straps. All larger offshore boats and workboats with Sns over 4 should have diagonal strapping.
- Strapping must be of silicon bronze or the equivalent, with a minimum tensile strength of 60,000 psi (413 mPa).
- Straps of somewhat differing proportions may be used, as long as their net cross-sectional area equals that of the strap recommended by the formula.
- Strapping is installed over the frames and under the plank. The frames are mortised just enough at the strap so the top of the strap lies flush under the plank.
- Screw-fasten the strap to the inside of each plank, using round-head screws. On very large boats, lag bolts may be used. Use two rows of fasteners along each edge of the strap. Where straps cross, fasten down through the inner strap, through the outer strap, and into the plank. Use one standard plank fastener to hold the strap to each frame. Fasten standard plank fas-

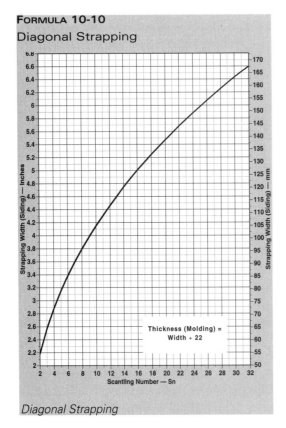

FORMULA 10-10
Diagonal Strapping

Diagonal Strapping

teners through the plank and the strap.

- Straps are installed at approximately a 45-degree angle to the fore-n-aft axis.
- There should be a pair of diagonal straps (running at approximately right angles to each other) at each mast, on the hull sides, and on the deck. Additional straps are used on larger hulls.
- The hull straps start together at the sheer and angle 45 degrees fore-n-aft.
- Deck straps form an **X** on the deck, with the center of the **X** either immediately in front or aft of the mast at the partners. The deck straps should be through-bolted to the partners.
- On boats with Sns higher than 6, three pairs of straps (six total) should be used on each side.
- All boats, power and sail, should use straps per side (and on deck) equal in number to the Sn rounded up to the nearest whole number, but not to exceed six straps per side and not less than two.
- Plywood decks have torsional rigidity and do not require diagonal strapping.
- Because of the edge-nailing and gluing of the planks on strip-plank hulls, the planks will not slide fore-n-aft relative to each other. This introduces torsional stiffness. Strip-plank hulls do not require diagonal strapping. For the same reason, lapstrake hulls do not require diagonal strapping.

In *Logger Bobber*'s case, its Sn is under 4, so straps are optional but recommended. With an Sn of 2.97, we would round up to three straps per side. If it were a cutter or a sloop, we would install a pair of straps on each side of the hull, starting at the sheer athwartships from the mast. The third strap would start aft near the cockpit and angle for-

ward. If, however, *Bobber* were a ketch, we would use four straps per side: two at the foremast and two at the mizzenmast. Alternately, if *Logger Bobber* were a powerboat, we would use three straps, with a pair starting at the sheer, a little forward of midships; the third strap would start at the sheer, aft near the cockpit, and angle forward. Dimensions would be as follows:

$$Width\ (Siding) = 1.65 \times 2.97^{0.4} = 2.55;$$
$$use\ 2\tfrac{1}{2}\ in.$$

$$Width\ (Siding) = 41.9 \times 2.97^{0.4} = 64.7;$$
$$use\ 65\ mm$$

$$Thickness\ (Molding) = \tfrac{1}{8}\ in.\ (3\ mm)$$

$$Fastener\ Diameter = 0.17\ in.;\ use\ No.\ 9\ or$$
$$No.\ 10\ screws\ (4.5\ mm\ screws)$$

$$Fastener\ Spacing = 1\ in.\ (25\ mm)$$

$$Fastener\ in\ from\ Edge = 0.59\ in.;\ use\ \tfrac{9}{16}\ in.$$
$$(1.25\ mm)$$

$$Fastener\ Length = \tfrac{7}{8}\ in.\ (20\ mm)$$

FORMULA 10-11

Breasthook and Quarter Knees

  Molding = deck-beam molding

  Breasthook Length = approximately 1.75 × frame spacing

  Quarter-Knee Length = approximately 1.3 × frame spacing

The quarter knees and breasthook are bolted down onto the shelf and clamp, and to the inside face of the stem and transom.

- Fastenings should be the same diameter as the floor-to-frame fasteners in Formula 10-6.
- Metal knees can be substituted; silicon bronze or Monel is the first choice, stainless-steel is the second choice, and hot-dip galvanized steel is a distant third.

correct   incorrect

Driving square-cut boat nails. Square-cut boat nails must be driven so the thin dimension is aligned with the grain. (Courtesy Tremont Nail Company)

- Metal-Knee-Siding Molding = wooden-knee molding ÷ 6
- Metal-Knee Bolt-Flange Length = frame molding

BOAT NAILS, CLENCH NAILS, AND RIVETS

Modern round wire nails should not be used for structural fastenings in a hull. Stainless-steel wire nails can be used, however, for edge-nailing strip-plank and for tacking and clamping together laminated hull components. Bronze or Monel annular-ring boat nails are superior, though, and much preferred.

If square-section, hot-dip-galvanized boat nails can be found, they are acceptable for plank-fastening. Bronze or Monel annular-ring boat nails are excellent. The old rule-of-thumb for sizing U.S. boat nails is as follows:

FORMULA 10-12
Boat Nail Size

- *For hardwood: The penny of the nail equals the number of eighths of an inch in the plank thickness.*
- *For extremely hard woods (e.g., well-seasoned white oak or hickory), the penny of the nail can be one less than the eighths of an inch in the plank thickness.*
- *For softwoods: The penny of the nail should equal the number of eighths of an inch in the plank thickness plus a quarter-inch.*
- *See Tables 10-13A and 10-13B for nail dimensions relative to the penny or length of the nail.*

Clench-nail length should equal the combined thickness of the plank plus the frame, plus a quarter-inch (6.5 mm) if bunged and a half-inch (13 mm) if not bunged. Because clench nails are *turned over* (i.e., hammered back around into a U shape on the inside of the hull), they must be from a soft malleable material. The old standard was soft wrought-iron, hot-dip galvanized. The current alternative is copper or some of the softer bronzes.

Built by the Covey Island Boatworks, the Gerr 42-foot (12.8 m) tunnel-drive motor cruiser Summer Kyle/Belle Marie *cruises the Chesapeake. The boat's construction is wood-epoxy strip-plank with heavy exterior hull sheathing exactly as detailed in the scantling rule. Drawing just 21 inches (53 cm), the boat has repeatedly weathered rough seas offshore and numerous groundings, all without the slightest difficulty.* (Courtesy Starke Jette)

Clench nails can be turned over on the inside without a washer, but a washer is preferable on larger vessels. The washer on a clench nail or rivet is usually termed a *rove* or a *burr*. In lapstrake construction, clench nails and rivets are not counter-bored or bunged, but rather are left flush with the surface even on bright-finished hulls.

Nail diameter is roughly proportional to length, and length—in the English system—is termed penny, which is abbreviated as "d." Tables 10-13A and 10-13B give standard lengths and diameters for U.S. boat nails.

- As a rule, heavy boat nails should be used in hardwood and light boat nails in soft-wood.
- All nail holes must be pre-bored before driving.

Copper rivets are about the same diameter as boat nails and slightly shorter than clench nails. Copper rivets are always hammered down on the inside over a rove or burr. The rove is a tight fit over the shank of the rivet, and is driven down on top of the plank inside with a roving iron. Excess rivet length is cut off and the remaining interior rivet is hammered down tight on top of the rove, forming the inside head.

Knees and Details

HANGING AND LODGING KNEES

Hanging knees are knees installed vertically, such as between the underside of the deck beams and the side of the frames on the hull topsides. *Lodging knees* are knees that are installed horizontally, usually under the deck. For example, a knee between the strong deck beam ahead of the mast and the sheer clamp would be a lodging knee.

TABLE 10-13A
Heavy Boat Nails

Penny	Length, in. (mm)	Diameter, in. (mm)
4d	1.50 (38)	¼ (6.3)
6d	2.00 (51)	¼ (6.3)
8d	2.50 (63)	¼ (6.3)
10d	3.00 (76)	⅜ (9.5)
12d	3.25 (83)	⅜ (9.5)
16d	3.50 (89)	⅜ (9.5)
20d	4.00 (101)	⅜ (9.5)

TABLE 10-13B
Light Boat Nails

Penny	Length, in. (mm)	Diameter, in. (mm)
4d	1.50 (38)	3/16 (4.7)
6d	2.00 (51)	3/16 (4.7)
8d	2.50 (63)	3/16 (4.7)
10d	3.00 (76)	¼ (6.3)
12d	3.25 (83)	¼ (6.3)
16d	3.50 (89)	¼ (6.3)
20d	4.00 (101)	¼ (6.3)

Hanging knees are sided fore-n-aft; their thickness, however, is up and down, which is their molding.

FORMULA 10-14
Hanging and Lodging Knees

Knee Thickness = frame siding

Hanging-Knee Length Along the Arms = approximately 1.5 × frame spacing

Lodging-Knee Length Along the Arms = slightly less than frame spacing

Hanging and lodging knees present a conundrum: They are common in many traditional plank-on-frame hulls, and they do strengthen the structure; however, they also form crevices and pockets where decay can begin. Generally, vessels built to this scantling rule with Sns of 9 or less do not require hanging or lodging knees. This is particularly so if the hull has been diagonally strapped and tie rods are installed at the mast and partners. Craft with Sns greater than 9 will benefit from installing knees (see photo on p. 340).

Some of these drawbacks can be reduced or eliminated by using cast or welded metal knees. These do not shrink, swell, or decay.

FORMULA 10-15
Metal Knees

- *Metal knees should be silicon bronze or Monel (first choice), stainless-steel (second choice), or hot-dip galvanized steel (a distant third).*

- *Metal-Knee Thickness = wooden-knee thickness ÷ 6*

- *Metal-Knee Bolt-Flange Length = frame molding*

Knees are installed as follows:

- Hanging knees at each strong deck beam.
- Lodging knees facing in opposing directions at every other strong deck beam.

Logger Bobber, with an Sn of 2.97, is not large enough for the added strength of lodging knees to be worth the cost in potential future decay. Again, this is particularly so if *Logger*'s hull is diagonally strapped.

FORMULA 10-16
Backing Blocks

Backing blocks should be installed under all highly loaded deck hardware. The highest loads are experienced by windlasses and sampson posts. The backing blocks for these items should be nearly identical to the mast partners, including the through-bolting to the deck beams. The width of these backing blocks need be no more than 12 percent wider than the width of the windlass base. In the case of sampson posts, the backing block should be at least as wide as the transverse width of the sampson post, on each side of the post. Windlasses must have aluminum, stainless-steel, or bronze backing plates under the backing block. These plates should be at least 5 percent larger in every dimension than the footprint of the windlass. Backing plates should be at least 0.375 times the thickness of the through-bolts and never less than ³⁄₁₆ inch (5 mm).

Mooring and docking cleats are best fastened to similar backing blocks; however, they may be fastened through plywood backing blocks instead. These should be at least 75 percent of the thickness of the plywood deck. They should be at least 12 percent larger in footprint than the footprint of the cleat on deck. All fasteners must be through-bolted with large washers.

Special attention must be paid to backing blocks and associated reinforcement for all other highly loaded deck hardware, including davits, fighting chairs, fishing gear, winches, rigging cleats, genoa, and traveler track.

ELEVEN

Modern Wood-Epoxy Construction

*D*uring the last 30 years or so, wooden-boat construction has undergone something of a revolution. As rugged and efficient as traditional plank-on-frame construction is, it still has several significant drawbacks: (1) the structure is no stronger than the individual fasteners holding it together; (2) most importantly, the wood structure is subject to decay; (3) wood is relatively soft, particularly when compared to metal—hulls can be damaged by impact and abrasion; (4) the swelling-shrinkage cycles in the wood lead to loose fasteners and deterioration of the timber; and (5) the very high-quality lumber necessary for first-rate plank-on-frame construction is becoming increasingly difficult to locate and increasingly expensive to buy.

Modern epoxy glues and coatings are so tenacious, elastic, and water-vapor-impermeable that they have solved (or helped to solve) all these drawbacks. A boat that has been entirely glued together with epoxy is not limited in strength by its metal fasteners. The glue joints are far stronger than individual metal fasteners, and the structure forms a large one-piece assembly—*monocoque* construction.

Sealing and coating every piece of wood all around with epoxy roughly freezes the timber at the moisture content it had at the time of the coating. Neither water vapor nor oxygen pass freely through the sealing barrier. (There is some slight permeability, but it's too slow for decay.) This not only eliminates almost all possibility for rot, but it also stabilizes the structure against swelling/shrinkage cycles—they simply don't occur.

Finally, sheathing the hull with fiberglass laid in epoxy—or other appropriate fibers—vastly increases abrasion and impact resistance. Early attempts at hull sheathing used polyester resin, but these attempts were usually unsuccessful. Polyester simply does not have the elasticity and peel strength required. Epoxy has both and does a splendid job. Furthermore, the sheathing itself is not subject to the extensive shrinkage and swelling on a hull with its wood structure stabilized by epoxy saturation.

Lumber Specification

Epoxy's sealing of the wood and the greater strength achieved by monocoque construction permit a far wider selection of woods to be used in epoxy-saturated hulls. Furthermore, the quality of the lumber need not be as high, nor does the wood have to be a species that is naturally highly rot-resistant. Generally, you can use virtually any conveniently available wood that meets the following requirements.

FORMULA 11-1

Wood-Epoxy Lumber-Density Specifications

- *Planking Wood—Small Boats (Hulls with Sns Less than 2.5): between 24 and 32 lb./cu. ft. (384 to 512 kg/m³)*

- *Planking Wood—Large Boats (Hulls with Sns of 2.5 or Higher): between 32 and 44 lb./cu. ft. (512 to 704 kg/m³)*

- *Frames, Keel, and All Framing Timber (All Size Boats): between 32 and 44 lb./cu. ft. (512 to 705 kg/m³)*

- *Lumber should be relatively clear and straight-grained; rift-sawn is greatly preferred. (If plain-sawn lumber is used extensively, scantlings should be increased by 8 to 10 percent.)*

- *Wood must not contain natural oils or acids that interfere with good epoxy-glue bonds; teak and oak are two such woods. Although you can glue teak and oak successfully with epoxy, longevity is suspect and more extensive joint preparation and practical gluing experience is required—not recommended for structural applications.*

Construction Methods

Almost all types of wooden-boat construction can be built with wood-epoxy-saturated techniques. Even plank-on-frame hulls can be fully saturated (if and only if they're built this way from scratch). A wood-epoxy carvel-plank hull would have individual timbers saturated with epoxy—the frames, floors, keel structure, deck beams, clamp, and stringers would all be glued together as well as metal-fastened. A plywood deck and cabin structure would be fully epoxied together and coated. The planks, however, would be individually installed with normal screws and caulking (not glued). If traditional cotton and oakum caulking is used, the planks must not be epoxy-saturated. This is so the planks will take up properly to make the seams watertight. Alternately, the planks could be individually coated all around with epoxy and installed with screw fasteners, but not glued. In this case, the seams should be sealed with epoxied-in-place *splines* (i.e., slender triangular-section wedges glued into the seam openings).

Epoxy-saturated carvel-plank hulls can be built, but they would be rather labor-intensive. The three standard wood-epoxy hull constructions are strip-plank, sheet-plywood, and cold-molded (i.e., multiple diagonal veneers). We examine each of these in turn.

WOOD-EPOXY STRIP-PLANK CONSTRUCTION

Wood-epoxy strip-plank construction runs the continuum from boats that are completely traditional plank-on-frame strip-plank-built vessels to hulls that are extensively glassed inside and out and devoid of most traditional framing. The latter are really strip-plank, cored-composite hulls and are much more akin to cored FRP than to traditional wooden boats. One of the lightest forms of fiberglass-skin, wood-epoxy, strip-plank construction is Baltek's proprietary DuraKore construction. A complete detailed scantling rule for Dura-Kore—devised by the author—is available in the *Baltek DuraKore Scantling Handbook*.

Conventional Wood-Epoxy Strip-Plank Construction

Conventional wood-epoxy strip-plank construction is identical to traditional plank-on-frame construction. Follow the formulas and recommendations in chapters 9 and 10. The difference is that every component of the entire wooden structure is glued together with marine-epoxy grout. Additionally, every component is coated and sealed with three coats (minimum) of unthickened marine epoxy.

Substantial labor savings can be achieved as follows:

- You don't have to bevel the planks or even make convex/concave edges on the planks to get a tight joint. Cut all the planks square and strip them on the hull, allowing the gaps created in the seams (plank edges) to form as they will. These gaps are simply filled with the thickened epoxy grout/glue as each plank is installed.
- It is not necessary to scarf the planks into long lengths. Simply butt each short length of plank to the next. Edge-nail down into the strip below at each butt. Be sure to stagger each butt by at least six planks vertically, and by at least three frames fore-n-aft. (This butt-only strip-joint may raise eyebrows in some circles. It works because—taken as a whole—the

well-staggered individual butts essentially form a "finger join" in the hull shell, which is quite strong.)

- It is not necessary to *spile* (i.e., taper) the strip-planks to get a consistent plank run that harmonizes with the sheer. It is permissible to let the planks simply run out at any angle or curve they naturally take as they are installed from sheer to garboard or vice versa. Alternately—if you want a fair, harmonious plank run in the topsides—you can mark a constant distance on the frames, measured from the sheer down to roughly the turn of the bilge. Then install the bottom strip-planks, starting at the keel, until you reach the marks. Allow these bottom strip-planks to take any angle or curve they want, but cut them off in a neat, smooth, continuous line fore-n-aft at the marks. This cut line will now run parallel to the sheer. Start strip-planking the topsides from this cut plank line up to the sheer. All the topside planks will run parallel to the sheer.
- On many boats, you can use permanent structural bulkheads instead of standard frames. In this case, the bulkheads are structural members similar to their use in FRP hulls. Bulkheads should be sized (but not spaced) according to Formula 5-5. Wherever the bulkhead can be located close to the calculated strip-plank frame spacing—and where the bulkhead is essentially an unbroken ring (molded at least 6.75 times its thickness at the deepest cutout)—a separate frame is not required (see photo on p. 340).
- Watertight/collision bulkheads should be according to Formula 9-29. These may be tabbed in place according to Formula 5-5

or they may be glued and screwed to frames, or some combination of the two. Tabbing should be from a bi-axial stitch-mat-style fabric that is compatible with epoxy.

- Frames may be laminated in place against the strip-planked hull shell. In this case, the sheer clamp may also be laminated in place against the inside of the planking (instead of against the inside of the frames). A shelf is not required, but the clamp should be sized according to the rule for sheer clamps without shelves (see Formula 9-15).

Wood-Epoxy Strip-Plank Exterior Hull Sheathing

All wood-epoxy hulls and decks should be covered with glass cloth or a similar material (e.g., Dynel or Vectra). This enhances abrasion resistance and gives a much thicker outer layer of epoxy-fiber matrix, which further protects the wood from degradation.

The minimum glass layer on hulls and cabin structures that are to be finished bright should use one layer of 8- to 10-oz./sq. yd. (270 to 339 g/m²) glass cloth laid in epoxy. Very small boats (e.g., canoes and rowing skiffs) would use 5-oz./sq. yd. (170 g/m²) cloth. For Dynel, Vectra, or Xynole polyester, the minimum is 4 oz./sq. yd. (135 g/m²) for all size boats.

Decks and cabin roofs should be covered with glass cloth, as specified in Formulas 9-19 through 9-26.

Better abrasion resistance, torsional strength, and longevity is achieved with heavier exterior sheathing on the hull; however, such hulls must be painted because the laminate is too thick to show attractive wood-grain. Even better—as we'll see—the torsional

strength and increased abrasion resistance of the sheathing allows the use of thinner strip-plank (see photo on p. 341).

FORMULA 11-2

Heavy Exterior Hull Sheathing for Strip-Plank Hulls

For hulls with Sns of 0.6 or higher:

Hull-Sheathing Fabric Weight, oz./sq. yd. = 30.8 + (8.3 × Sn) (English)

Hull-Sheathing Fabric Weight, g/m² = 1,044 + (281.4 × Sn) (Metric)

For Hulls with Sns Less than 0.6:

Hull-Sheathing Fabric Weight, oz./sq. yd. = 0.11 + (59.45 × Sn) (English)

Hull-Sheathing Fabric Weight, g/m² = 3.73 + (2,015 × Sn) (Metric)

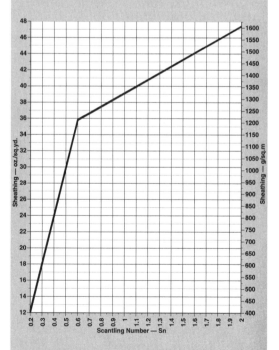

Heavy Exterior-Sheathing-Only Strip-Plank Hulls Sheathing Weight: Small Boats

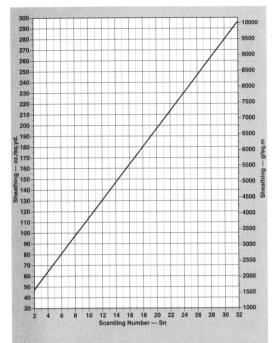

Heavy Exterior-Sheathing-Only Strip-Plank Hulls Sheathing Weight: Large Boats

- Vessels with Sns over 2 should use a sheathing laminate composed of bi-axial uni-di E-glass. With the uni-di layers installed at plus and minus 45 degrees to the fore-n-aft axis, such sheathing acts as diagonal strapping. In this way, the sheathing not only increases abrasion resistance but also torsional stiffness as well.
- Vessels with Sns less than 2 can use glass cloth instead of bi-axial fabric.
- Increase sheathing weight on bottom by 1 percent for every knot over 25 knots.
- Boats with Sns under 1.0 will not see much benefit from this construction method. Standard wood-epoxy strip-plank with lighter sheathing will work well.
- Increase sheathing weight by 10 percent on workboats and offshore cruisers.

- With internal frames, bulkheads, and backbone structure, no internal hull sheathing is required or recommended.

To sheath the exterior of *Logger Bobber's* hull, we would apply

Hull-Sheathing Fabric Weight = 30.8 + (8.3 × 2.97) = 55.4; use 55 oz./sq. yd.

Hull-Sheathing Fabric Weight = 1,044 + (281.4 × 2.97) = 1,879.7; use 1,880 g/m²

FORMULA 11-3
Exterior-Only Sheathed Strip-Plank Thickness

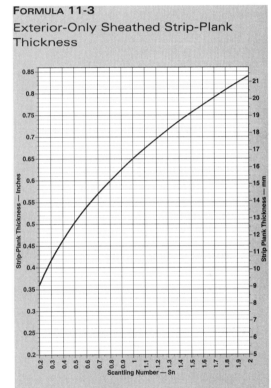

Exterior-Only Sheathed Strip-Plank Thickness: Small Boats

To determine the reduced strip-plank thickness that can be used with wood-epoxy strip-plank hulls that have the heavy exterior bi-axial E-glass sheathing specified in Formula 11-2, we would use the following:

(continued)

Strip-Plank Thickness, in. = 0.65 × Sn$^{0.3}$ (English)

Strip-Plank Thickness, mm = 16.51 × Sn$^{0.3}$ (Metric)

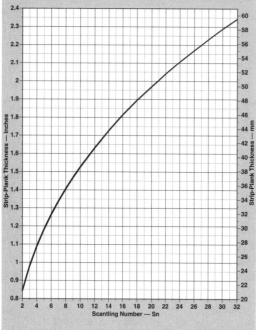

Exterior-Only Sheathed Strip-Plank Thickness: Large Boats

If our *Bobber* were so built, it would have

Strip-Plank Thickness = 0.65 × 2.97$^{0.3}$ = 0.97; use 1-in. plank

Strip-Plank Thickness = 16.51 × 2.97$^{0.3}$ = 24.7; use 25 mm plank

This is as opposed to the 1$^{1}/_{8}$-inch or 28 mm plank we specified for unsheathed strip-plank or conventional carvel-plank.

Double-Diagonal Exterior Wood Veneers on Wood-Epoxy Strip-Plank Hulls

An alternative to the heavy FRP exterior sheathing is double-diagonal layers of wood veneer—a layer of double-diagonal cold-molding. The outside of the hull must still be sheathed with a minimum 8- to 12-oz./sq. yd. (270 to 407 g/m^2) glass cloth. (For Dynel or Vectra, the minimum is 4 oz./sq. yd. [135 g/m^2].) With this construction, the double-diagonal cold-molded layers provide the same torsional stiffness that the heavy exterior hull sheathing provides. Because the veneers add appreciable thickness to the shell, the underlying strip-plank is reduced proportionately.

Boats with Sns less than 2.0 will not benefit much from this construction technique. Standard wood-epoxy strip-plank will serve best.

There are two drawbacks to external-wood diagonal layers on strip-plank hulls: the process of applying the diagonal wood layers is more labor-intensive than the FRP sheathing; and the heavy exterior FRP sheathing provides greater impact and abrasion resistance. Nevertheless, double-diagonal wood veneers over strip-plank is an excellent construction.

Note that although the method specifies two diagonal layers, there is no reason you cannot employ four or six layers, each proportionately thinner, to generate the total veneer thickness specified.

FORMULA 11-4

Strip-Plank Exterior Diagonal Wood-Veneer Thickness

Use the following to determine the thickness of the diagonal layers:

Thickness, Both Diagonal Layers Combined, in. = (0.43 × Sn$^{0.2}$) − 0.32 (English)

Thickness, Both Diagonal Layers Combined, mm = (10.92 × Sn$^{0.2}$) − 8.13 (Metric)

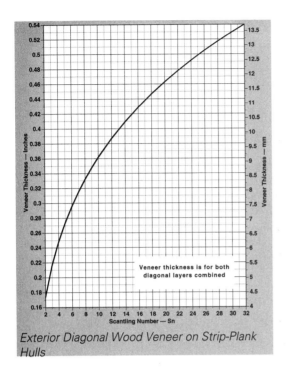

Exterior Diagonal Wood Veneer on Strip-Plank Hulls

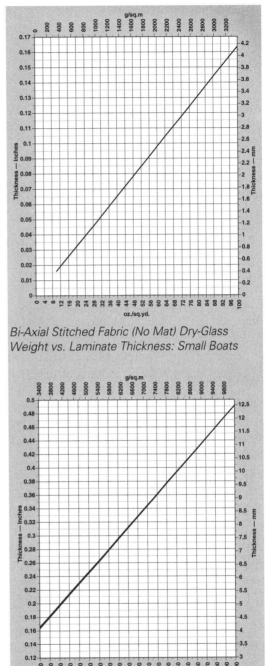

Bi-Axial Stitched Fabric (No Mat) Dry-Glass Weight vs. Laminate Thickness: Small Boats

Bi-Axial Stitched Fabric (No Mat) Dry-Glass Weight vs. Laminate Thickness: Large Boats

(continued)

Thus, *Logger Bobber* would use the following:

Thickness, Both Diagonal Layers Combined = $(0.43 \times 2.97^{0.2}) - 0.32 = 0.21$; use two diagonal layers ⅛-in. veneer, totals ¼ in.

Thickness, Both Diagonal Layers Combined = $(10.92 \times 2.97^{0.2}) - 8.13 = 5.44$; use two diagonal layers 3 mm veneer, totals 6 mm

To determine how much we can reduce the underlying strip-plank thickness, we have to know the thickness of the bi-axial sheathing laminate called for in Formula 11-2.

FORMULA 11-5

Bi-Axial Glass Laminate Thickness vs. Weight of Dry Glass

(English)

Weight of Dry Glass (oz./sq. yd.) = (Laminate Thickness [in.] × 610) − 0.3

We found an exterior sheathing for *Logger Bobber* of 55 oz./sq. yd. (1,880 g/m²). The laminate thickness would then be

(55 oz./sq. yd. – 0.3) ÷ 610 = 0.09 in.

(1,880 g/m² – 9.7) ÷ 813 = 2.3 mm

FORMULA 11-6
Reducing Underlying Strip-Plank Thickness with Diagonal Wood Veneers
The thickness of the strip-plank is reduced relative to the total shell thickness of the all-strip-plank hull with heavy hull-exterior sheathing.

Accordingly, *Logger Bobber*'s underlying strip-plank thickness—with the exterior diagonal wood veneers—can be reduced to ⁷/₈ inch (22 mm).

0.97-in. strip-plank + 0.09-in. sheathing = 1.06 in., and 1.06 in. – 0.25-in. veneers = 0.81; use ⁷/₈ in.

or

24.7 mm strip-plank + 2.3 mm sheathing = 27 mm, and 27 mm – 6 mm veneers = 21; use 22 mm

Thus, we have specified a hull shell composed of the following:

• One external layer of 8- to 12-oz./sq. yd. glass cloth (or one 4-oz./sq. yd. Dynel or Vectra layer).

• Two diagonal veneers, ¹/₈ inch each (¹/₄ inch total).
• Strip-plank ⁷/₈ inch.

or

• One external layer of 270 to 407 g/m² glass cloth (or one 135 g/m² Dynel or Vectra layer).
• Two diagonal veneers, 3 mm each (6 mm total).
• Strip-plank 22 mm.

Diagonal-Veneer or External-Glass-Sheathed Strip-Plank Hull Internal Structure

Adding the diagonal veneers or heavy bi-axial sheathing to the strip-plank allows you to eliminate much internal framing. Interior hull structure should follow the rules for FRP internal hull structure for cored FRP construction, as described in chapter 5, with the following comments and adjustments:

• No topsides longitudinals are required.
• Engine beds/stringers should be installed as described. They may be of foam- or balsa-core FRP or they may be of solid laminate, wood-screwed, bolted, and epoxy-glued to the hull. The solid-wood engine beds/stringers should be the same dimensions as the foam or balsa cores.
• Where a chine log is used, no other chine reinforcing is required.
• Alternately, an epoxy-chine may be used. (See the discussion on liquid joinery, page 166.)
• Bulkheads and ring frames do not require elastometric spacers under the CFR (Code of Federal Regulations, for passenger vessels or T-boats).
• Floors should be located as described in

the FRP rule. Solid-wood floors are made to the dimension of the foam or balsa core specified.

- It is possible to omit the keel and stem completely in this form of construction. Instead, the strip-planking and exterior-wood diagonal veneers are run right across the stem and keel. If this is done, the sheathing laminate at the keel and stem must be equal to 1.8 times the standard exterior-hull-sheathing laminate outside and 1.2 times the standard exterior-hull-sheathing laminate inside. A hull like this is really a wood-epoxy/FRP composite hull.
- Another approach to keel/backbone structure is to use a laminated plywood keel (see Formula 11-9C).

NOTE: All laminates and sheathing must be bonded in epoxy, using fabric styles compatible with epoxy (i.e., without binders) —usually stitch-mat bi-axial styles.

Internal/External FRP-Sheathed Strip-Plank

Yet another possibility with wood-epoxy strip-plank construction is to use heavy bi-axial sheathing both inside and outside of the hull shell in conjunction with an ordinary strip-plank core and with no diagonal wood veneers. This also allows you to eliminate the traditional frames and structure. Again, you should use the internal framing for cored FRP hulls described in chapter 5. (Note the comments and adjustments noted for strip-plank construction.)

FORMULA 11-7
Internal/External FRP-Sheathed Strip-Plank Thicknesses

The internal/external strip-plank construction uses a heavy internal sheathing or laminate in conjunction with the heavy external sheathing specified in Formula 11-2. This construction is true cored-composite construction. Because the strip-plank acts as a core, it can be reduced still further in thickness, as follows:

Strip-Plank Thickness, in. = $0.6 \times Sn^{0.34}$ (English)

Strip-Plank Thickness, mm = $15.24 \times Sn^{0.34}$ (Metric)

Thus, *Logger Bobber*'s internal and external sheathed strip-plank hull would have

$$\text{Strip-Plank Thickness} = 0.6 \times 2.97^{0.34} = 0.86;$$
$$\text{use } 7/8 \text{ in.}$$

$$\text{Strip-Plank Thickness} = 15.24 \times 2.97^{0.34} = 22 \text{ mm}$$

FORMULA 11-8
Interior-Hull Sheathing for Internal/External Strip-Planked Hulls

The internal hull sheathing is also bi-axial E-glass on boats with Sns over 2. On boats with Sns less than 2, the internal sheathing may be of glass cloth. The internal sheathing should be 66 percent of the thickness or weight of the external sheathing found in Formula 11-2.

Returning to *Logger Bobber*,

$$\text{Internal-Hull-Sheathing Fabric Weight} = 0.66 \times 55 \text{ oz./sq. yd.} = 36 \text{ oz./sq. yd.}$$

$$\text{Internal-Hull-Sheathing Fabric Weight} = 0.66 \times 1,880 \text{ g/m}^2 = 1,240 \text{ g/m}^2$$

Cored-Strip-Plank Construction vs. Cored-FRP Construction

Unlike the very low-strength (low-modulus) cores used in conventional cored-FRP construction, the wood strip-plank core itself provides substantial longitudinal strength, as well as local flexural strength and impact resistance. Furthermore, the wood-strip core has vastly greater sheer strength than the low-modulus cores used in conventional FRP. Additionally, the bi-axial E-glass/epoxy laminates have higher mechanical properties (they're stronger) than standard mat/roving polyester layups. Accordingly, although the total shell thickness of cored strip-plank and cored-FRP construction will work out similarly using the rules in this book, the interior and exterior laminates are thinner for wood-strip-cored construction than they are for cored-FRP construction.

Diagonal (Herringbone) Strip-Plank on Hard-Chine Hull Bottoms

On hard-chine hull bottoms—particularly those that have not been designed for plywood construction—it is sometimes more convenient to strip-plank the bottom diagonally, herringbone fashion. Plank thickness should be the same as given previously, unless the hull was intended for herringbone construction with minimal bottom framing. In this case, increase the bottom strip-plank thickness by 1.5 times.

Lindsay Lord's Ultralight Sheathed Strip-Plank Construction

Up until now, we've been designing conservative rigid-hull shells. Rigidity with safety requires considerable stiffness. There's another approach: allow the shell to flex slightly. If this sounds risky, it's not. Naval architect Lindsay Lord developed what is probably the lightest system of strip-planking (and one of the lightest approaches to boatbuilding ever) in the period after World War II. Although Lord designed and extensively tested several boats ranging from 22-foot (6.7 m) runabouts

to 80-foot (24.4 m), 40-knot patrol boats in this method, for some reason his whole approach is little known. This is odd, because the Lord system is inexpensive in both materials and labor, and it's amazingly tough. What's more, Lord wrote about his results at the time.

The Lord-type strip-plank boat is also a cored-composite hull. Its core is strip-planked of softwood (e.g., pine, cedar, or fir). This core serves as just that—a true core—so it can be of quite low-grade lumber. It is simply lightly tacked together as strip-planking (well glued with epoxy grout) over temporary molds. Then it is sheathed on the inside and the outside with Vectra polypropylene or Dynel (a modacrylic) from Union Carbide. All sheathing and gluing is done in marine epoxy, as with standard wood-epoxy strip-plank; no other resin is elastic enough for this application.

The critical point is that ordinary fiberglass is not used. Vectra and Dynel have much higher elongation (i.e., they will stretch much farther before they break) than FRP. When bonded as skins to a moderately thin wood-strip core, the resulting composite panel can deflect to absorb shocks and impacts, and bend and twist with extreme loading. This deflection/flexure is harmless with Dynel or Vectra. In epoxy resin, the skins and the strip-plank core bend together and spring back without any damage. This means that a thinner, lighter structure can absorb as much energy as a thicker, stiffer one.

FORMULA 11-9A
Lord's Sheathed Strip-Plank Core
Modified in format to match the procedures in this book, Lord's rules for determining scantlings are as follows:

Core:

Strip-Plank Hull-Core Thickness, in. = $0.34 \times Sn^{0.44}$ (English)

Strip-Plank Hull-Core Thickness, mm = $8.63 \times Sn^{0.44}$ (Metric)

Core not to be less than $\frac{3}{8}$ in. (9.5 mm).

Strip-plank deck and walk-on roofs to be 1.5 to 2 times the hull-core thickness.

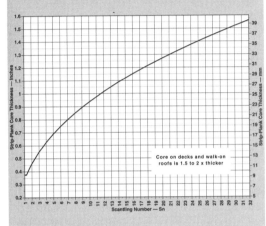

Lord's Strip-Plank Core Thickness

FORMULA 11-9B

Lord's Sheathed Strip-Plank Sheathing

Sheathing:

Both Vectra and Dynel come in 4-oz./sq. yd. (135 g/m²) fabric styles standard. In the following rule, one ply is one layer of either 4 oz./sq. yd. (135 g/m²) of either of these fabric styles. (Don't mix the two—use one or the other.)

Outside Laminate, oz./sq. yd. = $11.1 \times Sn^{0.43}$ (English)

Inside Laminate, oz./sq. yd. = $7.36 \times Sn^{0.36}$ (English)

or

Outside Laminate, g/m² = $376 \times Sn^{0.43}$ (Metric)

Inside Laminate, g/m² = $249 \times Sn^{0.36}$ (Metric)

Reverse the outside and inside layers for decks and cabin roofs.

Round up exterior laminate remainders over 2 oz./sq. yd. (68 g/m²) to one more full ply.

Round down interior laminate remainders less than 3 oz./sq. yd. (101 g/m²) to one ply.

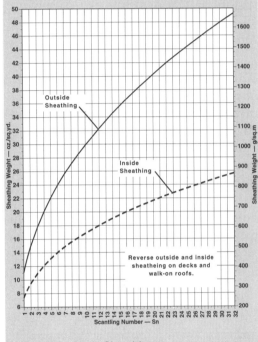

Lord's Strip-Plank Sheathing

To construct *Logger Bobber* using Lord's strip-plank method, we would use the following:

Core:

Strip-Plank Hull-Core Thickness = $0.34 \times 2.97^{0.44} = 0.55$; use $\frac{1}{2}$ in.

Strip-Plank Hull-Core Thickness = $8.63 \times 2.97^{0.44} = 13.9$; use 14 mm

Sheathing:

> *Outside Laminate = 11.1 × 2.97$^{0.43}$ = 17.7 oz./sq. yd.; use four plies Vectra or Dynel*

> *Inside Laminate = 7.36 × 2.97$^{0.36}$ = 10.89 oz./sq. yd.; use two plies Vectra or Dynel*

> *or*

> *Outside Laminate = 376 × 2.97$^{0.43}$ = 600 g/m²; use four plies Vectra or Dynel*

> *Inside Laminate = 249 × 2.97$^{0.36}$ = 368 g/m²; use two plies Vectra or Dynel*

Internal Structure:

Lord uses neither regular frames nor much other traditional internal structure; however, he does employ numerous bulkheads: "about every 8 to 10 feet, plus partial bulkheads, on an 80-footer (24.4 m)" (*Naval Architecture of Planing Hulls*). Also, Lord uses well-placed integral tanks, cabin soles, and such as additional hull stiffeners. Basically, you can use the standard internal FRP structure for cored hulls discussed in chapter 5, with the comments and adjustments noted in the previous section on internal structure for cored strip-plank hulls.

Keel/Backbone:

For the keel, stem, deadwood, and horn-timber backbone, Lord uses layers of plywood that are cut to the outline (profile) of the keel and stem, and glued together to the required thickness (siding). Butts between layers must be well staggered. The strip-plank-core garboard (and the planking at the stem) simply lands on a small furring strip tacked and epoxy-glued to each side of the keel at what would be the rabbet. Little beveling and no spiling to speak of are required. Any gaps or voids are filled with epoxy-putty grout or

foam (for large voids). All is tacked and glued in place, and all joints are generously radiused off using epoxy-grout putty and foam fillers of very large radii. Then the entire plywood backbone and strip-core structure is sheathed with the specified laminate inside and out. Really, this keel construction could be described as a keel or backbone core.

FORMULA 11-9C

Lord's Plywood-Keel-Core Siding (Thickness)

> *Scantling LOA between 20 and 30 feet, use two layers ⅝-in. ply*

> *Scantling LOA between 30 and 40 feet, use two layers ¾-in. ply*

> *Add one layer ¾-in. ply for every 10 feet over 40 feet*

> *or*

> *Scantling LOA between 6 and 9 m, use two layers 15 mm ply*

> *Scantling LOA between 9 and 12.2 m, use two layers 18 mm ply*

> *Add one layer (18 mm) ply for every 3 m over 12.2 m*

Thus, an 80-footer (24.4 m) would have six layers of ¾-inch (18 mm) ply comprising its keel/backbone, and would be sided 4½ inches (108 mm).

- If desired—instead of Lord's cored-strip construction—any portion of the decks and cabins can be made of epoxy-sheathed plywood, as described in Formulas 9-19 through 9-26.
- It is important that the internal hull sheathing/laminate run continuous and unbroken inside for the full length of the hull. Standard construction procedure is to

fabricate the permanent plywood-keel core and erect it upside down on temporary station molds. Strip the hull over the molds and permanently attach the strips to the keel core but not (of course) to the molds. Fill all voids and radii, and fill the corner fillets at the garboard, stem, and transom. Apply the outside sheathing and fair. Roll the hull right side up. Install a few temporary *exterior* molds to hold the hull in shape. Remove the temporary molds from inside. Smooth and fillet the hull interior core and its intersection with the keel/backbone. Apply the interior sheathing continuously and uninterrupted from bow to stern and athwartships. Now add the permanent bulkheads and internal structure.

- Unusual shapes, fairings, and nacelles can be built up out of wood core, foam, epoxy, and balsa, as required, and sheathed with the appropriate interior or exterior laminate.
- Lord even fabricates rudders and struts from plywood and/or pine strips, simply tacked together or to the hull, and faired-in with epoxy grout and foam as required. This then is sheathed with appropriate plies of Dynel or Vectra laminate.
- Add additional plies to the keel bottom and stem face as follows:

    Boats under 40 feet (12.2 m), add one ply

    Boats between 40 and 80 feet (12.2 and 24.4 m), add two plies

    Boats over 80 feet (24.4 m), add three plies

- A common problem with Dynel or Vectra layups is that these fabrics are so light (their specific gravity is so low) that they tend to float on the resin during layout.

The Gerr-designed 28-foot (8.5 m) offshore skiff is a good example of tape-seam sheet-plywood construction. (Courtesy Iain Neish)

The trick here is to use as little resin as required to wet-out each ply—no more and no less. Work a few test panels to get the hang of it, and you should have no difficulty. Vacuum-bagging the laminate would be an even better solution.

EPOXY/PLYWOOD CONSTRUCTION AND LIQUID JOINERY

Plywood hulls lend themselves very well to epoxy-saturated and glued construction. The large sheets of plywood are already more dimensionally stable than ordinary planks (although plywood has about half the tensile strength). Furthermore, the large sheets are easy to coat and glue in place.

Plywood planking thickness for wood-epoxy construction should be the same as determined in Formula 9-1. When subjected to repeated flexing, plywood's laminated construction is too prone to internal failures to allow any additional reductions in thickness. Decks and cabins should be sized according to Formulas 9-19 through 9-26.

Epoxy Chines (Tape-Seam Construction)

Plywood lends itself particularly well to tape-seam or epoxy-chine construction; however, tape-seam construction also can be used successfully at chines in epoxy strip-plank hulls, at great labor savings (see photo on p. 341). In tape-seam construction, the intersection between the topsides and the bottom plank is made—to start with—simply by allowing the two plank edges to touch each other. Usually, the bottom plank runs off past the topsides plank and is trimmed back flush. Because of epoxy-grout's gap-filling abilities, little beveling is required (and that of the roughest kind); a moderately sloppy fit is acceptable.

The exterior of the chine corner is radiused off and then an epoxy-grout fillet is applied smoothly, continuously, and evenly over the full length of the inside of the chine. Any exterior gaps or voids are filled with epoxy grout and smoothed off. The whole is then painted and sealed, inside and out, with a layer of unthickened epoxy. Finally, layers of glass-cloth tape are applied to both the inside and outside of the chine, all laid in epoxy. The resulting chine is smooth, fair, and watertight; it is quite strong. Better still, it is quick and easy to make, requiring little skill or painstaking measurements. By comparison, conventional chine logs—formed from solid wood—often require exacting beveling, plus they have edgeset, bend, and twist.

Liquid Joinery

This whole process can be called *liquid joinery* (a term attributed to multihull designer Jim Brown). Although we're discussing chines, the same *liquid-joinery* principle can be applied—with common sense—wherever strong corner joints must be made in wood-epoxy construction; for example, the corner intersection between the transom and the hull sides and bottom; the intersection between the bottom plank (garboard) and the keel (discussed in Lord's strip-plank rule); centerboard trunks; the cabin and coachroof joints; and even the hull-to-deck joint (in place of a clamp). In locations where it is relatively easy to work and to attach and shape solid wood (e.g., at the sheer clamps), the liquid-joinery or tape-seam approach doesn't add up to much time or labor savings and is probably not warranted. Chines and similar complex longitudinal joints, however, will be substantially easier to make in tape-seam.

Applications of Liquid Joinery

Other items that lend themselves well to liquid joinery are integral fuel and water tanks built into wood-epoxy hulls (these fuel tanks can be for diesel only), as well as built-in refrigerator and icebox compartments, shower sumps, bait wells, and even wood-epoxy sinks. In addition to (and on top of) the taped corner joints, fuel tanks must be completely sealed on the inside with a minimum of 8- to 12-oz./sq. yd. (270 to 407 g/m²) glass cloth or 4-oz./sq. yd. (135 g/m²) Vectra or Dynel. Twice this amount of sheathing should be used as a minimum on tanks over 100 gallons (455 l).

Laminated-Plywood Keel and Epoxy Sheet-Plywood Hull

A tape-seam sheet-plywood hull can have a laminated-plywood keel per Lord's strip-plank rule (see Formula 11-9C). If this is done, the interior of the keel should be generously filleted and taped to the plywood planking. Additional sheathing should also run athwartships over the plywood keel to completely cover it.

FORMULA 11-10

Tape-Seam Fabric Weight

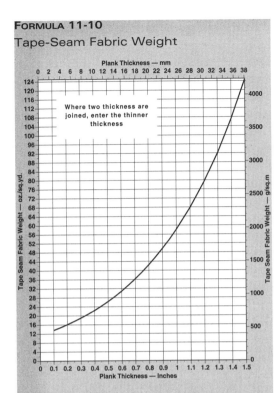

Tape-Seam Fabric Weight

The total weight of the fabric reinforcement used in a tape-seam chine (or other structural tape-seam joint) should be proportioned according to the plank thickness, as follows:

Fabric Weight, oz./sq. yd. = (1.13 + [plank thickness, in. ÷ 10.5])[20] (English)

Fabric Weight, g/m² = (1.345 + [plank thickness, mm ÷ 220])[20] (Metric)

- Where two planks of different thicknesses are joined, use the thickness of the thinner plank.
- The total fabric weight given is the maximum formed by the overlap of all the layers, inside and outside combined.
- When the individual layers applied are 10 oz./sq. yd. (340 g/m²) or less, it is usually applied as glass cloth. When the individual layers are greater than 10 oz./sq. yd. (340 g/m²), the fabric should be bi- axial E-glass.
- The tape is applied in roughly equal weights inside and out; however, when the total weight does not balance out per ply, the extra layers are installed on the interior because the overall exterior hull sheathing adds exterior strength.

If our old *Logger Bobber* were hard-chine sheet plywood, its topsides plank would be 1 inch (25 mm) thick (see Formula 9-1). Accordingly, its tape-seam chines would require the following:

Fabric Weight = (1.13 + [1-in. plank ÷ 10.5])[20] = 58.1; use 60 oz./sq. yd.

Fabric Weight = (1.345 + [25 mm plank ÷ 220])[20] = 1,900 g/m²

For *Logger*, we would then use

Three plies of 12-oz./sq. yd. (406 g/m²) bi-axial tape on the inside and two plies of 12-oz. (406 g/m²) bi-axial tape on the outside. This happens to total exactly 60 oz./sq. yd. (2,030 g/m²), although such precision is not necessary.

FORMULA 11-11

Tape-Seam Fabric Runout

The fabric reinforcement is applied to the joint in overlapping layers that build up to the required thickness at the chine and taper away along the plank.

The total tape reinforcement should extend away from the center of the joint at each side for a distance of nine times the plank thickness.

- The throat depth necessarily decreases as the angle the two panels make increases. When the angle is 180 degrees, the joint is a butt joint and there can be no throat depth at all.

COLD-MOLDED CONSTRUCTION (MULTIPLE DIAGONAL VENEERS)

Up until now, we've been using diagonal layers of wood as a portion of the hull shell only (when we used them at all). It is quite possible to use nothing but diagonal layers for the hull shell. This construction is usually termed *cold-molding*. Epoxy strip-plank methods could technically fit this term as well; however, it's seldom used in connection with strip-planking. Cold-molding originally referred to laminating up an entire wooden-hull shell (regardless of planking method) using glues that cured at room temperature (i.e., cold temperatures). This was in contrast to early laminated hulls, which were glued and cured in a massive female mold in an autoclave under pressure. Of course, most autoclave-laminated hulls employed some version of diagonal planking; thus—when room-temperature glues arrived on the scene—the term *cold-molding* came to refer to diagonal-veneer hull shells.

Only a light layer of exterior glass sheathing is used with most cold-molded hulls. Its purpose is not structural, but rather simply to add some abrasion and impact resistance. The interior of cold-molded hulls, however, must be reinforced with longitudinal stringers. These give the required fore-n-aft strength, plus they act as a form over which the planking veneers are laid. Widely spaced frames—installed inside the stringers—and/or bulkheads complete the structure. These members supply transverse strength.

Generally, cold-molded hulls are the lightest wooden-boat hulls you can build, except for boats built to Lord's strip-plank rule or of DuraKore. Cold-molded construction has many adherents; however, I usually find the labor required is not justified. Although the hulls are somewhat lighter than standard sheathed- or diagonal-veneer strip-plank, there are considerably more skill and hours required to properly spile, fit, staple down, and glue all the many diagonal veneers. On a larger boat—over 50 feet (15 m)—this can be many layers indeed. In fact, several experienced builders I know tried cold-molding and found it so labor-intensive that they no longer build in epoxy-saturated wood at all. Instead, these yards switched to aluminum for large vessels. This is a shame, because—although aluminum certainly has many excellent points—in contrast to cold-molding, many of the strip-plank building methods are very economical of labor and materials.

My experience has been that—using proper methods—wood-epoxy strip-plank is the most cost-effective way to build a one-off round-bilge hull. Labor considerations aside, however, cold-molded hulls are excellent structures—light, strong, and long-lived. For high-performance boats—race boats, sail and power; high-speed motor yachts; and patrol boats—the extra labor may well be worth the cost for the relatively modest gain in performance at the top end of the envelope.

- Shell thicknesses of $1/2$ inch (13 mm) or less generally consist of just two diagonal layers.
- Shell thicknesses between $1/2$ and 1 inch (13 to 25 mm) should consist of at least three layers. When three layers are used, the outer layer is laid on fore-n-aft.
- Shell thicknesses more than 1 inch (25 mm) should consist of four or more layers. When an odd number of layers is used,

the outer layer is laid on fore-n-aft; however, this is not mandatory.

- Hulls 1 inch (25 mm) and less should be sheathed with a minimum of one layer of 8- to 10-oz./sq. yd. (270 to 339 g/m²) glass cloth laid in epoxy. Very small boats (e.g., canoes and rowing skiffs) would use 5-oz./sq. yd. (170 g/m²) cloth. For Dynel, Vectra, or Xynole polyester, the minimum is 4 oz./sq. yd. (135 g/m²).
- Hulls more than 1 inch (25 mm)—and all boats running over 25 knots—should increase the bottom sheathing to a minimum of 16- to 20-oz./sq. yd. (542 to

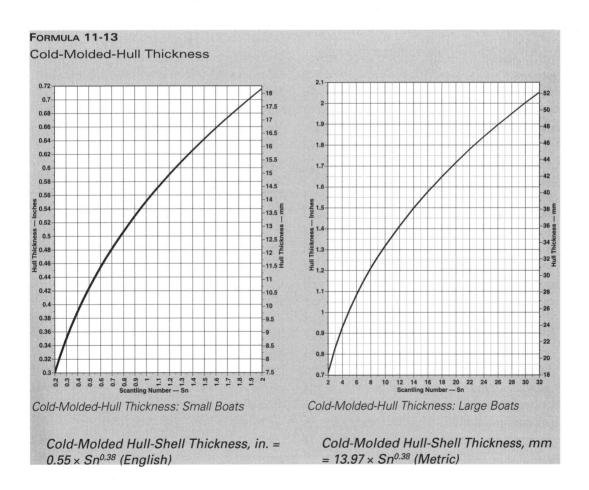

FORMULA 11-13
Cold-Molded-Hull Thickness

Cold-Molded-Hull Thickness: Small Boats

Cold-Molded-Hull Thickness: Large Boats

Cold-Molded Hull-Shell Thickness, in. = $0.55 \times Sn^{0.38}$ (English)

Cold-Molded Hull-Shell Thickness, mm = $13.97 \times Sn^{0.38}$ (Metric)

678 g/m²) glass cloth laid in epoxy on the bottom. For Dynel, Vectra, or Xynole polyester, the minimum is 8 oz./sq. yd. (271 g/m²) on the bottom. The topsides on these hulls may still use the lighter sheathing employed on hulls under 1 inch (25 mm) thick.

Thus, a cold-molded *Logger Bobber* would have the following shell scantlings:

Cold-Molded Hull-Shell Thickness =
0.55 × 2.97⁰·³⁸ = 0.83; use ⅞ in.

$$\textit{Cold-Molded Hull-Shell Thickness} = 0.55 \times 2.97^{0.38} = 0.83; \text{use } \tfrac{7}{8} \text{ in.}$$

Cold-Molded Hull-Shell Thickness =
13.97 × 2.97⁰·³⁸ = 21.1; use 22 mm

$$\textit{Cold-Molded Hull-Shell Thickness} = 13.97 \times 2.97^{0.38} = 21.1; \text{use } 22 \text{ mm}$$

So, we would use four diagonal layers, each ⁷/₃₂ inch (5.5 mm) thick.

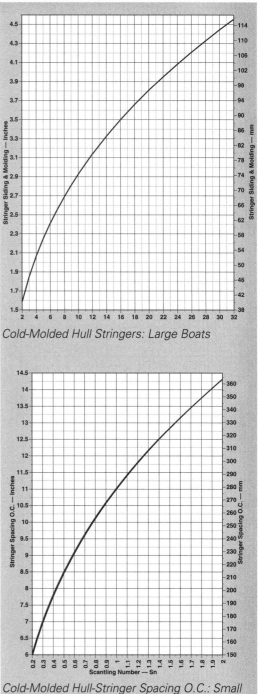

Cold-Molded Hull Stringers: Large Boats

FORMULA 11-14
Cold-Molded-Hull Stringers

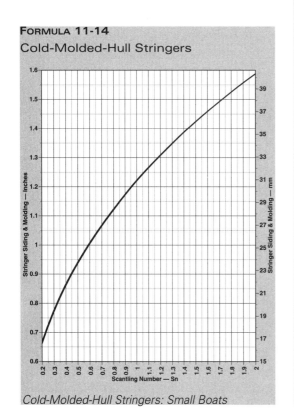

Cold-Molded-Hull Stringers: Small Boats

Cold-Molded Hull-Stringer Spacing O.C.: Small Boats

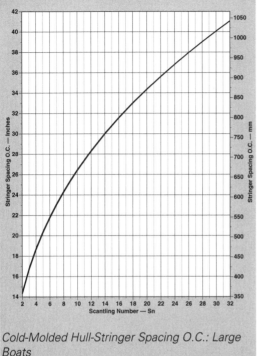

Cold-Molded Hull-Stringer Spacing O.C.: Large Boats

Stringers Sided and Molded, in. =
1.22 × Sn$^{0.38}$ (English)

Stringers Sided and Molded, mm =
31 × Sn$^{0.38}$ (Metric)

Stringers Spaced O.C., in. = 11 × Sn$^{0.38}$
(English)

Stringers Spaced O.C., mm = 279.4 ×
Sn$^{0.38}$ (Metric)

- Stringer siding may be tapered to 66 percent of the maximum siding, at the fore-n-aft thirds of the stringer's length.
- The stringers must be fastened to each other and to the stem with breasthooks and to the transom with quarter knees (see Formula 10-11).
- Stringers are laid out so that the maximum spacing center-to-center (O.C.) is at midships. The hull shape will naturally bring

the stringers closer together as they run toward the ends. This is desirable, at the bow in particular, because the impact loads are greatest here.

- The stringer immediately adjacent to the keel should be spaced only half the standard O.C. distance from the side of the keel.
- Decrease stringer spacing by 1 percent for every knot of boat speed over 25 knots.
- Although not required, it will often work out best to run the stringers along diagonals worked out on the line-drawing section view or body plan and then transferred to the inside of the plank along the length of the hull. This eliminates edgeset in the stringers, leaving only bend and twist to deal with during construction.
- Planing powerboats should install nearly full-length laminated engine beds sized according to Formulas 9-31 and 9-32. The engine beds on cold-molded hulls should be fastened directly to the inside of the hull shell. It is often possible and desirable to eliminate one or two standard bottom stringers where the engine beds perform essentially the same function (see photo on p. 341).

Returning to reliable old *Bobber*, we would find it as follows:

Stringers Sided and Molded = 1.22 × 2.97$^{0.38}$
= 1.84; use 1⅞-in. square

Stringers Sided and Molded = 31 × 2.97$^{0.38}$ =
46.8; use 48 mm square

Stringers Spaced O.C. (at Midships) =
11 × 2.97$^{0.38}$ = 16.6; use 16 in.

Stringers Spaced O.C. (at Midships) =
279.4 × 2.97$^{0.38}$ = 422.5; use 420 mm

If *Logger Bobber* were a 35-knot boat, we would decrease stringer spacing to 14³/₄ inches

(380 mm); (35 knots − 25 knots = 10 knots, so reduce spacing by 10 percent; 0.9×16.6 in. = 14.9 in. [422.5 mm $\times$ 0.9 = 380.2 mm]).

FORMULA 11-15
Cold-Molded-Hull Frames and Bulkheads

The longitudinal hull stringers are supported transversely on frames and bulkheads. Frames should be sized according to Formula 9-2 and spaced according to Formula 9-3; however, even for round-bilge cold-molded hulls, use the spacing for sawn frames, or 2.5 times the standard round-bilge plank-on-frame spacing. The frames are fastened to the inside of the stringers only; they don't touch the hull shell.

Bulkheads and watertight/collision bulkheads should be sized according to Formulas 5-5 and 9-29; however, the rule for spacing the bulkheads does not apply because regular frames are used. Wherever the bulkhead can be located close to the calculated frame spacing—and where the bulkhead is essentially an unbroken ring (molded at least 6.75 times its thickness at the deepest cutout)—a separate frame is not required. If as many bulkheads as specified in Formula 5-5 are used, then many of the frames can often be eliminated. Again, the bulkheads usually fasten only to the inside of the stringers; they need not touch the inside of the hull shell. Bulkheads can do so, however, wherever a watertight or vaportight seal is needed.

FORMULA 11-16
Cold-Molded-Hull Floors/Composite Metal-Strap Floors

Floors on cold-molded hulls with longitudinal stringers should end on top of one of the hull-bottom stringers.

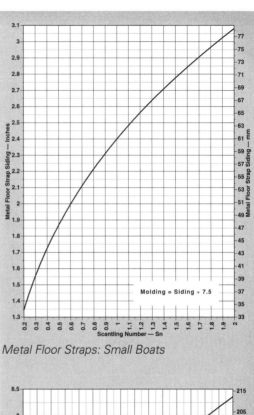

Metal Floor Straps: Small Boats

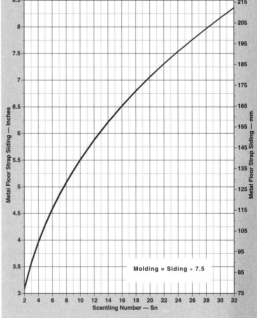

Metal Floor Straps: Large Boats

This avoids hard spots and distributes the stress from the floor ends longitudinally into the stringer. On powerboats, the floors should extend athwartships to at least the second stringer out from the keel, port and starboard. On sailboats—at the ballast keel and at the mast steps—the floors should extend out at least to the third stringer out from the keel. In other regards, the floors should be as described in Formulas 9-7 and 9-8.

An excellent alternative floor construction for use with cold-molded and longitudinal-stringer hulls is a composite floor (wood and metal combined), with a metal-strap floor plate bolted down on top of the stringers athwart-ships and wood blocking underneath, between the stringers. These floors are low in molding, easy to fabricate, and can be installed easily, either at a frame or where there is no frame.

The principal transverse strength is in the metal strap, which should be dimensioned as follows:

Metal-Strap Floor Siding, in. = 2.4 × $Sn^{0.36}$ (English)

Metal-Strap Floor Siding, mm = 60.9 × $Sn^{0.36}$ (Metric)

Molding = siding ÷ 7.5

- Silicon bronze and 316 stainless steel (second best) are the proper materials for metal-strap floors. Hot-dip galvanized mild steel, primed and painted all around before installation, can be used; however, it seems a poor economy after adding in the cost of galvanizing and painting and its lower life expectancy.
- Through-bolt the metal-strap floor into each stringer and into the keel.

- Through-bolt the metal-strap floor through the wood blocking and into the plank. On hulls with Sns less than 2, it may be easier to screw-fasten the blocking to the plank from outside, and then to screw-fasten (or lag-bolt) the metal strap down into the blocking from inside.

Install wood blocking under the metal strap at the same height, or a little higher, then the keel top athwartships. The blocking should be sided the same as the metal strap. Run the blocking out over the first stringer, out from the keel, and then taper the blocking height until it reaches the second stringer out and butts against it, flush with the stringer's top. The metal-strap floor runs on top of the blocking continuously from port to starboard. On sailboats, at the ballast keel and the mast steps, the blocking should be extended out to the third stringer out from the keel (or farther). The blocking height—outboard of the second stringer—will be the same height as the stringers, and the metal strap will extend out over the third stringer.

If *Logger Bobber* were fitted with metal-strap floors, we would install

Metal-Strap Floor Siding = 2.4 × $2.97^{0.36}$ = 3.55; use 3½ in.

Metal-Strap Floor Siding = 60.9 × $2.97^{0.36}$ = 90.1; use 90 mm

Molding = $7/16$ in. (12 mm)

The Metal Floor Option

In Formulas 9-7 and 9-8, we described traditional wooden floors. Formula 11-16 details the metal-composite alternative to the grown or laminated wooden floor. There is also an

An interesting and unusual variation of metal floors. Note the double-sawn frames alternating with every two steam-bent frames. (Courtesy Kortchmar & Willner)

Metal floors installed by Larry and Lin Pardey on their Taleisin. *(From* Details of Classic Boat Construction: The Hull, *by Larry Pardey, reproduced with permission.)*

excellent metal-composite alternative to the wooden sawn floor described in Formula 9-7. In this case, floors can be cast or welded up from bronze plate with angles to fasten or bolt down to the keel. In other respects, the overall dimensions and arrangements are similar to the Formula 9-7 sawn floors. Silicon bronze and Monel are the best materials for metal floors of this type, with stainless steel second best. Hot-dip galvanized steel can be used, but doesn't seem to be worth the slight economy in the long run.

FORMULA 11-17
Standard Metal Floors

Metal-composite floors should be dimensioned and fashioned exactly as described for standard sawn floor, with the following exceptions:

- *Siding = sawn-floor siding ÷ 6*

- *The length of the angle (i.e., bolt flange) along the keel to receive the keel bolts should be 1.1 times the standard sawn-floor siding.*

Metal floors can be formed to extend higher up along the frames' sides than sawn wooden floors because the metal can be trimmed back in the center, so that only the upper half of the floor continues up along the frames. The area between the frames thus opens and does not intrude on interior space. The metal floor can be cut down to 40 percent of the minimum molding for a standard sawn floor amidships to increase interior room, as long as the arms project up along the frames at least as high as the minimum sawn frame height (molding), or higher.

Metal floors can be used on either completely traditional plank-on-frame construction or on wood-epoxy construction. They do not shrink, swell, or decay. They provide more usable interior space and they are as strong or stronger than the best sawn floors. Labor is slightly greater than for sawn floors, but the added expenditure would be well justified.

TWELVE

Wood: Species, Type, and Application

Selection of Wood Species

In traditional wood hulls, the wood itself is subject to great variations in moisture content and temperature, and to complete immersion for extended periods. Therefore, to obtain long life and reliability, the wood species employed is critical. Generally, in the United States, the most common, plain-vanilla boat-building woods are as follows:

Small Boats to 20 Feet (6 m):

Keel/Backbone: Douglas fir, white oak, yellow pine
Frames: white oak, Douglas fir, elm
Deck-Beam Stringers, Carlins, etc.: cedar, spruce, Douglas fir, yellow pine
Planking: white cedar, Port Orford cedar, Honduras mahogany, Philippine mahogany (second-best)

Medium-Size Boats, 20 to 45 Feet (6 to 14 m):

Keel/Backbone: white oak, yellow pine, western larch, Douglas fir
Frames: white oak, elm
Deck-Beam Stringers, Carlins, etc.: Douglas fir, yellow pine, white or red oak
Planking: Honduras mahogany preferred, Philippine mahogany second-best, white cedar, Port Orford cedar, teak, yellow pine

Large Boats More Than 45 Feet (14 m):

Keel/Backbone: white oak, yellow pine, western larch
Frames: white oak, elm
Deck-Beam Stringers, Carlins, etc.: white or red oak, Douglas fir, yellow pine
Planking: Douglas fir, yellow pine, Honduras mahogany, white or red oak

These are, however, only the most common woods for these applications; many other wood species are suitable. Still other species, such as locust or lignum vitae, have specialized applications. Following is an alphabetical list of many of the common woods available in the United States and Europe. This list will serve as a general guide; however, many other local and imported species are suitable. It pays to investigate locally available woods.

Wood Species

Afromosia: *Afromosia spp.*, hardwood, 45 lb./cu. ft., 721 kg/m^3. Acceptable for planking and deck trim, good for small-boat keel/backbone, reasonably rot-resistant, tends to split.

Agba: *Gossweilerodendron balsamiferum*, hardwood, 30 lb./cu. ft., 481 kg/m^3. Acceptable for planking, decks, cabin sides, and joinerwork; fairly reliable all-around wood for boats with Sns less than 3.5 to 4.

Aptong: *Sipterocarpus spp.*, hardwood, 44 lb./cu. ft., 705 kg/m^3. Not well suited to boat use except for interior joiner cleats, etc.

Ash, White: *Fraxinum americana*, hardwood, 42 lb./cu. ft., 673 kg/m^3. Excellent deck beams, internal framing, and laminated frames; good for sawn frames, acceptable for bent frames; very strong for its density; not particularly rot-resistant; and it stains and discolors easily—not recommended for brightwork or deck trim.

Blue Gum (Eurrabbie): *Eucalyptus globulus*, hardwood, 56 lb./cu. ft., 897 kg/m^3. Good for sawn frames and keel/backbone parts that are reasonably straight.

Butternut: *Juglans cinera*, hardwood, 26 lb./cu. ft., 416 kg/m^3. Beautiful interior joiner wood but somewhat soft so mars easily; excellent thwarts and transoms on skiffs and rowboats.

Cedar, Port Orford: *Chamae cyparis*, softwood, 28 lb./cu. ft., 449 kg/m^3. Excellent planking for boats with Sns up to 3.5 or 4; aromatic, rot-resistant; good for scrubbed decks, light longitudinals.

Cedar, Red (Western Red): *Thuja plicata*, softwood, 23 lb./cu. ft., 368 kg/m^3. Good planking and secondary structure for boats with Sns up to 3; not especially strong for its density and swells more than most average woods.

Cedar, Spanish: *Thuja spp.*, softwood, 24 lb./cu. ft., 384 kg/m^3. Excellent small-boat planking; hard and strong for its density.

Cedar, White (Juniper): *Thuja occidentalis*, softwood, 21 lb./cu. ft., 336 kg/m^3. Excellent small-boat planking, rot-resistant, absorbs water and becomes heavier with long-term immersion.

Cedar, Yellow (Alaskan Cedar): *Chamaecyparis nootkatensis*, softwood, 31 lb./cu. ft., 496 kg/m^3. A rot-resistant, strong, and moderately hard cedar, more resistant to denting than other cedars; good for planking and general framing; sometimes hard to paint well.

Cypress, Bald: *Taxodijim distichum*, softwood, 34 lb./cu. ft., 545 kg/m^3. Good for ceiling and secondary structures, acceptable for planking, highly rot-resistant, can have a strong smell.

Douglas Fir: (see Fir)

Elm, English: *Ulmus campestris*, hardwood, 37 lb./cu. ft., 593 kg/m^3. Excellent small-boat planking, light and flexible.

Elm, Rock: *Ulmus thomasii*, hardwood, 44 lb./cu. ft., 705 kg/m³. Good for steam-bent frames, deck beams, keel/backbone; tough, hard, and abrasion-resistant; does not absorb much water so makes excellent bottom planking.

Elm, White (American): *Ulmus americana*, hardwood, 37 lb./cu. ft., 593 kg/m⁵. Good for deck beams, bent frames, table and counter tops; excellent for grates; gets whiter as it is scrubbed; does not bend well; not as strong as ash or fir; acceptable for small-boat frames.

Eurrabbie: (see Blue Gum)

Fir, Douglas (Oregon Pine): *Pseusdotsuga menziesii* (previously *taxifolia*), softwood, 36 lb./cu. ft., 577 kg/m³. Excellent planking wood, particularly for boats with Sns over 2; excellent for longitudinals, stringers, clamps, shelves; good for heavier spars; acceptable for keel/backbone; very good all-around structural wood; pronounced grain can be hard to paint.

Gabon: (see Okoume)

Green Heart: *Ocotea rodiaei*, hardwood, 61 lb./cu. ft., 977 kg/m³. Hard and dense, similar to locust, but with still higher strength.

Hackmatack: (see Larch)

Iroko (Bang, Tule, Odum, Nigeria Teak, Kambala, Intuile, Mareira): *Chlorophora excelsa*, hardwood, 41 lb./cu. ft., 657 kg/m³. Acceptable as a substitute for mahogany but not as durable or as strong; still available in wide boards; resistant to borers.

Ironbark: *Eucalyptus sp.*, hardwood, 64 lb./cu. ft., 1,025 kg/m³. Excellent for ice sheathing and similar abrasion protection.

Juniper: (see Cedar, White)

Khaya: (see Mahogany)

Larch, Eastern (Hackmatack, Tamarack): *Larix laricina*, softwood, 38 lb./cu. ft., 609 kg/m³. Roots make excellent grown knees, floors, and frames, as well as stems and sternposts with curvature.

Larch, European: *Larix decidua*, softwood, 35 lb./cu. ft., 561 kg/m³. Good for frames and beams; acceptable for planking; a popular all-around wood; sometimes termed *Scots boatbuilder's timber*.

Larch, Western: *Larix occidentalis*, softwood, 39 lb./cu. ft., 625 kg/m³. Good general boatbuilding lumber; good for keel/backbone; similar to Eastern Larch.

Lignum Vitae: *Guaiacum sp.*, hardwood, 78 lb./cu. ft., 1,249 kg/m³. Excellent for fairleads, deadeyes, lizards, pulley blocks, sheaves; the old standard for water-lubricated propeller-shaft bearings; contains oils that resist rot and act as a lubricant; extremely tough and abrasion-resistant; hard but brittle if longer lengths are bent.

Locust, Black: *Robina pseudacacia*, hardwood, 51 lb./cu. ft., 817 kg/m³. Excellent for cleats, tillers, butts, sampson posts, chafing boards, belaying pins, stanchions, deck trim; hard, dense, and abrasion-resistant.

Lauan: (see Mahogany)

Mahogany, African (Khaya and many other species): *Khaya ivorensis*, hardwood, 37 lb./cu. ft., 593 kg/m³. Excellent planking; good for coamings, cabin sides; good for joinerwork; hard to plane; can stain at metal fasteners.

Mahogany, Honduras (Mexican): *Swietenia macrophylla*, hardwood, 35 lb./cu. ft., 561 kg/m³. Excellent for planking, coamings, cabin sides; good for joinerwork.

Mahogany, Philippine (Red Lauan): *Shorea negrosensis*, hardwood, 31 lb./cu. ft., 496 kg/m³. Acceptable for planking, coamings, cabin sides; does not take large bends; tendency to split; good for joinerwork. NOTE: White Lauan, *Pentacame contorta*, is not as strong or as rot-resistant as Red Lauan, and should not be used for structural work, but is acceptable for joinerwork.

Mahogany, Philippine (Tangile): *Shorea polysperma*, hardwood, 41 lb./cu. ft., 567 kg/m³. Similar to Red Lauan, but somewhat denser and stronger; slightly superior for planking. NOTE: Tiaong, *Shorea teysmanniana* (also called Philippine mahogany) is not as strong or as rot-resistant as Tangile, and should not be used for structural work, but is acceptable for joinerwork.

Meranti, Red (Red Seraya): *Shorea*, hardwood, 42 lb./cu. ft., 673 kg/m³. Good for planking and frames (in smaller boats); a reasonably useful all-around wood, but must be carefully selected for quality and grain.

Oak, Black: *Quercus velutina*, hardwood, 43 lb./cu. ft., 689 kg/m³. Similar to white oak, but not quite as strong and not as rot-resistant.

Oak, European: *Quercus spp.*, hardwood, 46 lb./cu. ft., 737 kg/m³. Good for frames, keel/backbone, beams, stringers; hard and durable; not as rugged as white oak.

Oak, Red: *Quercus rubra*, hardwood, 43 lb./cu. ft., 689 kg/m³. Similar to white oak, but not quite as strong and not as rot-resistant.

Oak, White: *Quercus alba*, hardwood, 48 lb./cu. ft., 769 kg/m³. Excellent for keel/backbone and bent frames; crooks in roots make best knees; may be used for almost any part of a larger boat; expands and contracts greatly; prone to rot if not seasoned with great care. White oak is *the* standard all-around structural boat wood.

Okoume (Gabon): *Aucoumea klaineana pierre*, hardwood, 25 lb./cu. ft., 400 kg/m³. Acceptable for plywood and for laminated (cold-molded) planking; acceptable for secondary joiner cleats, etc.; neither strong for its weight nor rot-resistant.

Pine, Eastern White: *Pinus strobus*, softwood, 27 lb./cu. ft., 432 kg/m³. Excellent for scrubbed decks; good for planking; durable; good for joinerwork and secondary structures.

Pine, Oregon: (see Fir, Douglas)

Pine, Pitch: *Pinus spp.*, softwood, 40 lb./cu. ft., 641 kg/m³. Acceptable all-around wood for longitudinals, deck beams, decking, cabin sides, and framing; resin makes gluing, finishing, and painting difficult.

Pine, Ponderosa: *Pinus ponderosa*, softwood, 28 lb./cu. ft., 449 kg/m³. Rot prone, not good for boat use.

Pine, Scots (Scots Fir, Redwood, Red Deal): *Pinus sylvestris*, softwood, 32 lb./cu. ft., 513 kg/m³. Not strong or rot-resistant; not suitable for boat use, except for interior joiner cleats and similar light use.

Pine, Sugar: *Pinus lambertiana*, softwood, 27 lb./cu. ft., 432 kg/m³. Excellent for carving casting patterns and half models; similar to white pine.

Pine, Yellow (Longleaf Yellow): *Pinus palustris*, softwood, 44 lb./cu. ft., 705 kg/m³. Excellent planking for boats with Sns higher than 2.5; high resin content resists water absorption and rot; excellent all-around structural wood for longitudinals, deck beams, and all heavy framing; good for keel/backbone when white oak is unavailable; believed to be more rot- and borer-resistant than white oak in tropical waters.

Red Meranti: (see Meranti)

Redwood: *Sequoia sempervirens*, softwood, 28 lb./cu. ft., 449 kg/m³. Good for planking and cabin framing.

Spruce, Eastern: *Picea spp.*, softwood, 29 lb./cu. ft., 465 kg/m³. Not decay-resistant; seldom used in boats.

Spruce, Sitka: *Picea sitchensis*, softwood, 27 lb./cu. ft., 432 kg/m³. Excellent for masts and spars; good for beams, stringers, and secondary framing on light boats; prone to decay.

Tamarack: (see Larch)

Tangile: (see Mahogany)

Teak: *Tectona grandis*, hardwood, 45 lb./cu. ft., 721 kg/m³. Excellent for planking, cabin sides, coamings, transoms, and joinerwork; not as strong as commonly believed; high oil content makes it very rot- and check-resistant; does not glue well.

Plywood

PLYWOOD WATERPROOF BOIL-TEST
All plywood used in boats *must* be laminated with glues rated waterproof by the boil test. The standard test to establish a glue as truly "water*proof*" (not simply water-resistant) is a complete cycle of boiling fully immersed for 4 hours, drying at 140°F (60°C) for 20 hours, boiling again for 4 hours, allowing to cool in the water, and then sheer-testing wet. This roughly duplicates the extreme swings in moisture content all boats experience repeatedly throughout their service life. Plywood that doesn't withstand this boil test can't be used *anywhere* onboard. No amount of coating or sealing, with any wonder material, can *ever* make up for nonwaterproof glue. Plywood rated "exterior grade" is waterproofed by the boil test.

MARINE PLYWOOD FOR HULL PLANKING
In almost all cases, plywood used for hull planking should be American Plywood Association (APA) marine plywood, with A-A, A-B, or B-B face veneers, five plies minimum. It is made only from Douglas fir or western larch, with solid jointed cores and strict limitations on gaps and defects in the core veneers. Indeed, all the interior plies must be at least B-grade, with no gaps over ⅛ inch (3.1 mm). An A-grade surface is the highest grade—smooth with no knots or knotholes—but it may have wood or synthetic patches. B-grade surfaces are the next step down—

they may have knots but no knotholes. Marine ply is sanded on both surfaces.

Such marine ply is quite expensive. As a result, some builders use ordinary APA Exterior A-A- and A-B-grade ply for hull planking. Although there are success stories, I recommend against compromising on the integrity of the hull planking in this way. The defects permissible in the interior plies of exterior grade form hidden danger zones. Decay and localized glue-line failures can develop undetected until a catastrophic failure occurs. For example, APA-exterior-ply cores can have knotholes up to $1^1/_2$ inches (38 mm) across, and can have gaps between veneer butts as much as 1 inch (25.4 mm) wide. The cores only need to meet C-grade requirements, and they can be from other, less tough species of wood than Douglas fir or western larch.

EXTERIOR-GRADE PLYWOOD FOR BOATS

Throughout the remainder of the boat's structure (i.e., any place but the hull planking), you need not use true marine plywood; ordinary exterior A-A or A-B plywood can be employed safely. Decks, cabins, bulkheads, floors, interior joiner panels, solid cores on FRP-laminated stringers, and engine beds can all be fabricated from exterior ply. This is, of course, a cost-saving option and all marine ply throughout is the best.

OVERLAY PLYWOOD

One of the drawbacks to fir plywood—in any grade—is that the fir-veneer surface (even in A-grade) shows ripple and grain unless there is extensive surface preparation before painting. An apparently little-known but excellent solution is to use a medium-density overlay plywood (MDO). APA MDO exterior ply is identical to exterior B-B, but with a laminated surface of opaque resin-treated fiber sheet. This is tough, abrasion-resistant, highly weather-resistant, and provides a very smooth, clean painting surface, with virtually no preparation. MDO ply is substantially less expensive than marine grade. It can be used at will, anywhere but for the hull planking. Of course, MDO is not warranted where the ply will be sheathed with glass laid in epoxy, such as decks; however, it can still be used to advantage with the MDO side down. This makes a very smooth, easily painted overhead between the deck beams. MDO usually comes with the overlay on one side only, but can be found with the overlay on both sides, which saves even more time on interior finish. High-density overlay (HDO) is also available, and is even more abrasion- and weather-resistant. APA marine-grade plywood is also available with MDO and HDO overlays on either or both sides. Overlay marine-grade ply can be used for hull planking. The reduction in finish time may well be worth the added cost.

NON-APA "BOAT PLIES"

Various manufacturers produce non-APA plywood for the marine industry under product names like "Boat Ply." These plies generally fall somewhere between APA marine and exterior grade in quality. Hulls should not be planked with this unless heavily sheathed; however, it is excellent for all other applications on a boat.

THIRTEEN

Aluminum and Steel Construction Materials and Methods

*I*n this and following chapters, we examine metal-boat construction. As a practical matter, this means steel or aluminum. Bronze is too expensive and wrought iron, although it makes a long-lasting (if heavy) hull material, has long been unavailable. There is really only one other suitable modern boatbuilding metal; this little-known alternative is copper-nickel. It is very expensive like bronze, but it has the remarkable advantage of being totally nonfouling and virtually inert in a marine environment. Copper-nickel hulls have been built quite recently, and—under some circumstances—may make good economic sense. We take a brief look at copper-nickel in chapter 19.

Development of Metal Boats

EARLY METAL BOATS
Although older than fiberglass, metal boats are quite a modern development compared to wood construction. The first known all-metal boat was a riveted-iron barge built in 1787 by J. Wilkinson, Ironmaster. Although this barge

was successful, when Richard Trivithick and Robert Dickenson later proposed all-iron ships in 1809, they were met with incredulity and mirth. After all, everyone knew that iron was heavier than water and would sink!

It was nine years later—as best as can be determined—in 1818 that the first all-metal commercial self-propelled boat, the *Vulcan*, was constructed at Faskine, near Glasgow. Despite being a new concept and built of a radical material, it was stout enough to remain in active service through 1875—a good run for a commercial boat of any material or era. Finally, the *Aron Manbu* was built by the Horsely Iron Works, near Birmingham, in 1821. At 106 feet (32.3 m) with a 17-foot (5.18 m) beam, a newspaper described the boat as the "most complete specimen of workmanship in the way of iron that has ever been witnessed." Metal hulls were now fully accepted, particularly for craft over 200 feet (60 m), because they were stronger than nailed, screwed, and bolted wooden structures could ever hope to be.

STEEL TAKES CHARGE

Of course, all the early metal boats were entirely of iron. Iron was an improvement on wood for large boats and for supporting the incredible weight of the colossal steam-boilers of the day, but iron isn't particularly strong for its weight. Steel has much higher tensile strength and greater elongation. Probably the earliest steel boat was the *Ma Robert*, constructed in 1858 for David Livingstone's expedition to the Zambezi, in Africa. The tensile strength of her puddled steel was about 51,000 psi (351 mPa), which is approximately the same as the steel used on the liners *Mauritania* and *Lusitania*. Today, standard mild steel is about 60,000 psi (413 mPa).

The *Ma Robert* and another contemporary steel boat both went off to Africa, where they were out of sight of the public and made little impression on European boatbuilders. Accordingly, it wasn't until 1879, when the *Rothomahana*, built by W. Denny and Bros. for service in New Zealand, was launched that the age of steel ships really began in earnest. By 1891, more than 80 percent of the new steamers under construction were made of steel rather than iron or wood. Wooden ships would soon be, well . . . history.

EARLY ALUMINUM

Perhaps surprisingly, experiments with aluminum vessels started not long after steel. The first all-aluminum boat is believed to be a leeboard sailboat built in 1890. Probably the first all-aluminum powerboat was the *Mignon* (see photos on p. 342). Constructed in Switzerland in 1892, it was driven by a 2-hp (1.5 kW) naphtha engine. In 1894, several 18-foot (5.48 m) surfboats were built of aluminum in the United States for a polar expedition. Weighing in at 375 pounds (170 kg)—compared to 1,700 pounds (773 kg) for the equivalent screw-fastened wood—they were the first aluminum boats built in North America.

PROBLEMS WITH CORROSION

Naturally, there were problems. Even in the 1890s, there was more than just iron, steel, and aluminum to choose from; bronze, brass, and lead—the traditional boatbuilding metals—were still available as well. This opened all sorts of interesting possibilities in construction, but it also presented new and little-understood pitfalls. Indeed, the best designers could run into difficulty.

One of these was none other than the Wizard of Bristol, Captain Nat Herreshoff. Using his considerable high-tech expertise, he designed an all-metal boat for the America's Cup defense of 1895. Herreshoff's construction for his 123-foot (37.5 m) *Defender* was truly remarkable. The foundation was the heavy-bulbed lead keel, on top of which was a cast-brass keel plate in three sections, joined by bronze bolts through flanges on the upper side; this keel plate was fastened by bronze lag screws to the lead keel. The stem and stern-post were of cast bronze, as was the frame of the rudder. The plating, down from a little above the water, was of manganese bronze. The topsides were of aluminum, with a 4 percent alloy of nickel, $5/16$ and $3/8$ inch thick (7.9 and 9.5 mm), with a steel plate in the way of the chainplates. The rivets were bronze and the frames were steel.

Well, you get the idea—a lot of different metals all mixed together in salt water. Not good! In fairness to Captain Nat, all-metal hull construction was such a new concept that the corrosion problems just weren't fully understood. More important, *Defender* not only held together through her entire racing campaign, she also won it. Still, her problems were—to say the least—severe. The U.S. Navy inspected *Defender* to see about using aluminum in shipbuilding:

the topsides in bad condition, with the paint peeling and corrosion visible at the juncture of the aluminum and bronze. In spite of a special paint prepared by a local painter after the usual yacht paints had failed, it was difficult to maintain a satisfactory surface.

After a later inspection, the report continued:

In June, she showed more serious corrosion and the heads of many bronze rivets had fallen off. . . . The cast fittings about the deck were so corroded that many might be broken by hand.

Fully a hundred years have passed, and we have at last gained a firm understanding of how to build boats of metal and how to employ metal fittings. (There was a time when even ordinary metal fittings were nearly unheard of, and most cleats, chocks, brackets, and even rudder stocks were of wood.) The key is to keep dissimilar metals separated, which we take a closer look at in chapter 14.

Aluminum and Steel Materials

TYPES OF STEEL

Iron is no longer competitive (or available) for boat construction and bronze, which could make a fine boat hull, is far too expensive. This leaves steel as the only practical ferrous material; however, steel comes in many flavors; that is, alloys. Basically, steel is iron alloyed with carbon and other trace elements to adjust its characteristics. Generally, the higher the carbon content, the stronger and harder the steel. Too much carbon, though, makes the steel brittle and difficult to weld, particularly in a marine environment where carbide byproducts in the weld can cause corrosion. Steels are thus divided into categories based on their carbon content.

- Low-carbon steel has no more than 0.15 percent carbon.
- Structural carbon steel, or "mild steel," has between 0.15 and 0.30 percent carbon.
- Medium-carbon steel has between 0.30 and 0.50 percent carbon.
- High-carbon steel has between 0.50 and 1.00 percent carbon.

Medium- and high-carbon steels require pre- and post-heat treatment and/or low-hydrogen welding. They aren't suited to boatbuilding. Mild steel is most commonly used, with the exception of Cor-Ten steel, which at 0.09 percent carbon is a low-carbon steel.

The most common boatbuilding steel alloys are listed in Table 13-1.

An Eckold machine for rapid, precise bending of metal shapes and plate. A MIG welder is to the left and a grinder to the right.

TABLE 13-1 Steel Boatbuilding Alloy Physical Properties

Alloy	UTS, psi × 1,000 (mPa)	Yield, psi × 1,000 (mPa)	Elongation	Endurance Limit, psi × 1,000 (mPa)
A242 (Cor-Ten)	70 (482)	50 (345)	19%	35 (241)
A373	58 (400)	32 (221)	24%	28 (193)
A36	60 (414)	36 (248)	23%	28 (193)
ABS/A	58 (400)	34 (234)	21%	28 (193)
A440	75 (517)	50 (345)	18%	39 (269)
A441	70 (482)	50 (345)	18%	42 (289)

Note: Modulus of elasticity E = 29,000,000 psi (199,862 mPa)

UTS = Ultimate Tensile Strength

Elongation is a percent of an 8-inch (200 mm) sample.

A242 is manufactured by U.S. Steel under the trademark name Cor-Ten.

A36 is the most common standard structural steel or mild-steel alloy.

STEELS USED IN THE SCANTLING RULE

In general, the steel scantling rule assumes that A36, ABS/A, or A373 alloys will be used. It is intended for steels with a tensile strength between 58,000 and 60,000 psi (400 and 414 mPa) and a yield strength between 32,000 and 36,000 psi (221 and 248 mPa). These are *mild steels,* a term that originally indicated that these steels were not brittle.

Endurance Limit

All materials lose strength when they are flexed repeatedly. The more times and the farther they are bent, the weaker they get, until—eventually—they break. (This applies to elastic bending, where the material is not bent so much that it won't naturally spring back to its original shape. Plastic bending stretches the material so far that it deforms permanently and won't snap back. Plastic bending causes even more severe weakening, but it follows different rules than the endurance limit and fatigue strength considered here.)

Imagine bending a thin steel plate back and forth. It will be stiff at first, then grow easier to bend, and finally snap. Vibration and repeated slamming by waves cause just such repeated bending or flexure. Over time, all materials (including wood, fiberglass, and aluminum) grow gradually weaker from continued bending. This is measured as their *fatigue strength*, and it decreases with the number of cycles or the "age" of the structure. Of course, the weakening process can take a long time. For example, after 100,000 cycles of bending, an average aluminum alloy will lose about 15 percent of its original strength; after 200,000 cycles, 25 percent; after 400,000 cycles, 32 percent. Although 400,000 cycles might correspond to more than 50 years of hard use, this loss of strength continues indefinitely.

Steel is a unique exception to this rule. At some point, it ceases to lose any more strength no matter how many additional flexures it experiences. This is the "endurance limit"; obviously, it applies only to steel. The higher the endurance limit of the alloy, the stronger the hull will be many years in the future, all other things being equal. Unfortunately, steel's corrosion is a much bigger factor than its fatigue strength or endurance limit in small-craft applications.

Handbooks list "endurance limits" for other materials; however, read the fine print. These nonsteel "endurance limits" are really the fatigue strength after an arbitrarily defined number of cycles of testing—usually around 500,000 cycles.

HIGHER-STRENGTH STEELS

A440 and A441 steels have higher strength but lower elongation than the more common steels. They also have a higher endurance limit. However, in the thin plate used on boats under 100 feet (30 m), there is little to be gained by employing these steels. Their increased strength cannot be used to reduce thickness because the thinner plate will still corrode at the same rate as the standard structural steels; therefore, it would corrode away too fast. Because A440 and A441 are somewhat more expensive and a little harder to work (because they're stiffer), there's little advantage in using them for hulls. (However, certain high-strength fittings might benefit from these alloys.) Nevertheless, you can certainly build with them if convenient, using the same thickness specified in the standard scantling rule.

Cor-Ten (A242) Steel: Thinner Plate

Cor-Ten steel has strength properties similar to A440 and A441, but it also has improved corrosion resistance. You can reduce the plate thickness from the scantling rule that follows. Calculate the plate thickness and multiply by 0.88 for Cor-Ten. If, for example, the rule called for a $3/16$-inch (4.76 mm) topsides plate, you could reduce that to 0.165-inch (4.19 mm), which is equal to 8-gauge plate.

Don't be misled by its somewhat improved corrosion properties—Cor-Ten steel is not a stainless steel. It requires the same intensive paint and anodic protection against rust and corrosion that ordinary mild steel does. If not properly maintained, it will weep rust stains at about the same frequency, and can rust away nearly as rapidly as mild steel. Cor-Ten's corrosion advantage is that the rust—once it starts—progresses more slowly on well-maintained hulls, and tends to seal itself against further penetration (for a time).

TYPES OF ALUMINUM

Pure aluminum is not very strong. To increase its mechanical properties, it is alloyed with other elements. There is a wide assortment of aluminum alloys. Only true marine aluminum alloys will stand up to corrosion in salt water. You absolutely cannot use, for example, aircraft or cooking-utensil alloys for marine applications. Serious corrosion will destroy such a hull in short order.

Almost all marine aluminum alloys are in the 5000 series, which is aluminum alloyed with magnesium. The 6000 series—aluminum alloyed with magnesium and silicon—is used for spars and is suitable for some extrusions and structural shapes in hull construction.

ALUMINUM ALLOYS USED IN THE SCANTLING RULE

The temper of an alloy plays a significant role in determining its physical properties, and

Table 13-2 Aluminum Boatbuilding Alloy Physical Properties

Alloy	Temper	Form	UTS, psi × 1,000 (mPa)	Yield, psi × 1,000 (mPa)	Elongation
5083	H111	extrusions	40 (276)	24 (165)	16%
	H321	sheet & plate: U.S. Coast Guard now advises against marine use			
	H323	sheet	45 (310)	34 (234)	
	H324	sheet	50 (345)	39 (269)	
	H321	plate: U.S. Coast Guard now advises against marine use			
5086	H111	extrusions	35 (241)	21 (145)	
	H112	plate	35 (241)	16 (110)	14%
	H32	sheet & plate	40 (276)	28 (193)	12%
	H34	drawn tube	44 (303)	34 (234)	10%
5054	H111	extrusions	33 (227)	19 (131)	14%
	H112	extrusions	31 (214)	12 (83)	18%
	H32	sheet & plate	36 (248)	26 (179)	10%
	H34	sheet & plate	39 (269)	29 (200)	10%
5456	H111	extrusions	42 (289)	26 (179)	18%
	H112	extrusions	41 (283)	19 (131)	22%
	H321	sheet & plate	46 (317)	33 (227)	16%
	H323	plate	48 (331)	36 (248)	
	H324	sheet	53 (365)	41 (283)	
6061	T6	sheet & plate	42 (289)	35 (241)	17%
	T6	extrusions	38 (262)	35 (241)	17%
	T6	rod & bar	42 (289)	35 (241)	17%
	T6	drawn tube	42 (289)	35 (241)	17%
	T6	pipe	42 (289)	35 (241)	17%

Note: Modulus of elasticity E = 10,000,000 psi (68,918 mPa)

UTS = Ultimate Tensile Strength

Elongation is a percent of a 2-inch (50 mm) sample.

temper varies with the way the alloy is worked to form it into the shapes you purchase. Allowing for this, 5083, 5086, and 5456 are the alloys applicable to the scantling rule that follows. The 5054 alloy is somewhat weaker. It can be used, but—when given the choice—round up on the thickness given in the rule.

6061 Aluminum and Heat- Versus Non-Heat-Treatable Alloys

Aluminum 6061-T6 is the standard material for masts and spars, and is perfectly acceptable for specialized extrusions and stanchions. However, avoid 6061-T6 for hull construction whenever possible. It can be used for framing but not for plating at all, for two rea sons: 6061 contains 0.25 percent copper and the 5000 series has no copper, so the 6061 is somewhat less corrosion-resistant; and 6061 is a heat-treatable alloy, again compared to the 5000 series alloys, which are non-heat-treatable. Therefore, 6061 is stiffer and more difficult to bend into complex shapes without heating it first—although it can be done effectively and frequently is. The sweeping curves of longitudinals are little or no problem for 6061, for instance.

Even with these two drawbacks, however, in the real world it is often either too hard to find specific shapes in the 5000 series or too expensive. In this case, use the 6061; it will give acceptable service for internal hull framing—it is simply the second choice. For the deck, superstructure, and interior framing (e.g., sole beams), there is no practical difference, and 6061 can be considered interchangeable with the 5000-series alloys. However, on the exterior or where water can collect, it is still marginally more prone to corrosion.

Isotropic Materials for Uniform Strength
Both wood and fiberglass are similar in that they are made up of individual fibers held together by some binding agent and run in clearly defined directions. Wood fibers run with the grain; fiberglass fibers run according to the weave and construction of the cloth, but are clearly directional. The strength of steel and aluminum is uniform in every direction. No matter which way you orient a plate, it has the same strength up or down, fore-n-aft, diagonally, and even through the thickness of the plate. This is called *isotropy*, and steel and aluminum are both *isotropic* materials.

The nice thing about this is that you don't have to pay special attention in design or construction to the alignment of the fibers.

As we've seen, this takes much careful thought in wood and fiberglass.

Comparing Aluminum and Steel

ADVANTAGES OF ALUMINUM

Frankly, of the four standard boatbuilding materials covered in this book—fiberglass, wood, aluminum, and steel—steel is my least favorite. Aluminum has many advantages over steel, which we examine later. Before steel aficionados condemn me for this view, let me say clearly that steel is still a fine material from which to build a boat (or it wouldn't be included in this book). I have designed boats in steel and will continue to do so. In fact, as I write this, my office is designing a 65-foot (19.8 m) steel dinner/cruiser charter boat (see illustration on p. 193, top).

Nevertheless, aluminum has several significant advantages over steel:

1. **Light aluminum.** Aluminum is lighter than steel for the same strength. For example (roughly speaking and neglecting corrosion allowance in steel), aluminum plate should be between 1.25 and 1.5 times thicker than steel for the same strength. Aluminum, however, weighs 168 lb./ft.^{3} (2,691 kg/m^3) versus steel's 490 lb./ft.^{3} (7,849 kg/m^3)—only 34 percent of steel's weight. Even taking the larger thickness's multiplier of 1.5, this means that aluminum is about half the weight for the same strength—a huge difference (i.e., 1.5 times thicker × 0.34 lighter = 0.51, or 51 percent)! Indeed, aluminum structural weight compares favorably to wood or fiberglass. Steel hulls in vessels under 100 feet (30 m)

are nearly impossible to make both really light and long-lasting. Aluminum hulls, in contrast, can even be built extra heavy, resulting in a hull that is literally stronger than steel and still weighs significantly less.

2. **More stable and faster aluminum boats.** The light weight obtainable from aluminum construction lowers the center of gravity of a boat, making it more stable and thus more seaworthy. Less weight also means you can go faster with the same power or sail area, or have a higher ballast ratio in a sailboat for more sail area and improved performance. Alternately, you can use less power for the same speed or get greater range with the same tankage. Of course, you have more cargo capacity or allowable weight for joinerwork and auxiliary machinery with aluminum construction.

3. **Aluminum superstructures on steel hulls.** It is so difficult to make steel light enough that most vessels with Sns under 8 (roughly under 60 feet [18 m]) must use wood, FRP, or aluminum superstructures rather than steel. If they don't, it is nearly impossible to keep the boat's center of gravity low enough for adequate stability. Even larger steel craft benefit from lighter superstructures and frequently use this approach.

4. **Light weight equals labor-saving.** The lighter weight of the components makes building in aluminum less labor-intensive than steel. A $^3/_{16}$-inch, 400-sq. ft. (4.7 mm, 37.1 m²) steel plate would weigh 3,000 pounds (1,363 kg) and would require careful

handling and heavy gear. Roughly equivalent $^1/_4$-inch, 400-sq. ft. (6.3 mm, 37.1 m²) aluminum plate would weigh just 1,408 pounds (640 kg)—again, a vast difference.

5. **Easier to work in aluminum.** Aluminum is softer and easier to bend, cut, and form. It cuts about three times faster than steel. Aluminum bends so easily, in fact, that round-bilge hulls in aluminum are little problem. It can be cut with ordinary woodworking equipment, and quickly and easily drilled, sanded, and filed to exact dimensions. Steel, by comparison, takes heavy grinders and specialized cutting and bending tools. Larger building yards, of course, have specialized machinery for either aluminum or steel, but for aluminum it is simply to make the work go faster still.

6. **No compromise on hull shape.** The freedom to build inexpensively nearly any hull shape in aluminum means that the hull form doesn't have to be compromised with developable surfaces or chines when they're not wanted (see photo on p. 343). This translates into more efficient hydrodynamics for better performance and increased seakindliness.

7. **Faster welding.** Welding aluminum is roughly three times faster than welding steel. Even allowing for somewhat heavier welds (i.e., more passes) for the comparably thicker aluminum plate of the same strength, the total hours in welding aluminum should be about half that for a similar steel hull.

8. **No rust, lower maintenance.** Aluminum doesn't rust at all. Yes, alu-

minum can corrode when in contact with dissimilar metals or from stray electrical currents, but so can steel. Aluminum is so corrosion-resistant and totally rust-free that it doesn't even have to be painted above the waterline or on the inside. (Antifouling bottom paint is still a must.) Many workboats are routinely left bare above the waterline, but most vessels are painted for appearance. The net savings in maintenance over the life of the boat as a result of freedom from rust and generally reduced corrosion is substantial.

9. **No added plate thickness to allow for corrosion.** Even more important, rusting wastes away the steel so the plates get thinner with age. This is why on small craft you can't make effective use of most higher-strength alloys. Indeed, the plate thicknesses for small-boat steel hulls are somewhat heavier than required for basic strength to allow for corrosion—the *corrosion allowance*.

   A good rule-of-thumb is that a steel hull will lose about 0.004 inch (0.1 mm) of thickness every year. A well-maintained and properly built steel boat will do a little better than this in most places. Still, in those hard-to-reach areas—such as inside the bilge at the base of bulkheads, near stiffeners and other obstructions—this rule is close.

   Another old saying is that steel boats rust from the inside out. This is because it's just these hard-to-reach areas, which are difficult to inspect and maintain, that waste away fastest.

All this means is that in 25 years, $3/16$-inch (4.7 mm) shell plate would be reduced to 0.09 inch (2.2 mm) thick in several areas, approaching just $1/16$ inch left. To get adequate life in small craft, steel plates must be made heavier than needed for strength, with a corrosion allowance to accommodate this *wastage*.

10. **Aluminum is nonsparking and nonmagnetic.** Being nonsparking makes aluminum safer both in the building shop and in operation. Fires can't be ignited by the friction spark of some heavy object falling or scraping against the aluminum structure. The lack of magnetic interference is a great plus for navigation and electronics.

11. **Aluminum deforms to absorb more energy.** Aluminum deforms or stretches beyond its elastic limit more than steel before rupturing. This is why dents in aluminum canoes and runabouts seldom split open, and can usually be hammered out again. Such plastic deformation accords aluminum still more energy absorption for its weight than steel.

12. **Aluminum is less sensitive to stress risers.** Aluminum's plastic deformation offers another benefit as well. Steel is particularly sensitive to sharp corners in construction. This is called *notch sensitivity*; the notches or sharp corners are called *stress risers*. Although it is still recommended practice to radius corners and avoid hard spots on aluminum, in fact, aluminum is much more resistant to stress concentrations caused by stress risers than steel. Before the aluminum can fail at

such a hard corner, it deforms—absorbing some of the energy and relieving the stress.

Steel, on the other hand, develops cracks that further increase the stress concentration, which then, in turn, extends the crack and generates new ones as well—a progressively worsening downward spiral in strength. Large ships have literally broken in half and sunk at sea from small stress-riser cracks propagated at a sharp-corner hatch opening on deck. A World War II liberty ship, with square-corner deck openings, broke in half at its loading berth!

13. **Custom extrusions.** Custom dies are possible for aluminum to make specialized shapes. This is generally too costly for small one-off projects; however, production yards often find it economical and practical to have a few specialized extrusions made up for standard rubrails and similar details. This is not possible in steel.

14. **No attack by bacteria.** Aluminum hulls are not subject to attack by sulfate-reducing bacteria. These little-known bacteria can accumulate in bilges, ballast tanks, and fuel tanks—usually in commercial vessels—and eat their way through $5/16$ inch (8 mm) of steel plate in a year! Colonies of microorganisms, sulfate-reducing bacteria speed up corrosion by digesting sulfates and producing sulfides. They can cause catastrophic corrosion quickly if not detected.

15. **Higher scrap value.** Aluminum has higher scrap value than steel, recouping some of its added initial material cost.

16. **Reduced labor costs compensate for increased material costs.** The much greater ease of working with and forming aluminum substantially reduces labor costs. Usually, the labor-cost reduction—combined with the lower total weight of metal purchased—can be enough to offset the substantially higher cost of the aluminum itself.

DISADVANTAGES OF ALUMINUM
No material is perfect and, in spite of the many pluses listed previously, aluminum does have some drawbacks compared to steel.

1. **Aluminum is considerably more expensive.** Recently, I got prices for steel at around 29 cents and aluminum at $1.50 per pound. Although the relationship shifts with commodity-market vagaries, aluminum will always be significantly more costly. Still, it's not quite what it seems. Remember that an aluminum structure weighs only half as much as a steel structure of comparable strength. So, for proper boat-to-boat comparison, you need to cut the total weight of aluminum purchased to half that of steel, or—for convenience—figure on the same weight of metal for both, but half the price for aluminum. At today's prices, this is 29 cents versus 75 cents.

2. **Less abrasion-resistant.** Aluminum is softer than steel. This is a big plus for working and forming, but aluminum hulls are less resistant to abrasion. Still, aluminum is considerably more abrasion-resistant, however, than standard wood or fiberglass construction,

so this isn't much of a drawback for most boats. In fact, aluminum runabouts are routinely run up on rough concrete launching ramps on their bottom. Although not the best practice, aluminum hulls can survive such abuse, which most wood and FRP vessels could not. Still, when it comes to pure abrasion abuse, it's impossible to beat steel. For tugs, canal boats, barges, and dredges, steel becomes more attractive.

3. **Aluminum can melt and burn in a fire.** For a structural metal, aluminum has a low melting point, at approximately 1,080°F (592°C). It can even burn in an exceptionally intense fire. Steel, with a melting point of approximately 2,600°F (1,427°C), is the only truly fireproof boatbuilding material. Once again, aluminum is vastly more fire-resistant than wood or FRP; however, steel is clearly superior in this regard.

4. **Welding equipment is more expensive.** The gas-shielded welding equipment required for aluminum is more expensive than the stick/electrode welding used for steel. What's more, aluminum really should be welded in an enclosed building. If not, breezes will blow the gas shield away from the arc, causing defective welds. Builders have had good success setting up temporary windscreens for outdoor construction, but this is second-best for aluminum construction compared to having a properly enclosed building shed.

5. **Qualified workers and equipment are harder to find.** There are fewer yards and welders qualified for and experienced in welding aluminum than steel. Especially when voyaging to out-of-the-way corners of the globe, it may be difficult to find places to make repairs. Of course, most damage to aluminum can be temporarily patched by hammering the holed area as smooth as possible, drilling holes in the surrounding shell, and then bolting on a patch sealed with bedding compound.

6. **Aluminum alloy is harder to locate.** Aluminum alloys are frequently tough to find in many regions outside of North America and Europe. Even where aluminum suppliers and manufactures are common, it can be difficult to purchase the sizes and quantities of material necessary for a small-boat project.

Larger building yards will not have too much difficulty with this through their regular suppliers, due to their high annual purchase volume. Small yards and home builders, however, often have to expend great amounts of effort searching for adequate supplies at reasonable cost, and they may be compelled to import materials from distant sources. Even with this extra effort, compromises on more readily available sizes and shapes may become unavoidable. Steel, by comparison, is obtainable quickly and inexpensively—in small and large quantities—all over the world.

Construction Considerations

WELDING VERSUS RIVETING

Until the 1930s, virtually every part of every metal boat was fastened together with rivets and occasionally with bolts or screws. Riveting is labor-intensive and slow compared to welding, and leaves seams that can start and leak on impact. Probably the most structurally complicated and most carefully engineered boats anywhere are submarines. The stress that their hulls experience exceeds anything surface ships encounter, and even the smallest failure can be deadly. Naturally, the very finest and newest technology is used throughout.

It is interesting so see how, at the beginning of World War II, U.S. fleet subs were of nearly all-riveted construction, but by the end of the war they were entirely welded. Not only could they be built faster, but the extra strength from both all-welded construction and newer high-strength steels also enabled them to dive to deeper depths than had ever been possible before. All-welded boat construction really came into its own in the early 1940s, barely 15 years before the beginning of modern fiberglass boat construction.

WELDING DISTORTION

For all its advantages, welding does have some drawbacks. The most important of these is distortion. Every time you weld, you melt a portion of the structure, which then re-cools and resolidifies. This tremendous fluctuation in temperature distorts and warps the hull. Controlling and limiting weld distortion is critical to good boat construction. (More about this in chapter 18.)

Minimum Practical Plate Thicknesses for Welding

Another consideration, however, is that the thinner the plate, the more prone it is to distortion during welding. Generally, the thinnest aluminum plate that can be welded with standard gas-shielded equipment—

without distortion or burn-through—is $3/16$ or 0.1875 inch (4.75 mm). For steel, the minimum is 10-gauge (0.1345 inch [3.4 mm]). Using pulse-arc welding, aluminum down to $1/8$ inch (3.2 mm) and steel down to 11- or even 12-gauge (0.1196 to 0.1046 inch [3.0 or 2.7 mm]) can be welded. However, such thin plates take very careful attention to detail by experienced welders.

Except where both experienced welders and pulse-arc equipment are available (with the increased cost they represent), you're largely limited to a minimum of $3/16$ inch (4.75 mm) for aluminum and 10-gauge (3.4 mm) for steel.

In the scantling rules that follow—where the results give thinner plate than can be welded—simply round up to the $3/16$ inch in aluminum or 10-gauge in steel.

RIVETING THIN PLATE FOR SMALL BOATS

This is where riveted construction is still useful. Airplanes are made of aluminum rather than steel because aluminum offers so much lighter a structure. Even so, the plate in airplane shells must be well under $3/16$ inch (3.4 mm) and can't be effectively welded—instead, it's riveted.

It isn't practical to make small boats under 30 feet (9 m) light enough in steel, but it certainly is possible—even superior—in aluminum. Such small runabouts and skiffs are nearly universally riveted. Larger, high-performance aluminum sail and power-boats can also benefit from thin plate on their superstructure. There's an overall savings in weight (thus an increase in speed) and improved stability. Light, riveted super-structures are practical where performance is an overriding criterion—but it adds cost.

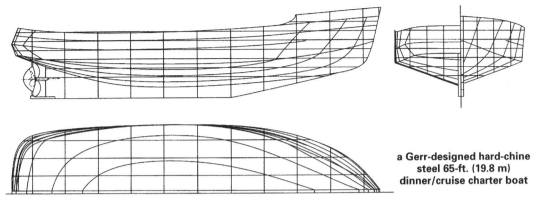

**a Gerr-designed hard-chine
steel 65-ft. (19.8 m)
dinner/cruise charter boat**

*This hull's lines show the characteristic convexity in the forefoot resulting
from conic development for easy plating in steel.*

Hull Shapes and Metal Construction

STEEL HULL SHAPES

Whereas aluminum can be bent into virtually any hull shape, steel hulls usually require compromise. Most small U.S. yards aren't familiar with the techniques required to build true round-bilge hulls with full compound curvature in steel. This is a shame because it is not as difficult as many believe. The standard steel hull is hard chine with *developable surfaces*, which can be rolled along the surface of a theoretical cone or a cylinder, or a series of cones and cylinders, joined smoothly together. Because the lines radiating along the surface of a cone—from its tip to its base—are straight, these *conic surfaces* curve only in one direction and are easy to plate up. (The lines are referred to as *radians*.)

In practice, steel plate can be bent, hammered, and heated into considerable curvature on a hard-chine hull—curvature that is not developable. More complex shapes (which usually occur at the forefoot) can be made up by installing the plate in smaller wedge sections. The only drawback here (besides the added labor) is some further distortion from the extra welding.

Even without any special torturing of the plate, steel can be bent in compound curvature on a hard-chine hull as long as the depth of the transverse curve is less than $1/40$ of the width of the plate athwartships. The fact is that such slight compound curvature actually makes the hull shell stiffer, and also keeps it fairer, reducing the tendency to get that hungry-horse look between frames. Furthermore, it looks nicer than pure slab-sided hulls.

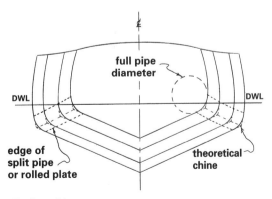

Radius chine

RADIUS-CHINE STEEL CONSTRUCTION

This leads us to an extremely useful intermediate path between true hard-chine and round-bilge construction. The hard corner, where the topsides and the bottom plate meet, can be replaced with a split pipe or a large-radius rolled plate. Such plates can be rolled to spec at a mill with rolling equipment, cut to moderately short lengths fore-n-aft, and then trucked to the building site, where they are welded in place to form the soft chine. Also, the slight convexity or concavity can be worked into steel along the topsides and bottom without special forming equipment using the $^1/_{40}$ rule and—properly faired—such a hull is essentially true round bilged specifically designed for easy construction in steel. Not surprisingly, this method is called *radius-chine construction*.

The pre-rolled bilge (chine) plates cannot be bent in the fore-n-aft direction, so they must be installed in many small segments, usually starting midships and working alternately fore-n-aft.

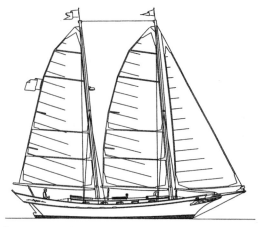

Papoo, a 51-foot (14.4 m) radius-chine steel pinky schooner

A Radius-Chine Example

The drawings show the author's radius-chine steel design, *Papoo*, a 51-foot (14.4 m) length-on-deck steel pinky schooner displacing 30 tons. Her sections show what a sweet round-bilge hull shape can be achieved with radius-chines combined with small amounts of convexity elsewhere. You can also see how the hard-chine hull design is converted to a radius-chine hull. On this hull, portions of the forefoot and after-end of the underbody do have considerable twist to the plate—it's not at all developable. In these regions, plate will need to be fitted in several triangular wedges of steel, heated as required and pulled in to the frames.

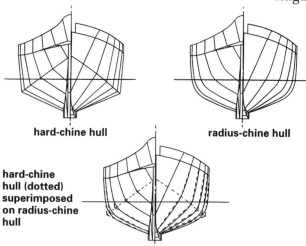

hard-chine hull   **radius-chine hull**

hard-chine hull (dotted) superimposed on radius-chine hull

Radius chine and hard chine compared

Developable and Radius-Chine Aluminum
Of course, any hull form that makes construction easier in steel makes it easier still in aluminum. Hard-chine, developable-surface hulls are common in aluminum but are far less necessary. Remember that usually a developable- or conic-surface hard-chine hull is somewhat less than the ideal form for best performance or seakindliness; however, with good design, the losses can be slight indeed. Still, for aluminum hard-chine planing hulls, it makes good sense to design substantial portions of the hull topsides and superstructure developable simply to reduce labor. Here, there is no compromise in performance, although occasionally there can be in appearance. Even the entire underbody can be developable, but again, often at some slight performance loss.

LINE-HEATING OF STEEL: FULL COMPOUND CURVATURE IN STEEL
The general belief is that true round-bilge steel construction requires heavy bending and forming equipment, furnaces, and other expensive machinery. Although such equipment can be used, it is not required and may not even be the quickest way to form compound-curved shell plates. Instead, a technique known as *line-heating* can be employed.

Line-heating uses the distortion caused be the heat of welding or by a welding torch to deliberately shrink the plate into exactly the compound curvature required. Basically, when you heat a portion of steel and it cools, it shrinks at that location. If you take a welding torch and pass it in a line down the length of a plate fairly quickly, it will heat the surface considerably, but—because you were moving fast—the heat will not penetrate fully through the plate. A section cut instantaneously through the hot plate would show a triangle of heat perhaps 1 inch (25 mm) wide at the torch surface, tapering to nearly zero at the opposite side. When the heated line cools, it shrinks, drawing the plate together. (Actually, it puckers in the top—surface—center, which draws the surface material together.)

Because a wider band was heated at the surface, it draws together more than does the side opposite the torch, which experienced little heat. The result is that the plate has bent or curled up slightly at right angles to the torch line. Repeating the process in parallel lines—closer together or farther apart as required—can introduce a great amount of controlled curvature into the plate with no force or heavy equipment. The depth of the curve in the plate is termed *backset*.

Compound Curvature with Line-Heating
If you ran the torch at right angles, in a cross, the plate would curl in both directions and give you compound curvature. If you wanted a plate curved convexly around the fore-n-aft axis and concavely around the transverse axis (e.g., at a garboard), you would turn the plate over and run the torch at a right angle to the curve direction on the opposing side. These

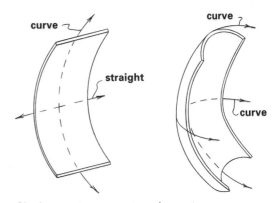

Single curvature, compound curvature

plates are called *saddle plates* because they vaguely resemble saddles.

Shrinking Plates with Line-Heating

Running the torch slowly along the plate allows the heat to penetrate evenly through its thickness. This contracts the plate at right angles to the torch line with little curvature. With practice—using varying torch speeds and directions, running lines closer together and farther apart and at differing orientations—a good fitter can make a steel plate match virtually any odd compound-hull shell with amazing precision.

Line-Heating to Curve Frames and Twist Plate

You can run up to four passes over exactly the same line to maximize curvature. You get less effect on each pass, and more than four passes generates virtually no additional bend. Curved frames can also be formed using line-heating. In this case, an equilateral triangle is marked on the web with the wide triangle base at the inside of the curvature. Start the torch at the apex until it gets cherry red, then cool off the apex end; weave the torch back and forth, heating the triangular area in widening passes to the wide edge of the triangle. Running your torch in diagonally crossing lines on opposite sides of a plate generates twist, which will help bend in the forefoot of nondevelopable forefoot plating, as on *Papoo*. For those knowledgeable in line-heating, this would be quicker and fairer than fitting the plate in several smaller triangular sections.

Using Heat and Restraint to Amplify Line-Heating Effects

Combining cold with heat and restraining the edges can further amplify the effects of line-heating. For example, it will help increase the difference in temperature between the torch side and the opposite side of the plate by spraying water on the opposite side during heating. This amplifies the resulting curvature.

Templates for Line-Heating Complex Plates

For relatively simple plates, experienced craftsmen will work to the hull framing, and then pull in the edges to fit. More complex steel hulls require wooden fitting molds made of widely spaced wooden mold frames called *sight-line templates*. The plate can be line-heated to the approximate shape, then placed on the fitting mold to check. Fine adjustments can be made conveniently and accurately on these light molds to get the best possible fit. Yards that do much of this work may fabricate adjustable sight-line templates that can be used repeatedly on different boat projects.

Line-Heating to Remove Distortion

Just as line-heating can form compound-curved plates deliberately (and help with making tight curves even in a single-curved plate), it can also be used to remove distortion from installed plating. Even a basic understanding of line-heating will help you build better, fairer steel hulls. To learn more about line-heating, refer to naval architect Chris Barry's excellent articles published in *Boatbuilder Magazine*.

Line-Heating Cannot Be Used on Aluminum

Aluminum is easy enough to form without line-heating, which is a good thing. Heating aluminum plate in this way causes stresses and weakens the grain structure of the metal. You cannot use line-heating on aluminum.

Structural Arrangement of Metal Hulls

MAKING THIN PLATE RIGID

Although aluminum and especially steel are very stiff—having high moduluses of elasticity compared to wood or FRP—they are so dense or heavy compared to wood and FRP that the hull shell or plating must be very thin to reduce weight. This is acceptable because both aluminum and steel are quite strong and abrasion-resistant, but it sets the background for the design of metal-boat structures. The aim is to create a structure that is strong enough to withstand the loads of service with plate thin enough to keep the boat light. The problem is that such thin plates are bendy. As we've seen, repeated bending reduces strength over time and will cause failure. It is also unsightly, uncomfortable, and noisy.

What we need to do, then, is support the thin hull-shell plate with a framework that divides the plate into panels small enough not to bend excessively under the expected loads. For example—using the identical 3/16-inch (4.75 mm) aluminum plate—a panel, say 10 by 30 inches (250 by 760 mm), will support a pressure loading of 12 psi (82.7 kPa), deflecting just 0.16 inch (4.0 mm) at its center.

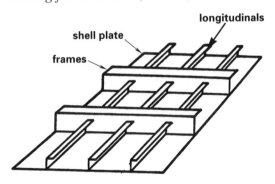

Plate stiffening

A larger panel, say 15 by 40 inches (380 × 1,000 mm), would deflect 0.78 inch (19.8 mm) with the same 12 psi (82.7 kPa) load.

TRANSVERSE FRAMING

Most early metal boats used simple transverse framing. This is exactly analogous to the ribs on traditional plank-on-frame hulls. A welded keel/stem backbone structure (most commonly, a vertical plate called the *centerline vertical keel* [*CVK*]) is laid down and numerous closely spaced transverse frames are attached to it. Transverse deck beams run athwartships at each frame, bulkheads are built in where required, and longitudinal sheer bar and a few longitudinal engine beds/girders round out the principal structure.

Transverse framing works and is covered in the scantling rule that follows. It has the advantage of defining the shape of the hull very tightly with the closely spaced frames, and the numerous frames are molded smaller than more widely spaced frames need to be. This gains some usable volume in the interior for accommodations, machinery, and cargo.

Welded metal-hull construction is, however, a monocoque construction. Transverse framing with few longitudinals is not as structurally efficient in such structures as extensive longitudinal stiffening. Also, longitudinal stiffening produces a fairer hull than all-transverse framing, which has a much greater tendency to get the hungry-horse ripple effect in the shell at each frame.

LONGITUDINAL FRAMING

The alternative to transverse framing is longitudinal framing. Here, widely spaced but deeper molded ring frames (or web frames) support numerous closely spaced longitudinal stringers. This is structurally the most effi-

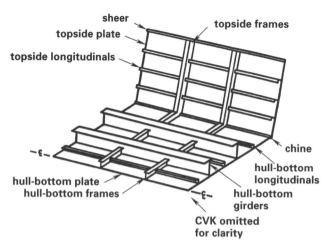

sheer
topside plate
topside longitudinals
topside frames
chine
hull-bottom longitudinals
hull-bottom plate
hull-bottom frames
hull-bottom girders
CVK omitted for clarity

Longitudinally framed chine-hull bottom and topsides

cient framework for a monocoque structure like a welded-boat hull. It is considerably easier to get a smooth, fair shell, and the framework goes together more quickly than using numerous transverse ring frames.

This is because fewer frames have to be cut exactly to shape. The many longitudinals are notched into the ring frames, and are simply bent and swept into place around the hull. The ring frames themselves are set on the same CVK as the transverse-framed hulls. Again, longitudinal en-

Magic Moment, built by Kanter Yachts. This Gerr-designed 52-foot (15.8 m) aluminum ketch clearly shows the transverse frames, flat-bar longitudinals, and CVK.

gine beds/stringers and secondary girders finish off the principal structure. The only disadvantage to full longitudinal framing is that the widely spaced ring frames must be molded quite deep, which steals some valuable volume from the interior.

Another disadvantage for longitudinal framing—for some larger vessels—stems from legal tonnage admeasurement considerations. On such craft, the legally admeasured tonnage must be kept low to ensure that the vessel meets the most economical commercial regulations—under 100 tons; under 300 tons; and the like. The depth of hull for admeasurement is defined to the top of the floors; however—as the rule is interpreted—floors penetrated by longitudinals don't count here. Accordingly, on large boats, when it's necessary to reduce admeasured tonnage, transverse framing may be the best approach.

TRANSVERSE FRAMING WITH LONGITUDINALS

To get the best combination of fairness with maximum interior volume, some builders use closely spaced transverse framing in combination with light longitudinals. The goal of this approach is to reduce the molding (depth) of the frames to increase usable interior volume, while simultaneously achieving the improved fairness and increased structural efficiency offered by the longitudinal stringers. The transverse frames in this construction can be slightly farther apart than if there were no longitudinals at all.

My personal preference is for true longitudinal framing as a first choice, falling back on transverse with longitudinals if the extra volume is necessary. Although perfectly good hulls can be crafted with all transverse framing, I think the drawbacks of slightly reduced longitudinal strength, somewhat increased labor, and a less fair hull make it generally the least attractive.

MIXING FRAMING TYPES

Although it is not common, it is permissible to mix framing types. For example, a trawler might use longitudinal framing in the fore-n-aft thirds of the hull, but all transverse or transverse with longitudinals in the middle third of the boat to maximize the fish-hold volume. If this approach is used, the transitions between the two types of framing must be at essentially full transverse metal bulkheads. In the case of our trawler, these bulkheads would likely form the fore-n-aft walls of the fish hold itself.

TORSIONAL STIFFNESS IN METAL HULLS

Because welded metal hulls are monocoque and because metal is isotropic, metal-hull plating has equal strength fore-n-aft, athwartships, and along the diagonal; this means that they have built-in torsional stiffness. Unlike wood and FRP—where special consideration has to be given to torsional strength either with diagonal strapping or by aligning some fibers or planks at plus and minus 45 degrees—this is not an issue for metal hulls.

FOURTEEN

Aluminum and Steel Design Considerations

*F*or both aluminum and steel boats, the details and procedures used to prevent corrosion, attach hardware, and insulate the hull are critical to longevity and usefulness. These factors must be kept in mind during design and construction, and throughout the process of determining the scantlings.

Corrosion Prevention

Corrosion in metal hulls occurs as three principal types: galvanic corrosion, stray-current corrosion, and rust.

GALVANIC CORROSION/DISSIMILAR METALS

When you connect two different metals or metal alloys together electrically and through an *electrolyte* (in this case, seawater), the electrons from the *less-noble* (i.e., *anodic*) metal will try to flow into the *more-noble* (i.e., *cathodic*) metal. This flow of electrons generates a real measurable force, exactly as you could measure, for example, the force in a stream of water flowing through a pipe from a tank with a high water level (the *anode*) to one with a low water level (the *cathode*). Where electrons are concerned, the force of flow is measured not in pounds but rather in volts, and is often referred to as *potential* (because it measures how great the potential is for a flow to occur).

The Galvanic Series

Of course, this potential is relative. Mild steel holds onto its electrons more strongly than marine aluminum, for example. If these two materials were in contact in seawater, the aluminum would corrode (too fast by half), but not nearly as fast as if the aluminum were in direct contact with silicon bronze, for example. Relatively speaking, silicon bronze holds more tightly to its electrons than mild steel, and far more tightly than marine aluminum.

The key word is *relative*, and the best way to keep tabs on these relative potentials is by listing the voltages of all materials with reference to a single test metal (electrode) in

TABLE 14-1 The Galvanic Series

Anodic or Least-Noble End (Active)	Millivolts (mV)
Magnesium (Mg)	−1,730
Magnesium (2% Manganese [Mn])	−1,670
Magnesium (9% Aluminum [Al], 1% Mn, 1.5% Zinc [An])	−1,580
Galvanized Iron (hot dip)	−1,140
Zinc Electroplating	−1,130
Cadmium (Cd) Zinc Solder (71%/29%)	−1,120
Zinc (Zn)	−1,050
Cadmium (Cd)	−860
Cadmium-Plated Steel (Cd 0.001 in.)	−860
Aluminum (Marine Alloys 5086, 5083, 6061)	−820
Mild or Structural Steel (A36)	−790
Alloy Steel	−740
Aluminum (forged alloy)	−730
Stainless Steel (316, 314, 304, 303, 302; active, oxygen-starved)	−550
Tin (Sn)	−500
Manganese Bronze, CA-464 Naval Brass (58% Cu, 39% Zn, 1% Aluminum, 0.25% Mg)	−450
Naval Brass (60% Copper, 39% Zinc)	−450
Yellow Brass	−450
Admiralty Brass (70% Copper, 29% Zinc)	−360
Copper CA-110 (Cu)	−340
Brass (60% Copper, 40% Zinc)	−330
Gunmetal (88% Copper, +Tin)	−310
Silicon Bronze (96% Cu, 1.5% Silicon)	−260
Tin Bronze	−260
Lead (Pb)	−240
Copper/Nickel (CA-715; 70% Cu, 30% Ni)	−200
Aluminum Bronze (90% Cu, 10% Aluminum)	−150
Stainless Steel (316, 317, 321, 347, 302, 304; passive, oxygenated)	−150
Monel 400 & 500	−110
Titanium (Ti)	−100
Silver (Ag)	−80
Graphite and Carbon Fiber (C)	(+250)
Platinum (Pt)	(+260)
Cathodic or Most-Noble End (Passive)	**Millivolts (mV)**

the electrolyte that you're concerned with—seawater, for our purposes. (The most stable and sensitive electrode material for this use is silver/silver chloride [Ag/AgCl]). The list of relative potentials generated this way comprises the *galvanic series* (see Table 14-1). (Electrical activity increases with temperature, so this is specified as well. Standard galvanic tables usually give voltages at 77°F or 25°C.)

- All measurements taken relative to an Ag/AgCl electrode, at 77°F (25°C).
- The sign of potential applies with the negative (black) probe of the voltmeter connected to the reference electrode, and positive (red) terminal connected to the fitting being tested.
- If using a zinc reference electrode, add 100 mV to the potential. For example, silicon bronze is −260mV; then + 100 mV = −160 mV.
- Average variability of potential is ±40 mV for alloys with iron and/or nickel; ±20 mV for copper-based alloys without nickel.
- Readings 200 to 400 mV more negative (i.e., more anodic) than given indicate the material is protected.
- Readings at or near those given up to 200 mV above those given indicate the material is unprotected and freely corroding.
- Readings over 400 mV more negative than given indicate over-protection.
- Stray-current corrosion is indicated by metals reading more cathodic (i.e., more positive) than indicated on the table.

Selecting Fittings and Alloys Using the Galvanic Series

There are two critically important uses for the galvanic series. First, you should refer to it when installing hardware and selecting alloys.

Make sure the voltage difference between any two metals—in direct contact in seawater—is less than 0.20 volt or 200 millivolts (mV). Metals that are less that 200 mV apart corrode each other fairly slowly and need little additional protection. If you must use two metals farther apart than 200 mV, you need to take steps to protect them, either by insulation or isolation (so they're not in contact) or by using anodes.

In metal hulls, the key is to have no dissimilar metals touching anywhere on the hull, and virtually nowhere in the rest of the boat structure. Stainless-steel hardware can mount directly to aluminum and steel on deck and in the cabin, for example. You can barely get by with some small brass joiner hardware in contact with aluminum on the interior (if and only if it doesn't contact any portion of the principal hull structure) and when there's absolutely no other choice. (Of course, brass, bronze, and stainless are all ideal for joiner hardware that is not in contact with aluminum at all.)

Isolating Bronze Seacocks and Fittings

This means that bronze seacocks must be isolated *exceptionally* well from the hull. In fact, these days, glass-fiber-reinforced-nylon plastic seacocks (sold by Forespar under the Marelon trade name) are approved for use by the ABS and Lloyds, and are recognized by the U.S. Coast Guard. I recommend using these exclusively to avoid any possibility of corrosion. Marelon is currently available in diameters up to 2 inches (50.8 mm) and, being a plastic, it can melt and burn in a fire. Some commercial regulations may demand metal seacocks.

Large engine-water intakes and other high-volume seawater pumps may require

3- or 4-inch (75 or 100 mm) diameters. You must not use ordinary PVC or similar alternate plastic valves for seacocks. Only plastic (and metal, for that matter) valves specifically certified for use as seacocks by Underwriters Laboratories, ABS, or Lloyds are rugged enough. A broken seacock can sink a boat fast. Accordingly, for such large-diameter inlets, solid-bronze seacocks are the only option. (Stainless is too subject to pitting corrosion, and aluminum is too soft.) The bronze seacocks must be insulated from the hull on a plastic or fiberglass pad, and bolted to the hull with stainless through-bolts. The bolts themselves must be isolated from the bronze by spacer tube/sleeves that completely surround each bolt, as well as with a plastic washer/spacer under the stainless washer under the nut on the seacock's interior flange. Similarly, cutless bearings must have fiberglass or plastic shells rather than brass or bronze.

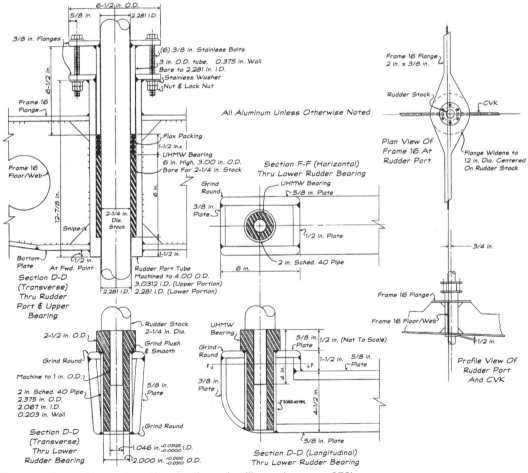

Noncorroding rudder port and bearing (see also illustration on p. 278)

Check Design and Fittings for Potential Corrosion

Careful thought must be given to rudder bearings and all other fittings that may contain dissimilar metals. I recently reviewed the plans of a 60-foot steel motor cruiser that had a dangerous detail for a lower rudder bearing in the rudder skeg. It contained a brass sleeve bearing with stainless-steel ball bearings under the end of the rudder stock to take the axial load. The combination of mild steel, brass, and stainless-steel balls rolling about would create a galvanic nightmare that would destroy this assembly in months, or less. Thordon makes a wide variety of plastic bearings that will not corrode and are water-lubricated. Ultra-high-molecular-weight polyethylene (UHMWPE) also makes an excellent bearing material and a perfect isolator/ spacer material. UHMWPE is strong, tough, very smooth, exceptionally abrasion-resistant, and—of course—totally inert electrically.

Stainless-Steel Hardware and Fittings

Stainless steel is quite useful for both aluminum and mild-steel hulls. Stainless is close enough galvanically not to cause too much of a problem. On aluminum under water, it must still be isolated, but it's the only choice for those rare instances when you must attach fittings or weldments to the aluminum hull below the waterline. (It's far better to fabricate these fittings entirely from aluminum, and usually there's little excuse not to do so.)

On the deck and superstructure, stainless-steel fittings can be bolted directly to the aluminum without problems—using no more than good bedding compounds. Stainless-steel bolts and screws are the standard fastener material for hardware attachment on both aluminum and steel vessels. On steel boats, it is also sometimes practical to weld stainless acorn nuts under the deck and inside the cabin to accept stainless through-bolts. Lightly welded all around, these won't leak and will permit easier removal and refastening without the need for a pair of hands below decks.

Stainless-Steel Inserts for Chafe and Corrosion Resistance on Mild-Steel Boats

On mild-steel hulls, stainless steel offers another option: It can be welded directly into the mild-steel structure using the proper welding rod/electrode (e.g., 309L). You must *not* do this anywhere that will be regularly below the waterline; it will lead to serious corrosion. Still, on the deck and cabin, stainless welded into the structure offers many advantages. Insert plates and riser weldments (e.g., winch bases) of stainless can be built in around areas of high chafe, such as at chocks, around winches, windlasses, mast bases, turning blocks, cleats, and hawseholes. You can even weld stainless-steel rod or heavy-wall tube around the interior perimeter of hawsehole openings.

You can also weld in stainless-steel plates or plugs in areas where you may have to fasten and unfasten hardware and fittings fairly regularly. The stainless itself can be drilled and taped for the bolts, which are then far less likely to freeze, and can be removed and refastened numerous times without losing the thread. All these welded-in stainless-steel areas should be painted to match the surrounding surface; however, when chafe occurs, you won't get the corrosion and rust weeps you would get on the basic mild steel of the hull proper.

The Best Stainless-Steel Alloys

All stainless steel is not created equal. For use below the waterline, only 316L (L for low carbon) steel should be used. All other stainless is too prone to localized pitting corrosion. (Even 316L can suffer from this is some cases.) The first choice for all marine stainless fittings is 316L, but it is the most expensive and sometimes hard to locate. On deck, 304 and 302 stainless is acceptable, although 302 is the most prone to light-brown rust discoloration and cosmetic pitting.

Isolate Wood from Metal to Prevent Corrosion

Wood also must be isolated from metal hulls. Moisture will collect under the wood, and the acids and oils in the wood mixed with the salt water generate poultice corrosion that can be quite severe. The solution is to bed the wood very well before fastening, and fasten it over a painted hull surface. At a minimum, the wood also must be painted or varnished on its mating surface before fastening it down. Better still is to saturate the wood with three coats of marine epoxy before fastening it down on bedding compound. Again, stainless is more resistant to this and, on mild-steel hulls, it can make sense to weld in stainless steel under wooden fittings and rails; however, this is expensive and not required.

Anodes Protect by Flooding with Electrons

After a good paint job and avoiding contact of dissimilar metals, anodes are the next line of defense against corrosion. There's a nice feature about anodic metals, if you use them correctly: as long as they're losing electrons, all the other more-noble (i.e., more-cathodic) metals they're connected to are protected from corrosion. For example, our *Aluma-Naught* had bronze seacocks. Even though you took care to isolate the bronze, there remains a possibility of electrical interaction. In this case, electrons would be tumbling from the less-noble aluminum to the bronze. *AlumaNaught's* hull would then quickly waste away near the seacocks. If a zinc anode were attached to the hull, however, its electrons would—roughly speaking—tumble toward both the aluminum and the bronze (it's far more anodic than both). It would flood the system with zinc electrons—again, roughly speaking. (Other anodic metals, such as magnesium and aluminum, are occasionally used as anodes. Zinc, however, offers the best trade-off between cost, reliability, and ease of manufacture. It's the standard marine-anode material.)

Making Your Zincs Work

It takes some smarts to make zincs work.

1. *You must install zincs to protect your boat's metal fittings or hull.*
2. *The zincs must be in tight, clean electrical contact with the metal components they're protecting. (If they're not electrically connected to the bonding system or metal hull, they're useless.)*
3. *The surface of the zincs must be exposed to the water. You can't paint a zinc anode—ever! You want it exposed and you want it to corrode. (They're not called "sacrificial zincs" for nothing!)*

Anode Installation

Anodes should be installed on all metal hulls to protect for corrosion. They even help protect against rust on steel hulls.

A converted army T-boat, this 60-foot (18.3 m), 100-ton steel tug was gutted and converted to a live-aboard home to the author's design. The numerous anodes are clearly visible. (Courtesy Sam Haigh)

It's possible to weld lugs projecting from some anodes directly to the hull. This, however, makes replacing anodes a difficult business. A better approach is to weld bolts to the hull to mate with the anode's fastener holes. Replacing anodes is then as simple as turning a wrench.

On aluminum craft, the best practice is to weld either a backing or doubler plate to the exterior of the hull, or a thick insert plate into the hull at the anode location. (The doubler or insert plate should be of the same aluminum alloy as the surrounding plate. The doubler thickness should be approximately 1.5 times the fastening-bolt diameter; the insert plate about 2.2 times the bolt diameter. Both should match the footprint of the anode or be slightly larger.) Drill the doubler for stainless threaded inserts and use standard 316-stainless hex-head machine bolts to fasten the anode. Be certain to install lock washers under each nut. Without these, engine vibration and corrosion will loosen the nuts.

To ensure good electrical contact and a firm mounting base, proper anodes are cast around a steel-bar core. Fastening bolts penetrate and land on this core. For aluminum hulls, the best practice is to use anodes with aluminum cores.

Amount of Zinc for Metal Hulls

A good estimate of the anode required can be made from the following formulas.

FORMULA 14-2

Steel Anode Quantity

For one year of protection of a steel hull with an average (i.e., less than perfect) paint job:

Steel-Hull Required Anode Weight (lbs.) = hull wetted surface (sq. ft.) ÷ 16.75

Steel-Hull Required Anode Weight (kg) = hull wetted surface (m²) ÷ 3.43

For two years of protection, use twice as much anode. For one year of protection for bare metal, use 2.5 times as much.

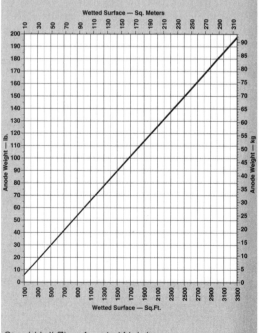

Steel-Hull Zinc Anode Weight

FORMULA 14-3

Aluminum Anode Quantity

For aluminum hulls, anodes are better selected by their surface area than by their weight.

For one year of protection:

Aluminum-Hull Required Anode Surface Area (sq. ft. or m²) = hull wetted surface (sq. ft. or m²) ÷ 220

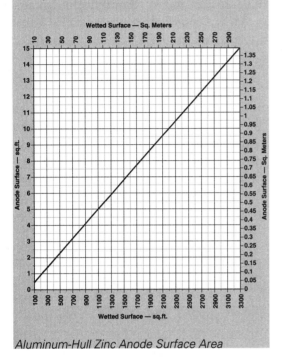

Aluminum-Hull Zinc Anode Surface Area

Remember, these formulas give estimates. Boats that operate in warm or highly polluted water may need more protection. Vessels that operate in cold clean waters can often get by with less.

FORMULA 14-4

Steel and Aluminum Anode Location

Anodes should be roughly evenly spaced on the hull under the waterline starting from the transom. Generally, they should be located about two-thirds of the waterline half-beam out from the centerline, port and starboard. On larger hulls, there is an additional anode pair aft, about one-third of the waterline half-beam out from the centerline, or mounted on the sides of the keel. Find the total amount of anodes you need from the previous formulas, then locate them roughly as follows (again, with all measurements starting at the transom):

25 Feet (7.5 m) and Under: 2: 1 each, port and starboard; one-third of WL

25 to 35 Feet (7.5 to 11 m): 4: 2 each, port and starboard; one-fifth of WL, and then 2 at 55% of WL

35 to 50 Feet (11 to 15 m): 6: 3 each, port and starboard; 2 at one-sixth of WL; 2 at 40% of WL; and 2 at 65% WL

50 to 65 Feet (15 to 20 m): 8: 6 of which are the same as for 35 to 50 feet (15 to 20 m), but with 2 additional closer to the centerline, at 14% of WL

65 to 85 Feet (20 to 26 m): 10: 8 of which are about evenly spaced, port and starboard, at about 17% of WL length O.C.; plus 2 at about 12% of WL, closer to the centerline

85 to 100 Feet (26 to 30 m): 12: 10 of which are about evenly spaced, port and starboard, at about 14% of WL length O.C.; plus 2 at about 11% of WL, closer to the centerline

Additional Anodes

Anodes should be installed on the rudder, sized according to the rudder's surface area.

Smaller rudders can have a single anode on one side; larger rudders should use one each, port and starboard. A collar-type shaft anode should be installed on the propeller shaft. Alternately, a commutator-type internal shaft brush can be used to contact the rudder, and then connect to the through-bolt and external anode on the hull bottom or keel side. Sea chests, bow thrusters, and similar recesses open to the sea each require their own small anode, which must be easily accessible and easy to replace.

FORMULA 14-5

Estimating Hull Surface

The boat's naval architect should be able to provide you with the exact wetted surface area of your hull. If this information is not available, however, you can guesstimate the hull's wetted surface as follows:

Area, in sq. ft. or m² = C × WL (sq. ft. or m²) × (Beam [sq. ft. or m²] + Draft [sq. ft. or m²])

C values are

1.2 for heavy-displacement tugs, dredgers, tankers

0.75 for medium-displacement vessels (i.e., most displacement yachts and charter vessels)

0.50 for light-displacement vessels (i.e., planing hulls, racing yachts)

Corrosion Monitors and Bonding

Larger metal boats, especially those with extensive electrical systems, should have a corrosion monitor installed. Corrosion monitors allow you to keep tabs on *AlumaNaught*'s hull potential, enabling you to be sure that its zincs are working properly, know when they need replacement, and identify overprotection and stray-current corrosion.

On still larger craft, the isolated fittings (e.g., bronze seacocks) should be connected to their own completely separate and isolated secondary internal-bonding system. The bonding conductors on these secondary systems must be insulated. Even the zinc anodes for this separate system must be completely isolated from the metal hull. Dual-metal corrosion monitors are available to monitor the hull anodes and to monitor the isolated secondary-bonding system. A reliable monitor, such as that made by Electrocatalytic of Union, New Jersey, is important.

STRAY-CURRENT CORROSION

Stray-current corrosion is the most dangerous form of corrosion to which any metal boat can be subjected. The voltages generated by dissimilar metals alone in salt water are measured in millivolts. Stray currents from faulty wiring—on board or from shore power—can reach more than 100 volts. Not only do these high voltages pose a serious electrocution hazard (particularly AC current), but they also can eat away large portions of metal hulls in just weeks, sometimes days (even at just a few volts, as compared to millivolts for galvanic corrosion). It is vital that the electrical system on all metal boats complies precisely with American Boat and Yacht Council Standards. There is just no point in building a strong beautiful hull only to have it eaten away by stray electrical currents.

Vital Isolation Transformer

All metal boats (except small runabouts, canoes, and skiffs) should be fitted with an isolation transformer at their shore-power inlet. If properly wired and installed, the isolation transformer nearly guarantees that faulty shore-side wiring cannot somehow short to the hull. Failure to install an isolation transformer is asking for serious trouble the first time your *AlumaNaught* or *Iron Maiden* spends a few days at an incorrectly wired dock—and there are plenty of those around. Simple galvanic isolators help in this regard, and may be adequate for metal runabouts with shore-side connection to a battery charger, but they're not sufficient insurance for larger metal boats. At this writing, the only *marine* UL-approved isolation transformer being manufactured comes from Charles Marine Products (Rolling Meadows, IL).

Isolate Electric Wiring from Hull

Great care must be taken with the DC system as well to ensure that it's entirely isolated. All wiring, both positive and the return negative wires, must be fully isolated from the hull. The sole exception is that the DC negative bus must be bonded to the hull. This is best accomplished as follows:

For aluminum hulls, weld a $^3/_8$-× 4-in. (10 × 100 mm) aluminum lug to convenient frame or hull stringer. Bolt $^1/_4$-× 4-in. (6.4 × 100 mm) stainless flat bar to this lug, with two $^1/_4$-in.-diameter (6.5 mm) stainless bolts, with lock washers. Attach a 00 DC ground cable, from the negative bus, to the stainless bar (at least 3 in. or 75 mm clear from aluminum), with a stainless bolt, with lock washer. Paint all bolts, the stainless bar, adjacent aluminum, and the terminal fitting of the 00 cable with three coats of marine varnish to seal out moisture. For a steel hull, weld the $^1/_4$-inch stainless flat bar directly to the hull framing.

At first glance, isolation of the DC system seems relatively easy to accomplish, but there are many potential pitfalls and hidden paths to short the negative return to the hull

structure. One of the most commonly overlooked paths is the engine block. Most automotive alternators (commonly found on many marine engines) use the engine block as the negative/ground. This can short the negative to the hull through the engine-mount bolts. Be certain to install isolated-negative-return marine alternators for engines and generators in metal boats. Then, go the next step and float the engine on rubber mounts, with a flexible rubber coupling to the shaft. This further isolates the engine from potential shorts to the hull. Another item often overlooked is engine instruments. Many of the standard senders also use the engine block for negative return. Again, be sure to use only senders that have isolated negative returns. Still another potential path for shorts is hose with embedded wire reinforcement. Should the wires wear through and make contact at both ends, again you have a potential electrical path to the hull.

AC Bonded to DC Bus

Like the DC electric system, the AC system must be completely isolated from the hull and from the DC system itself. Once again there is one, and only one, mandatory exception: The AC system green wire ground—from the isolation transformer (or the galvanic isolator on small boats)—*must* be bonded to DC negative bus. AC wiring must not make electrical contact with any other portion of the hull or the DC wiring.

RUST

Rust and excessive weight are the two central drawbacks to steel hulls. Both can be addressed to some degree, but never eliminated. It is difficult to say which is the more serious problem, but rust is the cause of more maintenance and expense throughout the life of the vessel than any other consideration in steel hulls. (Aluminum, as we've seen, doesn't rust at all.)

Basically, rust is the most common byproduct of the corrosion of most ferrous alloys, including boatbuilding steels. It is principally hydrated ferric oxide, but this varies slightly depending on the conditions and the alloy. Moisture and oxygen are the only two requirements for the rusting process to start. Salt increases the moisture's chemical efficiency at transmitting ions, and so considerably accelerates the oxidation reaction that produces rust, as do warm temperatures, which also encourage chemical activity. In other words, the environment most boats operate in is the best possible for making rust and the worst possible for preventing it! Given the slightest opportunity, rust *will* occur and *will* spread extensively.

Paint: The First Line of Defense against Rust

There is only one real preventative for rust in steel hulls: seal the steel away from the environment—from the moisture, the oxygen, and the salt. A superb paint system is critical. Reducing moisture and humidity in the hull interior also helps. Insulation assists here, as do various spray-on surfacing agents.

Because rust is a chemical reaction involving the exchange of electrons, anodes that flood the steel hull with their own electrons also help prevent rust. The anode's electrons flood the steel and combine with the ions in the salt-water/salt-air environment before the steel's own electrons can. This is the principle behind galvanizing, and hot-dip galvanized iron and steel fittings have a tolerable (although no better) life expectancy on boats.

Simply electroplated or painted-on zinc coatings (a cheap galvanizing) aren't up to marine applications.

Zinc or Aluminum Spraying (Galvanizing) Steel Hulls

Some builders essentially galvanize their hulls by sandblasting them to white metal and then flame-spraying on molten zinc or molten aluminum. A full paint job is applied over this zinc or aluminum surface. This can be effective but does have some drawbacks. First, it adds cost. Second, the flame-sprayed zinc or aluminum surface is roughish, with a faint stipple. You can't grind it smooth because you would remove the protection you just added. Accordingly, such hulls should be finished workboat-rough with matte paint. Third, when the paint and zinc or aluminum coating underneath is scratched through to the bare steel, that location can suffer accelerated local attack that usually shows up first as bubbles or blisters in the paint. On mild steel, sprayed-on aluminum is less reactive than zinc (it's closer on the galvanic series) and, therefore, is somewhat less likely to promote local attack. My opinion is that a high-quality paint finish inside and out, along with good insulation, sufficient anodes, and proper interior drainage, is the best approach. Using welded-in stainless-steel inserts at high-chafe areas helps still more.

Painting

On steel hulls, paint is the most essential barrier to rust. There are many paint systems, and most work well if carefully applied according to the manufacturer's instructions. The key to a long-lasting paint job on new steel construction is preparation. Spare no expense and reasonable labor on this—it will pay back many times over. Sandblast to near-white or pure-white metal, prime immediately—before there's any chance of surface contamination, and paint as soon as possible. Although there are a number of good paint systems available, I believe modern epoxy paints are the best for protecting steel.

For aluminum, the same recommendations apply. Although paint is really optional above the waterline, it is used on the overwhelming majority of boats. Even on aluminum, a good paint surface helps protect against both galvanic and stray-current corrosion by isolating the aluminum from the electrolyte (i.e., seawater) that carries half the "current"; that is, the ions needed for chemical reactions to occur.

Again, sandblasting to bare metal—as with steel—is one approach: Wash with fresh water, blow dry, and prime, followed by the fairing putty and topcoats as soon as possible. This is the key, along with religiously following the paint manufacturer's instructions. However, sandblasting aluminum is tricky. It is soft enough that too much pressure or too much flow will erode a significant thickness of metal. It will also leave a wavy pitted surface. Although you can use regular sand, the best "sandblasting" material for aluminum is crushed walnut shells or plastic beads, which are used in fine auto-refinishing and aren't excessively costly. Being softer, they don't pose the problems that harder silica sand does, although care is still needed with aluminum's soft surface.

Many builders prefer to prep aluminum hulls for paint with grinding rather than sandblasting. They grind the whole surface clean (and to give it tooth) with 24- to 36-grit disks. The bare metal is washed and/or blown clean, and then painted with an etching solution. The prime coat must be applied within an hour or two. Fairing putty follows on top of the primer as needed. During hull fairing—for both aluminum and steel—care must be taken to quickly touch up any bare metal that is exposed through the primer. The topcoats finish off the job.

Mud: Fairing Compound

Most yacht builders will expostulate at length about how little mud or fairing compound they use on their beautifully faired hulls and superstructures. Although there are a few exceptional boats and a few exceptional builders, in general I don't believe these claims and neither should you. I once had the opportunity to examine a damaged portion of a superstructure built by one of the finest luxury-yacht yards in the world. In some places, there was nearly $3/4$ inch (19 mm) of mud on the cabin roof! This was and still is a good builder, and clearly there had been a problem with distortion in this one location. Still, such problems occur—to greater or lesser degree—on most welded boats.

Many workboats, of course, don't bother with fairing. Some visible ripples, kinks, and dents are unimportant—only performance and economy count. On yachts and highly finished workboats—before you finish painting—you will need to fair your hull with mud. This is normal. The best fairing putties, in my opinion, are epoxy-based. Screeding on the mud, letting it cure, sighting along it, and long-boarding and hand-sanding are time-consuming, and these processes must be repeated over and over. If you're after a truly perfect, mirror-smooth finish, the labor involved can almost equal the labor in assembling the hull. You have to plan accordingly. You also need to allow for the weight of the mud. My experience has been that a good builder, obtaining an average but not perfect finish, uses fairing compound about equal to 3 percent of the weight of the aluminum hull structure, and about 2 percent of the weight of a steel hull structure (not the full displacement of the boat and not including deck or superstructure).

Construction Details

THREADED INSERTS FOR REMOVABLE FASTENERS

We previously discussed welded-in stainless-steel plates to accept fasteners and reduce chafe. For both steel and aluminum, stainless-steel threaded inserts are the best way to install bolts and screws of every type. In steel, the stainless threaded insert prevents corrosion and freezing of the fastener. In aluminum, the inserts additionally increase holding power in this softer material. All structural bolts that are not through-bolted should be bolted into stainless threaded in-

Stainless threaded insert. (Courtesy Camloc Fasteners)

serts. Helicoils or coil-thread inserts seem to be the easiest to install and have the greatest gripping power, but other forms of stainless threaded inserts are acceptable.

VOID AREAS IN HULLS

A conundrum on most metal hulls is what to do with the void areas in the keel, hollow rudders, under tanks, and so on. Traditional practice was to fill voids in the keel with bitumastic. It can be spread onto clean surfaces in layers of $1/2$ to 1 inch thick (12.5 mm to 25 mm), and it adheres very well. Massive solid buildups of bitumastic were often used to fill in deep areas of the keel. The buildups were applied in patterns and sloped to create a sump. The solid, hard, tarry mass lasts years and usually sticks tenaciously enough not to allow water to run in and collect between it and the inside of the plating. However, bitumastic is heavy and oily, and can have a noticeable odor. A lighter and more modern alternative is pour-in-place foam and various special filler chemicals.

However, there are difficulties with all these nearly permanent resilient materials in hard-to-get-at spots. You can't inspect under them, and—if you need to make repairs—you can't weld in these areas because the stuff smokes and/or burns. Before any work can be done, you have to get down into these inaccessible regions and remove the tenacious gooey mass—a nightmare.

Empty Voids Are Best

My preference for void spaces in the bilge and keel is to seal them off with a cover plate welded watertight all around. Install an access plate or two in the cover plate, in areas that are relatively easy to get at, using the same details as for a removable tank-manhole cover.

The access hole need only be a 6- or 7-inch (150 or 180 mm) clear opening (larger is better, if there's room). In this way, you can take a flashlight and a small mirror, remove the access panel, and inspect the interior to see if there are any leaks. A further refinement is a screw-in drain plug through the hull at the low point of the void space; this can be added later when any repairs are needed. By keeping the void space empty, you're free to make weld repairs with ease.

Oil-Filled Voids

On steel boats, some argument can be made for filling the void spaces with oil. The idea is that corrosion can't occur. Still, if the void space is sealed watertight (including the access panel—as it should be), the oxygen required for rust and corrosion will be quickly used up and further corrosion will be retarded. Fill and drain plugs should be installed at the high and low points if oil-fill is employed. (To comply with environmental regulations, only biodegradable vegetable oil should be used.) Keep in mind that oil-fill in the void spaces in the keel adds weight. Although this weight is low down, it does sink the boat lower and reduce performance potential to some degree.

A stronger case can be made for filling hollow-steel rudders and similar small fins or appendages with vegetable oil. These areas are difficult to inspect, and the weight of the oil is negligible. Still, no oil and a simple drain plug at the low point are really sufficient. Make it a practice to remove the plug at every haul-out. The void area should be bone dry. If any water leaks out, there is nothing to remove before welding a repair, not even drained oil. The leak can usually be located quickly by screwing an air-hose fitting into the drain-plug opening, pressurizing the void area (1.5 psi [10.3 kPa] is ample), then spraying the exterior with soapy water and looking for telltale bubbles.

On aluminum hulls, I see no reason to use any oil or a more solid void fill. Simple watertight cover plates with watertight inspection-access holes and outside drain plugs handle all eventualities and do not hinder repair.

INSULATION AND INTERIOR COATINGS

Because metal is such a superb conductor of heat and sound, extensive insulation of the hull, deck, and superstructure is required for comfortable interior accommodations. Without insulation, veritable rivers of condensation collect on the inside of the plating and run down into the bilge. The resulting high humidity promotes decay and damages wiring and electrical equipment. Even worse, on steel hulls it greatly accelerates rusting on the inside, where it's most difficult to inspect, locate, and repair. Finally, without insulation, the cabin spaces would be nearly impossible to heat in winter or cool in summer; they'd be noisy too.

Insulating the inside of a metal hull is a laborious and finicky job. Some builders are inclined to skimp here, but it must be done correctly, with patient attention to detail.

TYPES OF INSULATION

Standard insulation is either closed-cell foam, fiberglass batts or panels, or cork sheets. Of these, only fiberglass is truly fire-resistant and, therefore, is my first choice for safety. Nevertheless, foams are acceptable and have been installed in most of my metal designs. Cork is somewhat fire-retardant, especially compared to some of the foams available. It works well but is heavier than most foam or fiberglass. Cork is also a natural material and is subject to degradation from age and fungal attack.

Advantages of Spray-on Foam

The major question with insulating the hull interior is whether to use spray-in-place urethane foam or to apply sheets of material—either foam, fiberglass, or cork. Spray-in foam is difficult to blow onto the hull evenly. For this reason, it should only be installed by a professional with the right equipment and much experience. Its big advantages are maximum coverage and adhesion. If sprayed onto a steel hull correctly, the foam will adhere quite tenaciously and protect it well from both air and moisture—a good rust-inhibitor. You'll practically need a chisel to peel off the foam.

Drawbacks of Spray-on Foam

Spray-on urethane foam does give the maximum insulation effect because it covers every little nook and cranny, and can be built up quite thick. Its drawbacks are considerable, though. Spray-on foam burns fiercely and gives off very toxic gases. It should be coated with fire-retardant paint; however, even with protective paint, it can still burn. It also absorbs odors, which are impossible to eliminate, and can become quite unpleasant. Most intractable of all is that once in place, you can't weld anywhere near the foam without starting a real conflagration. One excellent boatbuilder I worked with lost a boat nearing completion in his shop in just this way. Any future welding repairs will require the difficult and messy job of scraping off this tenacious messy foam—all of which is inside,

behind joinerwork, and nearly impossible to reach.

INSULATION APPLIED IN SHEETS

Because of the drawbacks of spray-on foam, I prefer to insulate the hull with removable sheets/panels of foam or fiberglass. In this case, a steel hull should be blasted to near-white metal inside, primed immediately, and painted with a good epoxy paint. Then the foam or fiberglass sheets are glued in place between the frames and stringers. The stringers themselves should be covered with strips of foam glued over them in a U shape. Stringers with relatively low molding heights can simply be covered by running the sheets over them and pressing down as tightly as possible at the corners. Only the tops of the inside faces of the frames are left exposed. Yes, these bare spots do transmit some heat, but the square footage exposed is very small. (Aluminum hulls are not blasted or painted on the interior; rather, they are simply cleaned to ensure a good glue bond.)

These foam sheets are available from various manufacturers with excellent adhesive systems. They can be peeled off for repairs and—unlike spray-on foam, which is generally applied in one big job—the sheets can be added piecemeal during construction, permitting some portions of the boat to be insulated and finished off while other areas are still undergoing welding work. Fiberglass insulation panels are so fire-resistant that they actually help retard the spread of a blaze. All these insulating sheets/panels are available with mylar or aluminized mylar interior surfaces, which make the insulation much more resistant to absorbing odors and much easier to keep clean.

LOCATION OF INSULATION AND INTERIOR PAINT

In all cases, the insulation should start from the waterline, extend up the topsides, run under the deck, up the inside of the cabin sides, and under the cabin roofs. This should be done wherever there will be accommodations. Forepeaks, lazarettes, and cargo spaces need not be insulated, but—for steel—they must be painted. Aluminum requires no interior paint, although I like to paint the interior of aluminum hulls in the machinery spaces. This protects the aluminum from dropped pieces of copper or steel that might cause local corrosion inside, and it gives the compartment a more finished look. The inside of the hull topsides in the engine compartment should be insulated with foam or fiberglass. This is really a living space; you have to work in it regularly. What's more, without this insulation, the bare metal hull transmits and reflects engine noise fiercely.

ATTACHING THICK SOUND INSULATION

Insulation in machinery spaces also doubles as vital sound insulation. On larger boats, foam 3 to 6 inches (75 to 150 mm) may be used under the sole and along bulkheads to reduce noise. These thicker sheets can be held in place with inexpensive spiked fittings that have small base plates glued onto the hull or bulkhead. The insulation is jammed down on the spikes that penetrate it. Then the spikes are turned down (almost like a clench nail) over interior pads (similar to rivet roves). Again, I prefer fiberglass (mineral wool) insulation for its fire resistance but often end up using foam to please the builder because it's less expensive.

Extensive sound insulation in the engine room (still under construction) of the author's Imagine *design.*

DO NOT INSULATE THE BILGES

Never run insulation below the waterline. Any bilge water—and there's sure to be some eventually—will splash up onto the foam or fiberglass, where it will cause mildew, fungus, and a repulsive stench.

PAINTING THE INTERIOR OF STEEL-HULL BILGES

Except as desired in engine spaces and such, the bilge in aluminum hulls can be left bare. The bilge in steel hulls must be sandblasted, primed, and coated with epoxy paint. A more expensive but even tougher alternative is to paint the bilge, or the most inaccessible portions of it, with Isotrol, POR-15, or Pettit Rustlok 6980. These are thick specialty coatings for steel and usually contain aluminum or zinc powders for anodic protection. Although costly, they are remarkably tenacious and retard rust even better than ordinary paint.

INSTALLING BALLAST

Ballast is installed on almost all sailboats and on many displacement powerboats as well. Lead is—by far—the best material, and the only one acceptable for aluminum (steel or iron would cause corrosion). The ballast is almost always installed inside a hollow keel. Never pour all the lead in in molten form. The tremendous heat will distort any metal hull beyond salvaging. Instead, lay in as much of the ballast as possible in pigs. Then fill the gaps and corners with molten lead poured down around the pigs. On deep ballast keels, it may be necessary to do this in two or three layers to ensure maximum penetration and to reduce heat.

Scrap-Iron Ballast

Steel boats can also be ballasted with scrap iron. This is not as dense as lead, so its center of gravity will be higher, but it is cheaper. A mixture of large scrap bar stock with smaller steel shot and scrap nuts and bolts can be set in the bilge. It can be locked in place with a slurry of cement. Alternatively, you can lock it in place with a low-exotherm epoxy resin or bitumastic, but these have the drawback of being flammable and impeding future welding repairs.

External Bolted-on Ballast

It is possible to bolt cast-iron external ballast to steel hulls with stainless-steel bolts, although all stainless bolts are subject to pitting corrosion, even 316L. Nitronic 50 (Aquamet 22) is the best ballast-bolt material for steel. Bolt diameters should be determined using Formula 5-12. Lead external ballast can also be bolted externally to the bottom of aluminum or steel boats. Great care must be taken to isolate both the ballast and the bolts from the hull.

Use an external isolation pad between the entire ballast keel and hull bottom. It should be made of E-glass laminated in epoxy resin and vacuum-bagged to ensure that it's bubble-free. Similar isolation pads should be installed under the stainless-steel backing plates in the bilge (under the keel-bolt nuts), and sleeve isolation spacers are necessary around the bolts themselves. Except in the case of very high performance sailboats, there's little reason to use external ballast on most metal hulls.

LIGHTER-WEIGHT SUPERSTRUCTURES ON STEEL BOATS

As discussed previously, steel is so heavy that it is quite common to use wood, aluminum, or FRP deckhouses and superstructures fastened to a steel hull and deck. This reduces overall weight, and—more important—lowers the center of gravity for proper stability characteristics. FRP superstructures pose no corrosion problems, and wood only minor ones (nicely handled by proper bedding and fastening). The scantlings of the superstructure—whatever the material—can be determined using the scantling rule appropriate for that material.

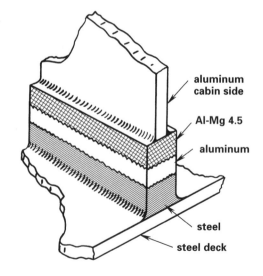

aluminum cabin side

Al-Mg 4.5

aluminum

steel

steel deck

Triclad

JOINING ALUMINUM SUPERSTRUCTURES TO STEEL HULLS

Joining an aluminum superstructure to a steel hull must be done so that the aluminum doesn't corrode, however. The old method was to weld a vertical flat bar of steel to the steel deck and then bolt the aluminum superstructure sides to that, insulating it with neoprene (or something similar), plus insulating each bolt with spacer sleeves. This is time-consuming and subject to degradation when the insulating material ages. This method has not proven very satisfactory over the long term.

The modern method uses a DeltaStrip or DeltaCouple from DuPont, also sold as Tri-Clad in Europe. This special strip is steel on one half and aluminum on the other, explosively bonded to an inert central core. Simply weld the steel lower half to the steel deck and the aluminum superstructure to the aluminum upper portion of the DeltaCouple.

STAINLESS FLAT-BAR JOINT BETWEEN ALUMINUM AND MILD STEEL

Another useful method is to weld a vertical flat bar of steel (just as with the traditional approach) to the deck, but use stainless instead. Then the aluminum superstructure is bolted to the stainless directly with stainless bolts. Ordinary bedding compound is all that is necessary to seal it.

FORMULA 14-6

Stainless Joint between Mild Steel and Aluminum

Stainless Vertical-Flat-Bar Thickness = 1.33 × steel-deck-plate thickness; not less than $^3/_{16}$ inch (4.75 mm)

Stainless Vertical-Flat-Bar Height = 12 × thickness; not less than $2^3/_4$ inches (70 mm)

The aluminum cabin-side plate's bottom edge must be 1 inch (25 mm) above the mild-steel deck for all but the smallest boats, and never less than $^3/_4$ inch (19 mm) even on small boats.

Stainless Through-Bolt Diameter = 1.5 × stainless-bar thickness

Stainless Through-Bolt Spacing, O.C. = 16 × bolt diameter; not more than 10 inches (250 mm)

If, for example, our steel *Iron Maiden* had $^3/_{16}$-inch steel deck plate and we were attaching an aluminum cabin to it, then its vertical stainless bar would be $^1/_4$ inch (6.4 mm) thick and 3 inches (75 mm) high; the through-bolts would be $^3/_8$ inch (9.5 mm) in diameter, spaced 6 inches (150 mm) O.C.

Plate Thickness and Weights

You can select plate thickness only from standard stock. Tables 14-7 and 14-8 give the common stock sizes and weights of steel and aluminum sheet or plate.

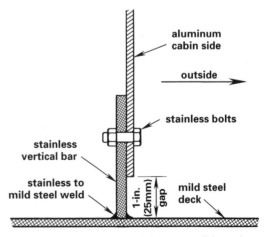

Stainless flat-bar joint: aluminum to mild steel

TABLE 14-7 Plate Thickness and Weights

Designation	Thickness, in.	Aluminum Weight, lb./sq. ft.	Steel Weight, lb./sq. ft.	Thickness, mm	Aluminum Weight, kg/sq. m	Steel Weight, kg/sq. m
16 gauge	0.0598	—	2.44	1.52	—	11.91
1/16 inch	0.0625	0.88	2.55	1.59	4.30	12.45
15 gauge	0.0673	—	2.75	1.71	—	13.41
14 gauge	0.0747	—	3.05	1.90	—	14.88
13 gauge	0.0897	—	3.66	2.28	—	17.87
12 gauge	0.1046	—	4.27	2.66	—	20.83
11 gauge	0.1196	—	4.88	3.04	—	23.82
1/8 inch	0.1250	1.76	5.10	3.18	8.60	24.90
10 gauge	0.1345	—	**5.49**	3.42	—	**26.79**
0.160 inch	0.1600	2.25	—	4.06	11.01	—
8 gauge	0.1644	—	6.71	4.18	—	32.75
7 gauge, 3/16 in.	0.1875	**2.64**	7.65	**4.76**	12.90	37.35
0.190 inch	0.1900	2.68	—	4.83	13.07	—
0.204 inch	0.2040	2.87	—	5.18	14.03	—
1/4 inch	0.2500	3.52	10.20	6.35	17.20	49.80
5/16 inch	0.3125	4.40	12.75	7.94	21.50	62.25
3/8 inch	0.3750	5.28	15.30	9.53	25.80	74.69
7/16 inch	0.4375	6.16	17.85	11.11	30.09	87.14
1/2 inch	0.5000	7.05	20.40	12.70	34.39	99.59
9/16 inch	0.5625	—	22.95	14.29	—	112.04
5/8 inch	0.6250	8.81	25.50	15.88	42.99	124.49
11/16 inch	*0.6875*	*9.69*	*28.05*	*17.46*	*47.29*	*136.94*
3/4 inch	0.7500	10.57	30.60	19.05	51.59	149.39
13/16 inch	*0.8125*	*11.45*	*33.15*	*20.64*	*55.89*	*161.84*
7/8 inch	0.8750	12.33	35.70	22.23	60.19	174.29
1 inch	1.0000	14.09	40.80	25.40	68.79	199.19
1 1/4 inch	1.2500	17.61	51.00	31.75	85.98	248.98
1 1/2 inch	1.5000	21.14	61.20	38.10	103.18	298.78
1 3/4 inch	1.7500	24.66	71.40	44.45	120.38	348.57
2 inch	2.0000	28.18	81.60	50.80	137.57	398.37
2 1/2 inch	2.5000	35.23	102.00	63.50	171.97	497.96

NOTES: Weights in **bold** indicate the thinnest size readily weldable with standard equipment. Sizes in *italic* are nonstandard and not usually stocked. Gaps in the weight columns indicate that material is not normally available in that thickness.

TABLE 14-8 English and Metric Plate Thicknesses

Designation	Thickness, in.	Nearest Metric Thickness, mm	Designation	Thickness, in.	Nearest Metric Thickness, mm
16 gauge	0.0598	1.50	—	0.4331	11.00
1/16 inch	0.0625	1.60	7/16 inch	0.4375	11.25
15 gauge	0.0673	1.70	—	0.4724	12.00
14 gauge	0.0747	1.90	1/2 inch	0.5000	13.00
—	0.0787	2.00	—	0.5512	14.00
13 gauge	0.0897	2.25	9/16 inch	0.5625	14.25
12 gauge	0.1046	2.70	—	0.5906	15.00
11 gauge	0.1196	3.00	5/8 inch	0.6250	16.00
1/8 inch	0.1250	3.20	—	0.6693	17.00
10 gauge	0.1345	3.40	11/16 inch	0.6875	17.50
0.160 inch	0.1600	4.00	—	0.7087	18.00
8 gauge	0.1644	4.20	3/4 inch	0.7500	19.00
7 gauge,			—	0.7874	20.00
3/16 inch	0.1875	4.75	13/16 inch	0.8125	20.50
0.190 inch	0.1900	5.00	—	0.8268	21.00
0.204 inch	0.2040	5.25	—	0.8661	22.00
—	0.2362	6.00	7/8 inch	0.8750	22.25
1/4 inch	0.2500	6.40	1 inch	1.0000	25.00
—	0.2756	7.00	1 1/4 inch	1.2500	32.00
5/16 inch	0.3125	7.90	1 1/2 inch	1.5000	38.00
—	0.3150	8.00	1 3/4 inch	1.7500	45.00
3/8 inch	0.3750	9.50	2 inch	2.0000	50.00
—	0.3937	10.00	2 1/2 inch	2.5000	65.00

FIFTEEN

Aluminum and Steel Shell Plate and Longitudinal Framing

*N*ow that we have reviewed the factors underlying sound metal-boat construction, we can proceed to determine the scantlings for aluminum and steel hulls. Before we can do this, however, we need to discuss the basic structural shapes used and how they are described.

Framing Methods

There are actually two common methods to framing a standard metal hull. I'll call them the old and the new methods.

OLD METHOD

The old method largely (although by no means exclusively) uses standard shapes (usually angles and Ts) to form the frames and deck beams. These off-the-shelf extrusions might be cut or trimmed somewhat where appropriate, but are generally simply bent carefully to the shape of each frame. At their bottom, the frames are welded to floor plates, and at their top to knees that connect to deck beams, which are also made using standard extrusions.

NEW METHOD

The new method has been gaining popularity steadily as plate-cutting has become quicker and more accurate. The advent of *NC cut* (numerically controlled cut, or NCC), computer-driven, automatic cutting machines has accelerated this trend. In this new method, the frame—usually including the deck beams and sometimes even the superstructure—is cut out as a single ring of flat plate from individual pieces as needed. These individual plates are welded together into a single-unit ring. Next, the interior flange of the frame is welded to the inside of its ring. Most commonly, this forms a simple T; however, it can also form an angle, if that's more convenient for some reason. The T-ring frame as a unit is erected on the CVK, and braced in position temporarily until longitudinals and plating lock it permanently in place. Often, the

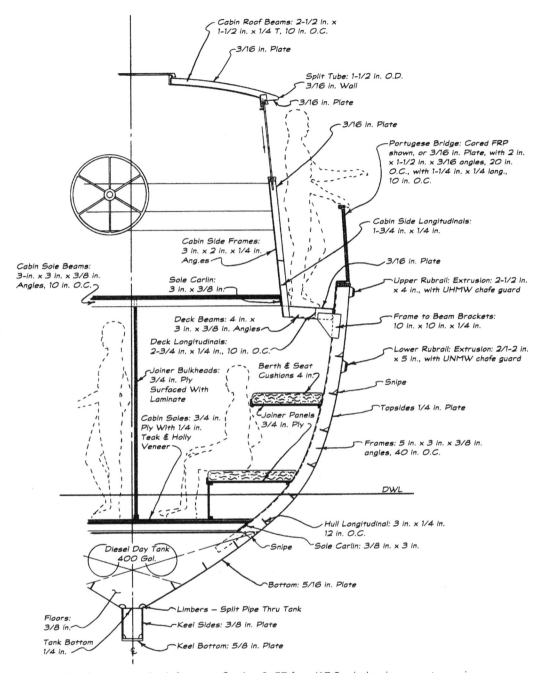

Old framing method, frame at Station 3, 57-foot (17.3 m) aluminum motor cruiser

The labels in the figure read:

Cabin Roof Beams: 2-1/2 in. x 1-1/2 in. x 1/4 T, 10 in. O.C.

3/16 in. Plate

Split Tube: 1-1/2 in. O.D. 3/16 in. Wall

3/16 in. Plate

3/16 in. Plate

Portugese Bridge: Cored FRP shown, or 3/16 in. Plate, with 2 in. x 1-1/2 in. x 3/16 in. angles, 20 in. O.C., with 1-1/4 in. x 1/4 long., 10 in. O.C.

Cabin Side Longitudinals: 1-3/4 in. x 1/4 in.

Cabin Side Frames: 3 in. x 2 in. x 1/4 in. Ang.es

3/16 in. Plate

Cabin Sole Beams: 3-in. x 3 in. x 3/8 in. Angles, 10 in. O.C.

Sole Carlin: 3 in. x 3/8 in.

Upper Rubrail: Extrusion: 2-1/2 in. x 4 in., with UHMW chafe guard

Deck Beams: 4 in. x 3 in. x 3/8 in. Angles

Frame to Beam Brackets: 10 in. x 10 in. x 1/4 in.

Deck Longitudinals: 2-3/4 in. x 1/4 in., 10 in. O.C.

Lower Rubrail: Extrusion: 2/1-2 in. x 5 in., with UNMW chafe guard

Berth & Seat Cushions 4 in.

Joiner Bulkheads: 3/4 in. Ply Surfaced With Laminate

Snipe

Joiner Panels 3/4 in. Ply

Topsides 1/4 in. Plate

Cabin Soles: 3/4 in. Ply With 1/4 in. Teak & Holly Veneer

Frames: 5 in. x 3 in. x 3/8 in. angles, 40 in. O.C.

DWL

Hull Longitudinal: 3 in. x 1/4 in. 12 in. O.C.

Diesel Day Tank 400 Gal.

Snipe

Sole Carlin: 3/8 in. x 3 in.

Bottom: 5/16 in. Plate

Floors: 3/8 in.

Limbers — Split Pipe Thru Tank

Keel Sides: 3/8 in. Plate

Tank Bottom 1/4 in.

Keel Bottom: 5/8 in. Plate

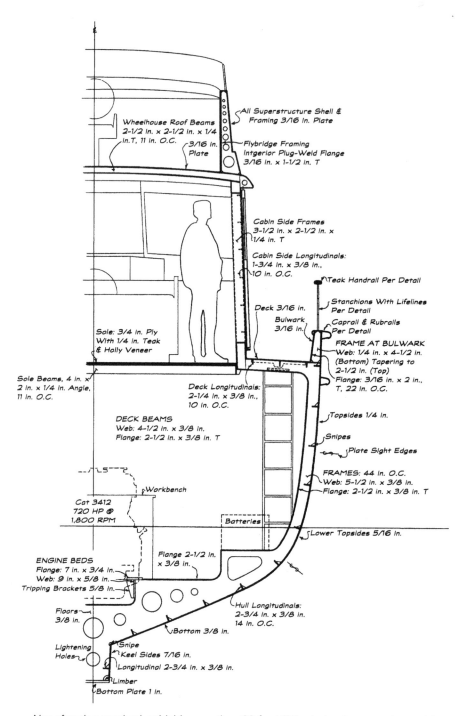

Wheelhouse Roof Beams 2-1/2 In. x 2-1/2 In. x 1/4 In.T, 11 In. O.C.

All Superstructure Shell & Framing 3/16 In. Plate

3/16 In. Plate

Flybridge Framing Intgerior Plug-Weld Flange 3/16 In. x 1-1/2 In. T

Cabin Side Frames 3-1/2 In. x 2-1/2 In. x 1/4 In. T

Cabin Side Longitudinals: 1-3/4 In. x 3/8 In., 10 In. O.C.

Teak Handrail Per Detail

Stanchions With Lifelines Per Detail

Deck 3/16 In.

Bulwark 3/16 In.

Caprail & Rubrails Per Detail

FRAME AT BULWARK
Web: 1/4 In. x 4-1/2 In. (Bottom) Tapering to 2-1/2 In. (Top)
Flange: 3/16 In. x 2 In., T, 22 In. O.C.

Sole: 3/4 In. Ply With 1/4 In. Teak & Holly Veneer

Topsides 1/4 In.

Snipes

Plate Sight Edges

Sole Beams, 4 In. x 2 In. x 1/4 In. Angle, 11 In. O.C.

Deck Longitudinals: 2-1/4 In. x 3/8 In., 10 In. O.C.

DECK BEAMS
Web: 4-1/2 In. x 3/8 In.
Flange: 2-1/2 In. x 3/8 In. T

FRAMES: 44 In. O.C.
Web: 5-1/2 In. x 3/8 In.
Flange: 2-1/2 In. x 3/8 In. T

Workbench

Cat 3412 720 HP @ 1,800 RPM

Batteries

Lower Topsides 5/16 In.

ENGINE BEDS
Flange: 7 In. x 3/4 In.
Web: 9 In. x 5/8 In.
Tripping Brackets 5/8 In.

Flange 2-1/2 In. x 3/8 In.

Hull Longitudinals: 2-3/4 In. x 3/8 In. 14 In. O.C.

Floors 3/8 In.

Bottom 3/8 In.

Lightening Holes

Snipe

Keel Sides 7/16 In.

Longitudinal 2-3/4 In. x 3/8 In.

Limber

Bottom Plate 1 In.

New framing method, midships section, 82-foot (25 m) aluminum motor yacht

frames are prenotched for the longitudinal stringers as well.

NEW FRAMING METHOD IS USED IN THESE SCANTLING RULES

There is no real difference between the scantlings of the two methods. If the frame were to have a web $^1/_4$ by 4 inches (6.4 by 100 mm), with a flange of $^1/_4$ by 2 inches (6.4 by 50 mm), then it makes no difference if this is welded up out of cut plate as in the new method or bent out of standard T-bar stock. However, throughout the following rule, we assume that the modern method is being used.

Describing Shapes Used in the Metal Scantling Rule

MANMADE SHAPES

Metal is different from wood and fiberglass in that it comes in a bewildering variety of manmade shapes—not only in plates of varying thicknesses, but also in flat bar, angles with equal and unequal legs, Ts of varying proportions, H- or I-beams, Z sections, channels, square and round tubes, bulb-angles and bulb-Ts, and more. It is necessary to be able to define the dimensions of these shapes.

Ts AND ANGLES

Although they are less common in use with metal-boat structures, I will continue to refer to molded and sided dimensions occasionally, where it helps in clarification (see chapter 9). Still, the standard method of describing metal shapes is by referring to the *flange* and the *web* of the shape. The web of a T or angle is its "vertical" portion that is welded at right angles to the hull, deck, or cabin-roof shell— it extends in the molded dimension and its

siding is small. (Properly speaking, the web is parallel to the direction of load.) The flange is the "horizontal" part of the T or angle. It extends in the fore-n-aft (sided) dimension, and its molding is small. (Again, speaking more precisely, the flange is at right angles to the direction of load.)

SHAPES USED IN THESE RULES

The fact is, there is a nearly endless combination of shapes that can quite properly be employed for framing a hull. To simplify the scantling rule, however, I will almost exclusively use Ts for the frames (angles of the same web and flange dimensions can be substituted at will) and flat bar for longitudinal stiffeners.

There are two reasons for this: these shapes are easy to define and easy to purchase or fabricate; and hulls framed with T or angle frames and flat-bar longitudinal stringers are the most common. There is no reason at all why other shapes of comparable section properties can't be substituted. Indeed, where ultimate weight savings and/or maximum strength are required, shapes like bulb angles or trimmed-flange I-beams can be structurally more efficient.

Some builders also prefer to use Ts (or channels or angles) for longitudinals because they are somewhat easier to control when bending into place. This too is fine— although I personally don't like the large notches such longitudinals cut into a frame. Chiefly, however, almost all the builders I have dealt with recently prefer the modern cut-plate method, using built-up T or angle frames and flat-bar longitudinals. (They employ standard Ts or angles whenever there is little curvature and where little cutting or bending would be required.)

FLOATING-FRAME CONSTRUCTION

The overwhelming majority of metal hulls are built with their longitudinals notched into the frames. In this way, both the longitudinals and the frames lie against the inside of the shell plate, and both are welded to the shell. It is also possible to run the longitudinals over the outside face or edge of the frames without notching them into the frames. Then the shell plate is laid on top of the longitudinals. In this construction, the frames don't touch the shell plate anywhere. Indeed, they are separated from it by the molding of the longitudinal stringers. (These stringers need to be Ts or angles.)

This less-common building method is known as *floating-frame construction*, which is *not* covered in these scantling rules. Properly engineered, it is an acceptable building method, but it requires different proportions than the scantlings given here. It also has the drawback of stealing the more interior volume from a metal hull, because the inside of the frames must be quite far from the plate.

Our Example Boats

In previous chapters, we used *Fish 'n Squish* and *Logger Bobber* as our examples. They were both 40 feet (12.19 m) LOA. Metal boats can be quite small; indeed, aluminum boats can be efficiently built as diminutive as in any other material. Nevertheless, most welded-metal vessels tend to be larger custom or semi-production projects. Accordingly, our metal example boats will be huskier at 64 feet (19.50 m). We've named them *AlumaNaught* in aluminum and *Iron Maiden* in steel.

AlumaNaught and *Iron Maiden* have the following characteristics:

LOA	64.00 ft.	19.50 m
WL	54.42 ft.	16.58 m
Beam	17.67 ft.	5.38 m
Depth of Hull	8.33 ft.	2.54 m

This gives an Sn of 8.71 (see Formula 1-1).

ALUMINUM AND STEEL FORMULA NUMBERS

Generally, both aluminum and steel have the same components and are assembled in the same way in this scantling rule; therefore, we consider them together in the following formulas. To help differentiate between them, I have added the suffix "A" to all aluminum formula numbers and the suffix "S" to all steel formula numbers. Formulas without a suffix apply equally to aluminum and steel.

Small Boats and the Limits of These Scantling Rules

Because steel is such a heavy construction material, all the steel scantling rules apply exclusively to boats with Sns greater than 1.0—approximately equal to 28 feet (8.5 m). I would say that building steel craft with dimensions that generate an Sn of less than 3.0 (around 40 feet [12.2 m]) results in a vessel

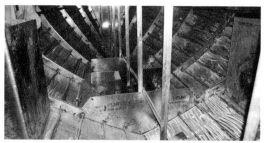

Midships in Imagine, looking forward. The integral diesel day tank is in the center of the photo; integral water tanks are port and starboard. The vertical angles are temporary braces and alignment aids.

with either poor performance or low life expectancy.

Using aluminum, really tiny boats—such as canoes and rowing skiffs—can be fabricated quite efficiently. The aluminum rules that follow generally apply to vessels with Sns greater than 0.50—roughly equivalent to boats greater than 20 feet (6 m). For smaller boats, follow the recommendations given in chapter 19 and Table 19-1.

Plate Thickness

FORMULA 15-1A
Aluminum Bottom Plate

Aluminum Bottom-Plate Thickness, in. = $0.2 \times Sn^{0.2}$ (English)

Aluminum Bottom-Plate Thickness, mm = $5.08 \times Sn^{0.2}$ (Metric)

Where

Sn = scantling number

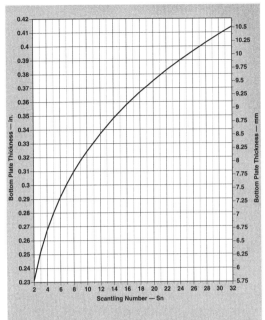

Aluminum Bottom-Plate Thickness: Large Boats

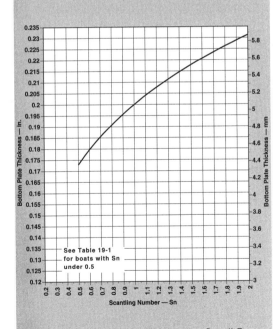

Aluminum Bottom-Plate Thickness: Small Boats

The bottom plate should extend down from the BLH to the keel (see Formula 4-3). This is heavy bottom plate and it is most definitely optional on displacement hulls or boats operating under 15 knots. Even planing hulls operating under 25 knots can opt to go with the lighter topsides plate on the bottom. However, if this is done to save weight (not an unreasonable consideration), the boat will have a shorter life and will sustain more damage on grounding or striking flotsam at speed. Over 25 knots, this heavier bottom plate is required.

On powerboats, it is recommended practice to increase the plate thickness by one standard size in the aft 20 to 25 percent of the hull bottom, over the propellers; the thicker plate is more rigid and therefore vibrates less. The result is a quieter boat and less fatigue in the shell at this location.

Displacement boats that have opted not to go with the heavy bottom plate should use this heavy plate in the aft underbody, but further thickness is not usually called for. High-powered, high-speed planing hulls should use the thicker bottom plate and then go up one standard size over the props. Again, this extra thickness above the heavier bottom plate is optional, but will reduce noise and increase life.

On *AlumaNaught*, we would find

Aluminum Bottom-Plate Thickness = 0.2 × 8.71^{0.21} = 0.315 in.; use ⅝₁₆ in.

Aluminum Bottom-Plate Thickness = 5.08 × 8.71^{0.21} = 8.00; use 8 mm

For heavy-displacement workboats and ocean voyagers, the heavier bottom plate throughout is recommended. The weight in the hull bottom actually increases stability, in addition to adding strength and corrosion allowance.

In *Iron Maiden*'s case,

Sn of 8.71 is between 3 and 12, so C = ⅟₁₆ in. (0.0625 in.) (3.2 mm)

Steel Bottom Plate = 0.0625 in. + 0.206 in. = 0.268; use ¼ in.

Steel Bottom Plate = 1.6 mm + 5.24 mm = 6.84 mm; use 6.4 mm

(See Formula 15-2S for steel shell-plate thickness.)

FORMULA 15-1S

Steel Bottom Plate

Steel Bottom Plate = C + shell plate

C = 0 for Sns under 3

C = ⅟₁₆ in. (1.6 mm) for Sns between 3 and 12

C = ⅛ in. (3.2 mm) for Sns greater than 12

The bottom plate should extend down from the BLH to the keel (see Formula 4-3). Cor-Ten steel can be 0.88 of this thickness. (See Formula 15-2S for steel shell-plate thickness.)

Thicker bottom plate on steel is optional for all boats, including planing hulls. The extra thickness does increase longevity and impact resistance, but it also adds weight. Even if the heavy bottom plate isn't used for most of the hull, it is advisable to use this extra thickness in the aft 20 percent of the hull bottom, over the propellers, on high-powered boats.

FORMULA 15-2A

Aluminum Topsides (Shell) Plate

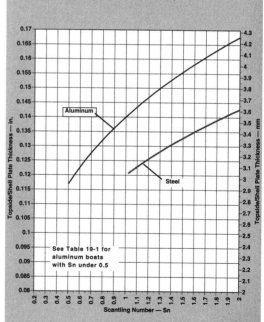

Topsides/Shell-Plate Thickness, Aluminum and Steel: Small Boats

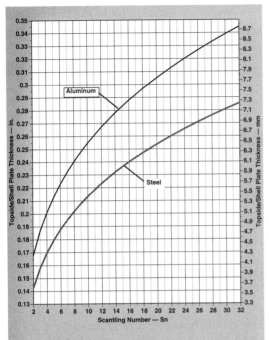

Topsides/Shell-Plate Thickness, Aluminum and Steel: Large Boats

Aluminum Topsides-Plate Thickness, in. = 0.14 × Sn^{0.26} (English)

Aluminum Topsides-Plate Thickness, mm = 3.55 × Sn^{0.26} (Metric)

The topsides plate can be run right around into the hull underbody and form the bottom plate, with no additional thickness, as described in Formula 15-1A.

For *AlumaNaught*,

Aluminum Topsides-Plate Thickness = 0.14 × 8.71^{0.26} = 0.245; use ¼ in.

Aluminum Topsides-Plate Thickness = 3.55 × 8.71^{0.26} = 6.23; use 6.4 mm

The upper-topsides plate—the upper third of the topsides below the sheer—can be reduced in thickness to that of the deck plate for maximum weight savings. Aluminum

plate is light enough, however, so this is not necessary and it is seldom done.

FORMULA 15-2S

Steel Topsides (Shell) Plate

Steel Shell Plate, in. = 0.12 × Sn^{0.25} (English)

Steel Shell Plate, mm = 3.05 × Sn^{0.25} (Metric)

Cor-Ten steel can be 0.88 of this thickness.

Iron Maiden would use

Steel Shell Plate = 0.12 × 8.71^{0.25} = 0.206; use 3/16 in. (0.1875 in.)

Steel Shell Plate = 3.05 × 8.71^{0.25} = 5.24; use 4.75 mm

Here, we have faced a common question in selecting plate thickness: 0.206 in. (5.24 mm) doesn't correspond to any standard plate or sheet size. In both English and Metric, sizes closest are thinner, so we rounded down. This is preferable in steel to control weight and permissible because steel is so strong. If the boat has great initial stability and is intended for rugged workboat use, you may want to round up instead of down, however. Switching to Cor-Ten for this plate, though, would put thickness in better agreement with the rule and increase its life at this thinner size. If Cor-Ten steel were used, then

Cor-Ten Shell Plate = 0.206 × 0.88 = 0.181; use 3/16 in.

Cor-Ten Shell Plate = 5.24 mm × 0.88 = 4.61; use 4.75 mm

Steel is stronger and stiffer than aluminum, so (as described in Formula 15-2A) the topsides plate can be used as bottom plate on all boats, even planing hulls. Accordingly, *shell plate* rather than *topsides plate* is a more accurate name.

Because it is necessary to keep weight low on steel boats, vessels with shell plate over $3/16$ in. (4.75 mm) should reduce the thickness of the shell plate in the upper topsides to the next standard plate size down. The upper topsides are roughly the upper third of the side of the hull, below the sheer. Any plate above the sheer is either bulwark or raised-deck cabin side. It should be reduced to the thickness of the deck plate (see Formula 15-4S).

On *Iron Maiden*, using mild steel, we already rounded down on the shell-plate thickness, so a further reduction in the upper topsides is not recommended. However, on a Cor-Ten-hull *Iron Maiden*,

Cor-Ten Upper Topsides = 8-gauge (0.1644 in.)

Cor-Ten Upper Topsides = 4.20 mm

Obviously, tugs, barges, and other vessels that will experience extensive abrasion and heavy impact loads on their topsides should use the full standard shell plate up to the sheer.

FORMULA 15-3

Aluminum and Steel Transom and Transom Framing

Aluminum Transom Plate = (bottom plate + ⅛ in.) (English)

Aluminum Transom Plate = (bottom plate + 3.2 mm) (Metric)

Steel Transom Plate = (bottom plate + ¹⁄₁₆ in.) (English)

Steel Transom Plate = (bottom plate + 1.6 mm) (Metric)

For boats with Sns less than 2.5, transom plate = topsides plate

Stiffeners on the inside of the transom run vertically. They are the same dimensions as the hull-bottom longitudinals (see Formulas 15-7A and S) without speed adjustment, and are spaced O.C. using the longitudinal spacing for the transom's plate thickness (see Formulas 15-6A and S). Install the stiffeners starting at the centerline, with the centerline stiffener welded to the top of the CVK at the stern and reinforced with a bracket (i.e., knee), with legs about 1.5 times the stiffener height. The knee should be the same thickness as the stiffener.

Except for the centerline stiffener, none of the other transom framing needs to be welded to the hull's longitudinal stiffeners. The stiffeners and the transom frames can end several inches or centimeters in from the hull side. However, it may be convenient to weld some or all of the transom's frames to suitable hull longitudinals. In this way, the curved frames and the centerline stiffener define the shape of the transom. The remaining stiffeners and frames are then added, and the plate scribed to fit and welded in place.

Transom frames run athwartships inside the transom and are notched out for the vertical transom stiffeners. The transom frames are spaced at half the O.C. spacing of the non-speed-adjusted hull frames (see Formula 15-9). This spacing is measured along the face of the transom, which is usually sloped either fore or aft. Transom-frame dimensions should be the same as the topsides frames (at their deepest web) (see Formula 15-10).

FORMULA 15-4A

Aluminum Deck and Superstructure Side Plate

Aluminum Deck- and Cabin-Side-Plate Thickness, in. = 0.14 × $Sn^{0.20}$ (English)

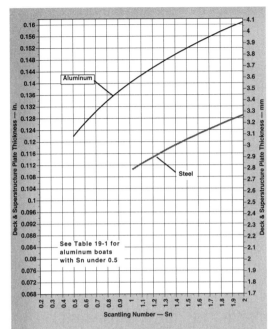

Deck- and Superstructure-Plate Thickness, Aluminum and Steel: Small Boats

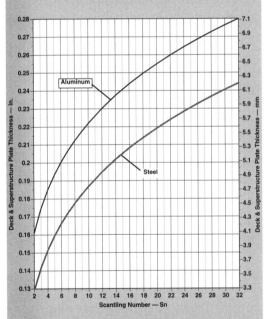

Deck- and Superstructure-Plate Thickness, Aluminum and Steel: Large Boats

On oceangoing craft, cabin-house fronts in the forward third of the vessel should use the next standard plate size up. Good old *AlumaNaught* would fit as follows:

Aluminum Deck- and Cabin-Side-Plate Thickness, in. = 0.14 × 8.71^0.20 = 0.22; use 3/16 or 7/32 in.

Aluminum Deck- and Cabin-Side-Plate Thickness, mm = 3.55 × 8.71^0.20 = 5.47; use 4.75 (5.55 mm)

Aluminum plate 7/32 inch (5.55 mm) thick is also difficult to find, although it fits the calculation best. It is better to round down—to the nearest standard plate—to decrease weight high up. Even with the light alloy aluminum, this is still a consideration. Assuming easy availability, ideally, the decks would be 7/32 inch (5.55 mm) and the cabin sides 3/16 inch (4.75 mm). Heavy workboats should round up in plate size rather than down.

FORMULA 15-4S

Steel Deck and Superstructure Side Plate

Steel Deck Plate, in. = 0.11 × Sn^0.23 (English)

Steel Deck Plate, mm = 2.79 × Sn^0.23 (English)

Cabins sides to be 90 percent of the deck thickness.

Cor-Ten steel can be 0.88 of this thickness.

Iron Maiden would then have

Steel Deck Plate = 0.11 × 8.71^0.23 = 0.181; use 3/16 in.

Steel Deck Plate = 2.79 × 8.71^{0.23} = 4.59; use 4.75 mm

Steel Superstructure Side Plate = 0.181 in. × 0.9 = 0.163; use 8-gauge

Steel Superstructure Side Plate = 4.59 mm × 0.9 = 4.12; use 4.2 mm

Because we rounded down *Iron Maiden's* shell-plate thickness, we ended up with the same thickness for both deck and shell plate. Except for the hardest usage, you could slim down deck thickness to 8-gauge (0.1664 in. [4.2 mm]). In Cor-Ten, we would get this anyway, with longer life and higher stiffness:

Cor-Ten Deck Plate = 0.181 in. × 0.88 = 0.159 in.; use 8-gauge (0.1664 in.)

Cor-Ten Deck Plate = 4.59 in. × 0.88 = 4.03 mm; use 4 mm

Cor-Ten Superstructure Side Plate = 0.163 in. × 0.88 = 0.143; use 10-gauge (0.1345 in.)

Cor-Ten Superstructure Side Plate = 4.12 mm × 0.88 = 3.62; use 3.4 mm

You can see that the 8- and 10-gauge (4.2 and 3.4 mm) plates we're getting for *Iron Maiden's* superstructure are near the limit that can be welded practically. Yet, *Iron Maiden*—at 64 feet (19.5 m) with an Sn of 8.71—is a fairly large vessel, which is why smaller steel craft should usually use wood, aluminum, or FRP superstructures. If they don't, the thicker plate required for welding raises the center of gravity too high. Of course, some smaller boats are built with steel superstructures anyway. These boats must be beamier and heavier than otherwise, however, to compensate for the higher weight distribution.

Note that because we rounded the aluminum deck plate and superstructure plate down some to match stock plate sizes, and

rounded the steel deck plate up a little, we ended up with the same deck-plate thickness for both materials. This is an anomaly. In most cases, aluminum plate will be thicker. Indeed, the Cor-Ten-steel deck and superstructure are thinner than even the rounded-down aluminum, though still heavier.

FORMULA 15-5

Butt and Seam Locations in Plate

Minimum Butt-Joint Distance from Transverse Frame = 24 × plate thickness

Minimum Seam-Joint Distance from a Longitudinal = 12 × plate thickness

The smooth joints in the shell plating are all made with butt welds; however, convention calls the vertical or transverse joints *butts* (like butt joints in planks) and the horizontal or fore-n-aft joints *seams*. Where practical, these joints should be separated from frames and longitudinals by the following recommended distance to avoid stress concentrations.

On some transverse-framed hulls and at the bow of some longitudinally framed hulls, it can be nearly impossible to achieve these minimums. In this case, try to locate the butts and seams about midway between each frame or longitudinal.

Longitudinal-Construction Framing

FORMULA 15-6A

Aluminum Longitudinal-Stiffener Spacing

Aluminum Longitudinal-Stiffener Spacing O.C., in. = 4 + (plate thickness, in. × 32) (English)

Aluminum Longitudinal-Stiffener Spacing O.C., mm = 101.6 + (plate thickness, mm × 32) (Metric)

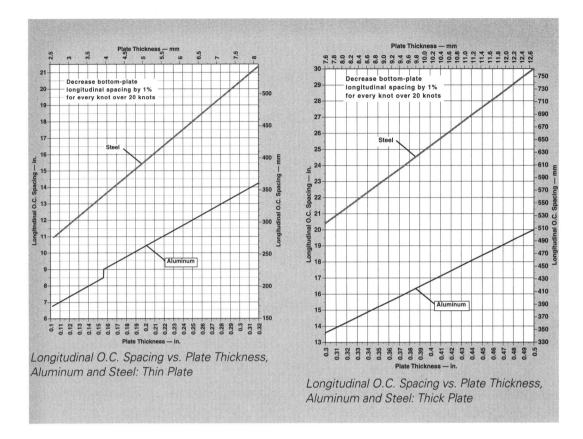

Longitudinal O.C. Spacing vs. Plate Thickness, Aluminum and Steel: Thin Plate

Longitudinal O.C. Spacing vs. Plate Thickness, Aluminum and Steel: Thick Plate

For plate under ⁵/₃₂ inch (4 mm), subtract ¹/₂ inch (12.7 m) from the O.C. spacing. (Such thin plate should be welded with pulse-arc equipment.) The spacing must decrease to 85 percent of the formula value at the forefoot in the bow, from around Station 3.5 forward.

Use O.C. spacing for the topsides plate on the heavier bottom plate. Use the thickness of the plate actually installed after rounding or other adjustments, not the calculated plate thickness. In the case of *AlumaNaught*, the shell plating we settled on yields the following stiffener spacing:

Aluminum Bottom Plate: ⁵/₁₆ in. (8 mm)
Bottom-plate longitudinals will be spaced the same as the thinner topsides plate.

Aluminum Topsides Plate: ¹/₄ in. (6.4 mm)

Longitudinal O.C. = 4 + (0.25 in. × 32) = 12 in.

Longitudinal O.C. = 101.6 + (6.4 mm × 32) = 306.4; use 300 mm

Aluminum Deck and Superstructure Plate: ³/₁₆ in. (4.75 mm)

Longitudinal O.C. = 4 + (0.1875 in. × 32) = 10 in.

Longitudinal O.C. = 101.6 + (4.75 mm × 32) = 253.6; use 250 mm

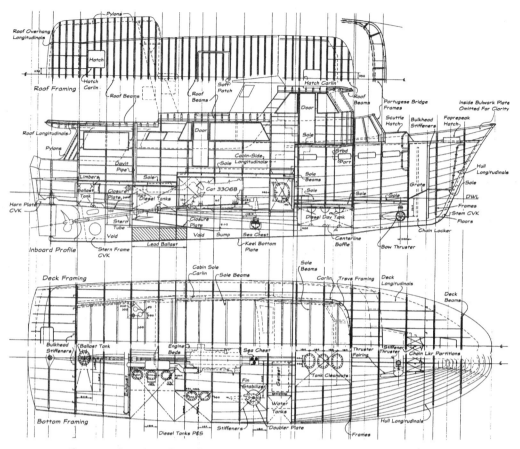

Construction plan of the Gerr 57-foot (17.3 m) aluminum motor yacht Imagine

FORMULA 15-6S
Steel Longitudinal-Stiffener Spacing

Steel Longitudinal-Stiffener Spacing O.C., in. = 6 + (plate thickness, in. × 48) (English)

Steel Longitudinal-Stiffener Spacing O.C., mm = 152.4 + (plate thickness, mm × 48) (Metric)

The spacing must decrease to 85 percent of the formula value at the forefoot in the bow, from around Station 3.5 forward.

Use O.C. spacing for the topsides plate on the heavier bottom plate (when heavier bottom plate is installed). Use the thickness of the plate actually installed after rounding or other adjustments, not the calculated number. In the case of *Iron Maiden*, the shell plating we settled on yields the following stiffener spacing:

Steel Bottom Plate (if used) = ¼ inch (6.4 mm)

Bottom-plate longitudinals will be spaced the same as the thinner topsides plate.

Steel Shell Plate $^3/_{16}$ inch (4.75 mm) Cor-Ten:

Longitudinal O.C. = 6 + (0.1875 in. × 48) = 15 in.

Longitudinal O.C. = 152.4 + (4.75 mm × 48) = 380.4; use 380 mm

Steel Upper Topsides and Bulwark Plate 8-Gauge (0.1644 in. [4 mm]) Cor-Ten:

Longitudinal O.C. = 6 + (0.1644 in. × 48) = 13.89; use 13 in.

Longitudinal O.C. = 152.4 + (4.0 mm × 48) = 344.4; use 340 mm

Steel Deck and Superstructure Plate 8-Gauge (0.1644 in. [4 mm]) Cor-Ten:

Same as previous upper topsides and bulwark.

BOTTOM LONGITUDINAL O.C. SPACING ADJUSTMENT FOR SPEED

Decrease bottom longitudinal O.C. spacing—up to the BLH (or to the chine) (see Formula 4-3)—by 1 percent for every knot over 20 knots. If good old *AlumaNaught* were a 35-knot boat, we would adjust its bottom longitudinals as follows:

Aluminum 35-Knot Bottom Longitudinal O.C., in. = 35 – 25 = 10; therefore, reduce by 10%, or 0.90 × 12 in. = 10.8; use 10 in.

Aluminum 35-Knot Bottom Longitudinal O.C., in. = 35 – 25 = 10; therefore, reduce by 10%, or 0.90 × 300 mm = 270; use 250 mm

For *Iron Maiden*, as a 35-knot boat, we would adjust its bottom longitudinal as follows:

Steel 35-Knot Bottom Longitudinal O.C., in. = 35 – 25 = 10; therefore, reduce by 10%, or 0.90 × 15 in. = 13.5; use 13 in.

Steel 35-Knot Bottom Longitudinal O.C., in. = 35 – 25 = 10; therefore, reduce by 10%, or 0.90 × 380 mm = 342; use 340 mm

NOTES ON ALUMINUM AND STEEL LONGITUDINALS

You can see in this scantling rule that the longitudinal spacing is directly controlled by the plate thickness. Thus, when we round down (or up) on plate thickness, the rule adjusts the stiffener spacing accordingly. Unless otherwise called for, the longitudinal O.C. spacing formulas apply to all panels everywhere on the vessel.

Always round the stiffener spacing *down* to the nearest convenient even distance. Decreasing the spacing from 13.8 to 13 inches (350 to 330 mm), for example, will add at most one or two stringers to the hull. This is little increase in weight, in proportion to the overall structure, while ensuring adequate panel stiffness.

Using the closer spacing of the thinner topsides plate on the heavier bottom plate decreases the panel size in proportion to the plate thickness for further increased strength and stiffness.

HULL LONGITUDINAL LAYOUT

My preferred practice on the hull is to run the longitudinals along the inside surface of the plate, in diagonals laid out on the body plan. The previous O.C. spacing is used as the governing distance between stiffeners at midships. Because the diagonals sweep closer together at the bow and stern, the longitudinal spacing will decrease at the bow and stern, which gives increased stiffness at the bow where slamming loads are greatest, and aft where propeller vibration is a factor. This also automatically gives the 85 percent decreased

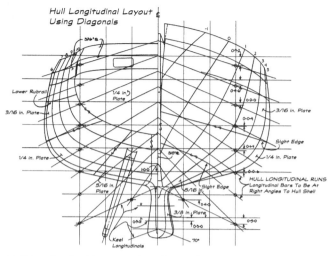

Hull longitudinal layout using diagonals

O.C. spacing at the forefoot. Other advantages to the diagonal stiffener layout is that the longitudinals naturally take smooth fair curves, they are very easy to lay out on the frames, and they experience only bend and twist but no edgeset. This makes flat-bar longitudinals easier to lay in.

DECK AND CABIN LONGITUDINAL LAYOUT

On decks, I most frequently run the longitudinals dead straight fore-n-aft, in plan view, at the specified O.C. spacing. Where the cabin sides meet the deck, they form a very substantial longitudinal-strength member. Adjust the longitudinals somewhat to work around these at close to or slightly less than the formula O.C. Sometimes it is convenient to sweep some of the deck longitudinals parallel to the sheer (or close to that). Again, any arrangement that results in smooth fair runs and O.C. equal to or less than specified is fine.

The same goes for cabin sides. Usually, straight fore-n-aft longitudinals are easiest, but sometimes it's more convenient for some (or all) to run with the curve of the deck or cabin roof in plan view.

OTHER LONGITUDINAL LAYOUTS AND ENDING LONGITUDINALS

It is possible—particularly on hard-chine vessels—to run the longitudinals in other patterns, including at constant-width spacing. Any system of laying out the stringers is acceptable as long as the O.C. spacing is less than or equal to the spacing called for in the formula, including closing together in the forefoot.

Longitudinals that will run out of the hull should be ended at the nearest frame inside the hull, where practical. Don't simply end a longitudinal under the middle of a deck panel; this would cause a hard spot. It sometimes works out best to sweep otherwise straight and parallel deck longitudinals in at their ends to maximize their run, and end them on a frame.

FORMULA 15-7A

Aluminum Hull-Longitudinal Dimensions

Aluminum Flat-Bar Hull-Longitudinal Height, in. $= 1.05 \times Sn^{0.4}$ *(English)*

Aluminum Flat-Bar Hull-Longitudinal Thickness, in. $= 0.23 \times Sn^{0.21}$ *(English)*

Aluminum Flat-Bar Hull-Longitudinal Height, mm $= 26.67 \times Sn^{0.4}$ *(Metric)*

Aluminum Flat-Bar Hull-Longitudinal Thickness, mm $= 5.84 \times Sn^{0.21}$ *(Metric)*

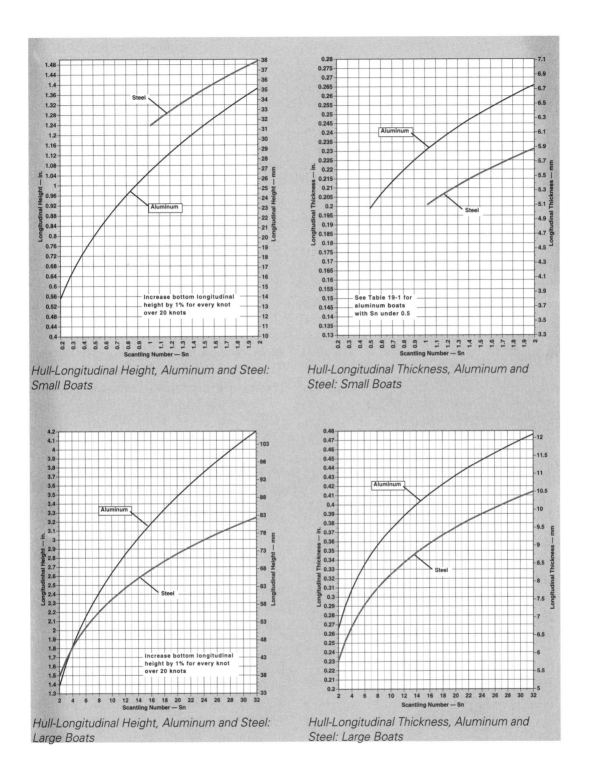

Hull-Longitudinal Height, Aluminum and Steel: Small Boats

Hull-Longitudinal Thickness, Aluminum and Steel: Small Boats

Hull-Longitudinal Height, Aluminum and Steel: Large Boats

Hull-Longitudinal Thickness, Aluminum and Steel: Large Boats

To stiffen *AlumaNaught*, we would employ

Aluminum Flat-Bar Hull-Longitudinal Height = $1.05 \times 8.71^{0.4} = 2.49$; use $2\frac{1}{2}$ in.

Aluminum Flat-Bar Hull-Longitudinal Thickness = $0.23 \times 8.71^{0.21} = 0.36$; use $\frac{3}{8}$ in.

Aluminum Flat-Bar Hull-Longitudinal Height = $26.67 \times 8.71^{0.4} = 63.39$; use 65 mm

Aluminum Flat-Bar Hull-Longitudinal Thickness = $5.84 \times 8.71^{0.21} = 9.2$; use 9.5 mm

---

FORMULA 15-7S

Steel Hull-Longitudinal Dimensions

Steel Flat-Bar Hull-Longitudinal Height, in. = $1.23 \times Sn^{0.28}$ (English)

Steel Flat-Bar Hull-Longitudinal Thickness, in. = $0.20 \times Sn^{0.21}$ (English)

Steel Flat-Bar Hull-Longitudinal Height, mm = $31.24 \times Sn^{0.28}$ (Metric)

Steel Flat-Bar Hull-Longitudinal Thickness, mm = $5.04 \times Sn^{0.21}$ (Metric)

To stiffen *Iron Maiden*, we would employ

Steel Flat-Bar Hull-Longitudinal Height = $1.23 \times 8.71^{0.28} = 2.25$; use $2\frac{1}{4}$ in.

Steel Flat-Bar Hull-Longitudinal Thickness = $0.20 \times 8.71^{0.21} = 0.315$; use $\frac{5}{16}$ in.

Steel Flat-Bar Hull-Longitudinal Height = $31.24 \times 8.71^{0.28} = 57.26$; use 58 mm

Steel Flat-Bar Hull-Longitudinal Thickness = $5.04 \times 8.71^{0.21} = 7.9$; use 8 mm

INCREASE BOTTOM-LONGITUDINAL HEIGHT FOR SPEED

Increase bottom-longitudinal height up to the BLH or chine (see Formula 4-3) by 1 percent for every knot over 20 knots.

On a 35-knot *AlumaNaught*, we would use

Aluminum 35-Knot Bottom-Longitudinal Height, in. = $35 - 20 = 15$; therefore, increase by 15% or 1.15×2.5 in. = 2.875; use $2\frac{7}{8}$ or 3 in.

Aluminum 35-Knot Bottom Longitudinal Height, in. = $35 - 20 = 15$; therefore, increase by 15% or 1.15×65 mm = 74.7; use 75 mm

If *Iron Maiden* were driven 35 knots, it would have

Steel 35-Knot Bottom-Longitudinal Height, in. = $35 - 20 = 15$; therefore, increase by 15% or 1.15×2.25 in. = 2.58; use $2\frac{5}{8}$ in.

Steel 35-Knot Bottom-Longitudinal Height, in. = $35 - 20 = 15$; therefore, increase by 15% or 1.15×57.26 mm = 65.8; use 68 mm

PRACTICAL MINIMUM LONGITUDINAL THICKNESS

On small boats, the rule generates flat-bar longitudinals that are quite thin. Structurally, these will work fine. As a practical matter, however, such thin flat-bar is difficult to bend and fabricate into smooth fair members. Generally, aluminum flat-bar longitudinals under $\frac{1}{4}$ inch and steel under $\frac{3}{16}$ inch will be inconvenient to work with; however, it can be done if weight-saving considerations call for it.

DECREASING LONGITUDINAL HEIGHT ON UPPER TOPSIDES

To maximize weight reduction, you can gradually reduce the topsides longitudinals' height to the height of the deck longitudinals, decreasing each longitudinal from bilge to sheer (see Formulas 15-8A and S). This is seldom done, however, because the weight savings is minimal.

FORMULA 15-8A
Aluminum Deck-Longitudinal Dimensions

Aluminum Flat-Bar Deck-Longitudinal Height, in. = 0.77 × Sn$^{0.32}$ (English)

Aluminum Flat-Bar Deck-Longitudinal Thickness, in. = 0.19 × Sn$^{0.21}$ (English)

Aluminum Flat-Bar Deck-Longitudinal Height, mm = 19.55 × Sn$^{0.32}$ (Metric)

Aluminum Flat-Bar Deck-Longitudinal Thickness, mm = 4.83 × Sn$^{0.21}$ (Metric)

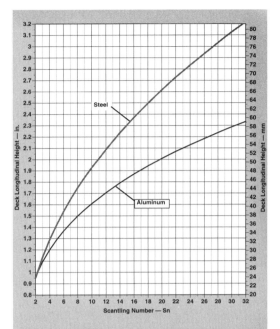

Deck-Longitudinal Height, Aluminum and Steel: Large Boats

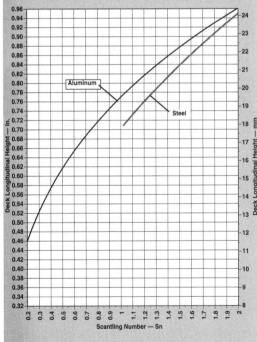

Deck-Longitudinal Height, Aluminum and Steel: Small Boats

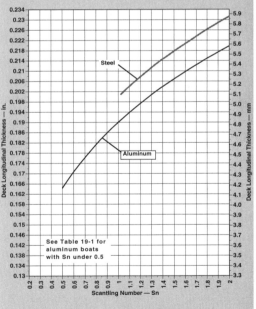

Deck-Longitudinal Thickness, Aluminum and Steel: Small Boats

(continued)

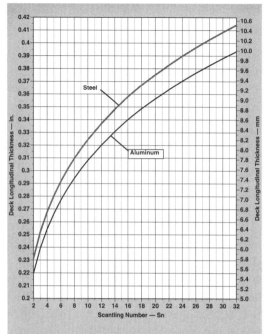

Deck-Longitudinal Thickness, Aluminum and Steel: Large Boats

Applying this to *AlumaNaught:*

Aluminum Flat-Bar Deck-Longitudinal Height = 0.77 × 8.71^{0.32} = 1.53; use 1½ in.

Aluminum Flat-Bar Deck-Longitudinal Thickness = 0.19 × 8.71^{0.21} = 0.29; use ⁵⁄₁₆ in.

Aluminum Flat-Bar Deck-Longitudinal Height = 19.55 × 8.71^{0.32} = 39.07; use 40 mm

Aluminum Flat-Bar Deck-Longitudinal Thickness = 4.83 × 8.71^{0.21} = 7.63; use 7.9 mm

FORMULA 15-8S

Steel Deck-Longitudinal Dimensions

Steel Flat-Bar Deck-Longitudinal Height, in. = 0.7 × Sn^{0.44} (English)

Steel Flat-Bar Deck-Longitudinal Thickness, in. = 0.2 × Sn^{0.21} (English)

Steel Flat-Bar Deck-Longitudinal Height, mm = 17.78 × Sn^{0.44} (Metric)

Steel Flat-Bar Deck-Longitudinal Thickness, mm = 5.08 × Sn^{0.21} (Metric)

Or, on *Iron Maiden*, this yields

Steel Flat-Bar Deck-Longitudinal Height = 0.7 × 8.71^{0.44} = 1.81; use 1⅞ or 2 in.

Steel Flat-Bar Deck-Longitudinal Thickness = 0.2 × 8.71^{0.21} = 0.315; use ⁵⁄₁₆ in.

Steel Flat-Bar Deck-Longitudinal Height = 17.78 × 8.71^{0.44} = 46.08; use 48 mm

Steel Flat-Bar Deck-Longitudinal Thickness = 5.08 × 8.71^{0.21} = 8.00; use 8 mm

FORMULA 15-9

Ring-Frame Spacing O.C. (Longitudinal Construction)

Aluminum and steel have the same ring-frame spacing:

Transverse Ring Frames O.C., in. = 33 × Sn^{0.15} (English)

Transverse Ring Frames O.C., cm = 83.8 × Sn^{0.15} (Metric)

We would then build *AlumaNaught* or *Iron Maiden* with the following:

Transverse Ring Frames O.C. = 33 × 8.71^{0.15} = 45.6; use 46 in.

Transverse Ring Frames O.C. = 83.8 × 8.71^{0.15} = 115.9; use 115 cm

ADJUSTING RING-FRAME SPACING FOR SPEED

Decrease Frame O.C. by 1 percent for every knot over 15 knots.

Applying this to a 35-knot *AlumaNaught* or *Iron Maiden* gives the following:

35 knots – 15 knots = 20 knots, so decrease O.C. by 20%

Speed-Adjusted Ring-Frame O.C. = 45.6 in. × 0.80 = 36.48; use 36 in.

Speed-Adjusted Ring-Frame O.C. = 115.9 mm × 0.80 = 92.7; use 90 cm

FORMULA 15-9A

Aluminum Ring-Frame Dimensions: Hull Bottom

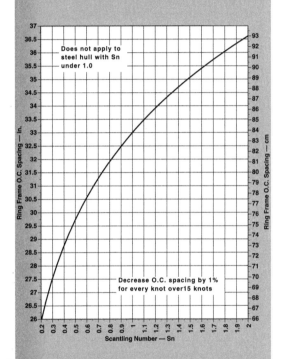

Ring-Frame Spacing and Dimensions for Aluminum and Steel in Longitudinally Framed Hulls
(1) Ring-Frame O.C. Spacing: Small Boats

Aluminum Hull-Bottom Ring-Frame Web Height, in. = 2.33 × $Sn^{0.4}$ (English)

Aluminum Hull-Bottom Ring-Frame Web Thickness, in. = 0.23 × $Sn^{0.21}$ (English)

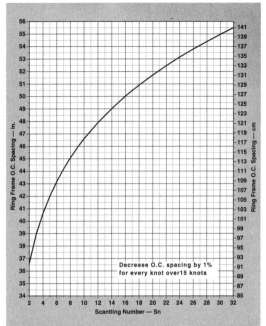

(2) Ring-Frame O.C. Spacing: Large Boats

Aluminum Hull-Bottom Ring-Frame Flange Width, in. = 1.75 × $Sn^{0.4}$ (English)

Aluminum Hull-Bottom Ring-Frame Flange Thickness, in. = 0.29 × $Sn^{0.21}$ (English)

Aluminum Hull-Bottom Ring-Frame Web Height, mm = 59.18 × $Sn^{0.4}$ (Metric)

Aluminum Hull-Bottom Ring-Frame Web Thickness, mm = 5.84 × $Sn^{0.21}$ (Metric)

Aluminum Hull-Bottom Ring-Frame Flange Width, mm = 44.45 × $Sn^{0.4}$ (Metric)

Aluminum Hull-Bottom Ring-Frame Flange Thickness, mm = 7.37 × $Sn^{0.21}$ (Metric)

(continued)

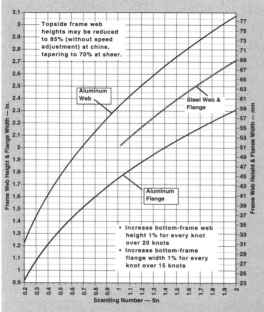

(3) *Ring-Frame Web Heights and Flange Widths: Small Boats*

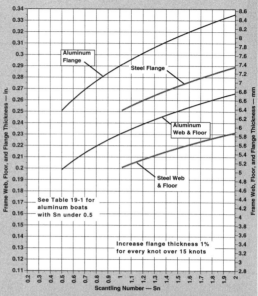

(5) *Ring-Frame Web and Flange Thicknesses and Floor Thickness: Small Boats*

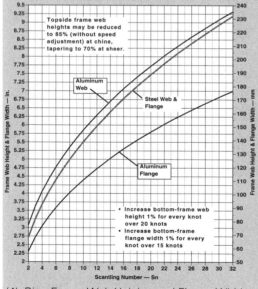

(4) *Ring-Frame Web Heights and Flange Widths: Large Boats*

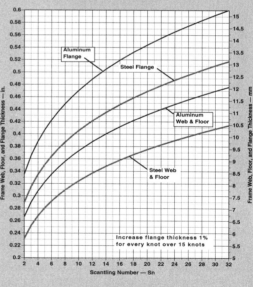

(6) *Ring-Frame Web and Flange Thicknesses and Floor Thickness: Large Boats*

Note that the flange's thickness is 1.25 times greater than the web. This maximizes the stiffness of the section while reducing its intrusion into the interior volume, and improves access to welding at the "closed bevel" side of the frame. If you prefer to use a flange the same thickness as the web, then increase the flange width 1.25 times.

The hull-bottom ring-frames on our reliable old *AlumaNaught* then work out as follows:

Aluminum Hull-Bottom Ring-Frame Web Height = $2.33 \times 8.71^{0.4} = 5.53$; use 5½ in.

Aluminum Hull-Bottom Ring-Frame Web Thickness = $0.23 \times 8.71^{0.21} = 0.36$; use ⅜ in.

Aluminum Hull-Bottom Ring-Frame Flange Width = $1.75 \times 8.71^{0.4} = 4.15$; use 4 in.

Aluminum Hull-Bottom Ring-Frame Flange Thickness = $0.29 \times 8.71^{0.21} = 0.45$; use $^7/_{16}$ or ½ in. (Alternately, use a ⅜ × 5 in. flange.)

Aluminum Hull-Bottom Ring-Frame Web Height = $59.18 \times 8.71^{0.4} = 140.6$; use 140 mm

Aluminum Hull-Bottom Ring-Frame Web Thickness = $5.84 \times 8.71^{0.21} = 9.2$; use 9.5 mm

Aluminum Hull-Bottom Ring-Frame Flange Width = $44.45 \times 8.71^{0.4} = 105.5$; use 100 mm

Aluminum Hull-Bottom Ring-Frame Flange Thickness = $7.37 \times 8.71^{0.21} = 11.61$; use 11.25 mm (Alternately, use a 9.5 × 125 mm flange.)

FORMULA 15-9S
Steel Ring-Frame Dimensions: Hull Bottom

Steel Hull-Bottom Ring-Frame Web Height, in. = $2.0 \times Sn^{0.44}$ (English)

Steel Hull-Bottom Ring-Frame Web Thickness, in. = $0.20 \times Sn^{0.21}$ (English)

Steel Hull-Bottom Ring-Frame Flange Width, in. = web height (English)

Steel Hull-Bottom Ring-Frame Flange Thickness, in. = $0.25 \times Sn^{0.21}$ (English)

Steel Hull-Bottom Ring-Frame Web Height, mm = $50.8 \times Sn^{0.44}$ (Metric)

Steel Hull-Bottom Ring-Frame Web Thickness, mm = $5.08 \times Sn^{0.21}$ (Metric)

Steel Hull-Bottom Ring-Frame Flange Width, mm = web height (Metric)

Steel Hull-Bottom Ring-Frame Flange Thickness, mm = $6.35 \times Sn^{0.21}$ (Metric)

As with the aluminum rule, the flange is 1.25 times thicker than the web. You can use a flange the same thickness as the web by increasing the web's width by 1.25 times. Applying this to *Iron Maiden*, we get the following:

Steel Hull-Bottom Ring-Frame Web Height = $2.0 \times 8.71^{0.44} = 5.18$; use 5¼ in.

Steel Hull-Bottom Ring-Frame Web Thickness = $0.20 \times 8.71^{0.21} = 0.31$; use $^5/_{16}$ in.

Steel Hull-Bottom Ring-Frame Flange Width = web height

Steel Hull-Bottom Ring-Frame Flange Thickness = $0.25 \times 8.71^{0.21} = 0.39$; use ⅜ in. (Alternately, use a $^5/_{16}$ × 6½ in. flange.)

Steel Hull-Bottom Ring-Frame Web Height = $50.8 \times 8.71^{0.44} = 131.6$; use 130 mm

Steel Hull-Bottom Ring-Frame Web Thickness = $5.08 \times 8.71^{0.21} = 8$ mm

Steel Hull-Bottom Ring-Frame Flange Width = web height

Steel Hull-Bottom Ring-Frame Flange Thickness = $6.35 \times 8.71^{0.21} = 10$ mm (Alternately, use 8 × 160 mm flange.)

ADJUSTING HULL-BOTTOM RING-FRAME SCANTLINGS FOR SPEED

Increase web height by 1 percent for every knot over 20 knots.

Increase flange width by 1 percent for every knot over 15 knots. Increase flange thickness by 1 percent for every knot over 15 knots. Only the bottom-frame scantlings are adjusted for speed in this way; the topsides frames and deck beams are unaffected.

In the case of our 35-knot *AlumaNaught*, the bottom frames would be adjusted to the following:

35 knots – 20 knots = 15 knots; therefore, increase web height by 15%

Bottom-Web Height = 1.15 × 5.53 in. = 6.35; use 6⅜ in.

35 knots – 15 knots = 20 knots; therefore, increase flange by 20%

Bottom-Flange Width = 1.20 × 4.15 in. = 4.95; use 5 in.

Bottom-Flange Thickness = 1.20 × 0.45 in. = 0.54; use ½ in.

or

35 knots – 20 knots = 15 knots; therefore, increase web height by 15%

Bottom-Web Height = 1.15 × 140.6 mm = 161.7; use 160 mm

35 knots – 15 knots = 20 knots; therefore, increase flange by 20%

Bottom-Flange Width = 1.20 × 105.5 mm = 126.6; use 125 mm

Bottom-Flange Thickness = 1.20 × 11.61 mm = 13.9; use 14 mm

The same approach would be used on a 35-knot *Iron Maiden*; however, it's rare to have steel hulls this size that are light enough to achieve such speeds efficiently.

VARYING FLANGE DIMENSIONS

The section properties of the combined frame, web, and flange determine its strength and stiffness. For the same web height and web thickness, a flat-plate flange will yield nearly identical section properties (i.e., moment of inertia and section modulus) if its area is the same. In other words—for any of the flat-bar flanges called for in the rule—you can substitute another flat bar that has the same total cross-section area. The resulting flange width, however, cannot exceed 12 times its thickness for aluminum or 15 times its thickness for steel.

For example, we found that *Aluma-Naught*'s speed-adjusted bottom flanges were 4.95 by 0.54 inches, which is 2.67 square inches. If you wanted to use a ⁷/₁₆-inch (0.4375-inch) flange instead of a ¹/₂-inch flange, you would divide 2.67 square inches by 0.4375 to get the new required flange width of 6.1 inches. Check to be sure this isn't too thin, as follows:

7.12 in. ÷ 0.375 in. = 13.9:1. This is greater than 12:1; therefore, it is too thin and can't be used.

or

For example, we found that *Aluma-Naught*'s speed-adjusted bottom flanges were 126.6 by 13.9 mm, which is 1,759 m². If you wanted to use a 11 mm flange instead of a 14 mm flange, you would divide 1,759 m² by 11 mm to get the new required flange width of 160 mm. Check to be sure this isn't too thin:

160 mm ÷ 11 mm = 14.59:1. This is greater than 12:1; therefore, it is too thin and can't be used.

In this example, you can't go much thinner than the speed-adjusted flange thickness from the rule. You could go thicker, though, reducing the flange width accordingly.

FORMULA 15-10
Aluminum and Steel Ring-Frame Dimensions: Topsides

On displacement and semi-displacement boats, the bottom frames are often carried up and around, unchanged, along the topsides to the sheer. However, you can save weight by reducing the web height as follows:

Web Height at Chine or Bilge = 0.85 × bottom-web height (not speed-adjusted)

Web Height at Sheer = 0.70 × bottom-web height (not speed-adjusted)

The flange can also be reduced in thickness, as follows:

Flange Thickness = Web Thickness

The weight saved here is minor, but well worth doing on high-speed craft; the lower web heights (moldings) gain an extra 1 or 2 inches (25 to 50 mm) of interior space.

CHANNEL AND SQUARE-TUBE HULL FRAMING

Some builders use channels welded open-end down against the inside of the plate, or square tube for hull frames, and even for longitudinals, deck beams, and cabin-roof beams. The sizing of such beams isn't covered in this rule, but I recommend against this practice. Water can get into or behind these shapes where corrosion can take place, but you can't ever see it to inspect.

TOPSIDE FRAMES ON SAILBOATS NEAR MAST AND CHAINPLATES

On sailboats, additional strength is required at the masts and shroud chainplates. The top-sides frames at the mast and chainplates should be the same dimensions as the hull-bottom frame (not the reduced topsides-frame dimensions). In addition—on boats with Sns greater than 3—the web thickness should be increased to the next standard plate size up. Usually, the two or three frames athwartships from the mast should meet this requirement; however, if shrouds fall at some other location, the topside frame there should be increased as well (see photo on p. 343).

FORMULA 15-11A
Aluminum Deck-Beam Dimensions

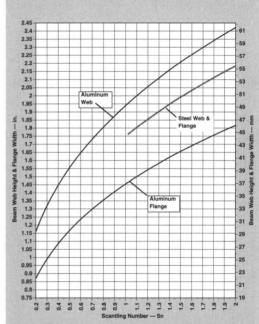

Deck-Beam-Web Heights and Flange Widths in Longitudinally Framed Hulls, Aluminum and Steel: Small Boats

Aluminum Deck-Beam-Web Height, in. = $1.94 \times Sn^{0.32}$ (English)

Aluminum Deck-Beam-Web Height, mm = $49.27 \times Sn^{0.32}$ (Metric)

(continued)

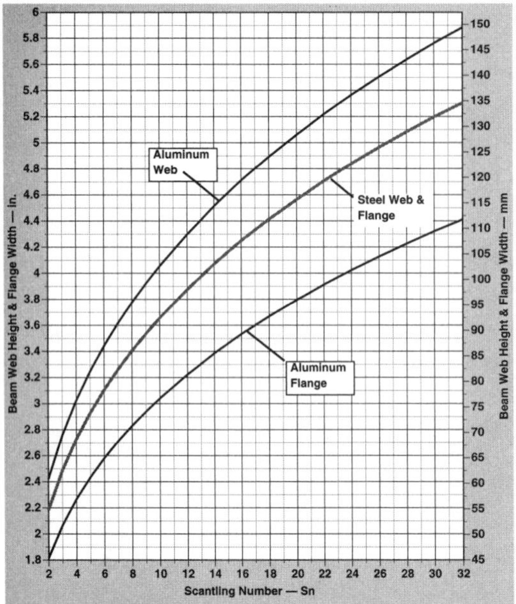

Deck-Beam-Web Heights and Flange Widths in Longitudinally Framed Hulls, Aluminum and Steel: Large Boats

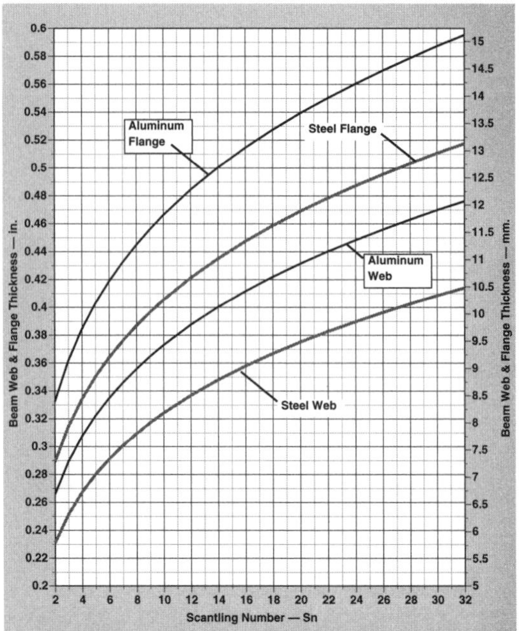

Deck-Beam-Web and Flange Thicknesses in Longitudinally Framed Hulls, Aluminum and Steel: Large Boats

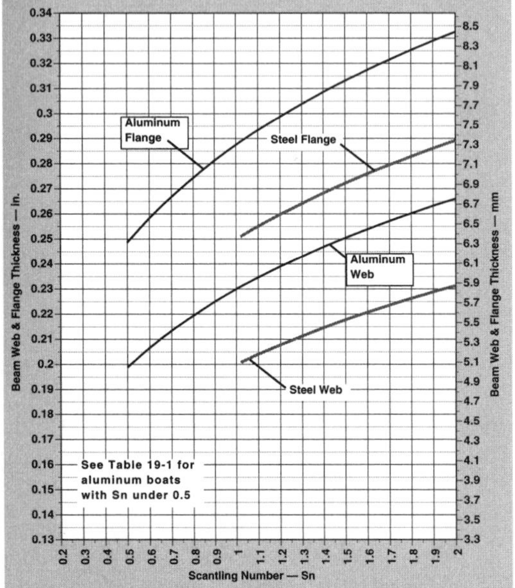

Deck-Beam-Web and Flange Thicknesses in Longitudinally Framed Hulls, Aluminum and Steel: Small Boats

Aluminum Deck-Beam-Web Thickness, in. = same as bottom and topsides web

Aluminum Deck-Beam-Flange Width, in. = 0.75 × web height

Aluminum Deck-Beam Flange Thickness, in. = 1.25 × web thickness

Here again, you can choose a flange that is the same thickness as the web, but then increase the flange width by 1.25 times. *AlumaNaught*'s deck beams then would be

Aluminum Deck-Beam-Web Height, in. = $1.94 \times 8.71^{0.32} = 3.87$; use 3⅞ or 4 in.

Aluminum Deck-Beam-Web Height, mm = $49.27 \times 8.71^{0.32} = 98.49$; use 100 mm

Aluminum Deck-Beam-Web Thickness, in. = ⅜ in. (9.5 mm)

*Aluminum Deck-Beam-Flange Width, in. =
3 in. (75 mm)*

*Aluminum Deck-Beam-Flange Thickness, in.
= 7/16 or 1/2 in. (11.25 mm) (Alternately, use
3/8 × 4 7/8 in. or 5 in. flange [9.5 × 125 mm].)*

FORMULA 15-11S
Steel Deck-Beam Dimensions

Steel Deck-Beam-Web Height, in. = 1.75
× $Sn^{0.32}$ (English)

Steel Deck-Beam-Web Height, mm =
44.45 × $Sn^{0.32}$ (Metric)

Steel Deck-Beam-Web Thickness, in. =
same as bottom and topsides web

Steel Deck-Beam-Flange Width =
web height

Steel Deck-Beam-Flange Thickness =
1.25 × web thickness

If you want the flange to be the same thickness as the web, multiply its width by 1.25. This means that our *Iron Maiden* should have

Steel Deck-Beam-Web Height, in. = 1.75 ×
$8.71^{0.32}$ = 3.49; use 3 1/2 in.

Steel Deck-Beam-Web Height, mm = 44.45 ×
$8.71^{0.32}$ = 88.8; use 90 mm

Steel Deck-Beam-Web Thickness, in. =
5/16 in. (8 mm)

Steel Deck-Beam-Flange Width =
web height

Steel Deck-Beam-Flange Thickness =
3/8 in. (10 mm) (Alternately, use 5/16 × 4 3/8 in.
flange [8 × 110 mm].)

NOTES ON RING FRAMES
The ring frames in this rule are Ts. It is assumed that they'll be built up in the new

method from cut plate welded together. On hard-chine vessels—where the hull curvature of the frames may be slight, or if you prefer to bend standard extrusions—you'll need to use the rule results for a flange with a thickness equal to that of the web. Keep in mind, however, that the formula web height doesn't include the flange thickness. You have to add flange thickness to web height to get the height for an off-the-shelf extrusion.

OPEN- OR CLOSED-BEVEL FRAMES
Angles are also perfectly acceptable for frames. Their webs and flanges should be sized exactly the same as the Ts. An important consideration with angles is that if their flange projects aft from the web forward of midships, and forward of the web aft of midships, then the angles project farther into the hull interior and steal room. At the same time, though, the frame's welds are easier to get at, both during construction and for later

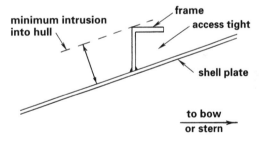

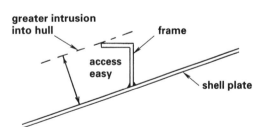

Top: Closed-bevel frame. Bottom: Open-bevel frame.

painting, inspection, and repairs. Angle frames installed in this orientation are termed *open-bevel* frames.

Because of the necessity to clean, paint, and inspect under the flanges, open-bevel frames are strongly recommended on steel hulls. On aluminum vessels, though, *closed-bevel* frames (i.e., flanges pointing forward, forward of midships; and pointing aft, aft of midships) will increase interior volume. Be sure there is enough clearance to get a MIG welding gun in to work on the frames up in the bow.

An approach that can help in this regard with Ts is to locate the flange of the T off-center, with either a fourth or a third of the flange either fore or aft of the web. In this way, you can produce open- or closed-bevel Ts. On a steel hull, an open-bevel T aids in painting and inspection; on an aluminum hull, a closed-bevel T increases usable volume.

On Ts, the knee is welded to the underside of the flanges; however, on angle frames, the knees are welded to the opposite sides from the flanges. Here, the knee lies on top of the web, forming an overlap.

Minimum Overlap of Knee onto Both Deck-Beam Web and Topsides-Frame Web = 0.3 × non-speed-adjusted bottom-frame-web height

On sailboats, the frames at the mast and chainplates need extra strength. The minimum radius should be 1.3 times the non-speed-adjusted bottom-frame-web height on these frames, or

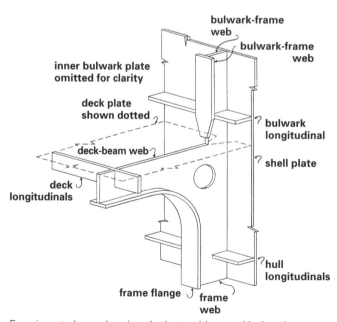

Framing at sheer showing deck, topsides, and bulwark

the knee should be 1.7 times the bottom-web height. Thus, *AlumaNaught* would be fitted with the following:

Minimum Frame-Web Radius at Sheer = 5.5 in. (140 mm)

Minimum Knee Length = 5.5 in. × 1.3 = 7.15; use 7 in.

Minimum Knee Length = 140.6 mm × 1.3 = 182.7; use 180 mm

Minimum Knee Overlap = 5.5 in. × 0.3 = 1.65; use 1⅝ in.

Minimum Knee Overlap = 140.6 mm × 0.3 = 42.18; use 42 mm

Precisely the same approach would be used on our steel *Iron Maiden*.

FORMULA 15-13A

Aluminum Centerline Vertical Keel (CVK) and Stem

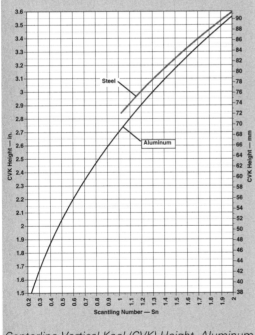

Centerline Vertical Keel (CVK) Height, Aluminum and Steel: Small Boats

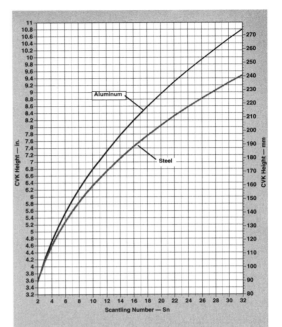

Centerline Vertical Keel (CVK) Height, Aluminum and Steel: Large Boats

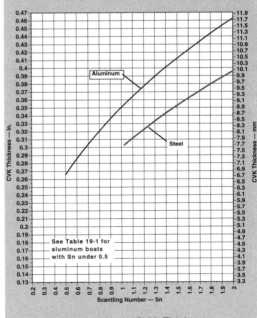

Centerline Vertical Keel (CVK) Thickness, Aluminum and Steel: Small Boats

(continued)

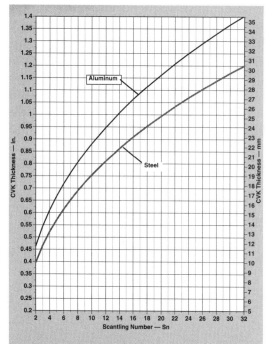

Centerline Vertical Keel (CVK) Thickness, Aluminum and Steel: Large Boats

For standard flat-plate CVKs:

Aluminum CVK Height, in. = 2.7 × Sn$^{0.4}$ (English)

Aluminum CVK Height, mm = 68.58 × Sn$^{0.4}$ (Metric)

Aluminum CVK Thickness = height ÷ 7.7

Horn plates are the same as the CVK—the CVK aft of the deep keel. Stems are the same thickness, but may taper in height (molding) to 60 percent of the CVK maximum at the sheer. *AlumaNaught*'s CVK backbone then works out as

Aluminum CVK Height = 2.7 × 8.71$^{0.4}$ = 6.41; use 6½ in.

Aluminum CVK Height = 68.58 × 8.71$^{0.4}$ = 163; use 165 mm

Aluminum CVK Thickness = 6.41 in. ÷ 7.7 = 0.83; use ⅞ in.

Aluminum CVK Thickness = 163 mm ÷ 7.7 = 21.1; use 22 mm

FORMULA 15-13S
Steel CVK and Stem

For standard flat-plate CVKs:

Steel CVK Height, in. = 2.82 × Sn$^{0.35}$ (English)

Steel CVK Thickness, in. = 0.30 × Sn$^{0.4}$ (English)

Steel CVK Height, mm = 71.62 × Sn$^{0.35}$ (Metric)

Steel CVK Thickness, mm = 7.62 × Sn$^{0.4}$ (Metric)

Horn plates are the same as the CVK—the CVK aft of the deep keel. Stems are the same thickness, but may taper in height (molding) to 60 percent of the CVK maximum at the sheer. The upper 60 percent of the stem CVK can also be 80 percent of the CVK maximum thickness. This means that *Iron Maiden* would have

Steel CVK Height = 2.82 × 8.71$^{0.35}$ = 6.01; use 6 in.

Steel CVK Thickness = 0.30 × 8.71$^{0.4}$ = 0.71; use ¾ in.

Steel CVK Height = 71.62 × 8.71$^{0.35}$ = 152.7; use 150 mm

Steel CVK Thickness = 7.62 × 8.71$^{0.4}$ = 18.1; use 18 mm

The upper-stem CVK thickness could be reduced to ⅝ inch (16 mm).

CVKs AS EXTERNAL SKEGS
The CVK can be entirely in the boat or it may extend some distance below the bottom

plate to form an exterior skeg keel. In this case, it is normal for the CVK height to be much greater than the minimum specified by the rule.

FORMULA 15-14
Stern Frame

The stern frame is the CVK where it is split by the stern tube at the aft end of the keel—on single-screw vessels. It runs roughly vertically from the bottom of the keel or skeg, up the trailing edge of the keel to the horn timber, to which it is welded. Twin-engine craft do not require a heavier stern frame; their CVK is constant thickness along the hull bottom.

Stern-Frame Thickness = 1.42 × CVK thickness

AlumaNaught's stern frame would then be

> *0.83 in. × 1.42 = 1.17 in.; use 1¼ in.*
> *21.1 mm × 1.42 = 29.9; use 30 mm*

Iron Maiden's stern frame works out to

> *0.71 in. × 1.42 = 1.07; use 1 in.*
> *18 mm × 1.42 = 25.5; use 25 mm*

Fore-n-aft, the stern frame should extend to at least a full ring-frame length. It should be welded to a floor for at least twice the height of the CVK, which will butt against and be welded to the forward face of the same floor.

FORMULA 15-15
Floors

Floors connect the frames from both sides of the vessel across the CVK, just as in wood construction.

Floor Thickness = same as speed-adjusted bottom-frame webs

Floor Height = at least the same as the CVK

Floors can be integral with the new-method built-up ring-frame or welded to the faces of frames made of angles. If the frames consist of Ts, the Ts are cropped and the floor butt is welded to them.

Preferably, the floors should extend at least 60 percent of the bottom-frame-web height above the CVK, with the bottom-frame flange extending across the top of the floor. On some boats with deep box keels, this almost happens naturally. Other craft, with shallow bilges and no box keel, may lose too much interior height to such deep floors. In this case, floors the same height as the CVK are acceptable. Run the bottom-frame flange along the top of the floors; in any case, continuously athwartships across the top of the CVK.

BOX KEELS

Most displacement vessels have deep box keels. These deep-section keels are far stronger than the standard CVK plate, so the CVK can be eliminated wherever the box keel exists. The true CVK stem runs down into the box keel at its leading edge, and is welded to the top of the keel-bottom plate and to the floors. The stem should extend at least one full frame bay aft of the front of the box keel.

At the aft end of the box keel, the stern frame is welded to the top of the keel-bottom plate and to the aft floors. The box keel's side plates usually sweep in to join to the stern frame, port and starboard. Aft of the box keel, the CVK reappears as the horn plate, which is welded to the top of the stern frame.

Weight in the keel of displacement hulls is not detrimental, so I usually round up on

Welding on box-keel steel sideplates. (Courtesy Treworgy Yachts)

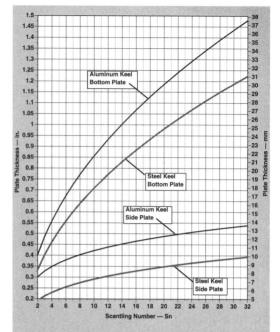

Box-Keel Side- and Bottom-Plate Thickness, Aluminum and Steel: Large Boats

the keel plate to maximize corrosion and impact resistance. In addition, on sailboats and many voyaging motor cruisers, the weight of the box-keel plating can be deducted from the lead ballast.

FORMULA 15-16A
Aluminum Box-Keel Sides

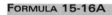
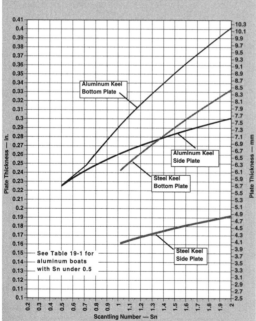

Box-Keel Side- and Bottom-Plate Thickness, Aluminum and Steel: Small Boats

> **Aluminum Box-Keel-Side Plate, in. = $0.26 \times Sn^{0.21}$ (English)**
>
> **Aluminum Box-Keel-Side Plate, mm = $6.6 \times Sn^{0.21}$ (Metric)**

AlumaNaught's box-keel-side plate should then be

> **Aluminum Box-Keel-Side Plate = $0.26 \times 8.71^{0.21} = 0.41$; use $^{7}/_{16}$ in.**
>
> **Aluminum Box-Keel-Side Plate = $6.6 \times 8.71^{0.21} = 10.39$; use 11 mm**

FORMULA 15-16S
Steel Box-Keel Sides

> **Steel Box-Keel-Side Plate, in. = $0.16 \times Sn^{0.26}$ (English)**
>
> **Steel Box-Keel-Side Plate, mm = $4.06 \times Sn^{0.26}$ (Metric)**

Thus, the box-keel-side plate on *Iron Maiden* would be

Steel Box-Keel-Side Plate = 0.16 × 8.71^0.26 = 0.28; use ⁵⁄₁₆ in.

$$Steel\ Box\text{-}Keel\text{-}Side\ Plate = 0.16 \times 8.71^{0.26} = 0.28;\ use\ \tfrac{5}{16}\ in.$$

$$Steel\ Box\text{-}Keel\text{-}Side\ Plate = 4.06 \times 8.71^{0.26} = 7.12;\ use\ 7.9\ mm$$

BOX-KEEL-BOTTOM PLATE

The bottom plate of the box keel takes all the grounding loads and abrasion imposed by the weight of the entire hull. It should be quite heavy. Again, the weight can be deducted from the lead ballast. On steel hulls, the combined weight of the heavy box-keel-side plate and the bottom plate can make a substantial contribution to the total ballast weight.

FORMULA 15-17A

Aluminum Box-Keel-Bottom Plate

$$Aluminum\ Box\text{-}Keel\text{-}Bottom\ Plate,\ in. = 0.29 \times Sn^{0.4}\ (English)$$

$$Aluminum\ Box\text{-}Keel\text{-}Bottom\ Plate,\ mm = 7.37 \times Sn^{0.4}\ (Metric)$$

Accordingly, *AlumaNaught's* box-keel-bottom plate would be

$$Aluminum\ Box\text{-}Keel\text{-}Bottom\ Plate = 0.29 \times 8.71^{0.4} = 0.80\ in.;\ use\ \tfrac{7}{8}\ or\ 1\ in.$$

$$Aluminum\ Box\text{-}Keel\text{-}Bottom\ Plate = 7.37 \times 8.71^{0.4} = 20.3;\ use\ 20\ to\ 25\ mm$$

Thicker doesn't hurt here, so I might even use a $1^1/_4$-inch (30 mm) box-keel-bottom plate. The thickness from the formula should be about minimum.

For Sns less than 0.65, the bottom-plate formula gives smaller thicknesses than for the side plate. Use the thicker side plate on the bottom, or refer to the box-keel-thickness chart.

FORMULA 15-17S

Steel Box-Keel-Bottom Plate

$$Steel\ Box\text{-}Keel\text{-}Bottom\ Plate,\ in. = 0.24 \times Sn^{0.4}\ (English)$$

$$Steel\ Box\text{-}Keel\text{-}Bottom\ Plate,\ mm = 6.09 \times Sn^{0.4}\ (Metric)$$

The keel-bottom plate on *Iron Maiden* is then

$$Steel\ Box\text{-}Keel\text{-}Bottom\ Plate = 0.24 \times 8.71^{0.4} = 0.66;\ use\ \tfrac{5}{8}\ in.$$

$$Steel\ Box\text{-}Keel\text{-}Bottom\ Plate = 6.09 \times 8.71^{0.4} = 16.8;\ use\ 17\ mm$$

Once again, thicker bottom plates are usually better (within reason); therefore, $^7/_8$ or 1 inch (22 to 25 mm) would certainly be worth considering. Even thicker bottom plates still could be installed for ballast purposes.

CHINE ROD

On hard-chine craft, some builders use a chine rod or round bar at the corner between the bottom and topsides plate. The argument for this is that it is somewhat easier to make a fair joint and the heavy rod can take more abuse than a sharp welded corner. Still, it is perfectly acceptable to simply weld the topsides and bottom plates together with no chine rod. Indeed, a drawback to chine rods is that they form a narrow crevice (against the inside of the topside plate) where water can collect and corrosion can start—which is particularly troubling in steel.

FORMULA 15-18A

Aluminum Chine-Rod Diameter

$$Aluminum\ Chine\text{-}Rod\ Diameter,\ in. = 0.42 \times Sn^{0.38}\ (English)$$

$$Aluminum\ Chine\text{-}Rod\ Diameter,\ mm = 10.66 \times Sn^{0.38}\ (Metric)$$

(continued)

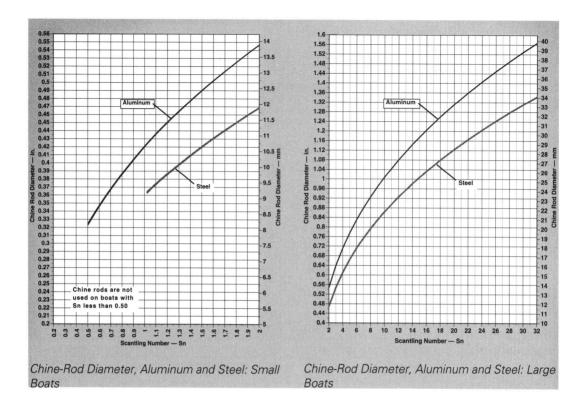

Chine-Rod Diameter, Aluminum and Steel: Small Boats

Chine-Rod Diameter, Aluminum and Steel: Large Boats

The chine rod on *AlumaNaught* is

*Aluminum Chine-Rod Diameter = 0.42 ×
8.71$^{0.38}$ = 0.95; use 1-in. diameter*

*Aluminum Chine-Rod Diameter = 10.66 ×
8.71$^{0.38}$ = 24.2; use 25 mm diameter*

Chine rods are not used on boats with Sns less than 0.50.

FORMULA 15-18S
Steel Chine-Rod Diameter

*Steel Chine-Rod Diameter, in. = 0.36 ×
Sn$^{0.38}$ (English)*

*Steel Chine-Rod Diameter, mm = 9.14 ×
Sn$^{0.38}$ (Metric)*

The chine rod on *Iron Maiden* is

*Steel Chine-Rod Diameter = 0.36 × 8.71$^{0.38}$ =
0.81; use ⅞-in. diameter*

*Steel Chine-Rod Diameter = 9.14 × 8.71$^{0.38}$ =
20.8; use 20 mm diameter*

SIXTEEN

Aluminum and Steel Structural Details

*A*lthough the plate and framing discussed in chapter 15 describe the basic hull structure—as we've seen for other materials—there are numerous secondary structures and details required to complete a strong and long-lasting vessel. Bulkheads, cabin roofs, mast partners, engine beds, and more: we examine these items in this chapter.

Bulkheads

Bulkheads fall into one of the following three categories:

- joiner bulkheads (wood, nonstructural)
- metal structural bulkheads, watertight or not (not rated for full head)
- metal watertight collision bulkheads (rated for full head of water to 1 foot [30 cm] above the top of the bulkhead)

JOINER BULKHEADS

These days, joiner bulkheads are almost exclusively from sheet ply (i.e., marine, exterior grade, or MDO). On boats between 35 and 100 feet (10 to 30 m), joiner bulkheads are from $1/2$ to $3/4$ inch (12 to 20 mm) thick, with $3/4$ inch (20 mm) being most common. On vessels under 35 feet (10 m), joiner bulkheads as thin as $3/8$-inch (9.5 mm) ply may be used; however, $1/2$ or $5/8$ inch (12 or 16 mm) are stiffer and easier to hold in plane and fasten to.

Old practice was to fabricate joiner bulkheads out of tongue-and-groove lumber. This still works well, but is more costly and noticeably heavier than ply. The minimum practical thickness is about $1^1/2$ to 2 inches (38 to 50 mm), which also steals a little more interior room.

METAL STRUCTURAL BULKHEADS (WATERTIGHT AND NOT)

Most larger metal hulls have several metal structural bulkheads separating the machinery spaces, the lazarette, and the forepeak. These may or may not be watertight. Although it increases safety to have several fully watertight bulkheads in the hull, it also complicates the bilge piping system and can break up the accommodations unacceptably.

Even nonwatertight structural metal bulkheads help prevent the spread of fire and combustion byproduct gases. A nonwatertight bulkhead between machinery and accommodations spaces, which has a combined opening area of less than 0.01 percent of the area of the bulkhead separating the accommodation and machinery, is considered effective at containing the spread of both noxious gases and fire.

Unlike FRP hulls and some forms of wood-epoxy hulls, even the so-called "structural" bulkheads on a metal boat aren't required for strength. The basic framing and plate alone are quite robust enough by themselves. Bulkheads on aluminum and steel craft are principally to divide the vessel into compartments to separate machinery, accommodations, and cargo spaces, and to increase watertight integrity in case of a hull breach.

For strength purposes, full structural bulkheads are called for under exceptionally heavy-load deck machinery, such as cranes, dredges, and similar heavy lifting equipment.

Common Locations of Metal Bulkheads

On boats under 60 feet (18 m), I usually use a full watertight collision bulkhead at the aft end of the forepeak (between 5 and 15 percent of WL aft of the WL at the bow) and another aft at the forward end of the lazarette, if the arrangement permits (i.e., no aft cabin in the hull). Under 40 feet (12 m), it's difficult even to work in a collision bulkhead forward.

Vessels over 60 or 70 feet (18 or 20 m) can often fit two additional bulkheads, one forward and one aft of the engine compartment.

It's tempting to make these watertight; however, there are drawbacks. All the penetrations through these centrally located bulkheads (including propeller shaft, wires, hoses, and vent ducts) must be made watertight, which is time-consuming and costly. Fully watertight access doors are heavy and cumbersome, and awkward to fit in. This extra investment should be made for serious ocean-voyaging yachts and workboats; however, it's not usually warranted for ordinary yachts.

Bulkhead Stiffeners

Bulkhead stiffeners should not touch the hull. They should end about three to four times the stiffener's web thickness from the hull shell, inside. Their flanges should be sniped back or beveled at their ends to avoid sharp projecting corners. Alternately, the vertical stiffeners can be aligned with and welded to the deck longitudinals. It may not be convenient to do this, though, and the added strength is not required.

Decreasing Weight on Steel Bulkheads

To decrease weight on steel bulkheads, the upper 40 percent of the bulkhead is usually reduced in thickness to the next standard plate size down. This can only be done, of course, when the resulting lighter upper-bulkhead plate won't be too thin to weld. Aluminum bulkheads can be treated the same way, but this is appropriate only on the lightest and highest-performance aluminum vessels.

FORMULA 16-1A

Aluminum Bulkheads (Not Rated for Full Head)

Aluminum Bulkhead Plate = same as deck plate

Aluminum Bulkhead Vertical Stiffeners O.C., in. = 5 + (plate thickness, in. × 38) (English)

Aluminum Bulkhead Vertical Stiffeners O.C., mm = 127 + (plate thickness, mm × 38) (Metric)

Aluminum Bulkhead Stiffener: web height, in. = 15 × plate thickness (does not include flange thickness)

Aluminum Bulkhead Stiffener: flange and web thickness = plate thickness + 1/16 in. (English)

Aluminum Bulkhead Stiffener: flange and web thickness = plate thickness + 1.6 mm (Metric)

Aluminum Bulkhead Stiffener: flange width = web height ÷ 1.4

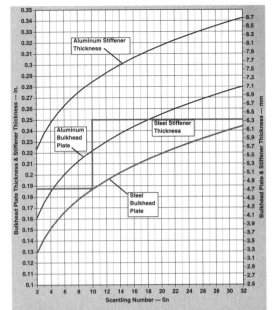

Bulkhead Plate and Stiffener Thickness, Aluminum and Steel: Large Boats (Not Rated for Full Head)

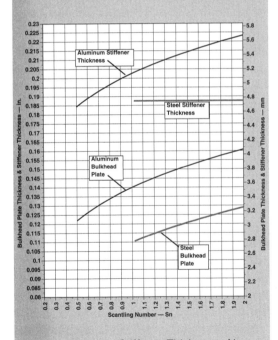

Bulkhead Plate and Stiffener Thickness, Aluminum and Steel: Small Boats (Not Rated for Full Head)

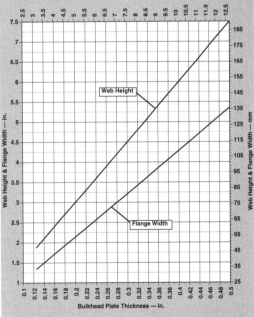

Aluminum Bulkhead Stiffener, Web Heights and Flange Widths (Not Rated for Full Head)

(continued)

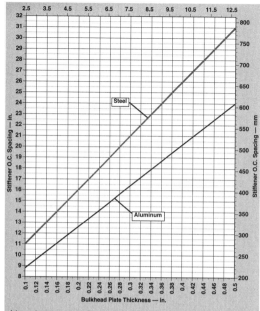

Aluminum and Steel Bulkhead-Stiffener O.C.
Spacing (Not Rated for Full Head)

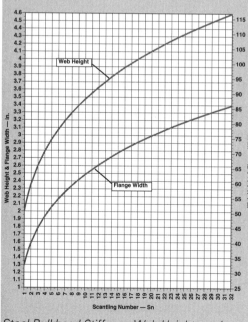

Steel Bulkhead Stiffener, Web Heights and
Flange Widths (Not Rated for Full Head)

In the previous chapter, *AlumaNaught's* deck plate was $3/16$ inch (4.75 mm). Accordingly, its bulkheads would be

Aluminum Bulkhead Plate = $3/16$ in.
(0.1875 in.)

Aluminum Bulkhead Vertical Stiffeners O.C.
= 5 + (0.1875 in. × 38) = 12.1; use 12 in.

Aluminum Bulkhead Vertical Stiffeners O.C.
= 127 + (4.75 mm × 38) = 307.5; use 300 mm

Aluminum Bulkhead Stiffener: web height =
15 × 0.1875 = 2.81 in.

Aluminum Bulkhead Stiffener: web height =
15 × 4.75 = 71.2

Aluminum Bulkhead Stiffener: flange and
web thickness = $3/16$ + $1/16$ in. = $1/4$ in.

Aluminum Bulkhead Stiffener: flange and
web thickness = 4.75 + 1.6 mm = 6.35;
use 6.4 mm

Aluminum Bulkhead Stiffener: flange width
= 2.81 in. ÷ 1.4 = 2 in.

Aluminum Bulkhead Stiffener: flange width
= 71.2 mm ÷ 1.4 = 50.8; use 50 mm

Bulkhead stiffeners can be Ts or angles interchangeably. Angles are most common, because—being straight—there's no reason to make these up. It's quicker and less expensive to use off-the-shelf extrusions. We have to add the flange thickness to the web height to get the full extrusion height

2.81 in. web + 0.25 in. flange = 3.06;
use 3 in. height

71.2 mm web + 6.4 mm flange = 77.6; use
78 mm height

Thus, $1/4$ in. × 3 in. × 2 in. angles, 12 in. O.C.
would fill the bill;

or

6.4 mm × 80 mm × 50 mm, 300 mm O.C.
would fill the bill

Steel Bulkheads (Not Rated for Full Head)

Steel Bulkhead Plate = same as deck plate

Steel Upper-Bulkhead Plate = next standard plate size down on the upper 40% of the bulkhead

Steel Bulkhead Vertical Stiffeners O.C., in. = 6 + (plate thickness, in. × 50) (English)

Steel Bulkhead Vertical Stiffeners O.C., mm = 152.4 + (plate thickness, mm × 50) (Metric)

Steel Bulkhead Stiffener: web height, in. = (2 × $Sn^{0.24}$) – 0.4 (including flange thickness) (English)

Steel Bulkhead Stiffener: web height, mm = (50.8 × $Sn^{0.24}$) – 10.16 (including flange thickness) (Metric)

Steel Bulkhead Stiffener: flange and web thickness = ¼ in. for all bulkheads with plate thicker than $3/16$ in.; $3/16$ in. for plate $3/16$ in. or less (English)

Steel Bulkhead Stiffener: flange and web thickness = 6.4 mm for all bulkheads with plate thicker than 4.75 mm; 4.75 mm for plate 4.75 mm or less (Metric)

Steel Bulkhead Stiffener: flange width, in. = (0.81 × web height in.) – 0.33 (English)

Steel Bulkhead Stiffener: flange width, mm = (0.81 × web height, mm) – 8.38 (Metric)

In the last chapter, *Iron Maiden*'s deck plate was $3/16$-inch mild steel or 8-gauge Cor-Ten (0.1664 in.) (4.75 mm mild steel or 4 mm Cor-Ten). Using Cor-Ten to reduce weight, *Iron Maiden*'s bulkheads work out as

Steel Bulkhead Plate = Cor-Ten 8-gauge (0.1664 in.) (4 mm)

Steel Upper-Bulkhead Plate = Cor-Ten 10-gauge (0.1345 in.) (3.4 mm)

Steel Bulkhead Vertical Stiffeners O.C. = 6 + (0.1664 in. × 50) = 14.3; use 14 in.

Steel Bulkhead Vertical Stiffeners O.C. = 152.4 + (4 mm × 50) = 352.4; use 350 mm

Steel Bulkhead Stiffener: web height = (2 × $8.71^{0.24}$) – 0.4 = 2.96; use 3 in.

Steel Bulkhead Stiffener: web height = (50.8 × $8.71^{0.24}$) – 10.16 = 75.2; use 75 mm

Steel Bulkhead Stiffener: flange and web thickness = $3/16$ in.

Steel Bulkhead Stiffener: flange and web thickness = 4.75 mm

Steel Bulkhead Stiffener: flange width = (0.81 × 2.96 in.) – 0.33 = 2.06; use 2 in.

Steel Bulkhead Stiffener: flange width = (0.81 × 75.2 mm) – 8.38 = 52.5; use 50 mm

Bulkhead stiffeners can be Ts or angles interchangeably. Angles are most common, because—being straight—there's no reason to make these up. It's quicker and less expensive to use off-the-shelf extrusions. The rule for steel bulkhead stiffeners *does include* the thickness of the flange in the web height, so we would find that

$3/16$ n. × 3 in. × 2 in. angles, 14 in. O.C. would do the job

or

4.75 mm × 75 mm × 50 mm, 350 mm O.C. would do the job

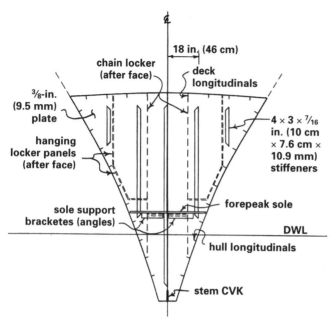

Forward-collision bulkhead, 10-foot (3 m) head, looking aft

WATERTIGHT COLLISION BULKHEADS AND TANK WALLS

The bulkheads from Formulas 16-1A and S may or may not be strong enough to rate as full watertight collision bulkheads. The controlling factor is the head or the height of water that the bulkhead can withstand with adequate safety. Formulas 16-1A and S simply estimate approximate strength based on the Sn. For wide shallow-bodied boats—where the head will be low—it will give over-strength bulkheads in terms of head. For deep bodied hull, Formulas 16-1A and S bulkheads may not be strong enough.

To ensure that a bulkhead can withstand a head of water 1 foot (30 cm) above the top of the deck, use the following tables. The head in feet or meters is the distance from the bottom-most point of that bulkhead on the keel to the underside of the deck at the centerline. Watertight collision bulkheads in the middle of a deep-bodied hull need to be beefier than the shallower bulkheads at the ends of such a hull.

TABLE 16-2A   Aluminum Watertight Collision Bulkheads and Tanks (English)

Head, ft.	Plate Thickness, in.	Stiffener			
		O.C., in.	Web, in.	Flange, in.	Thickness, in.
4	0.1875	12	2.0	1.0	0.1875
6	0.2500	18	2.5	2.0	0.2500
8	0.2500	18	3.5	2.5	0.3750
10	0.3750	18	4.0	3.0	0.4375
12	0.3750	18	6.0	3.0	0.4375
14	0.4375	18	6.0	4.0	0.6250
16	0.4375	18	8.0	4.0	0.6250

See table note on page 260.

TABLE 16-2A Aluminum Watertight Collision Bulkheads and Tanks (Metric)

Head, m	Plate Thickness, mm	Stiffener			
		O.C., mm	Web, mm	Flange, mm	Thickness, mm
1.22	4.75	300	50	25	4.75
1.83	6.40	450	65	50	6.40
2.44	6.40	450	90	65	9.50
3.05	9.50	450	100	75	11.25
3.66	9.50	450	150	75	11.25
4.27	11.25	450	150	100	16.00
4.88	11.25	450	200	100	16.00

See table note on page 260.

TABLE 16-2S Steel Watertight Collision Bulkheads and Tanks (English)

Head, ft.	Plate Thickness, in.	Stiffener			
		O.C., in.	Web, in.	Flange, in.	Thickness, in.
4	0.1345	12	1.25	1.00	0.1250
6	0.1644	12	2.00	1.00	0.1875
8	0.1875	18	3.00	1.75	0.2500
10	0.2500	18	4.00	2.50	0.2500
12	0.2500	18	5.00	2.25	0.3750
14	0.2500	18	5.00	4.00	0.3750
16	0.3125	18	6.00	4.75	0.3750

See table note on page 260.

TANKS DESIGNED FOR HEAD (PRESSURE)

The walls of integral tanks need to meet the same criteria for head; therefore, the tables also give wall thickness and stiffeners for tanks. Because large tanks need baffles, every other stiffener should be replaced with an internal baffle so that no area measures more than 36 inches (92 cm) of free surface in any direction. (As much as 44 inches [112 cm] in the fore-n-aft direction is acceptable, as long as there are adequate stiffeners on the walls.) Baffles must have large snipes that double as limbers cut out in all four corners, with a central hole as well. The total cut-out area should be about 18 to 20 percent of the baffle's square area; more would reduce the baffles effectiveness and less could impede fluid flow.

TABLE 16-2S Steel Watertight Collision Bulkheads and Tanks (Metric)

			Stiffener		
Head, m	Plate Thickness, mm	O.C., mm	Web, mm	Flange, mm	Thickness, mm
1.22	3.40	300	32	25	3.20
1.83	4.20	300	50	25	4.75
2.44	4.75	450	75	45	6.40
3.05	6.40	450	100	64	6.40
3.66	6.40	450	130	58	9.50
4.27	6.40	450	130	100	9.50
4.88	8.00	450	160	120	9.50

For fuel tanks—regardless of the height of the plumbing—in no case should a total pressure head of less than 3 psi or 20.7 kPa (6.9 feet or 2.1 m) be used for yachts, and never less than 5 psi or 34.5 kPa (11.5 feet or 3.5 m) for charter vessels and workboats.

Determining Tank Head

The curious and most critical thing about pressure head on tanks is that it is not mea-

Engine-room bulkhead, 5-foot (1.5 m) head

sured to the top of the tank but rather to the top of the highest plumbing point. For instance, say that you have an integral diesel tank in the bilge. Its top is just 3 feet (0.91 m) "deep" above the keel and 1 foot (0.30 m) below the waterline. However, the fill is on deck 4 feet (1.22 m) above the WL, and the vent is on the cabin roof 5 feet (1.52 m) above that. You need to use the height from the bottom of the tank to the top of the vent for head. (You can't just use the height to the fill because, if the tank were topped up with cold fuel and capped off, the fuel will then warm up on a hot summer day. The fluid will expand and rise to fill a surprising portion of the vent tube.) This works out to the remarkable head of

3 ft. deep tank + 1 ft. to WL + 4 ft. WL to deck + 5 ft. to cabin top vent = 13 ft.!

or

0.91 m deep tank + 0.3 m to WL + 1.22 m WL to deck + 1.52 m to cabin top vent = 3.95 m!

Thin-Plate Bulkheads and Tanks and Structural Penetrations

Small tanks with low heads require plate thickness too thin to weld except with pulse-arc equipment. Usually, you simply use the smallest conveniently weldable thickness. Adequate plate thickness for welding is critical on tanks and watertight bulkheads because the welds must be tight. It's much easier to ensure a proper seal on a heavier weld. Indeed, on penetrations of the watertight bulkhead and tanks—with thinner plate—it's good practice to weld in an insert plate of twice the plate thickness surrounding the penetrating member. This allows quite heavy and, therefore, tight welding around the corners of stringers and pipes. On integral fuel tanks, in particular, my preference is to cut the longitudinal framing at the tank wall and butt-weld these to the tank-wall plate fore-n-aft.

Superstructure Framing and Cabin Roofs

CABIN FRAMING

The cabin and superstructure sides are framed out much like the hull. The ring frames—wherever possible—continue up into the cabin sides, and longitudinal stiffeners are notched into these fore-n-aft.

Formula 16-3A

Aluminum Cabin-Side Framing

Aluminum Cabin-Side Plate from Formula 15-4A

Aluminum Cabin-Side-Frames O.C. = hull frame O.C.

Aluminum Cabin-Side-Frame Web Height, in. = $2.1 \times Sn^{0.21}$ (English)

Aluminum Cabin-Side-Frame Web Height, mm = $53.34 \times Sn^{0.21}$ (Metric)

Aluminum Cabin-Side-Frame Web and Flange Thickness = web height ÷ 11.67

Aluminum Cabin-Side-Flange Width = $0.55 \times$ web height

Aluminum Cabin-Side-Longitudinal Height = $0.52 \times$ web height

Aluminum Cabin-Side-Longitudinal Thickness = web thickness

Aluminum Cabin-Side-Longitudinal O.C. from Formula 15-6A

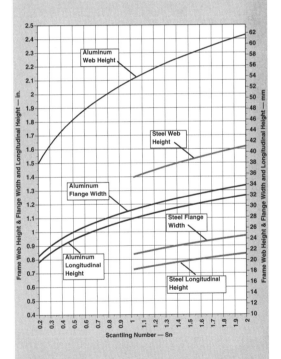

Cabin-Side-Frame Web and Flange Widths and Longitudinal Height, Aluminum and Steel: Small Boats

(continued)

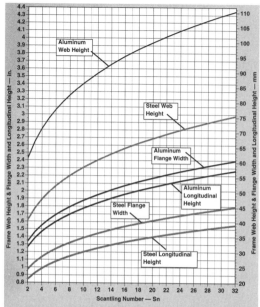

Cabin-Side-Frame Web and Flange Widths and Longitudinal Height, Aluminum and Steel: Large Boats

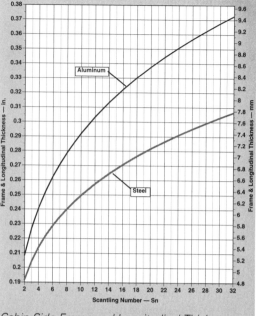

Cabin-Side-Frame and Longitudinal Thickness, Aluminum and Steel: Large Boats

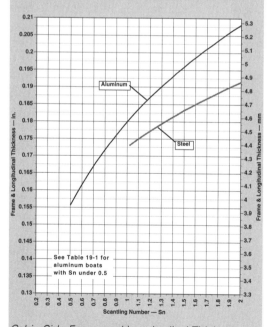

Cabin-Side-Frame and Longitudinal Thickness, Aluminum and Steel: Small Boats

Applying this to our trusty *Aluma-Naught*, we would use the following:

Aluminum Cabin-Side Plate = ³⁄₁₆ in. (4.75 mm) (see Formula 15-4A)

Aluminum Cabin-Side-Frames O.C. = hull frame O.C. = 46 in. for the displacement version and 36 in. for the 35-knot version

Aluminum Cabin-Side-Frame Web Height = 2.1 × 8.71^{0.21} = 3.3; use 3³⁄₈ in.

Aluminum Cabin-Side-Frame Web Height = 53.34 × 8.71^{0.21} = 84 mm

Aluminum Cabin-Side-Frame Web and Flange Thickness = 3.3 in. ÷ 11.67 = 0.28; use ¼ in.

Aluminum Cabin-Side-Frame Web and Flange Thickness = 84 mm ÷ 11.67 = 7.19; use 7.5 mm

Aluminum Cabin-Side-Flange Width = 0.55 × 3.3 in. = 1.81; use 1⅞ or 2 in.

Aluminum Cabin-Side-Flange Width = 0.55 × 84 mm = 46.2; use 45 mm

Aluminum Cabin-Side-Longitudinal Height = 0.52 × 3.3 in. = 1.71; use 1¾ in.

Aluminum Cabin-Side-Longitudinal Height = 0.52 × 84 mm = 43.6; use 45 mm

Aluminum Cabin-Side-Longitudinal Thickness = ¼ in. (7.5 mm)

Aluminum Cabin-Side-Longitudinal O.C. = 4 + (³⁄₁₆ in. × 32) = 10 in.

Aluminum Cabin-Side-Longitudinal O.C. = 101.6 + (4.75 mm × 32) = 253.6; use 250 mm

FORMULA 16-3S

Steel Cabin-Side Frames

Steel Cabin-Side Plate from Formula 15-4S

Steel Cabin-Side-Frames O.C. = hull frame O.C.

Steel Cabin-Side-Frame Web Height, in. = 1.39 × Sn⁰·²² = (English)

Steel Cabin-Side-Frame Web Height, mm = 35.3 × Sn⁰·²² = (Metric)

Steel Cabin-Side-Frame Web and Flange Thickness = cabin-side plate thickness (in mild steel) + ¹⁄₁₆ in. (English)

Steel Cabin-Side-Frame Web and Flange Thickness = cabin-side plate thickness (in mild steel) + 1.6 mm (Metric)

Steel Cabin-Side-Flange Width = 0.6 × web height

Steel Cabin-Side-Longitudinal Height = 0.52 × web height

In the previous chapter, we settled on 10-gauge (0.1345 inch) (3.4 mm) Cor-Ten plate for *Iron Maiden*'s cabin sides. We use the actual thickness of the Cor-Ten plate installed for the longitudinal spacing, but the equivalent thickness of mild-steel plate to determine the cabin-framing thickness. Therefore, we would determine the following:

Steel Cabin-Side Plate = Cor-Ten 10-gauge (0.1345 in.) (3.4 mm) Equivalent mild steel, from Formula 15-4S = 0.163 in. (4.59 mm)

Steel Cabin-Side Frames O.C. = hull frame O.C. = 46 in. for the displacement version and 36 in. for the 35-knot version

Steel Cabin-Side-Frame Web Height = 1.39 × 8.71⁰·²² = 2.23; use 2¼ in.

Steel Cabin-Side-Frame Web Height = 35.3 × 8.71⁰·²² = 56.8; use 58 mm

Steel Cabin-Side-Frame Web and Flange Thickness = 0.163 in. (in mild steel) + ¹⁄₁₆ in. = 0.225; use ¼ in.

Steel Cabin-Side-Frame Web and Flange Thickness = 4.59 mm (in mild steel) + 1.6 mm = 6.19; use 6.4 mm

Steel Cabin-Side-Flange Width = 0.6 × 2.23 in. = 1.33; use 1⅜ in.

Steel Cabin-Side-Flange Width = 0.6 × 56.8 mm = 34.08; use 34 mm

Steel Cabin-Side-Longitudinal Height = 0.52 × 2.23 in. = 1.15; use 1⅛ in.

Steel Cabin-Side Longitudinal Height = 0.52 × 56.8 mm = 29.54; use 30 mm

Steel Cabin-Side-Longitudinal Thickness =
¼ in. (6.4 mm)

Steel Cabin-Side-Longitudinal O.C. = 6 +
(0.1345 in. Cor-Ten × 48) = 12.45; use 12 in.

Steel Cabin-Side-Longitudinal O.C. = 152.4 +
(3.4 mm Cor-Ten × 48) = 315.6; use 300 mm

CABIN ROOFS

Cabin roofs are the highest large structure on any boat. Accordingly, for both aluminum and steel vessels, it is vital to make these as light as possible to keep the center of gravity low. Usually—even on an otherwise longitudinally framed craft—it is more convenient to fabricate the cabin roofs transversely framed, with no longitudinals at all. In this construction, the transverse frames are quite closely spaced. (Longitudinals are added at fore-n-aft ends to support overhangs here, if required.)

Use the following tables to select the proper cabin-roof scantlings, based on the *span* (i.e., the beam or width athwartships) of the cabin roof at its widest point. In general, there are two somewhat conflicting goals. Thinner plate makes for lighter weight, but deeper cabin beams either steal headroom or force you to raise the roof slightly, thus raising the center of gravity. You need to select the thinnest roof plate you can weld that will give the maximum acceptable roof-beam depth, for headroom.

Keep in mind that even on the largest steel boat, aluminum, wood, or FRP cabin roofs—even when the cabin sides are steel—are lighter and will lower the center of gravity. Such nonsteel roofs are almost a necessity for proper stability on vessels with Sns under 6. Tables 16-4A and 16-4S are based on 200 lb./sq. ft. (976 kg/m²) loading, with a safety factor of 1.5 over yield.

TABLE 16-4A Aluminum Transverse-Frame Cabin-Roof Construction (English)

Cabin Span, ft.	Roof Beams O.C., in.	Beam Height, in.	Beam Flange, in.	Beam Thickness, in.
⅛-in. Roof Plate				
4	7.5	1.50	1.00	0.1250
6	7.5	2.00	1.00	0.1250
8	7.5	2.25	1.50	0.1875
10	7.5	2.50	2.00	0.1875
12	7.5	3.00	2.00	0.2500
5/32-in. Roof Plate				
6	9	2.00	1.00	0.1875
8	9	2.50	1.25	0.1875
10	9	3.00	1.50	0.1875

TABLE 16-4A Aluminum Transverse-Frame Cabin-Roof Construction (English) *(Cont.)*

Cabin Span, ft.	Roof Beams O.C., in.	Beam Height, in.	Beam Flange, in.	Beam Thickness, in.
$5/32$-in. Roof Plate (con't.)				
12	9	3.00	2.00	0.2500
14	9	3.50	2.50	0.2500
$3/16$-in. Roof Plate				
6	10	2.00	1.00	0.1875
8	10	2.00	1.50	0.2500
10	10	2.75	1.50	0.2500
12	10	3.00	2.00	0.2500
14	10	3.50	2.50	0.2500
16	10	4.00	2.75	0.2500
18	10	4.00	3.00	0.3125
$1/4$-in. Roof Plate				
8	12	2.25	1.50	0.2500
10	12	2.75	1.75	0.2500
12	12	3.00	2.50	0.2500
14	12	3.00	2.75	0.3125
16	12	3.75	2.75	0.3125
18	12	4.00	2.75	0.3750
20	12	4.50	3.00	0.3750
22	12	4.75	3.50	0.3750
$5/16$-in. Roof Plate				
10	12	2.50	1.75	0.2500
12	12	3.00	1.50	0.3750
14	12	3.50	1.75	0.3750
16	12	3.75	2.00	0.3750
18	12	4.00	2.75	0.3750
20	12	4.50	2.75	0.3750
22	12	4.75	3.25	0.3750
24	12	5.00	3.25	0.4375
26	12	5.25	4.00	0.4375

TABLE 16-4A Aluminum Transverse-Frame Cabin-Roof Construction (Metric)

| Cabin Span, m | Roof Beams O.C., mm | Beam | | |
		Height, mm	Flange, mm	Thickness, mm
3.2 mm Roof Plate				
1.22	190	40	25	3.20
1.83	190	50	25	3.20
2.44	190	60	40	4.75
3.05	190	60	40	4.75
3.66	190	75	50	6.40
4 mm Roof Plate				
1.83	230	50	25	4.75
2.44	230	65	30	4.75
3.05	230	75	40	4.75
3.66	230	75	50	6.40
4.27	230	90	65	6.40
4.75 mm Roof Plate				
1.83	250	50	25	4.75
2.44	250	50	40	6.40
3.05	250	70	40	6.40
3.66	250	75	50	6.40
4.27	250	90	65	6.40
4.88	250	100	70	6.40
5.49	250	100	75	8.00
6.4 mm Roof Plate				
2.44	300	58	40	6.4
3.05	300	70	45	6.4
3.66	300	75	65	6.4
4.27	300	75	70	8.0
4.88	300	100	70	8.0
5.49	300	100	70	9.5
6.10	300	115	75	9.5
6.71	300	120	90	9.5
7.9 mm Roof Plate				
3.05	300	65	45	6.4
3.66	300	75	40	9.5

TABLE 16-4A Aluminum Transverse-Frame Cabin-Roof Construction (Metric) *(Cont.)*

Cabin Span, m	Roof Beams O.C., mm	Beam		
		Height, mm	Flange, mm	Thickness, mm
7.9 mm Roof Plate (con't)				
4.27	300	90	45	9.5
4.88	300	75	50	9.5
5.49	300	100	70	9.5
6.10	300	115	70	9.5
6.71	300	120	80	9.5
7.32	300	130	80	11.0

TABLE 16-4S Steel Transverse-Frame Cabin-Roof Construction (English)

Cabin Span, ft.	Roof Beams O.C., in.	Beam		
		Height, in.	Flange, in.	Thickness, in.
⅛-in. Roof Plate				
4	12	1.0	1.00	0.1250
6	12	1.5	1.00	0.1875
8	12	2.0	1.25	0.1875
10	12	2.5	1.75	0.1875
12	12	3.0	2.00	0.1875
14	12	3.0	2.25	0.2500
16	12	3.5	2.50	0.2500
10-Gauge (0.1345 in.) Roof Plate				
6	12	1.5	1.50	0.1250
8	12	2.0	1.25	0.1875
10	12	2.5	1.50	0.1875
12	12	3.0	1.75	0.1875
14	12	3.5	2.25	0.1875
16	12	3.5	2.25	0.2500
18	12	4.0	2.50	0.2500
20	12	4.3	3.00	0.2500
8-Gauge (0.1644 in.) Roof Plate				
6	14	2.00	1.00	0.1250

(continued)

TABLE 16-4S Steel Transverse-Frame Cabin-Roof Construction (English) *(Cont.)*

Cabin Span, ft.	Roof Beams O.C., in.	Beam Height, in.	Flange, in.	Thickness, in.
8-Gauge (0.1644 in.) Roof Plate (con't)				
8	14	2.25	1.25	0.1875
10	14	2.50	2.00	0.1875
12	14	3.00	2.25	0.1875
14	14	3.50	2.75	0.1875
16	14	4.00	3.00	0.1875
18	14	4.00	3.00	0.2500
20	14	4.75	3.50	0.2500
7-Gauge (0.1875) 3/16-in. Roof Plate				
8	15	2.00	1.00	0.1875
10	15	2.50	1.50	0.2500
12	15	2.75	2.00	0.2500
14	15	3.00	2.50	0.2500
16	15	3.50	2.50	0.3125
18	15	4.00	2.50	0.3125
20	15	4.25	3.00	0.3125
22	15	4.50	3.50	0.3125
24	15	4.75	4.00	0.3125

TABLE 16-4S Steel Transverse-Frame Cabin-Roof Construction (Metric)

Cabin Span, m	Roof Beams O.C., mm	Beam Height, mm	Flange, mm	Thickness, mm
3.2 mm Roof Plate				
1.22	300	25	25	3.20
1.83	300	40	25	4.75
2.44	300	50	30	4.75
3.05	300	65	45	4.75
3.66	300	75	50	4.75

| Cabin Span, ft. | Roof Beams O.C., in. | Beam | | |
		Height, in.	Flange, in.	Thickness, in.
3.2 mm Roof Plate (con't)				
4.27	300	75	60	6.40
4.88	300	90	65	6.40
3.4 mm Roof Plate				
1.83	300	40	40	3.20
2.44	300	50	30	4.75
3.05	300	65	40	4.75
3.66	300	75	45	4.75
4.27	300	90	60	4.75
4.88	300	90	60	6.40
5.49	300	100	65	6.40
6.10	300	110	75	6.40
4.2 mm Roof Plate				
1.83	350	50	25	3.20
2.44	350	55	30	4.75
3.05	350	65	50	4.75
3.66	350	75	60	4.75
4.27	350	90	70	4.75
4.88	350	100	75	4.75
5.49	350	100	75	6.40
6.10	350	120	90	6.40
4.75 mm Roof Plate				
2.44	380	50.00	25.00	4.75
3.05	380	65.00	40.00	6.40
3.66	380	70.00	50.00	6.40
4.27	380	75.00	65.00	6.40
4.88	380	90.00	65.00	8.00
5.49	380	100.00	65.00	8.00
6.10	380	110.00	75.00	8.00
6.71	380	115.00	90.00	8.00
7.32	380	120.00	100.00	8.00
7.92	380	130.00	100.00	9.50

Based on Tables 16-4, if *AlumaNaught* had a trunk cabin with a roof beam 12.2 feet (3.71 m) across the top of the cabin, we could select the following:

³⁄₁₆-in. roof plate, with beams 10 in. O.C., each ¼ in. thick, with 3-in. web and 2-in. flange

or

4.75 mm roof plate, with beams 250 mm O.C., each 6.4 mm thick, with 75 mm web and 50 mm flange

If *Iron Maiden* had a roof beam 12.2 feet (3.71 m) across the top of its cabin, we could use the tables to select the following:

10-gauge (0.1345 in.) roof plate, with beams 12 in. O.C., each ³⁄₁₆ in. thick, with 3-in. web and 1³⁄₄-in. flange

or

3.4 mm roof plate, with beams 300 mm O.C., each 4.75 mm thick, with 75 mm web and 45 mm flange

FORMULA 16-5
Longitudinally Framed Cabin Roofs

Occasionally, longitudinal framing makes more sense for cabin roofs. This is most likely for larger boats with wide cabins; for example, cabins that extend the full width of the deck. In this case, the following would apply:

Cabin-Roof Plate = one standard size down from the deck plate

Cabin-Roof-Longitudinals O.C. = use Formula 15-6A or 15-6S for the roof plate used

Cabin-Roof-Longitudinals Height = deck longitudinal height

Cabin-Roof-Longitudinal Thickness = deck longitudinal thickness

Cabin-Roof-Beams O.C. = speed-adjusted hull-frame O.C.

Cabin-Roof-Beam Web Height = 0.88 × deck-beam-web height

Cabin-Roof-Beam Web Thickness = deck-beam web thickness

Cabin-Roof-Flange Width and Thickness = same as deck beams

Engine Beds and Hull Girders

ENGINE BEDS

Displacement hulls and planing hulls require different engine beds and hull-bottom girders. Longitudinally framed displacement hulls don't need the added longitudinal strength of long bottom girders. Although the engine beds can extend down to meet the interior hull plate, this isn't necessary. The engine beds of displacement craft need only be welded to a minimum of three ring frames, or one full frame beyond the forward-most and after-most engine mounts, whichever extends a greater length. Engine beds can be made in many configurations; however, this rule will use made-up T-section beds with heavy vertical plate and still heavier flange plate on top to accept the engine-mount bolts. Tripping brackets are welded between the flange and the web for added rigidity.

FORMULA 16-6A
Aluminum Engine Beds

Aluminum Engine-Bed-Flange Thickness, in. = 0.012 × hp$^{0.66}$ (English)

Aluminum Engine-Bed-Flange Thickness, in. = 0.24 × Sn$^{0.24}$ (English)

Aluminum Engine-Bed-Flange Thickness, mm = 0.305 × hp$^{0.66}$ (Metric)

Aluminum Engine-Bed-Flange Thickness, mm = 6.09 × Sn$^{0.24}$ (Metric)

Whichever is greater, and never less than $^3/_8$ in. (9.5 mm)

Aluminum Engine-Bed-Flange Width = 9.5 × thickness

Aluminum Engine-Bed-Web Thickness = 0.83 × flange thickness

Aluminum Engine-Bed-Web Height = 14 × web thickness

Aluminum Engine-Bed Trip-Bracket Thickness = same as web thickness

Aluminum Engine-Bed Number of Trip Brackets = 2 + (hp ÷ 330), but not more than 5 (round down all decimals under 0.5; round up all decimals 5.0 and higher)

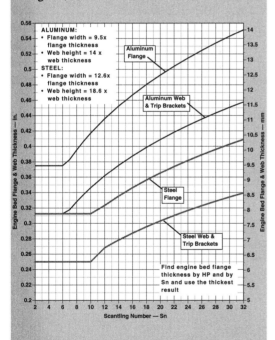

Engine-Bed-Flange and Web Thickness vs. Scantling Number, Aluminum and Steel

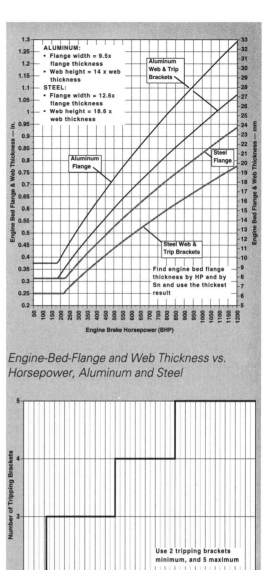

Engine-Bed-Flange and Web Thickness vs. Horsepower, Aluminum and Steel

Number of Engine-Bed Tripping Brackets

Say our reliable old *AlumaNaught* were fitted with a 300-hp (2224 kW) engine. We would then install engine beds as follows:

Aluminum Engine-Bed-Flange Thickness = 0.012 × 300 hp^{0.66} = 0.52 in.

Aluminum Engine-Bed-Flange Thickness = 0.24 × 8.71^{0.24} = 0.40 in.

Aluminum Engine-Bed-Flange Thickness = 0.305 × 300 hp^{0.66} = 13.2 mm

Aluminum Engine-Bed-Flange Thickness = 6.09 × 8.71^{0.24} = 10.2 mm

0.51 in. is greater, use ½ in.; or 13.1 is greater, use 13 mm

Aluminum Engine-Bed-Flange Width = 9.5 × 0.5 in. = 4.75 in.

Aluminum Engine-Bed-Flange Width = 9.5 × 13 mm = 123; use 125 mm

Aluminum Engine-Bed-Web Thickness = 0.83 × 0.5 in. = 0.41; use ⁷⁄₁₆ in.

Aluminum Engine-Bed-Web Thickness = 0.83 × 13.1 mm = 10.87; use 11 mm

Aluminum Engine-Bed-Web Height = 14 × 0.41 in. = 5.74; use 5¾ in.

Aluminum Engine-Bed-Web Height = 14 × 11 mm = 154; use 155 mm

Aluminum Engine-Bed Trip-Bracket Thickness = ⁷⁄₁₆ in. (11 mm)

Aluminum Engine-Bed Number of Trip Brackets = 2 + (300 hp ÷ 330) = 2.9; use 3

A 35-knot *AlumaNaught* would require heavier engine beds. It would have, for example, twin 1,200-hp (895 kW) engines. In this case, the following would apply:

Aluminum Engine-Bed-Flange Thickness = 0.012 × (1,200 hp)^{0.66} = 1.29.; use 1¼ in.

Aluminum Engine-Bed-Flange Thickness = 0.305 × (1,200 hp)^{0.66} = 32.8; use 32 mm

Aluminum Engine-Bed-Flange Width = 9.5 × 1.25 in. = 11.8; use 12 in.

Aluminum Engine-Bed-Flange Width = 9.5 × 33 mm = 313.5; use 310 mm

Aluminum Engine-Bed-Web Thickness = 0.83 × 1.25 in. = 1.03; use 1 in.

Aluminum Engine-Bed-Web Thickness = 0.83 × 33 mm = 27.3; use 25 mm

Aluminum Engine-Bed-Web Height = 14 × 1.03 in. = 14.4; use 14½ in.

Aluminum Engine-Bed-Web Height = 14 × 27.3 mm = 382; use 380 mm

Aluminum Engine-Bed Trip Bracket Thickness = 1 in. (25 mm)

Aluminum Engine-Bed Number of Trip Brackets = 2 + (1,200 hp ÷ 330) = 5.6; 5 is maximum, use 5

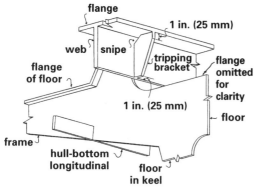

Engine-bed construction

FORMULA 16-6S

Steel Engine Beds

Steel Engine-Bed-Flange Thickness, in. = hp^{0.66} ÷ 115 (English)

Steel Engine-Bed-Flange Thickness, in. = 0.178 × Sn^{0.24} (English)

Steel Engine-Bed-Flange Thickness, mm = 0.22 × hp^{0.66} (Metric)

Steel Engine-Bed-Flange Thickness, mm = 4.52 × Sn^{0.24} (Metric)

Whichever is greater, and never less than ⁵⁄₁₆ in. (8 mm)

> *Steel Engine-Bed-Flange Width = 12.6 × thickness*
>
> *Steel Engine-Bed-Web Thickness = 0.83 × flange thickness*
>
> *Steel Engine-Bed-Web Height = 18.6 × web thickness*
>
> *Steel Engine-Bed Trip-Bracket Thickness = same as web thickness*
>
> *Steel Engine-Bed Number of Trip Brackets = 2 + (hp ÷ 330), but not more than 5 (round down all decimals under 0.5; round up all decimals 5.0 and higher)*

Fit *Iron Maiden* with a 300-hp (224 kW) engine and the boat would use the following:

> *Steel Engine-Bed-Flange Thickness = $(300 \text{ hp})^{0.66} \div 115 = 0.375$ in.*
>
> *Steel Engine-Bed-Flange Thickness = $0.178 \times 8.71^{0.24} = 0.299$ in*
>
> *Steel Engine-Bed-Flange Thickness = $0.22 \times (300 \text{ hp})^{0.66} = 9.49$ mm*
>
> *Steel Engine-Bed-Flange Thickness = $4.52 \times 8.71^{0.24} = 7.59$ mm*
>
> *0.375 in. is greater, use ⅜ in.; or 9.49 is greater, use 9.5 mm*
>
> *Steel Engine-Bed-Flange Width = 12.6 × 0.375 in. = 4.73; use 4¾ in.*
>
> *Steel Engine-Bed-Flange Width = 12.6 × 9.5 mm = 119.7; use 120 mm*
>
> *Steel Engine-Bed-Web Thickness = 0.83 × 0.375 in. = 0.31; use ⁵⁄₁₆ in.*
>
> *Steel Engine-Bed-Web Thickness = 0.83 × 9.49 mm = 7.88; use 8 mm*
>
> *Steel Engine-Bed-Web Height = 18.6 × 0.3125 in. = 5.81; use 5¾ in.*
>
> *Steel Engine-Bed-Web Height = 18.6 × 7.87 mm = 146.3; use 150 mm*

> *Steel Engine-Bed Trip-Bracket Thickness = ⁵⁄₁₆ in. (8 mm)*
>
> *Steel Engine-Bed Number of Trip Brackets = 2 + (300 hp ÷ 330) = 2.9; use 3*

HULL-BOTTOM GIRDERS

High-speed craft require additional longitudinal strength to stiffen the hull bottom against slamming impacts, and to resist the forces generated by the engine weight due to the accelerations caused by this slamming. The bottom girders should be welded to the inside of the bottom plate and extend from the transom forward to approximately Station 2, where they end aft and are welded to a convenient frame. Because these hull-bottom girders are so much deeper and stronger than the smaller hull-bottom longitudinals, you can eliminate the longitudinals where they run close to and/or cross the bottom girders.

The hull-bottom girders should run continuously over the top of the floors or frames for the minimum height given in Formulas 16-7A and S. Therefore, the hull-bottom girders' vertical webs are notched to fit over the floor's vertical plates, with an unnotched continuous portion above. This is capped with the girder's flange. The floor's transverse-running flange is cut at the girder's web, and then butted and welded to the girder web, port and starboard. Where the frames are from off-the-shelf sections, the minimum height of the girder's web is measured above the top of the floor's flange.

HULL-BOTTOM GIRDERS OR ENGINE-MOUNT FOUNDATIONS/ EXTENSIONS

The bottom girders double as extensions of the engine mounts. In other words, the engine-mount vertical web (see Formulas

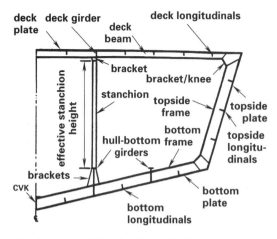

deck plate · deck · deck girder · deck beam · deck longitudinals · bracket · bracket/knee · stanchion · topside frame · topside plate · hull-bottom frame · bottom frame · topside longitudinals · effective stanchion height · bottom plate · brackets · CVK · bottom longitudinals · bottom plate

Section through hard-chine hull with stanchions

16-6A and S) is welded into the hull-bottom girder on high-speed craft (in addition to being welded to the floors). Accordingly, at the engine mounts, you'll have the vertical web plate of the hull-bottom girder extending up from the bottom plate. Then welded on edge on top of that, you have the heavier vertical engine-mount web plate, and—on top of all—the still thicker engine-mount flange plate.

The engine's mounting-bolt centers thus govern the transverse location of the hull-bottom girders. On twin-engine vessels, there will necessarily be four hull-bottom girders. On single-engine planing vessels, four hull-bottom girders are still required. The outer girders act simply as longitudinal-strength members about midway between the inner engine-bed/hull-bottom girder and the chine (or the turn of the bilge).

Keep in mind that hull-bottom girders are intended for high-speed craft. The basic Formulas 16-7A and S are really step one in determining their scantlings; step two is to make the speed adjustments given on page 277.

FORMULA 16-7A

Aluminum Hull-Bottom Girders

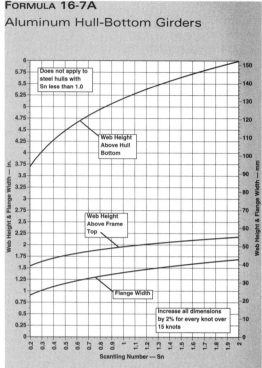

Bottom-Girder-Web Heights and Flange Width, Aluminum and Steel: Small Boats

Aluminum Hull-Bottom Girder-Web Thickness, in. = 0.2 × Sn^{0.24} (English)

Aluminum Hull-Bottom Girder-Web Height Minimum, in. = 5.18 × Sn^{0.21} (English)

Aluminum Hull-Bottom Girder-Web Height Above Top of Floor or Frame Minimum, in. = 1.96 × Sn^{0.15} (English)

Aluminum Hull-Bottom Girder-Flange Thickness, in. = 0.24 × Sn^{0.24} (English)

Aluminum Hull-Bottom Girder-Flange Width, in. = 1.4 × Sn^{0.27} (English)

or

Aluminum Hull-Bottom Girder-Web Thickness, mm = 5.08 × Sn^{0.24} (Metric)

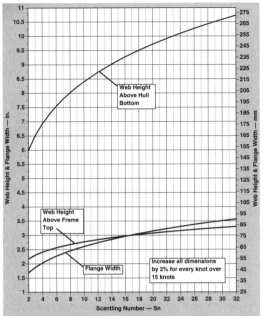

Bottom-Girder-Web Heights and Flange Width, Aluminum and Steel: Large Boats

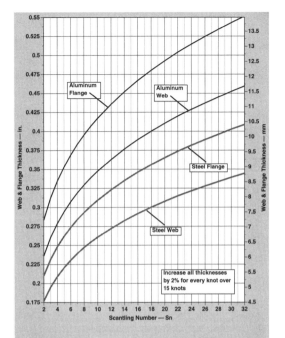

Bottom-Girder-Web and Flange Thickness, Aluminum and Steel: Large Boats

Aluminum Hull-Bottom Girder-Web Height Minimum, mm = 131.5 × Sn$^{0.21}$ (Metric)

Aluminum Hull-Bottom Girder-Web Height Above Top of Floor or Frame Minimum, mm = 49.8 × Sn$^{0.15}$ (Metric)

Aluminum Hull-Bottom Girder-Flange Thickness, mm = 6.09 × Sn$^{0.24}$ (Metric)

Aluminum Hull-Bottom Girder-Flange Width, mm = 35.5 × Sn$^{0.27}$ (Metric)

If *AlumaNaught* were a high-speed planing hull, we would install four hull-bottom girders in line with the engine mounts (which would be welded into the top of them), as follows:

Aluminum Hull-Bottom Girder-Web Thickness, in. = 0.2 × 8.71$^{0.24}$ = 0.34; use ⅜ in.

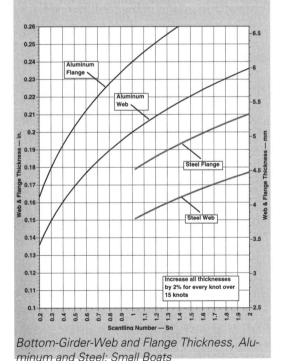

Bottom-Girder-Web and Flange Thickness, Aluminum and Steel: Small Boats

Aluminum Hull-Bottom Girder-Web Height, in. = 5.18 × 8.71^{0.21} = 8.16; use 8¼ in. minimum

Aluminum Hull-Bottom Girder-Web Height Above Top of Floor or Frame, in. = 1.96 × 8.71^{0.15} = 2.71 in.; use 2¾ in. minimum

Aluminum Hull-Bottom Girder-Flange Thickness, in. = 0.24 × 8.71^{0.24} = 0.40; use ⁷⁄₁₆ in.

Aluminum Hull-Bottom Girder-Flange Width, in. = 1.4 × 8.71^{0.27} = 2.51; use 2½ in.

or

Aluminum Hull-Bottom Girder-Web Thickness, mm = 5.08 × 8.71^{0.24} = 8.54; use 8.5 mm

Aluminum Hull-Bottom Girder-Web Height, mm = 131.5 × 8.71^{0.21} = 207.1; use 210 mm minimum

Aluminum Hull-Bottom Girder-Web Height Above Top of Floor or Frame, mm = 49.8 × 8.71^{0.15} = 68.9; use 70 mm

Aluminum Hull-Bottom Girder-Flange Thickness, mm = 6.09 × 8.71^{0.24} = 10.2; use 11 mm

Aluminum Hull-Bottom Girder-Flange Width, mm = 35.5 × 8.71^{0.27} = 63.6; use 64 mm

FORMULA 16-7S

Steel Hull-Bottom Girders

Steel Hull-Bottom Girder-Web Thickness, in. = 0.15 × Sn^{0.24} (English)

Steel Hull-Bottom Girder-Web Height Minimum, in. = 5.18 × Sn^{0.21} (English)

Steel Hull-Bottom Girder-Web Height Above Top of Floor or Frame Minimum, in. = 1.96 × Sn^{0.15} (English)

Steel Hull-Bottom Girder-Flange Thickness, in. = 0.178 × Sn^{0.24} (English)

Steel Hull-Bottom Girder-Flange Width, in. = 1.4 × Sn^{0.27} (English)

or

Steel Hull-Bottom Girder-Web Thickness, mm = 3.81 × Sn^{0.24} (Metric)

Steel Hull-Bottom Girder-Web Height Minimum, mm = 131.5 × Sn^{0.21} (Metric)

Steel Hull-Bottom Girder-Web Height Above Top of Floor or Frame Minimum, mm = 49.7 × Sn^{0.15} (Metric)

Steel Hull-Bottom Girder-Flange Thickness, mm = 4.52 × Sn^{0.24} (Metric)

Steel Hull-Bottom Girder-Flange Width, mm = 35.5 × Sn^{0.27} (Metric)

Our steel *Iron Maiden* would be unusual, indeed, if it could make high-planing speeds; but this can be done on steel hulls. The hull-bottom girders would then be

Steel Hull-Bottom Girder-Web Thickness, in. = 0.15 × 8.71^{0.24} = 0.252; use ¼ in.

Steel Hull-Bottom Girder-Web Height Minimum, in. = 5.18 × 8.71^{0.21} = 8.16; use 8 ¼ in. minimum

Steel Hull-Bottom Girder-Web Height Above Top of Floor or Frame Minimum, in. = 1.96 × 8.71^{0.15} = 2.71; use 2¾ in. minimum

Steel Hull-Bottom Girder-Flange Thickness, in. = 0.178 × 8.71^{0.24} = 0.299; use ⁵⁄₁₆ in.

Steel Hull-Bottom Girder-Flange Width, in. = 1.4 × 8.71^{0.27} = 2.51; use 2½ in.

or

Steel Hull-Bottom Girder-Web Thickness, mm = 3.81 × 8.71^{0.24} = 6.4 mm

Steel Hull-Bottom Girder-Web Height Minimum, mm = 131.5 × 8.71^0.21 = 207.1; use 210 mm minimum

Steel Hull-Bottom Girder-Web Height Above Top of Floor or Frame Minimum, mm = 49.7 × 8.71^0.15 = 68.7; use 70 mm

Steel Hull-Bottom Girder-Flange Thickness, mm = 4.52 × 8.71^0.24 = 7.59; use 8 mm

Steel Hull-Bottom Girder-Flange Width, mm = 35.5 × 8.71^0.27 = 63.6; use 64 mm

SPEED ADJUSTMENT FOR HULL-BOTTOM GIRDERS

Increase hull-bottom girder-web height by 2 percent for every knot over 15 knots. Increase hull-bottom girder-web thickness by 2 percent for every knot over 15 knots. Increase hull-bottom girder-web height above top of floor or frame by 2 percent for every knot over 15 knots.

Increase hull-bottom girder-flange width by 2 percent for every knot over 15 knots. Increase hull-bottom girder-flange thickness by 2 percent for every knot over 15 knots.

NOTE: If the speed-adjusted hull-bottom girder flange thickness is greater than the engine-mount thickness based on horsepower (see Formulas 16-6A and S), use the speed-adjusted flange thickness for the engine mount as well.

Returning to our 35-knot *AlumaNaught*, its hull-bottom girders would be adjusted to the following:

35 knots – 20 knots = 15 knots, then 15 knots × 2% per knot = 30%

Hull-Bottom Girder-Web Height = 1.30 × 8.16 in. = 10.6; use 10 5/8 in.

Hull-Bottom-Web Thickness = 1.30 × 0.33 in. = 0.429; use 7/16 in.

Hull-Bottom Girder-Web Height Above Top of Floor = 1.30 × 2.71 in. = 3.52; use 3 1/2 in.

Hull-Bottom Girder-Flange Width = 1.30 × 2.51 in. = 3.26; use 3 1/4 in.

Hull-Bottom Girder-Flange Thickness = 1.30 × 0.40 in. = 0.52; use 1/2 in.

or

35 knots – 20 knots = 15 knots, then 15 knots × 2% per knot = 30%

Hull-Bottom Girder-Web Height = 1.30 × 207.1 mm = 269.2; use 270 mm

Hull-Bottom-Web Thickness = 1.30 × 8.54 mm = 11.1; use 11 mm

Hull-Bottom Girder-Web Height Above Top of Floor = 1.30 × 68.9 mm = 89.5; use 90 mm

Hull-Bottom Girder-Flange Width = 1.30 × 63.6 mm = 82.6; use 85 mm

Hull-Bottom Girder-Flange Thickness = 1.30 × 10.2 mm = 13.2; use 13 mm

For the remarkably fast (for steel) 35-knot *Iron Maiden*, hull-bottom girders would be adjusted to the following:

35 knots – 20 knots = 15 knots, then 15 knots × 2% per knot = 30%

Hull-Bottom Girder-Web Height = 1.30 × 8.16 in. = 10.6; use 10 5/8 in.

Hull-Bottom-Web Thickness = 1.30 × 0.524 in. = 0.33; use 3/8 in.

Hull-Bottom Girder-Web Height Above Top of Floor = 1.30 × 2.71 in. = 3.52; use 3 1/2 in.

Hull-Bottom Girder-Flange Width = 1.30 × 2.51 in. = 3.26; use 3 1/4 in.

Hull-Bottom Girder-Flange Thickness = 1.30 × 0.299 in. = 0.388; use 3/8 in.

or

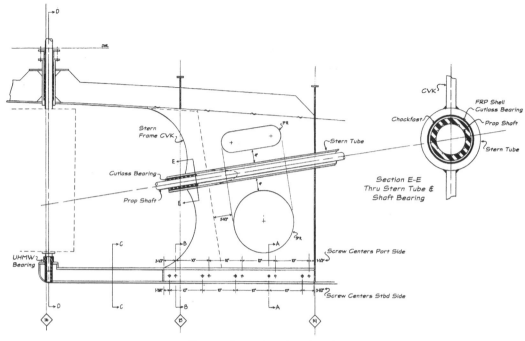

Stern tube and cutless bearing

35 knots – 20 knots = 15 knots, then 15 knots × 2% per knot = 30%

Hull-Bottom Girder-Web Height = 1.30 × 6.4 mm = 8.32; use 9 mm

Hull-Bottom Girder-Web Height Above Top of Floor = 1.30 × 68.9 mm = 89.5; use 90 mm

Hull-Bottom Girder-Flange Width = 1.30 × 63.6 mm = 82.6; use 85 mm

Hull-Bottom Girder-Flange Thickness = 1.30 × 7.59 mm = 9.86; use 10 mm

FORMULA 16-8
Stern Tube

Traditional commercial practice has been to use an exceptionally heavy-wall tube for the stern bearing and line-bore it exactingly for the cutless bearing. My opinion is that this practice is obsolete. It's vastly easier to use Schedule 80 pipe (or tube of roughly equivalent thickness) that has an inside diameter (I.D.) slightly larger that the outside diameter (O.D.) of the bearing housing. (Schedule 80 pipe is also known as "heavy-wall" or "extra-strong" pipe.) The bearing is slipped around the shaft and into the stern tube. Inside the boat, the shaft is run through all intermediate bearings and bolted to the engine coupling. The bearing itself is then set in Chockfast in the end of the stern tube, which—with the small play from the slightly oversize I.D.—takes the proper angle, ensuring perfect alignment when the Chockfast sets. All this, without the lengthy process of *precise line-boring. Remember to provide water input to lubricate the bearing. Most commonly, this is accomplished with a water-injected stuffing box.*

Deck Girders, Stanchions, and Brackets

DECK GIRDERS

Deck girders strengthen the deck in much the same way that hull-bottom girders reinforce the hull bottom. Such reinforcement is only required on larger vessels or boats that will carry heavy deck loads.

Vessels with Sns over 12 that run at speeds over 20 knots and that carry substantial cargoes or other loads on deck should install two girders each about a third of the way inboard from the maximum beam, and running straight fore-n-aft. All vessels with Sns between 10 and 15 should considered for installation of at least one girder on the centerline of wide decks. Yachts with Sns under 15 do not require deck girders, nor do high-speed vessels that don't carry deck cargo (with Sns less than 12). Boats with Sns under 12 require deck girders only if they are workboats that will routinely haul heavy loads on deck.

It is usually most convenient to adjust the athwartships location of a pair of deck girders to form the sides of cargo hatches and the deckhouse. Because stanchions are used to support the deck girder, it is sometimes more convenient to locate the deck girder directly over the hull-bottom girders, so that the stanchions can land on these.

FORMULA 16-9A
Aluminum Deck Girders

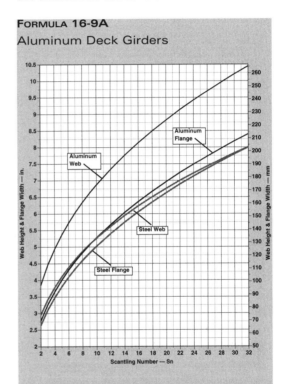

Deck-Girder Web Heights and Flange Width, Aluminum and Steel

Aluminum Deck-Girder-Web Thickness, in. = 0.23 × Sn^0.21 (English)

Aluminum Deck-Girder-Web Thickness, mm = 5.84 × Sn^0.21 (Metric)

Aluminum Deck-Girder Height, in. = 3 × Sn^0.36 (English)

Aluminum Deck-Girder Height, mm = 76.2 × Sn^0.36 (Metric)

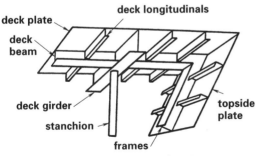

Longitudinal deck and topsides framing

(continued)

Aluminum Deck-Girder-Flange Thickness = 1.2 × web thickness

Aluminum Deck-Girder-Flange Width, in. = 2.1 × $Sn^{0.4}$ (English)

Aluminum Deck-Girder-Flange Width, mm = 53.34 × $Sn^{0.4}$ (Metric)

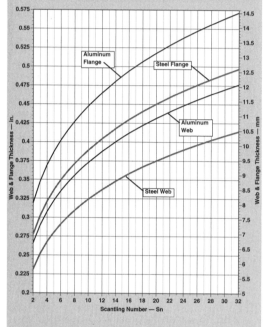

Deck-Girder-Web and Flange Thickness, Aluminum and Steel

At 64 feet (19.5 m) and with an Sn of 8.71, *AlumaNaught* is not large enough to require deck girders for most service. If, however, *AlumaNaught* were a crewboat that would be operating at speeds over 20 knots offshore and carrying deck cargo, that would be a different story. In that case, our boat would require

Aluminum Deck-Girder-Web Thickness = 0.23 × $8.71^{0.21}$ = 0.36; use ⅜ in.

Aluminum Deck-Girder-Web Thickness = 5.84 × $8.71^{0.21}$ = 9.2; use 9.5 mm

Aluminum Deck-Girder Height = 3 × $8.71^{0.36}$ = 6.53; use 6½ in.

Aluminum Deck-Girder Height = 76.2 × $8.71^{0.36}$ = 166; use 170 mm

Aluminum Deck-Girder-Flange Thickness = 1.2 × 0.36 in. = 0.42; use ⁷⁄₁₆ in.

Aluminum Deck-Girder-Flange Thickness = 1.2 × 9.2 mm = 11.04; use 11 mm

Aluminum Deck-Girder-Flange Width = 2.1 × $8.71^{0.4}$ = 4.99; use 5 in.

Aluminum Deck-Girder-Flange Width = 53.34 × $8.71^{0.4}$ = 126.7; use 125 mm

FORMULA 16-9S

Steel Deck Girders

Steel Deck-Girder-Web Thickness, in. = 0.2 × $Sn^{0.21}$ (English)

Steel Deck-Girder-Web Thickness, mm = 5.08 × $Sn^{0.21}$ (Metric)

Steel Deck-Girder Height, in. = 2.3 × $Sn^{0.36}$ (English)

Steel Deck-Girder Height, mm = 58.42 × $Sn^{0.36}$ (Metric)

Steel Deck-Girder-Flange Thickness = 1.2 × web thickness

Steel Deck-Girder-Flange Width, in. = 2.0 × $Sn^{0.4}$ (English)

Steel Deck-Girder-Flange Width, mm = 50.8 × $Sn^{0.4}$ (Metric)

A steel crewboat *Iron Maiden* would then have

Steel Deck-Girder-Web Thickness = 0.2 × $8.71^{0.21}$ = 0.31; use ⁵⁄₁₆ in.

Steel Deck-Girder-Web Thickness = 5.08 × $8.71^{0.21}$ = 8.0 mm

Steel Deck-Girder Height = 2.3 × $8.71^{0.36}$ = 5.0 in.

*Steel Deck-Girder Height = 58.42 × 8.71[0.36] =
127.3; use 130 mm*

*Steel Deck-Girder-Flange Thickness =
1.2 × 0.31 in. = 0.37; use ⅜ in.*

*Steel Deck-Girder-Flange Thickness =
1.2 × 8.0 mm = 9.6; use 10 mm*

*Steel Deck-Girder-Flange Width =
2.0 × 8.71[0.4] = 4.75; use 4¾ in.*

*Steel Deck-Girder-Flange Width =
50.8 × 8.71[0.4] = 120.4; use 120 mm*

STANCHIONS

The deck girders are supported underneath with stanchions—usually of pipe—that extend down to the bottom framing. All stanchions *must* land on a frame or hull-bottom girder; they can *never* run down and weld directly to the hull plate. Because of this, stanchions pose a problem for interior and machinery layout. If the deck girder doesn't lie directly above the hull-bottom girder, then the stanchions can only be located at a frame. In many cases, this may conflict with the interior arrangement and can be the source of much juggling.

If the deck girders, however, are immediately above the hull-bottom girders, then you can move the stanchions fore-n-aft along the length of the girders to any convenient location along their length. However, deck girders located over the hull-bottom girders may not be ideal for the deck openings and superstructure framing. There's no right or wrong here, simply a set of trade-offs for each vessel.

Solving Stanchion Location Problems

Smaller displacement vessels that carry heavy deck loads may require deck girders but no hull-bottom girders. Again, you're forced to

locate the stanchions on the frames. However, you can simply add hull-bottom girders for convenience. In fact, you can use a partial hull-bottom girder under the stanchions, which should extend between three frames. Its dimensions under the stanchion should be the full height of a hull-bottom girder (see Formulas 16-7A and S); however, the web height can be tapered down to the same height as the bottom frame's web, at the fore-n-aft ends.

In circumstances where there is no way to locate a stanchion over either a hull-bottom girder or a frame (even on a boat's full hull-bottom girders), this same partial girder approach can be used—adding an additional partial girder where it is required for that problem stanchion.

Stanchion Strength Governed by Moment of Inertia

Pipes come in a wide variety of diameters and wall thicknesses. When used as stanchions, however, what we're interested in is the pipe's ability to resist compression loads. Essentially, the deck load above the stanchions presses down on the stanchion, and—if it's not strong enough—it will bend over or buckle. The way engineers determine a member's resistance to buckling is by a section property called *moment of inertia* or *I*. To select the proper stanchions for your *AlumaNaught* or *Iron Maiden*, find the required moment of inertia from the formula, and then select a suitable pipe from the table in appendix 2 or from similar tables found in engineering handbooks and many manufacturers' brochures.

Moment of inertia is in units of in.[4] or cm[4] (i.e., inches to the fourth power or centimeters to the fourth power). To convert in.[4]

to cm⁴, multiply in.⁴ by 41.62. To convert cm⁴ to in.⁴, divide cm⁴ by 41.62.

Stanchions Don't Have to Be Pipe

You're not limited to pipe for stanchions—although it is the most common and usually the most convenient. You can select any shape that provides the required moment of inertia (I). Keep in mind, though, that pipes—being circles—are perfectly symmetrical. An H-beam or an angle, in contrast, will have different moments of inertia relative to different axes. Using such asymmetrical shapes, be certain that its *smallest* I is equal to or greater than the I from the formula.

Brackets Strengthen Stanchions

Most stanchions are reinforced at their top and at their base with brackets welded to the girders and frames. The stanchion rule assumes brackets top and bottom. If no brackets are used, the stanchion's I should be increased by 15 percent. Formulas 16-10A and S are based on a uniform deck loading of 300 lb./sq. ft. (1,465 kg/m²).

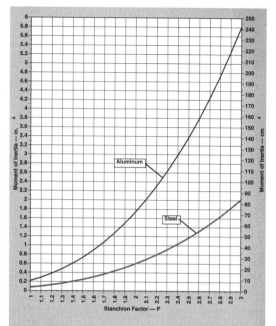

Stanchion Moment of Inertia, Aluminum and Steel

FORMULA 16-10A

Aluminum Stanchions (with Brackets)

Aluminum Stanchion I, in.⁴ = 0.22 × F²·⁹⁸ (English)

Aluminum Stanchion I, cm⁴ = 9.15 × F²·⁹⁸ (Metric)

Where

$F = [(\text{depth of hull, ft.})^2 \times \text{beam, ft.} \times \text{stanchion spacing, ft.}]^{0.34} \div 10$ *(English)*

or

$F = [(\text{depth of hull, m}/3.28)^2 \times \text{beam, m}/3.28 \times \text{stanchion spacing, m}/3.28]^{0.34} \times 10$ *(Metric)*

Stanchions are usually spaced about every second or third ring frame. Say our 35-knot *AlumaNaught*'s stanchions are spaced every two ring frames. They are then 2 × 36 inches (6 ft.) or 182.9 centimeters (1.83 m) apart. Our boat's stanchions would be as follows:

$F = [(8.33 \text{ ft. depth of hull})^2 \times 17.67 \text{ ft. beam} \times 6.0 \text{ ft. stanchion spacing, ft.}]^{0.34} \div 10 = 1.946$

$\text{Aluminum } I = 0.22 \times 1.946^{2.98} = 1.599 \text{ in.}^4$

$\text{Aluminum } I = 9.15 \times 1.946^{2.98} = 66.53 \text{ cm}^4$

Referring to the pipe table (see appendix 2), we find that a 2½-in. nominal Schedule 80 pipe (2.875-in. O.D., 0.276-in. wall) has a moment of inertia of 1.92 in.⁴ (79.9 cm⁴), which will do nicely.

Steel Stanchions (with Brackets)

> Steel Stanchion I, in.^{4} = F^3 ÷ 13.4
> (English)
>
> Steel Stanchion I, cm^4 = 3.1 × F^3 (Metric)
>
> Where
>
> F = [(depth of hull, ft.)^2 × beam, ft. ×
> stanchion spacing, ft.]$^{0.34}$ ÷ 10 (English)
>
> or
>
> F = [(depth of hull, m/3.28)^2 × beam,
> m/3.28 × stanchion spacing, m/3.28]$^{0.34}$
> × 10 (Metric)

If our displacement speed steel *Iron Maiden*'s stanchions are spaced every two ring frames, they are then 2 × 46 inches (7.667 feet) or 233.7 centimeters (2.33 m) apart. Its stanchions would be

$$F = [(8.33 \text{ ft. depth of hull})^2 × 17.67 \text{ ft. beam} \\ × 7.667 \text{ ft. stanchion spacing, ft.}]^{0.34} ÷ \\ 10 = 2.12$$

Steel Stanchion I = 2.12^3 ÷ 13.4 = 0.71 in.^{4}

Steel Stanchion I = 3.1 × 2.12^3 = 29.54 cm^4

Referring to the pipe table (see appendix 2), we find that a 1^1/$_2$-inch nominal Schedule 80 pipe (2.375-in. O.D., 0.218-in. wall) has a moment of inertia of 0.868 in.^{4} (36.12 cm^4), which will fill the bill.

BRACKETS

Brackets are angles welded (like knees) to support a structural component. We've already defined tripping brackets welded under the engine mounts and the knees (which are really brackets) at the joint between the topsides frames and the deck beams.

Brackets are also used to reinforce other miscellaneous structures, like generator mounts and stanchions. Brackets can be defined by the length of their legs, which form approximate right triangles—although other convenient proportions are fine. On stanchions, the bracket legs are usually about 1.25 to 1.50 times the stanchion diameter.

Brackets can be flanged or flat. Flanged brackets have a bent-over angle or a welded-on T on their hypotenuse (i.e., long edge). Flanged brackets are suited to heavy-load applications.

TABLE 16-11   Bracket Dimensions (English)

Hypotenuse, in.	Aluminum			Steel		
	Unflanged Thickness, in.	Flanged Thickness, in.	Flange Width, in.	Unflanged Thickness, in.	Flanged Thickness, in.	Flange Width, in.
Under 12	0.2500	0.1875	0.0	0.1875	0.1644	0.0
12 to 18	0.3125	0.2500	1.5	0.2500	0.1875	1.5
18 to 26	0.4375	0.3125	2.0	0.3125	0.2500	2.0
26 to 36	0.5000	0.4375	2.5	0.3750	0.3125	2.5
36 to 54	0.5625	0.5000	3.0	0.4375	0.3750	3.0

TABLE 16-11 Bracket Dimensions (Metric)

Hypotenuse, mm	Aluminum			Steel		
	Unflanged Thickness, mm	Flanged Thickness, mm	Flange Width, mm	Unflanged Thickness, mm	Flanged Thickness, mm	Flange Width, mm
Under 300	6.40	4.75	0	4.75	4.20	0
300 to 450	7.90	6.40	40	6.40	4.75	40
450 to 660	11.25	7.90	50	7.90	6.40	50
660 to 900	13.00	11.25	65	9.50	7.90	65
900 to 1400	14.25	13.00	75	11.25	9.50	75

Unless otherwise specified in a specific rule, bracket thickness can be selected based on hypotenuse length.

The hypotenuse of a triangle is found as follows:

$$hypotenuse = (a^2 + b^2)^{0.5} \ or \ \sqrt{a^2 + b^2}$$

Where

a and b are the length of each leg

In the case of *AlumaNaught*, we found 2.875-inch O.D. (73 mm) pipe stanchions; 1.25 × 2.75 inches = 3.59-inch leg (1.25 × 73 mm = 91.2 mm). It might be that there is only room for a 3-inch-high (75 mm) face along the stanchion, without projecting through the sole. Therefore, we choose a 3-inch-high bracket with a 4-inch base (75 × 100 mm).

The hypotenuse is then

$$(3^2 + 4^2)^{0.5} = 5 \ in.$$

and reading from Table 16-11, we see that a $^1/_4$-inch-thick unflanged aluminum bracket would do.

Or

$$(75^2 + 100^2)^{0.5} = 125 \ mm$$

and reading from Table 16-11, we see that a 6.4-mm-thick unflanged aluminum bracket would do.

The same procedure would be used for the steel stanchion brackets on *Iron Maiden*.

MAST STEPS

The compression loads on masts are immense. On a 52-footer (15.8 m) I have under construction at the moment, the compression load calculated to 21 tons—close to the displacement of the boat. Mast steps must be strong.

The mast step in this rule is a T with a heavy vertical web and flange on top. Usually, the web is a vertical extension of the CVK. This is ideal but not required. If the web is an extension of the CVK, then the mast step must extend fore-n-aft at least between two frames. If the mast step is not an extension of the CVK, then it must extend for at least three frames. (The mizzenmast step can extend to only two frames in either case.)

The mast step is braced underneath with tripping brackets. Be sure to check that the width of the mast section you will actually install against the calculated mast-step width.

FORMULA 16-12A
Aluminum Mast Steps

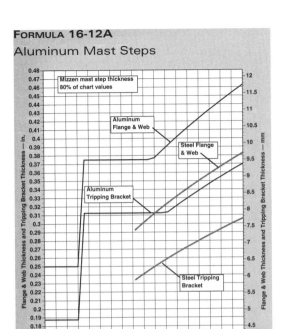

Mast-Step Web and Flange Thickness and Tripping-Bracket Thickness, Aluminum and Steel: Small Boats

Aluminum Mast-Step Web and Flange Thickness = CVK thickness (see Formula 15-13A), but not less than ⅜ in. (9.5 mm) (on boats with Sns less than 0.50, minimum thickness is ¼ in. [6.4 mm])

Aluminum Mast-Step Web and Flange Width and Height = 18 × thickness (on boats with Sns less than 0.50, width may be just 20 percent wider than the mast width)

Number of Tripping Brackets = 2.6 × (thickness, in.)$^{0.72}$ (English)

Number of Tripping Brackets = 0.25 × (thickness, mm)$^{0.72}$ (Metric)

Aluminum Tripping-Bracket Thickness = 0.8 × flange thickness, but not less than ⁵⁄₁₆ in. (8 mm)

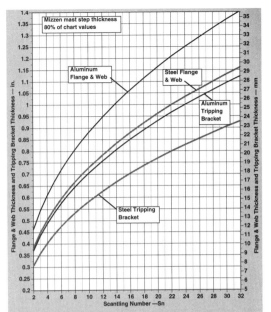

Mast-Step Web and Flange Thickness and Tripping-Bracket Thickness, Aluminum and Steel: Large Boats

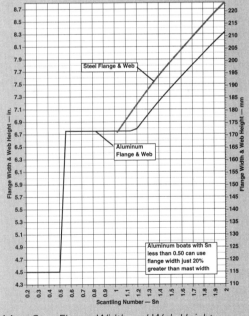

Mast-Step Flange Width and Web Height, Aluminum and Steel: Small Boats

(continued)

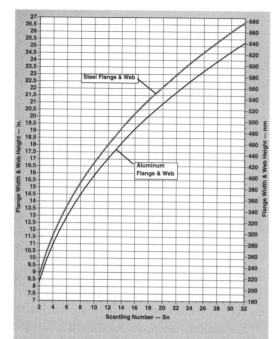

Mast-Step Flange Width and Web Height, Aluminum and Steel: Large Boats

For aluminum mizzenmast step, use 80 percent of this flange thickness and proportion everything else according to the reduced thickness. Schooner foremast steps are the same as mainmast steps.

AlumaNaught's mainmast step would then be as follows:

Aluminum Mast-Step Web and Flange Thickness = ⁷⁄₈ in. (22 mm)

Aluminum Mast-Step Web and Flange Width and Height = 15 ³⁄₄ in. (400 mm)

Number of Tripping Brackets = 2.6 × (0.875 in.)$^{0.72}$ = 2.36; use two—one just forward and one just aft of the mast

Number of Tripping Brackets = 0.25 × (22 mm)$^{0.72}$ = 2.31; use two—one just forward and one just aft of the mast

Aluminum Tripping-Bracket Thickness = 0.8 × 0.875 in. = 0.7; use ³⁄₄ in.

Aluminum Tripping-Bracket Thickness = 0.8 × 22 mm = 17.6; use 17.5 mm

FORMULA 16-12S
Steel Mast Steps

Steel Mast-Step Web and Flange Thickness = 0.29 × Sn$^{0.4}$ (English), but not less than ¼ in.

Steel Mast-Step Web and Flange Thickness = 7.36 × Sn$^{0.4}$ (Metric), but not less than 6.4 mm

Steel Mast-Step Web and Flange Width and Height = 23 × thickness

Number of Tripping Brackets = 2.94 × (thickness, in.)$^{0.72}$ (English)

Number of Tripping Brackets = 0.28 × (thickness, mm)$^{0.72}$ (Metric)

Steel Tripping-Bracket Thickness = 0.8 × flange thickness, but not less than ³⁄₁₆ in. (4.75 mm)

For steel mizzenmast steps, use 80 percent of this flange thickness and proportion everything else according to the reduced thickness. Schooner foremast steps are the same as mainmast steps. Fitting a mainmast step into *Iron Maiden* would give us the following:

Steel Mast-Step Web and Flange Thickness = 0.29 × 8.71$^{0.4}$ = 0.69; use ⁵⁄₈ in.

Steel Mast-Step Web and Flange Thickness = 7.36 × 8.71$^{0.4}$ = 17.49; use 17.5 mm

Steel Mast-Step Web and Flange Width and Height = 23 × 0.68 in. = 14.96; use 15 in.

Steel Mast-Step Web and Flange Width and Height = 23 × 17.5 mm = 402.5; use 400 mm

Number of Tripping Brackets = 2.94 ×
(0.68 in.)$^{0.72}$ = 2.22: use two—one just
forward and one just aft of the mast

Number of Tripping Brackets = 0.28 ×
(17.5 mm)$^{0.72}$ = 2.19; use two—one just
forward and one just aft of the mast

Steel Tripping-Bracket Thickness =
0.8 × 0.68 in. = 0.54; use ½ in.

Steel Tripping-Bracket Thickness =
0.8 × 17.49 mm = 13.99; use 14 mm

MAST PARTNERS

It is just as important to increase the
strength of the deck in the way of the mast
on a metal boat as it is on an FRP or wood
vessel. A doubler plate should surround the
mast hole under the deck. The doubler
should extend fore-n-aft to the closest deck
beams. A mast collar or ring surrounds the
opening, and the partners are usually diagonal stiffeners welded to the underside of the
deck between the collar and the deck beams,
fore-n-aft.

FORMULA 16-13A
Aluminum Mast Partners

Doubler-Plate Thickness = deck
thickness (see Formula 15-4A)

Doubler Width = 2.2 × mast width

Mast-Collar-Ring Thickness = deck plate
plus ⅛ in. (3.2 mm)

Mast-Collar-Ring Height = 16 × thickness

Mast Partners = frames the same as the
deck beams running diagonally from
the mast collar to the nearest deck
beams, fore-n-aft, port and starboard

AlumaNaught's mast partners are as follows:

Doubler-Plate Thickness = ³⁄₁₆ in. (5.55 mm)

Doubler Width = 2.2 × mast width

Mast Collar-Ring Thickness = ⁵⁄₁₆ in.
(8.5 mm)

Mast Collar-Ring Height = 5 in. (135 mm)

Mast Partners = frames the same as the
deck beams running diagonally from the
mast collar to the nearest deck beams,
fore-n-aft, port and starboard

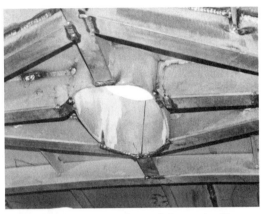

*Mast-partner ring or collar and diagonal stiffen-
ers. (Courtesy Topper Hermanson Boatbuilding)*

FORMULA 16-13S
Steel Mast Partners

Doubler-Plate Thickness = deck
thickness (see Formula 15-4S)

Doubler Width = 2.2 × mast width

Mast-Collar-Ring Thickness = deck plate
plus ¹⁄₁₆ in. (1.6 mm)

Mast-Collar-Ring Height = 21 × thickness

Mast Partners = frames the same as the
deck beams running diagonally from
the mast collar to the nearest deck
beams, fore-n-aft, port and starboard

Reinforcement at Imagine's stabilizer fin shaft penetrations. Note the doubler plate on the hull shell and the diagonal bracing to the frames.

Imagine's stabilizers installed.

Fitting partners in *Iron Maiden*, we would find

Doubler-Plate Thickness = Cor-Ten 8-gauge (0.1664 in.) (4 mm)

Doubler Width = 2.2 × mast width

Mast-Collar-Ring Thickness = ¼ in. (5.55 mm)

Mast-Collar-Ring Height = 5¼ in. (120 mm)

Mast Partners = frames the same as the deck beams running diagonally from the mast collar to the nearest deck beams, fore-n-aft, port and starboard

FORMULA 16-14
Doubler Plates and Insert Plates

Doubler plates should be installed under winch and windlass bases and at mooring cleats, chocks, and other high-load hardware. Underwater, insert plates should be installed at shaft-log penetrations, sea chests, and the like.

Doubler-Plate Thickness = shell plate thickness

Insert-Plate Thickness = 2 × shell plate thickness

The ends and corners of the doubler plate should be very well radiused, or the ends should be run into the nearest frames.

SEVENTEEN

Aluminum and Steel Alternate Construction Methods

*C*hapters 15 and 16 illustrate how to calculate scantlings for longitudinally framed boats—boats with widely spaced transverse ring frames and closely spaced longitudinals. In chapter 13, however, we saw that there are other standard framing approaches: transverse framing with longitudinals and transverse framing with no longitudinals at all.

Longitudinal Scantling Rules Form the Basis for Alternate Rules

We examine these alternatives—and some lightweight construction methods—in this chapter. Keep in mind throughout that the longitudinal scantling rules form the basis for all the variants that follow. You need to fully understand the longitudinal scantlings before you can use these transverse scantlings. Indeed, unless a change is specifically mentioned, the transverse or lightweight rules simply use the scantlings from the longitudinal rules. For example, the transverse-framing rules don't mention the CVK or the shell-

plating; accordingly, they are the same as specified for the longitudinal rule.

Aluminum Transverse Framing

OPTIONAL LONGITUDINALS

Because aluminum plate is usually between 1.25 and 1.5 times thicker than steel, it has greater stiffness for the same or less weight. As a result, the transverse-frame aluminum scantlings don't require longitudinal framing for strength. You can construct a boat with or without the longitudinals described.

Then why include longitudinals at all? The answer is weld distortion. Longitudinals—properly installed and welded—are the most effective method of reducing this problem. Some builders also find it is easier to fit plate on complex-curved hull surfaces to have both the closely spaced transverse frames and the closely spaced longitudinals. For this reason, most round-bilge yachts—built with closely spaced transverse frames—use the optional longitudinals. On workboats—where fairness is less of a consideration—it's somewhat more common to omit them.

FORMULA 17-1

Aluminum Transverse Frame Space O.C.

Transverse Bottom Frames O.C., in. =
$10.2 \times Sn^{0.24}$ (English)

Transverse Bottom Frames O.C., mm =
$259 \times Sn^{0.24}$ (Metric)

Decrease frame O.C. by 1% for every knot over 15 knots.

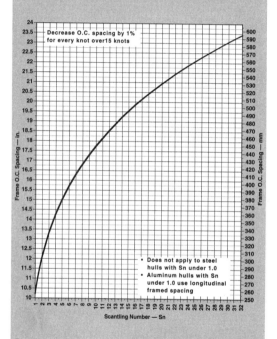

Frame O.C. Spacing in Transversely Framed Hulls, Aluminum and Steel

Hulls with Sns less than 1.0 should be built with longitudinal framing and frame spacing.

FORMULA 17-2

Aluminum Transverse Bottom-Frame Dimensions

Bottom-Frame-Web Thickness, in. =
$0.23 \times Sn^{0.21}$ (English)

Bottom-Frame-Web Thickness, mm =
$5.84 \times Sn^{0.21}$ (Metric)

Bottom-Frame-Web Height, in. =
$1.23 \times Sn^{0.46}$ (English)

Bottom-Frame-Web Height, mm =
$31.24 \times Sn^{0.46}$ (Metric)

Bottom-Frame-Flange Thickness =
$1.25 \times$ web thickness

Bottom-Frame-Flange Width, in. =
$0.92 \times Sn^{0.46}$ (English)

Bottom-Frame-Flange Width, mm =
$23.36 \times Sn^{0.46}$ (Metric)

Increase web height by 1% for every knot over 20 knots.

Increase flange width by 1% for every knot over 15 knots.

Increase flange thickness by 1% for every knot over 15 knots.

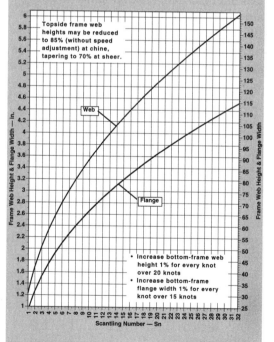

Frame-Web Heights and Flange Widths in Aluminum Transversely Framed Hulls

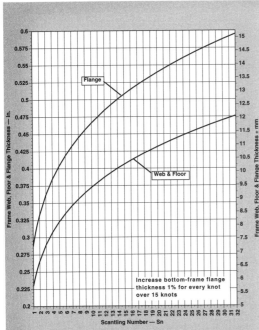

Frame, Deck-Beam and Cabin-Side Frame: Web, Floor, and Flange Thicknesses in Aluminum Transversely Framed Hulls

FORMULA 17-3

Aluminum Transverse Topsides-Frame Dimensions

Bottom frames can extend—unchanged in dimensions—from the bottom, up along the topsides, to the sheer. However, you can elect to save weight by reducing the web heights in the topsides, as follows:

Topsides-Frame-Web Height at Chine or Bilge = 0.85 × bottom web height (not speed-adjusted)

Topsides-Frame-Web Height at Sheer = 0.70 × bottom web height (not speed-adjusted)

On sailboats—at the masts and shroud chainplates—the topside frames should be the same dimensions as the hull-bottom frame (not the reduced topsides-frame dimensions). In addition, on sailing vessels with Sns greater than 3, the web thickness should be increased to the next standard plate size up from the reduced topsides-frame-web thickness.

FORMULA 17-4

Aluminum Transverse Deck-Beam Dimensions

Deck-Beam-Web Thickness, in. = same as bottom and topsides web

Deck-Beam-Web Height, in. = 1.05 × $Sn^{0.36}$ (English)

Deck-Beam-Web Height, mm = 26.67 × $Sn^{0.36}$ (Metric)

Deck-Beam-Flange Thickness = 1.25 × web thickness

Deck-Beam-Flange Width = 0.75 × web height

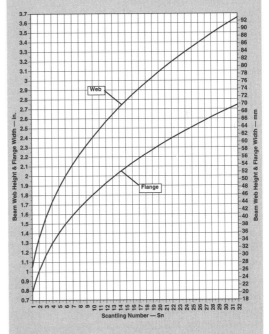

Deck-Beam-Web Heights and Flange Widths in Aluminum Transversely Framed Hulls

Aluminum Transverse-Framing Optional Longitudinals

> Longitudinal-Stiffener-Spacing O.C., in. = 4 + (plate thickness, in. × 32) (English)
>
> Aluminum Longitudinal-Stiffener-Spacing O.C., mm = 101.6 + (plate thickness, mm × 32) (Metric) (same as in Formula 15-6A)
>
> Longitudinal Height = 0.45 × frame or beam-web height
>
> Longitudinal Thickness = plate thickness or one standard size thicker
>
> On vessels with Sns less than 2.5, longitudinals are not usually used.

Aluminum Transverse-Framed Cabin-Side Frames

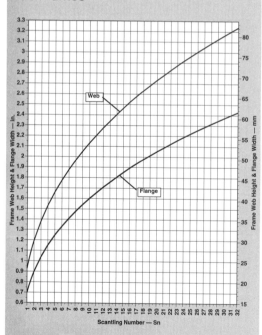

Cabin-Side-Frame Web Heights and Flange Widths in Aluminum Transversely Framed Hulls

> Cabin-Side-Frame Web Thickness = same as deck-beam-web thickness
>
> Cabin-Side-Frame Web Height, in. = $0.93 \times Sn^{0.36}$ (English)
>
> Cabin-Side-Frame Web Height, mm = $23.62 \times Sn^{0.36}$ (Metric)
>
> Cabin-Side-Frame Flange Thickness = 1.25 × web thickness
>
> Cabin-Side-Frame Flange Width = 0.75 × web height

Aluminum Transverse-Framed Stanchion Spacing

> Stanchions may be spaced as convenient using Formula 16-10A; however, the usual spacing is approximately every five frames.

Deck Girders

> Deck girders should be proportioned according to Formula 16-9A; however, in addition to the requirements from this formula, deck girders should be installed in all transverse-framed aluminum hulls with Sns greater than 8.

Aluminum Transverse-Framed Engine Beds and Bottom Girders

> The engine beds and bottom girders are the same as in longitudinal construction, except that the engine beds of displacement craft need to be welded to a minimum of four ring frames, or one full frame beyond the forward-most and after-most engine mounts, whichever extends a greater length.

Mast steps for transverse framing are the same as for longitudinal construction, except that if the mast step is not an extension of the CVK, then it must extend for at least four frames. (The mizzenmast step can extend to only three frames.)

CALCULATING AN EXAMPLE TRANSVERSE-FRAMED ALUMINUM HULL

Returning to our trusty old *AlumaNaught*, we would adjust the boat's structure as follows to frame it out transversely:

Transverse-Framed Hull Frames O.C. = 10.2 × 8.71^{0.24} = 17.1; use 17 in.

Transverse-Framed Hull Frames O.C. = 259 × 8.71^{0.24} = 435.4; use 430 mm

A 35-knot *AlumaNaught* would use

35 knots–15 knots = 20 knots; therefore, decrease O.C. by 20%

Speed-Adjusted-Frame O.C. = 17.1 in. × 0.80 = 13.68; use 13 in.

Speed-Adjusted-Frame O.C. = 430 mm × 0.80 = 344; use 340 mm

Bottom-Frame-Web Thickness = 0.23 × 8.71^{0.21} = 0.362; use ⅜ in.

Bottom-Frame-Web Thickness = 5.84 × 8.71^{0.21} = 9.2; use 9.5 mm

Bottom-Frame-Web Height = 1.23 × 8.71^{0.46} = 3.33; use 3⅜ in.

Bottom-Frame-Web Height = 31.24 × 8.71^{0.46} = 84.5; use 85 mm

Bottom-Frame-Flange Thickness = 1.25 × 0.362 in. = 0.45; use ⁷⁄₁₆ in.

Bottom-Frame-Flange Thickness = 1.25 × 9.2 mm = 11.5; use 11 mm

Bottom-Frame-Flange Width = 0.92 × 8.71^{0.46} = 2.48; use 2½ in.

Bottom-Frame-Flange Width = 23.36 × 8.71^{0.46} = 63.2; use 64 mm

For a 35-knot *AlumaNaught*, the bottom frames would be adjusted as follows:

35 knots–20 knots = 15 knots; therefore, increase web height by 15%

Bottom-Frame-Web Height = 1.15 × 3.32 in. = 3.818; use 3⅞ in.

35 knots –15 knots = 20 knots; therefore, increase flange by 20%

Bottom-Frame-Flange Width = 1.20 × 2.48 in. = 2.97; use 3 in.

Bottom-Frame-Flange Thickness = 1.20 × 0.362 in. = 0.434; use ⁷⁄₁₆ in.

or

35 knots–20 knots = 15 knots; therefore, increase web height by 15%

Bottom-Frame-Web Height =1.15 × 84.5 mm = 97.1; use 100 mm

35 knots–15 knots = 20 knots; therefore, increase flange by 20%

Bottom-Frame-Flange Width = 1.20 × 63.2 mm = 75.8; use 75 mm

Bottom-Frame-Flange Thickness = 1.20 × 9.2 mm = 11.04; use 11 mm

Topsides-Frame-Web Height at Chine or Bilge = 0.85 × 3.32 in. = 2.82; use 2⅞ in.

Topsides-Frame-Web Height at Chine or Bilge = 0.85 × 84.5 mm = 71.8; use 72 mm

Topsides-Frame-Web Height at Sheer = 0.70 × 3.32 in. = 2.32; use 2⅜ in.

Topsides-Frame-Web Height at Sheer = 0.70 × 84.5 mm = 59.1; use 60 mm

Deck-Beam-Web Thickness = ⅜ in. (9.5 mm)

Deck-Beam-Web Height = 1.05 × $8.71^{0.36}$ = 2.29; use 2¼ in.

Deck-Beam-Web Height, mm = 26.67 × $8.71^{0.36}$ = 58.1; use 58 mm

Deck-Beam-Flange Thickness = 1.25 × 0.362 in. = 0.45; use 7⁄16 in.

Deck-Beam-Flange Thickness = 1.25 × 9.2 mm = 11.5 mm

Deck-Beam-Flange Width = 0.75 × 2.25 in. = 1.68; use 1⅝ in.

Deck-Beam-Flange Width = 0.75 × 58.1 mm = 43.57; use 44 mm

In chapter 15, we found the following plate thickness for *AlumaNaught*:

Bottom: 5⁄16 in. (8 mm)
Topsides: 1⁄4 in. (6.4 mm)
Deck: 3⁄16 in. (4.75 mm)

Accordingly, the optional longitudinals would be spaced as follows:

Hull-Bottom-Longitudinal O.C. = 4 + (0.3125 in. × 32) = 14 in.

Topsides-Longitudinal O.C. = 4 + (0.25 in. × 32) = 12 in.

Deck-Longitudinal O.C. = 4 + (0.1875 × 32) = 10 in.

or

Hull-Bottom-Longitudinal O.C. = 101.6 + (8 mm × 32) = 357.6; use 350 mm

Topsides-Longitudinal O.C. = 101.6 + (6.4 mm × 32) = 306.4; use 300 mm

Deck-Longitudinal O.C. = 101.6 + (4.75 mm × 32) = 253.6; use 250 mm

or

Hull-Bottom-Longitudinal Height = 0.45 × 3.375 in. = 1.51; use 1½ in.

Hull-Bottom-Longitudinal Thickness = 5⁄16 or ⅜ in.

Topsides-Longitudinal Height = 0.45 × 2.75 in. at bottom = 1.23; use 1¼ in.

Topsides-Longitudinal Thickness = ¼ or 5⁄16 in.

Deck-Longitudinal Height = 0.45 × 2.25 in. = 1.01; use 1 in.

Deck-Longitudinal Thickness = 3⁄16 or ¼ in.

or

Hull-Bottom-Longitudinal Height = 0.45 × 85 mm = 38.2; use 38 mm

Hull-Bottom-Longitudinal Thickness = 8 or 9.5 mm

Topsides-Longitudinal Height = 0.45 × 72 mm at bottom = 32.4; use 32 mm

Topsides-Longitudinal Thickness = 6.4 or 8 mm

Deck-Longitudinal Height = 0.45 × 58 mm = 26.1; use 25 mm

Deck-Longitudinal Thickness = 4.75 or 6 mm

Cabin-Side-Frame Web Thickness = ⅜ in. (9.5 mm)

*Cabin-Side-Frame Web Height =
0.93 × 8.71$^{0.36}$ = 2.03; use 2 in.*

*Cabin-Side-Frame Web Height =
23.62 × 8.71$^{0.36}$ = 51.48; use 52 mm*

*Cabin-Side-Frame Flange Thickness =
1.25 × 0.362 in. = 0.45; use $^7/_{16}$ in.*

*Cabin-Side-Frame Flange Thickness =
1.25 × 9.2 mm = 11.5 mm*

*Cabin-Side-Frame Flange Width = 0.75 ×
2 in. = 1½ in.*

*Cabin-Side-Frame Flange Width = 0.75 ×
52 mm = 39; use 40 mm*

Lightweight Aluminum Scantlings

Both the longitudinal- and transverse-framed scantlings presented so far are generous with heavy plate. Aluminum, however, is so rust-free and tough (it absorbs so much energy by deforming) that both the longitudinal- and transverse-framed scantlings can be reduced still more. This may be done safely for most yachts and high-speed craft. The penalties are less reserve strength and a somewhat shorter operational life expectancy. The reward—and it is an important one—is improved performance: higher speed, longer range, greater cargo capacity, better fuel economy, higher ballast ratio.

On high-performance sailboats and high-speed planing hulls, weight savings is so critical to success that it can be well worth this trade-off in less reserve strength. Indeed, even at these lightweight scantlings, such hulls are still quite tough. Displacement boats (e.g., sailboats) can reduce the scantlings everywhere, including on their underbodies.

Extreme lightweight construction system pioneered by Derecktor Shipyards. Closely spaced ring frames and longitudinals allow very thin plate. Numerous carefully engineered lightening holes further reduce weight. This construction gives hull weights comparable to high-tech composite materials. (Courtesy Derecktor International)

Planing hulls, however, must use the standard bottom framing and bottom longitudinals and the standard heavier bottom plate on their underbodies—from the BLH or the chine down (see Formula 4-3).

Of course, heavy workboats and serious ocean-voyaging vessels would do well to build-in the reserve of strength from the standard scantlings in chapters 15 and 16. In aluminum—in larger, heavier-displacement hulls—the greater weight of the standard scantlings is modest in proportion with overall displacement, and therefore does not significantly affect performance.

The following formulas give the adjustments for lightweight aluminum construction suited to high-performance vessels.

Because $^3/_{16}$-inch (4.75 mm) plate is the thinnest conveniently weldable with standard equipment, no further reduction should be made below $^3/_{16}$ inch (4.75 mm), unless pulse-arc welding is available and economically viable or unless riveting is practical.

For displacement craft, the standard heavier bottom plate should be determined and then 88 percent of that thickness used. This heavier bottom plate is required—not optional—with the lightweight rule. Again, planing hulls must use the standard heavier bottom plate without reduction.

SCANTLINGS FOR A LIGHTWEIGHT ALUMANAUGHT

If our sleek *AlumaNaught* were a 35-knot planing hull, it would make good sense to use lightweight scantlings to ensure we achieved this high speed. Because it's a planing hull, we would keep the same standard heavier bottom plating and the same bottom framing calculated in chapter 15. We would adjust the following scantlings, however, to get a lightweight hull—in this case, longitudinally framed:

Lightweight Bottom Thickness = $^5/_{16}$ in. (8 mm) (same as standard)

Lightweight Topsides Thickness = 0.88 × 0.245 in. = 0.21; use 0.204 in.

Lightweight Topsides Thickness = 0.88 × 6.23 mm = 5.25 mm

Lightweight Deck and Cabin-Side Thickness = $^3/_{16}$ in. (4.75 mm)

These thicknesses were already rounded down and are the thinnest practical for standard welding; do not reduce.

Bottom Longitudinals = same as standard

Topsides-Longitudinal Spacing, O.C. = 4 + (0.21 in. × 32) = 10.72; use 10½ in.

Topsides-Longitudinal Spacing, O.C. = 101.6 + (5.25 mm × 32) = 269.6; use 265 mm

Deck- and cabin-longitudinal spacing will be unchanged as the plate thickness is unchanged.

Topsides-Longitudinal Height = 2.49 in. × 1.10 = 2.73; use 2¾ in.

Topsides-Longitudinal Height = 63.39 mm × 1.10 = 69.7; use 70 mm

Topsides-Longitudinal Thickness = ¼ in. (6.4 mm)

Deck-Longitudinal Height = 1.53 in. × 1.10 = 1.68; use 1⅝ in.

Deck-Longitudinal Height = 39.07 mm × 1.10 = 42.9; use 44 mm

Deck-Longitudinal Thickness = ¼ in. (6.4 mm)

Cabin-Side-Longitudinal Height = The plate is unchanged in thickness (cannot reduce below ³⁄₁₆ in.); therefore, use standard cabin-side longitudinals.

Frame Spacing, O.C. = same as standard

Bottom-Web-Frame Dimensions = same as standard for AlumaNaught's planing hull

Topsides-Frame-Web Thickness = ¼ in. (6.4 mm)

Topsides-Frame-Web Height = 1.10 × 5.53 in. non-speed-adjusted bottom height × 0.85 for standard topsides = 5.17; use 5.14 in. tapering to 0.75% of bottom or 4½ in. at sheer

Topsides-Frame-Web Height = 1.10 × 140.6 mm non-speed-adjusted bottom height × 0.85 for standard topsides = 131.4; use 130 mm tapering to 0.75% of bottom or 115 mm at sheer

Topsides-Frame-Flange Thickness = same as standard ⁷⁄₁₆ in. (11.25 mm)

Topsides-Frame-Flange Width = 1.10 × 4.15 in. = 4.56; use 4½ in.

Topsides-Frame-Flange Width = 1.10 × 105.5 mm = 116; use 115 mm

Deck-Frame-Web Thickness = ¼ in. (6.4 mm)

Deck-Frame-Web Height = 1.10 × 3.87 in. = 4.25; use 4¼ in.

Deck-Frame-Web Height = 1.10 × 98.49 mm = 108.3; use 110 mm

Deck-Frame-Flange Thickness = same as standard ⁷⁄₁₆ in. (11.25 mm)

Deck-Frame-Flange Width = 1.10 × 3 in. = 3.3; use 3⅜ in.

Deck-Frame-Flange Width = 1.10 × 75 mm = 82.5; use 85 mm

Steel Transverse Framing with Longitudinals

Like aluminum, steel can be built with closely spaced transverse frames and light longitudinals. Hulls built to these steel-transverse-framing-with longitudinal scantlings can do away with the small longitudinals completely if a pair of longitudinal hull girders are used. Also, in smaller craft (i.e., Sns less than 2.5), no longitudinals are required at all, although such vessels would be quite heavy in steel. Keep in mind that fewer longitudinals means greater difficulty in getting a fair hull.

As with the aluminum-transverse-framing rule, the longitudinal scantlings from chapters 15 and 16 are the basis for the steel-transverse scantlings. Unless a component is specifically changed, it is determined identically to the longitudinal scantlings. You must understand the scantlings selection in chapters 15 and 16 before using the following transverse-framing rules.

FORMULA 17-15

Steel Transverse-Framing with Longitudinals Frame Spacing

Frame Spacing O.C., in. = 10.2 × $Sn^{0.24}$ (English) (same as Formula 17-1)

Frame Spacing O.C., mm = 259 × $8.71^{0.24}$ (Metric) (same as Formula 17-1)

Decrease frame O.C. by 1% for every knot over 15 knots.

FORMULA 17-16

Steel Transverse Bottom-Frame Dimensions

Bottom-Frame-Web Height, in. = 1.25 × $Sn^{0.44}$ (English)

Bottom-Frame-Web Height, mm = 31.75 × $Sn^{0.44}$ (Metric)

Bottom-Frame-Web Thickness, in. = 0.20 × $Sn^{0.21}$ (English)

Bottom-Frame-Web Thickness, mm = 5.08 × $Sn^{0.21}$ (Metric)

Bottom-Frame-Flange Width = 0.75 × web height

Bottom-Frame-Flange Thickness = 1.25 × web thickness

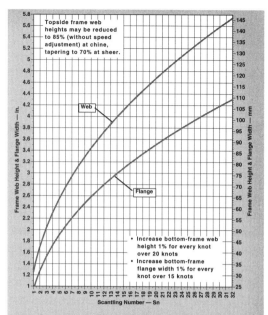

Frame-Web Heights and Flange Widths in Steel Transversely Framed Hulls

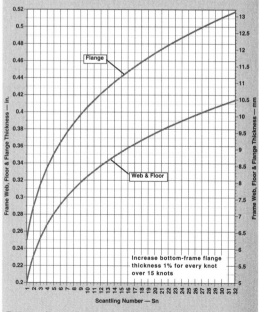

Frame, Deck-Beam, and Cabin-Side Frame: Web, Floor, and Flange Thicknesses in Steel Transversely Framed Hulls

Increase web height by 1 percent for every knot over 20 knots. Increase flange width by 1 percent for every knot over 15 knots. Increase flange thickness by 1 percent for every knot over 15 knots.

FORMULA 17-17

Steel Transverse Topsides-Frame Dimensions

The same as non-speed-adjusted bottom frames, except the web can be 0.85 × bottom-frame-web height at the chine or bilge, tapering down to 0.75 × bottom-frame web height at the sheer.

On sailboats—at the masts and shroud chainplates—the topsides frames should be the same dimensions as the hull-bottom frame (not the reduced topsides-frame dimensions). In addition—on boats with Sns greater than 4.5—the web thickness should be increased to the next standard plate size up from the reduced topsides-frame-web thickness.

FORMULA 17-18

Steel Transverse-Framed Hull Longitudinals

Longitudinal Thickness = frame web thickness

Longitudinal Height = 0.35 × frame web height

Longitudinals are not required on hulls with Sns less than 2.5.

FORMULA 17-19

Steel Transverse-Framed Deck-Beam Dimensions

Deck-Beam-Web Thickness = same as hull-bottom web

Deck-Beam-Web Height, in. = 1.05 × $Sn^{0.35}$ (English)

Deck-Beam-Web Height, mm = 26.67 × $Sn^{0.35}$ (Metric)

Deck-Beam-Flange Thickness, in. = 1.25 × web thickness

Deck-Beam-Flange Width, in. = 0.75 × web height

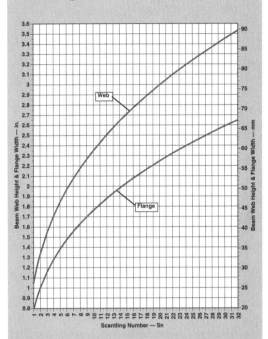

Deck-Beam-Web Heights and Flange Widths in Steel Transversely Framed Hulls

FORMULA 17-20

Steel Transverse-Framed Deck Longitudinals

Deck longitudinals are optional with transverse frames spaced this close; however, they are frequently used to improve fairness.

Deck-Longitudinal Thickness = plate thickness or the next standard size up (based on mild-steel plate, not Cor-Ten thickness)

Deck-Longitudinal Height = 0.35 × deck-beam-web height

FORMULA 17-21

Steel Web Frames or Deep Frames or Transverse-Framed Hulls

Transverse-framed vessels with Sns over 6 should install heavier or deeper frames at every third frame.

Web-Frame Thickness = same as standard transverse frame

Web-Frame Height = 1.8 × standard transverse frame web height (for topsides and bottom web, respectively)

Web-Frame-Flange Thickness = same as standard transverse frame

Web-Frame-Flange Width = 0.5 × web frame web height

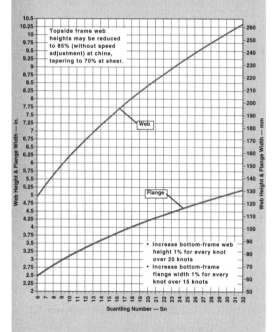

Deep Web Frames, Web Heights, and Flange Widths in Steel Transversely Framed Hulls

FORMULA 17-22

Steel Transverse-Framed Cabin-Side Frames

Cabin-Side-Frame Web Thickness = same as deck-beam-web thickness

Cabin-Side-Frame Web Height, in. = 0.92 × Sn$^{0.35}$ (English)

Cabin-Side-Frame Web Height, mm = 23.3 × Sn$^{0.35}$ (Metric)

Cabin-Side-Frame Flange Thickness = 1.25 × web thickness

Cabin-Side-Frame Flange Width = 0.75 × web height

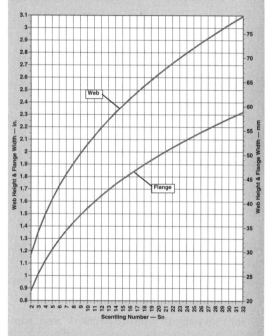

Cabin-Side-Frame Web Heights and Flange Widths in Steel Transversely Framed Hulls

Formula 17-23

Steel Transverse-Framed Longitudinal Stringer or Girder Plates in Lieu of Web Frames

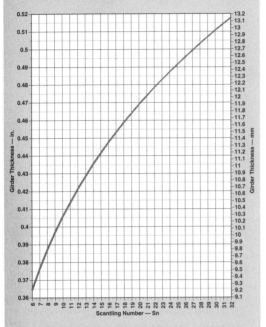

Hull Girder in Place of Deep Web Frame: Thickness in Steel Transversely Framed Hulls

Deep web frames every third frame interfere with one of the advantages of transverse-framed construction: reduced frame molding for increased interior room. The web frames can be dispensed with if two heavy longitudinal stringers or girder plates are installed. These are built in at roughly right angles to the hull plating at: one about half way out from the keel to the bilge or chine on the hull bottom; one about 35 percent of the topside height up from the bilge or chine, on the topside. These longitudinal girders are flat plate, as follows:

Girder Thickness, in. = $0.25 \times Sn^{0.21}$ (English)

Girder Thickness, mm = $6.35 \times Sn^{0.21}$ (Metric)

Girder Height, in. = $3.08 \times Sn^{0.36}$ (English)

Girder Height, mm = $78.23 \times Sn^{0.36}$ (Metric)

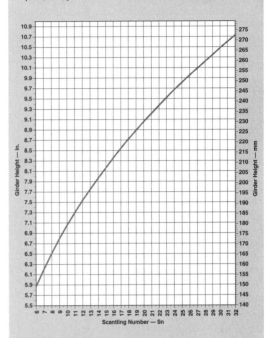

Hull Girder in Place of Deep Web Frame: Height in Steel Transversely Framed Hulls

It is unusual to produce larger steel hulls light enough to operate as high-speed planing craft. If this were done, however, the bottom girders would be the same as the high-speed hull girders from the longitudinal section. In this case, if you wanted to avoid deep web frames, you would only have to add the upper (topsides) girder specified previously.

Formula 17-24

Steel Transverse-Framed Stanchion Spacing

Stanchions may be spaced as convenient, using Formula 16-10S;

(continued)

however, the usual spacing is approximately every five frames.

FORMULA 17-25
Steel Transverse-Framed Deck Girders

Deck girders should be proportioned according to Formula 16-9S; however, in addition to the requirements in chapter 16, deck girders should be installed in all transverse-framed steel hulls with Sns greater than 8.

FORMULA 17-26
Steel Transverse-Framed Engine Beds and Bottom Girders

The engine beds and bottom girders are identical to longitudinal construction, except that the engine beds of displacement craft need to be welded to a minimum of four ring frames or one full frame beyond the forward-most and after-most engine mounts, whichever extends a greater length.

FORMULA 17-27
Steel Transverse-Framed Mast Step

Mast steps for transverse framing are the same as for longitudinal construction, except that if the mast step is not an extension of the CVK, then it must extend for at least four frames. (The mizzenmast step can extend to only three frames.)

WORKING THROUGH A TRANSVERSE-FRAMED DISPLACEMENT-SPEED *IRON MAIDEN*

If we decided to use transverse framing on our 10.5-knot (for example) *Iron Maiden*, we would get the following scantlings:

$$Frame\ Spacing\ O.C. = 10.2 \times 8.71^{0.24} = 17.1; use\ 17\ in.$$

$$Frame\ Spacing\ O.C. = 259 \times 8.71^{0.24} = 435.4; use\ 435\ mm$$

$$Bottom\text{-}Frame\text{-}Web\ Height = 1.25 \times 8.71^{0.44} = 3.23; use\ 3\tfrac{1}{4}\ in.$$

$$Bottom\text{-}Frame\text{-}Web\ Height = 31.75 \times 8.71^{0.44} = 82.2; use\ 84\ mm$$

$$Bottom\text{-}Frame\text{-}Web\ Thickness = 0.20 \times 8.71^{0.21} = 0.31; use\ \tfrac{5}{16}\ in.$$

$$Bottom\text{-}Frame\text{-}Web\ Thickness = 5.08 \times 8.71^{0.21} = 8\ mm$$

$$Bottom\text{-}Frame\text{-}Flange\ Width = 0.75 \times 3.23\ in. = 2.42; use\ 2\tfrac{1}{2}\ in.$$

$$Bottom\text{-}Frame\text{-}Flange\ Width = 0.75 \times 82.2\ mm = 61.6; use\ 65\ mm$$

$$Bottom\text{-}Frame\text{-}Flange\ Thickness = 1.25 \times 0.31\ in. = 0.38; use\ \tfrac{3}{8}\ in.$$

$$Bottom\text{-}Frame\text{-}Flange\ Thickness = 1.25 \times 8.0\ mm = 10\ mm$$

$$Topsides\text{-}Web\ Height, at\ Bilge\ or\ Chine = 0.85 \times 3.23\ in. = 2.74; use\ 2\tfrac{3}{4}\ in.$$

tapering to

$$Topsides\text{-}Web\ Height\ at\ Sheer = 0.75 \times 3.23\ in. = 2.42; use\ 2\tfrac{1}{2}\ in.$$

or

$$Topsides\text{-}Web\ Height, at\ Bilge\ or\ Chine = 0.85 \times 82.2\ mm = 69.8; use\ 70\ mm$$

tapering to

$$Topsides\text{-}Web\ Height\ at\ Sheer = 0.75 \times 82.2\ mm = 61.6; use\ 62\ mm$$

$$Hull\text{-}Longitudinal\ Thickness = \tfrac{5}{16}\ in.\ (8\ mm)$$

$$Hull\text{-}Longitudinal\ Height = 0.35 \times 3.23\ in. = 1.13; use\ 1\tfrac{1}{8}\ or\ 1\tfrac{1}{4}\ in.$$

$$Hull\text{-}Longitudinal\ Height = 0.35 \times 82.2\ mm = 28.7; use\ 30\ mm$$

Deck-Beam-Web Thickness = $\frac{5}{16}$ in. (8 mm)

Deck-Beam-Web Height = $1.05 \times 8.71^{0.35}$ = 2.24; use $2\frac{1}{4}$ in.

Deck-Beam-Web Height = $26.67 \times 8.71^{0.35}$ = 56.8, use 58 mm

Deck-Beam-Flange Thickness = 1.25×0.31 in. = 0.38; use $\frac{3}{8}$ in.

Deck-Beam-Flange Thickness = 1.25×8.0 mm = 10 mm

Deck-Beam-Flange Width = 0.75×2.23 in. = 1.67; use $1\frac{5}{8}$ in.

Deck-Beam-Flange Width = 0.75×56.8 mm = 42.6; use 42 mm

We found *Iron Maiden*'s deck to be 8-gauge (0.1664 in.) (4 mm) Cor-Ten, which equaled $\frac{3}{16}$-in. (4.75 mm) mild steel.

Deck-Longitudinal Thickness = $\frac{3}{16}$ or $\frac{1}{4}$ in. (4.75 or 6 mm)

Deck-Longitudinal Height = 0.35×2.23 in. $\times$ 0.78; use $\frac{3}{4}$ or 1 in.

Deck-Longitudinal Height = 0.35×56.8 mm = 19.88; use 20 or 25 mm

Web-Frame Web Thickness = $\frac{5}{16}$ in. (8 mm)

Web-Frame Web Height, Bottom = 1.8×3.23 in. = 5.81; use $5\frac{3}{4}$ in.

Web-Frame Web Height, Bottom = 1.8×82.2 mm = 147.9; use 145 mm

Web-Frame Web Height, Lower Topsides = 1.8×2.74 in. = 4.93; use 5 in.

Web-Frame Web Height, Lower Topsides = 1.8×69.8 mm = 125.6; use 125 mm

Web-Frame Web Height, Upper Topsides = 1.8×2.42 in. = 4.36; use $4\frac{3}{8}$ in.

Web-Frame Web Height, Upper Topsides = 1.8×61.6 mm = 110.8; use 110 mm

Web-Frame-Flange Thickness = $\frac{3}{8}$ in. (10 mm)

Web-Frame-Flange Width = 0.5×5.81 in. = 2.9; use 3 in.

Web-Frame-Flange Width = 0.5×147.9 mm = 73.9; use 74 mm

Cabin-Side-Frame Web Thickness = $\frac{5}{16}$ inch (8 mm)

Cabin-Side-Frame Web Height = $0.92 \times 8.71^{0.35}$ = 1.96; use 2 in.

Cabin-Side-Frame Web Height = $23.3 \times 8.71^{0.35}$ = 49.7; use 50 mm

Cabin-Side-Frame Flange Thickness = 1.25×0.31 in. = 0.38; use $\frac{3}{8}$ in.

Cabin-Side-Frame Flange Thickness = 1.25×8.0 mm = 10 mm

Cabin-Side-Frame Flange Width = 0.75×1.96 in. = 1.47; use $1\frac{1}{2}$ in.

Cabin-Side-Frame Flange Width = 0.75×49.7 mm = 37.2; use 38 mm

Girder Thickness = $0.25 \times 8.71^{0.21}$ = 0.39; use $\frac{3}{8}$ in.

Girder Thickness = $6.35 \times 8.71^{0.21}$ = 10 mm

Girder Height = $3.08 \times 8.71^{0.36}$ = 6.7; use $6\frac{3}{4}$ in.

Girder Height = $78.23 \times 8.71^{0.36}$ = 170.5; use 170 mm

Steel Transverse-Framing with No Longitudinals

It is possible to construct steel vessels with closely spaced transverse frames using no longitudinals at all. I'm not sure I see much advantage to this. Weld distortion is more difficult to control, which often results in rippled, hungry-horse plating. To minimize this problem, the plating should be thicker than normal. This adds weight, which is detrimental to stability and performance. Still, for heavy workboats such as trawlers, this heavy plate can increase the life of the steel hull, especially when maintenance may be poor. The thicker plate has a higher built-in corrosion allowance. Indeed, the plate for this rule is so thick that it qualifies as light ice-class, which also can be an advantage in some waters.

Because of the heavy plate and the resulting heavy hull, the scantlings from this all-transverse-framed rule are only suited to heavy-displacement vessels with Sns greater than 6.

The transverse-frame-with-no-longitudinal scantlings are based on the previously given standard transverse-frame scantlings.

FORMULA 17-28
Steel Transverse-Framed Hull Plate with No Longitudinals

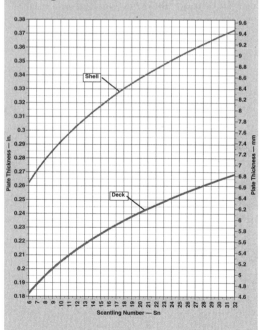

Heavy Shell and Deck Plate in Steel Transversely Framed Hulls

Hull Plate (Bottom and Topsides), in. = $0.18 \times Sn^{0.21}$ (English)

Hull Plate (Bottom and Topsides), mm = $4.57 \times Sn^{0.21}$ (Metric)

FORMULA 17-29
Steel Transverse-Frame Spacing

Transverse Framed Spacing O.C. = same as standard steel transverse-framed spacing (see Formula 17-15), except not to exceed 24 in. (610 mm)

FORMULA 17-30
Steel Transverse-Framed Deep Web Frames

With this construction, the deep web frames are not required.

FORMULA 17-31
Steel Transverse-Framed Deck Plate

Deck Plate, in. = $0.121 \times Sn^{0.23}$ (English)

Deck Plate, mm = $3.07 \times Sn^{0.23}$ (Metric)

(See chart 17-28.)

CONVERTING *IRON MAIDEN* TO TRANSVERSE-FRAMED WITHOUT LONGITUDINALS

Going back to our reliable *Iron Maiden*, we could convert the boat to transverse-framed without any longitudinals as follows:

Hull Plate (Bottom and Topsides) = $0.18 \times 8.71^{0.21} = 0.28$; use ¼ in.

Hull Plate (Bottom and Topsides) = $4.57 \times 8.71^{0.21} = 7.2$; use 7.2 mm

Transverse-Framed Spacing O.C. = same as standard steel transverse-framed spacing (see Formula 17-15), except not to exceed 24 in. (610 mm). The 17 in. (435 mm) that we found previously is acceptable.

Deck Plate, in. = 0.121 × 8.71^0.23 = 0.199; use ³⁄₁₆ in.

$$Deck\ Plate,\ in. = 0.121 \times 8.71^{0.23} = 0.199;\ use\ ^3/_{16}\ in.$$

$$Deck\ Plate,\ mm = 3.07 \times 8.71^{0.23} = 5.05;\ use\ 5\ mm$$

Lightweight Steel

You would expect that—like aluminum—we could make lightweight steel hulls by reducing plate thicknesses from those given for the standard construction method. Unfortunately, because of steel's rust problem, this is not generally a good idea. Such thin-plate steel hulls can lose too large a percentage of their hull thickness to rust and corrosion too quickly. Yes, a perfect construction job, with excellent engineering followed by superb paint and coating and with ongoing excellent and regular maintenance, can make even thin-plate steel last a very long time in saltwater. Achieving all these ideals in one boat—especially continuing the high-level of maintenance for years—is seldom a realistic prospect. In addition, because steel is so heavy to begin with, the standard rule already generates reasonably thin plates.

True round-bilge steel boats can *be built by yards that know how. Here, one comes together nicely at Treworgy Yachts.* (Courtesy Treworgy Yachts)

Remember, though, that Cor-Ten is not rustproof by any means. These thinner Cor-Ten members can corrode out and, if you lose ¹⁄₁₆ inch (1.6 mm) of plate from a ³⁄₁₆-inch-thick (4.75 mm) longitudinal, you have lost a third of its strength. The same ¹⁄₁₆-inch (1.6 mm) loss from a comparable ⁷⁄₃₂-inch (5.5 mm) longitudinal would be 28 percent. Still, Cor-Ten does rust more slowly than mild steel, so converting to all Cor-Ten is acceptable. Remember, reduce only thicknesses; the web and longitudinal heights should all remain the same. You must *increase* the flange widths by 1.13 times. Alternately, leave the flange dimensions unchanged from the standard scantlings.

FORMULA 17-32

Lightweight Steel: All Cor-Ten

So what is the answer to lightweight steel? The best I can come up with is Cor-Ten. We've already seen that using Cor-Ten, you can reduce plate thickness to 88 percent of the standard mild-steel calculated in the rule. Generally, I believe it is better to use mild steel for the interior framing; however, you can go the next step: convert all thicknesses to Cor-Ten by reducing them to 88 percent of mild steel.

EIGHTEEN

Welding, Small Openings, and Riveting Aluminum

Welding

TYPES OF WELDING

Except for thin sheet, which is riveted, almost every component of a metal boat is joined or fastened by welding. Originally, welding could be accomplished only on a forge. Not surprisingly, this is termed *forge welding*. Although at least a couple of thousand years old, forge welding is limited to parts small enough for you to heat them to near melting and then hammer together. Clearly, this is labor-intensive and hardly suited to welding a boat hull. Modern welding is either oxyacetylene or electric-arc welding. Oxyacetylene has little application for welding boats; however, the oxyacetylene-torch equipment does have important uses. Electric-arc welding—in one of several standard forms—is the welding method for modern steel- and aluminum-boat construction.

In this chapter, we discuss the different types of welding equipment appropriate to different materials, and we determine how to specify the correct size and frequency of weld bead to join various components; this is akin to determining fastener size in wood construction. We also discuss some of the principles underlying sound welding practice and joint design. This chapter is not a welding manual, however—welding is a craft that takes time, thought, and effort to acquire. No one should undertake building a metal hull without, at the minimum, taking a course in welding from a local technical school. For classed or U.S. Coast Guard–certified vessels, welders must be certified by ABS, Lloyds, or the Coast Guard.

OXYACETYLENE EQUIPMENT AND CUTTING PLATE

Oxyacetylene welding uses the heat of acetylene gas burned in combination with pure oxygen to melt the metal to be welded. Extra filler metal is added to the joint with hand-fed filler rods. Oxyacetylene is not efficient for welding hulls, but the equipment is essential for cutting steel plate and for pre- and post-heating special weldments. It's also useful for heating plate to ease bending and for line heating, brazing, and soldering.

Oxyacetylene torches are the standard method for cutting steel plate. It might seem odd that the same process can both weld and cut. To cut rather than weld, enough extra oxygen is forced through the torch so that the molten metal actually burns. This burning is the "cutting" action. Keep in mind at all times that both the oxygen and the acetylene are dangerously explosive. In many ways, the oxygen is more dangerous than the acetylene. Pure oxygen can transform normally inflammable or slow-burning materials into bombs. For instance, pure oxygen can cause oil or grease to ignite spontaneously. Use great care!

The fastest and most accurate method of cutting plate (aluminum or steel) is with a plasma cutting machine. These are quite expensive, however, and are usually found only in larger building yards.

ELECTRIC-ARC WELDING

The first patent on arc welding was issued to an Englishman named Wilde in 1865. It wasn't until the 1890s, however, that what is known as *carbon-arc* welding became a commercially viable process. In this form of arc welding, a carbon electrode is held close to the metal to be welded to create the hot electric arc that melts the metal, and any filler metal is added manually.

Modern *metal-arc welding* was invented in 1889, when N. G. Slavinoff and Charles Coffin were each granted patents—in Russia and the United States, respectively—on a new process. They replaced the carbon electrode with a metal rod. The rod not only acted as the electrode to generate the hot metal-melting arc, but the rod itself also melted away to form filler metal for the joint at the same time. This is basically the *metal-arc-welding* process, or simply the *arc-welding* or *stick-welding* process, used to fabricate most steel hulls.

ARC-WELDING ELECTRODES (RODS OR STICKS)

Still, there were difficulties. The early metal electrodes (i.e., the metal rods that doubled as electrode and filler metal) were the problem. When you heat metals to melting, they react chemically with oxygen in the atmosphere and with trace elements in the metal and the electrode. These reactions can cause brittleness and corrosion. Special formulations of flux coatings and proper weld-filler metal alloys were the solution. The flux coatings vaporize and shield the arc from oxygen, so this modern-arc or stick-welding is properly termed *shielded metal-arc welding*. Using this method, the first all-welded vessel was built in Charleston, South Carolina, in 1930. As discussed previously, World War II marked the transition. Before the war, almost all steel ships were riveted; by the end of the war, riveted ships were the exception.

Today, metal-arc electrodes come in a wide variety of alloys and flux coverings, each best suited for welding specific alloys, with specific welding equipment, in exact conditions. These shielded-arc electrodes are critical to the success of any metal-arc-welding project. It is vital to follow the recommendations of the rod manufacturer in using exactly the right electrodes for your machine and building circumstances.

WELDING ALUMINUM ALLOY: GAS-SHIELDED ARC WELDING

The flux-coated rods of metal-arc welding do not provide sufficient protection from undesirable chemical reactions when welding aluminum, which is far more chemically active than steel. The solution—which wasn't fully arrived at until the 1950s—is to shield the weld arc with an inert gas such as argon, nitrogen, helium, or carbon dioxide.

Tungsten Inert-Gas Welding

The first of these processes was *tungsten inert-gas (TIG) welding*, which employs a tungsten electrode with a helium-gas shield. A high-frequency, high-voltage AC current is superimposed on the welding current to stabilize the arc. TIG welding is somewhat slower than *metal inert-gas (MIG) welding*, but it generates a smoother weld bead, which minimizes or eliminates grinding on many surfaces. TIG welding is still useful, especially for fabricating small fittings and components; its drawback is that it requires a separate hand-held filler rod.

Metal Inert-Gas Welding

Metal inert-gas welding (MIG) is the process used for assembling most components of most aluminum boats. With MIG welding, the welder holds a gun with a nozzle that blows the shielding gas around the arc struck from a filler-metal wire electrode. This wire is fed continuously and automatically into the weld line through the center of the gun tip. A spool of filler/electrode wire is mounted on the welding machine and runs through to the gun, which is attached by hoses and cables to the welding machine many feet away (as convenient). This is the quickest and easiest welding technique for most aluminum boatbuilding applications.

MIG welding is faster than metal-arc or stick-welding and can be used on steel as well as aluminum. Most steel boats, however, are built entirely with shielded-metal-arc equipment (i.e., stick-welding). Although MIG equipment is considerably more expensive, large boatbuilding shops might well consider the potential economies from faster welding with MIG on steel hulls. A factor often overlooked in this evaluation is that the faster welding speeds with gas-shielded-arc welding such as MIG mean less heat is put into the structure, so there is less distortion. Of course, MIG and TIG welding should both be done indoors (or, less satisfactorily, with windscreens outdoors) to ensure that the gas shield isn't blown away from the weld.

TYPES OF WELDS

There are two basic types of welds: butt welds and right-angle welds. Joints made at right angles are usually made with fillet welds, although heavier plate can benefit from beveled V-groove welds. Welds can also be subdivided into continuous and intermittent welds. A continuous weld on a flange to a web that was 10 feet (3 m) long would run the full 10 feet (3 m), without interruption. An intermittent weld might run for perhaps 2 inches (50 mm), then skip 10 inches (250 mm), followed by 2 more inches (50 mm), and so on.

Fillet-Weld Dimensions

Because fillet welds are so common, most welds are defined with respect to them. A cross section through a standard fillet weld is roughly a section through a right triangle with equal legs. The throat of the weld is the line that slices through the widest portion of the triangle from the center of the hypotenuse to the 90-degree (inside) corner. It is the weld metal in the throat that determines the strength of a weld; however, it's not easy to measure throat size directly. For this reason, in the United States the custom is to specify weld size in terms of leg length—the length of the triangle sides against the welded parts. In Europe, throat size is often specified rather than leg length. We use leg length exclusively in this discussion.

The throat is equal in length to half the hypotenuse, so it is easy to convert leg length to throat size or vice versa.

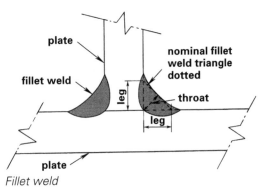

Fillet weld

FORMULA 18-1
Weld Leg-Length to Throat-Size Conversion

$Throat = 0.707 \times leg$

$Leg = 1.41 \times throat$

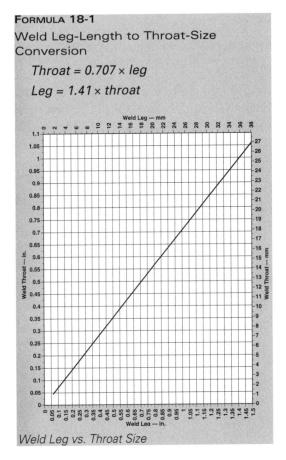

Weld Leg vs. Throat Size

Accordingly, a ¼-in. weld has a 0.176-in. throat; 0.25-in. leg × 0.707 = 0.176 in.

or

a 6.4 mm weld has a 45.2 mm throat; 6.4 mm × 0.707 = 45.2 mm

Minimizing Weld: Intermittent and Continuous Welds

There is a common misconception that metal hulls are welded continuously throughout. Nothing could be farther from the case! Because every additional bit of weld introduces extra heat into the structure, each extra weld length increases distortion. It is vital that no more weld be used than is necessary for strength. Excess welding does not make a boat stronger; in fact, the resulting locked-in stresses from distortion can make it weaker. It will also make the vessel lumpy, wrinkled, and unsightly.

Generally, the vast majority of the internal structure is intermittently welded. The exceptions are high-load components such as engine beds, mast steps, chainplates, and butt-joint welds in frame members. Of course, the shell, deck, tanks, and superstructure plate must all be continuously welded to make them watertight. This is naturally unavoidable, but is unfortunate because the continuous welding of all the shell plate is one of the principal sources of weld distortion in a hull.

Chain and Staggered Welds

Intermittent welds are further subdivided into two categories: *chain* and *staggered*. If you

A close-up of the stringers or longitudinals where they notch into the hull. The draining snipes in the frames at the longitudinal slots show clearly. The internal flat bar is temporary bracing. Note the chain weld of frame web to flange.

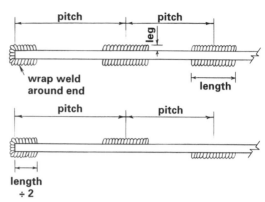

*Top: Chain weld. **Bottom:** Staggered weld.*

lay down, for example, 2 inches (50 mm) of weld on both sides of a web-to-flange joint, back to back, then skip 10 inches (250 mm) and lay down another 2 inches (50 mm) back to back, you've been doing chain welding. Staggered welding alternates the welds on opposite sides of the web. In this case, you would put down 2 inches (50 mm) on the left side (with nothing on the right side), skip 10 inches (250 mm) and lay down 2 inches (50 mm) on the right side (with no weld on the left), and so on. Because the pitch is the same for both chain and staggered welds, in this rule staggered welds have twice the total weld of chain welds. Both staggered and chain welding are sometimes referred to as *stitch welding*. My opinion is that this term should be properly applied only to staggered welds (not chain welds), but this convention isn't strictly observed.

The following table gives the type of weld—staggered, chain, or continuous—to be used on various structural components.

TABLE 18-2 Component Weld Selection Table

All standard webs to shell or bulkhead plate:	staggered
All standard longitudinals to shell plate:	staggered
All standard flanges to webs:	chain
Web to shell at mast partner and chainplate frames (for 6 × web height on longitudinally framed hulls, down topsides from sheer, and in from sheer along deck beam; for 8 × web height on transversely framed hulls, down topsides from sheer, and in from sheer along deck beam):	continuous
Floors to shell:	chain
Floors to frame:	continuous
Floors to keel-bottom plate:	continuous
Floors to shell in engine compartment:	continuous

TABLE 18-2 Component Weld Selection Table *(Cont.)*

Floors to shell at stern tube:	continuous
Floors to shell at mast step:	continuous
Floors to CVK:	continuous
CVK to stern frame:	continuous
Bottom girders to floors and frames:	continuous
Bottom-girder web to shell under engine mounts:	continuous
Bottom-girder web to shell:	chain
Frame webs to shell under engine beds	
(for at least 1.5 times length of engine and gear, or from CVK to	
chine or bilge, whichever is less):	continuous
Frame webs to shell at shaft logs:	continuous
For at least three longitudinals wide	
Engine-bed flange to web and engine bed to floors	continuous
and bulkheads:	
Engine beds to bottom girder:	continuous
Deck girder to beams:	continuous
Deck-girder web to shell:	chain
Bulkheads to shell:	continuous
Interior decks to shell (not watertight):	staggered
Stanchion tops and bases:	continuous
Brackets:	continuous
Doubler and insert plates:	continuous

All continuous welds are double continuous; that is, equal fillet welds on both sides. If access to one side is limited, a full-penetration, 60-degree bevel weld can be used instead, from the accessible side.

WELD SIZES

Welds are sized according to the thickness of the plates they join and the loads they will experience. The size of a fillet weld is specified by its leg; the spacing between intermittent welds is termed the *pitch*. Accordingly, to fully define a weld, you have to call out the following:

leg length
weld bead laid down (if intermittent)
pitch (if intermittent)
continuous (if continuous)

For example, the web of a $^1/_4$-inch (6.4 mm) aluminum frame would be fastened to $^3/_{16}$-inch (4.75 mm) shell plate with $^1/_8$-inch (3.2 mm) fillet welds, 1 inch (25 mm) long, with a 10-inch (250 mm) pitch, staggered (not chain).

FORMULA 18-3
Fillet-Weld Sizes

Fillet-weld size is based on the thinnest of the two plates being joined.

Weld Leg = thinnest plate – $^1/_{16}$ in. (for plates up to $^1/_2$ in.) (English)

Weld Leg = thinnest plate – 1.6 mm (for plates up to 13 mm) (Metric)

Weld Leg = thinnest plate – $^1/_8$ in. (for plates $^1/_2$ to 1 in.) (English)

(continued)

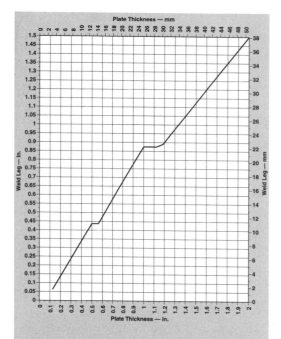

Fillet Weld Leg vs. Plate Thickness

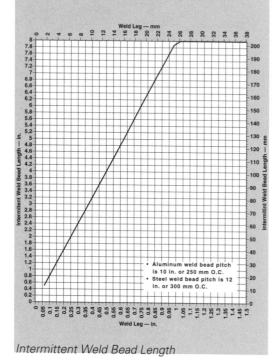

- Aluminum weld bead pitch is 10 in. or 250 mm O.C.
- Steel weld bead pitch is 12 in. or 300 mm O.C.

Intermittent Weld Bead Length

Weld Leg = thinnest plate − 3.2 mm (for plates 13 to 25 mm) (Metric)

Weld Leg = 0.75 × thinnest plate (for plates over 1 in. [25 mm])

Weld Length (Intermittent Welds) = 8 × leg, but not over 6 in. (152 mm)

Pitch O.C. = 10 in. (250 mm) for aluminum

Pitch O.C. = 12 in. (300 mm) for steel

Around the end of a member, say at a frame web at a limber hole, there should be a wraparound weld approximately equal to the standard weld-segment length.

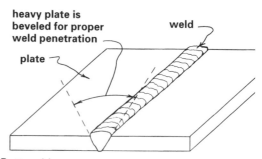

heavy plate is beveled for proper weld penetration

weld

plate

Butt weld

FORMULA 18-4

Butt Welds

For plates 1/16 to 1/8 in., the gap should be 0 to 1/16 in. (English)

For plates 1.6 to 3.2 mm, the gap should be 0 to 1.6 mm (Metric)

For plates 1/8 to 3/16 in., the gap can be 0 to 3/16 in. (English)

For plates 3.2 to 4.75 mm, the gap can be 0 to 4.75 mm (Metric)

Plates 3/16 to 5/16 in. should have a 60- to 100-degree groove in one face penetrating to within at least ⅛ in. of the opposite side (a single-groove butt weld) (English)

Plates 4.75 to 7.9 mm should have a 60- to 100-degree groove in one face penetrating to within at least 3.2 mm of the opposite side (a single-groove butt weld) (Metric)

Plates over ⁵⁄₁₆ in. require a 60- to 100-degree groove in both faces with a ¹⁄₁₆- to ⅛-in. flat in the center (a double-groove butt weld) (English)

Plates over 7.9 mm require a 60- to 100-degree groove in both faces with a 1.6 to 3.2 mm flat in the center (a double-groove butt weld) (Metric)

PLUG AND SLOT WELDS

There are usually several places on a hull where it is impossible to reach to weld from inside. Deep keels, hollow rudders and skegs, and enclosed superstructure pylons all have internal stiffeners but are closed in from both sides. To assemble these components, the framework is erected. Then the plate along one side is welded from the inside. Finally, the opposite plate is installed and plug- or slot-welded from the outside. However, you can't plug-weld from the outside to the thin-plate edge of an internal stiffener. Accordingly, the framing on the cover-plate side must have T flanges welded to the stiffener edges. These flanges are fillet-welded to the stiffeners from the side on which the first plate will be installed, before that plate is installed.

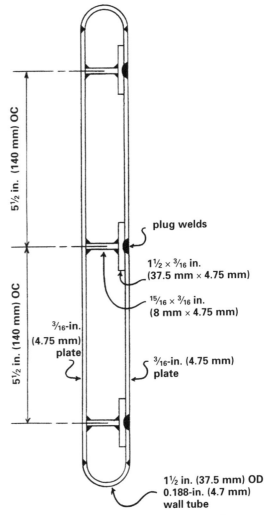

Section through pylon showing stiffeners and plug welds

(continued)

FORMULA 18-5

Plug- and Slot-Weld Sizes

A plug-weld is a round "rivet" weld from an outside plate through to the plate below.

Plug-Weld Diameter at Base = 2 × plate thickness (plate under ½ in. [12.7 mm])

Plug-Weld Diameter at Base = (2 × plate thickness) + ½ in. (plate over ½ in.) (English)

> *Plug-Weld Diameter at Base = (2 × plate thickness) + 12.7 mm (plate over 12.7 mm) (Metric)*
>
> *Plug-Weld Hole Beveled at 45 Degrees (wider at top than at base)*
>
> *Plug-Weld Pitch, Aluminum = 4.5 in. (115 mm)*
>
> *Plug-Weld Pitch, Steel = 5.5 in. (140 mm)*

Slot-welds are rectangular slots with round ends, through the outside plate to the plate below.

Slot-Weld Width = 2 × plate thickness (plate under ¼ in. [6.4 mm])

Slot-Weld Width = 2 × plate thickness with a 45-degree bevel (plate between ¼ and ½ in. [6.4 and 12.7 mm])

Slot-Weld Length = length for fillet weld of the same plate size

Slot-Weld Pitch = pitch of fillet weld for the same plate size

A FULL WELD SCHEDULE FOR ALUMANAUGHT

With this information, we can generate a complete weld schedule using, for example, our longitudinally framed, 35-knot, standard-scantling *AlumaNaught*.

Bottom-Frame Webs to Shell

$^5/_{16}$-in. (8 mm) plate, $^3/_8$-in. (9.5 mm) web: $^1/_4$-in. weld, 2-in. long, staggered, 10-in. O.C. (6.4 mm weld, 50 mm long, staggered, 250 mm O.C.)

Bottom-Frame Webs to Flange

$^3/_8$-in. (9.5 mm) floor, $^1/_2$-in. (14 mm) flange

$^5/_{16}$-in. weld, 2.5-in. long, chain, 10-in. O.C. (8 mm weld, 64 mm long, chain, 250 mm O.C.)

Bottom-Frame Webs to Shell under Engine Beds

$^5/_{16}$-in. (8 mm) plate, $^3/_8$-in. (9.5 mm) web: $^5/_{16}$-in. (8 mm) double-continuous weld for at least 1.5 times length of engine and gear, or from CVK to chine or bilge, whichever is less

Bottom-Frame Webs to Shell at Shaft Logs

$^5/_{16}$-in. (8 mm) plate, $^3/_8$-in. (9.5 mm) web: $^5/_{16}$-in. (8 mm) double-continuous weld, for at least three longitudinals

Floors to Shell

$^5/_{16}$-in. (8 mm) plate, $^3/_8$-in. (9.5 mm) floor: $^1/_4$-in. weld, 2-in. long, chain, 10-in. O.C. (6.4 mm weld, 50 mm long, chain, 250 mm O.C.)

Floors to Shell in Engine Compartment

$^5/_{16}$-in. (8 mm) plate, $^3/_8$-in. (9.5 mm) floor: $^1/_4$-in. (6.4 mm) double-continuous weld

Floors to Shell at Stern Tube

$^5/_{16}$-in. (8 mm) plate, $^3/_8$-in. (9.5 mm) floor: $^1/_4$-in. (6.4 mm) double-continuous weld

Floors to Frame

$^3/_8$-in. floor to $^3/_8$-in. frame (9.5 to 9.5 mm): continuous butt weld

Floors to Keel-Bottom Plate

$^3/_8$- to $^7/_8$-in. (9.5 to 20 mm) $^5/_{16}$-in. (8 mm) double-continuous weld

Floors to CVK

$^3/_8$-in. (9.5 mm) floor to $^7/_8$-in. (22 mm) bottom plate: $^5/_{16}$-in. (8 mm) double-continuous weld

CVK to Stern Frame

$7/8$-in. CVK to $1^1/4$-in. stern frame (22 to 30 mm): continuous 60-degree double-groove butt weld

Topsides–Frame Webs to Shell

$3/8$-in. web to $1/4$-in. plate (9.5 to 6.45 mm): $3/16$-in. weld, 1.5-in. long, staggered, 10-in. O.C. (4.75 mm weld, 38 mm long, staggered, 250 mm O.C.)

Topsides–Frame Web to Flange

$3/8$-in. web to $7/16$-in. (9.5 to 11.25 mm): $5/16$-in. weld, 2.5-in. long, chain, 10-in. O.C. (8 mm weld, 64 mm long, chain, 250 mm O.C.)

Deck–Beam Web to Shell

$3/8$-in. web to $3/16$-in. shell (9.5 to 4.75 mm): $1/8$-in. weld, 1-in. long, staggered, 10-in. O.C. (3.2 mm weld, 25 mm long, staggered, 10-in. O.C.)

Deck–Beam Web to Flange

$3/8$- in. web to $7/16$-in. flange (9.5 to 11.25 mm): $5/16$-in. weld, 2.5-in. long, chain, 10-in. O.C. (8 mm weld, 64 mm long, chain, 250 mm O.C.)

Hull-Bottom Longitudinals to Shell

$3/8$-in. longitudinals to $5/16$-in. shell (9.5 to 8 mm): $5/16$-in. weld, 2.5-in. long, staggered, 10-in. O.C. (8 mm weld, 64 mm long, staggered, 250 mm O.C.)

Topsides Longitudinals to Shell

$3/8$-in. longitudinals to $1/4$-in. shell (9.5 to 6.4 mm): $3/16$-in. weld, 1.5-in. long, staggered, 10-in. O.C. (4.75 mm weld, 38 mm long, staggered, 250 mm O.C.)

Deck Longitudinals to Shell

$5/16$-in. longitudinals to $3/16$-in. shell (8 to 4.75 mm): $1/8$-in. weld, 1-in. long, staggered, 10-in. O.C. (3.2 mm weld, 25 mm long, staggered, 250 mm O.C.)

Cabin–Frame Webs to Shell

$1/4$- to $3/16$-in. (6.4 to 4.75 mm): $1/8$-in. weld, 1-in. long, staggered, 10-in. O.C. (3.2 mm weld, 25 mm long, staggered, 250 mm O.C.)

Cabin–Frame Webs to Flange

$1/4$- to $1/4$-in. (6.4 to 6.4 mm): $3/16$-in. weld, 1.5-in. long, chain, 10-in. O.C. (4.75 mm weld, 38 mm long, chain, 250 mm O.C.)

Cabin Longitudinals to Shell

$1/4$-in. longitudinals to $3/16$-in. shell (6.4 to 4.75 mm): $1/8$-in. weld, 1-in. long, staggered, 10-in. O.C. (3.2 mm weld, 25 mm long, staggered, 250 mm O.C.)

Cabin-Roof-Beam Webs to Shell

$1/4$-in. web to $3/16$-in. shell (6.4 to 4.75 mm): $1/8$-in. weld, 1-in. long, staggered, 10-in. O.C. (3.2 mm weld, 25 mm long, staggered, 250 mm O.C.)

Cabin-Roof-Beams Web to Flange

$1/4$-in. web to $1/4$-in. flange (6.4 to 6.4 mm): $3/16$-in. weld, 1.5-in. long, chain, 10-in. O.C. (4.75 mm weld, 38 mm long, chain, 250 mm O.C.)

Hull-Bottom-Girders Web to Shell under Engine Mounts

$7/16$-in. web to $5/16$-in. shell (11 to 8 mm): $1/4$-in (6.4 mm) double-continuous weld

Hull-Bottom-Girder Web to Shell

$7/16$-in. web to $5/16$-in. shell (11 to 8 mm): $1/4$-in. weld, 2-in. long, chain, 10-in. O.C. (6.4 mm weld, 50 mm long, chain, 250 mm O.C.)

Hull-Bottom-Girder Web to Flange

$7/16$- to $1/2$-in. (11 to 12.7 mm): $3/8$-in. weld, 3-in. long, chain, 10-in. O.C. (9.5 mm weld, 115 mm long, chain, 250 mm O.C.)

Engine-Bed Web to Hull-Bottom Girder

$7/16$- to 1-in. (11 to 25 mm): continuous 60-degree double-bevel butt weld

Engine-Bed Web to Engine-Mount Flange

1-in. web to $1 1/4$-in. flange (25 to 30 mm): $3/4$-in. (19 mm) double-continuous weld

Bulkheads to Hull

$3/16$-in. bulkhead to $1/4$-, $3/16$-, and $5/16$-in. shell (4.75 mm bulkhead to 6.4, 4.75, and 8 mm shell): $1/8$-in. (3.2 mm) double-continuous weld

Bulkhead-Stiffener Webs to Bulkhead

$1/4$-in. web to $3/16$-in. plate (6.4 to 4.75 mm): $1/8$-in. weld, 1-in. long, staggered, 10-in. O.C. (3.2 mm weld, 25 mm long, staggered, 10-in. O.C.)

Bulkhead-Stiffener Web to Flange

$1/4$-in. web to $1/4$-in. flange (6.4 to 6.4 mm): $3/16$-in. weld, 1.5-in. long, chain, 10-in. O.C. (4.75 mm weld, 38 mm long, chain, 250 mm O.C.)

WELDING ACCESS

In both design and construction, access for welding in general is an important consideration. Boats are a glut of odd shapes and tight corners. An average MIG welding gun is about 15 inches (38 cm) long, with heavy hoses and cables fastened to one end; it can be difficult, even impossible, to get in to weld some areas. Careful thought must be given to the design of the structure so that welding is physically possible; equal thought must be given to the construction sequence to ensure that interior welds aren't made inaccessible.

WELDING SEQUENCE

The sequence or order of structural welding is critical to controlling distortion. There are three aspects to consider:

- Use back-step welding to minimize local distortion.
- Skip around the hull evenly from port to starboard and back, and fore-n-aft and back.
- The actual sequence in which the structural welds are completed must be selected to minimize distortion.

Back-Step Welding

Back-step welding eliminates local distortion. For example, take two plates 5 feet square (0.5 m²) and lay them just touching, parallel, side by side on a flat floor. If you joined them with a butt weld starting at one corner, running along the seam and working straight to the other end without stopping, you would end up with distorted plates. The corners you started at would cool first and shrink together. By the time you reached opposite corners to finish the seam, the once-parallel line between the plates would have spread open into a V shape. Where the plates were just touching to begin with, there might be an inch gap at the finishing corners. You would find it impossible to pull the plates together again; therefore, you would have to fill this gap with weld metal, meaning still more welding. This, in turn, would introduce yet more heat into the gapped-end, warping the plates.

To eliminate this, you must start in the middle of the plate. Weld several inches, with the gun moving in one direction. Then skip over to close to one end and weld several inches, running the welder in the opposite direction. Next, skip back to the opposite end and weld a few more inches, again switching the welding-pass direction. Then go back to an area near the middle for a few more inches still, and so on until the entire seam is complete. In this way, you draw the two plates together evenly without introducing a triangular gap or any warp.

In aluminum, you can weld up to 10 inches (255 mm) in a single pass, then skip about 15 inches (380 mm) away or more, and weld another 10 inches (255 mm), making the pass in the opposite direction. In steel—with the higher heat input required—weld no more than 3 or 4 inches (75 or 100 mm), then skip 12 inches (300 mm) or more, and weld running in the opposite direction.

Spreading Welds around the Boat

The principle of back-step welding applies not only at the local level for each plate, but also for the entire structure. Thus, if you were welding frames to the shell, you would start at the middle of the boat on starboard, and weld several inches. Next, switch to the same location on the port side. When this is done, don't go back to the same frame on the starboard side again; rather, skip forward or aft a few frames and repeat the process. Then go back to another frame next to your first one and do a few inches there. Again, you should spread the welds around in small increments to draw the structure together equally, without causing the same kind of large-scale distortion in the hull as you would by seaming two plates together in a single continuous pass.

Overall Welding Sequence

Keeping both local back-step welding and spreading welds around the boat in mind at all times, it is vitally important to follow a careful weld sequence in the final structural welding.

Except for backbone and framing components that won't be accessible later, all the frame and interior structure and all the plating should just be lightly tack-welded in place. Only when most of this structure is fitted and tacked can final structural welding begin.

Always start with the shell plate. Begin at the bilge or chine midships, gradually skipping your way outward toward the bow and stern and up to the sheer and down to the keel. Weld all the seams in this way, port and starboard (paying careful attention to back-step welding and weld-spreading). At the same time—skipping around as always—weld the shell plate to the backbone (i.e., stem, transom, and keel).

Next, break the longitudinals free from their tack welds to the frames and weld the longitudinals to the shell plating. Finally, weld the transverse frames to the shell plate and then to the longitudinals.

Aligning Plate Seams

To keep the plate seams in alignment (smooth and flush), it is often helpful to drill small holes along the seam and insert stainless steel bolts with heavy washers tightening them down to hold the plates flush and in line. These bolts are removed once most of the seam is welded and the holes are filled with weld metal. The bolts should be slightly larger in diameter than the plate thickness. Alternately, Ts with notches in them can be made up and slid through the seam. Wedges hammered in through the notch from the outside keep the plates aligned and knock out more quickly than unscrewing several bolts.

Clean Welds

Dirt, dust, slag, oil, rust, and scale play havoc with weld integrity. Edges to be welded have to be clean and free of contamination. In aluminum, even greasy handprints can make for local imperfections. Both rust and scale must be totally removed. In aluminum, for example, the oxide has nearly four times the melting point of the clean alloy. If you were to weld over aluminum oxide, you would have unwelded oxide flakes included in the weld and unwelded sections of alloy behind the flakes—not good!

JIGS

Because distortion can be such a serious problem, many yards fabricate on a massive steel strongback or jig. The intention is that the strongback will hold the structure in alignment against much weld distortion. I think this is good practice; however, I've worked with a builder who used virtually no strongback or jig at all. This builder simply hangs the transverse frames in place, attaching the CVK, gradually building up the internal framework including longitudinal stringers, and finally the plating. The result was quite fair. Jigs or strongbacks do help reduce distortion, but only within reason. Nothing on earth can resist the contraction in

a metal hull due to poor weld control and planing. Carefully thought-out weld sequences and widely spread back-step welding are the keys to success. Heavy jigs help minimize distortion still further and help reduce problems—to a limited degree—when they occur.

JOINING LIGHT PLATE TO HEAVY PLATE

Heavy welds to light plate is an inconsistency; it can't be done. Still, there are heavy components—like engine beds $5/8$ inch (16 mm) thick—that must be continuously welded in hulls with plate just $3/16$ inch (8 mm) thick. The trick is to build up to the heavier component with gradually thicker ones. The structure specified for bottom girders and engine beds is a good example. In our example 35-knot *AlumaNaught*, we called for $5/16$-inch (8 mm) bottom plate. Fastened vertically to that is the hull-bottom girder, which was $7/16$ inch (11 mm) thick. On top of this is welded the web of the engine bed itself which, for *AlumaNaught*, came to 1 inch (25 mm). On top of all is the engine-bed flange, which is $11/4$ inches (32 mm). This same approach should be used whenever possible for heavy components.

When thick plate has to be butt-welded to thin plate, the thick plate must be beveled down to the thickness of the thin plate on a 3:1 bevel. Then a standard butt weld for the thin plate is used.

ROTATING JIGS AND BUILDING RIGHTSIDE UP OR UPSIDE DOWN

Welding is always easiest downhanded. On vertical surfaces, it is fairly easy; overhead, it is comparatively difficult. Some large production builders, fabricating multiple hulls, employ specialized rotating jigs that hold the entire hull and revolve it so almost every weld can be downhanded—much like a rotating fiberglass production mold. Nevertheless, most larger metal hulls are one-off or short-run production operation. All the yards I've worked with on such hulls have elected to build them rightside up. Without the ability to rotate the boat, there's little advantage to building the hull upside down and then righting it to finish. However, there's nothing wrong with building a hull upside down if some special circumstances seem to favor it. Some yards do prefer to build upside down in steel because it's easier to muscle the heavy plate onto the hull bottom.

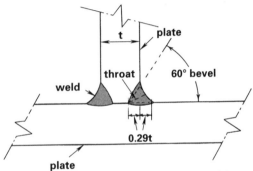

60-degree partial-penetration V-groove weld

V-GROOVE WELDS IN PLACE OF FILLET WELDS IN HEAVY PLATE

The majority of welding on boats is on plate under $1/2$ inch (25 mm). Nevertheless, there are a few heavier plates: CVK, horn plate, engine beds, chainplate, and lugs. When welding two plates over $3/4$ inch (19 mm), it is faster to use partial-penetration, double-bevel, V-groove welds. Even better, these welds use less weld metal, so they introduce less heat and less distortion.

The web plate should be beveled to 0.29 times the thickness of the thinner plate at a 60-degree angle on both sides. This is welded flush, and a fillet weld with a base leg of 0.29 thickness is added outside.

Where space is at a premium on heavy plate weldments, fillet welds can be replaced with double V-groove welds that penetrate nearly to the center of the web. Bevel the groove at 45 degrees and fill flush with weld metal. This does not reduce total weld or heat, but it keeps the base plate free of external fillet weld.

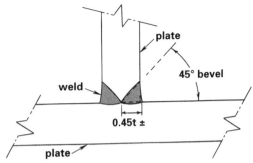

45-degree full-penetration V-groove weld

AVOID WELD GRINDING

On the hull exterior, welds must be ground smooth and flush. Everywhere else, though, weld grinding should be minimized. Grinding welds removes weld metal and weakens them; in tight corners, it can also create new crevices for corrosion.

RIGHT-ANGLE PLATE JOINTS PREFERRED

Where two plates meet at roughly right angles, they are joined with a fillet weld. Fillet welds, in fact, are easiest to make and strongest and close to right angles. In the odd shapes found in boat hulls, sole plates and tank walls often make obtuse or acute angles rather than right angles with the hull shell. Wherever possible, modify the shapes of such components to approximate a right-angle joint for maximum strength and ease of assembly.

Snipes, Rat Holes, and Limbers (Small Openings)

SNIPES

Snipes are cut-out corners where three welded plates meet at right angles so that weld lines don't cross each other. For instance, the CVK is welded to the hull-bottom plate. At right angles to these two are the floors. If the floor were welded continuously to the bottom plate and to the CVK, the longitudinal weld of the CVK to the bottom plate would cross the transverse weld of the floor to the bottom plate and the CVK. This causes tri-axial stress in the weld line and should be avoided as much as possible. (There is no avoiding it at watertight bulkheads, tanks, and such.) Accordingly, the corner of the floor (or any plate where weld lines could cross at right angles) should be snipped away in a snipe.

Close-up of longitudinal slot with snipe in frame. Note the rat hole in the longitudinal and the chain weld of the frame flange to the web.

In the previous example, the snipe doubles as a limber hole, which we need in this location anyway. In fact, snipes double as limber holes throughout, and help avoid areas where water can collect. Almost every right-angle plate intersection in the hull should be installed with a snipe. All the ring frames, for example, should have a snipe where each longitudinal passes through them—except, of course, at tanks and watertight bulkheads. The longitudinal snipe should be on the upper face of the longitudinal. This allows water to drain fore-n-aft along the stringers.

LIMBER HOLES AND RAT HOLES

Snipes are usually simply cropped back in a straight line, making a triangular opening. In the case of main limber holes in the floors—as discussed previously—this triangular opening is not as large in cross section as a quarter-circle cut out of the same height and width (same radius). Principal limber holes in the floors should be true quarter-circle cutouts. These naturally double as snipes.

The longitudinals themselves require limbers to drain the water so it can't pool on top. Limbers in stringers are usually termed *rat holes* because that is what they resemble. They are half-circles cut in the longitudinal against the inside of the shell plate. Stringers that are vertically oriented or overhead (e.g., deck and cabin-roof stringers) don't need rat-hole limbers because they shed water freely.

Rat holes in stringers also serve to avoid tri-axial weld stresses caused by crossing welds. The stringer should have a rat hole centered over any vertical butt seams in the shell plate to avoid weld lines crossing. This is recommended practice, but because the stringers are only welded intermittently to the plate, I find it is enough simply to instruct the

Limbers in floors.

welders to slightly adjust the weld spacing, as required, so that no stringer-to-plate weld crosses a plate's seam weld.

FORMULA 18-6

Snipes, Rat Holes, and Limbers

Snipes—General Applications = roughly right-triangle legs one-fourth the depth of the member or 1¼ in. (32 mm), whichever is less

Snipes—in Frames for Longitudinals = roughly right-triangle legs 0.6 × the longitudinal's height

Limbers to be 1¾ in. (44 mm) radius or radius one-third the depth of the member, whichever is less

Rat-Hole Radius = ¼ × longitudinal height

Rat-Hole Location = one between every frame

LIGHTENING HOLES

Large webs in girders and in floors are usually penetrated by *lightening holes*. This term is a little misleading. Yes, the holes do reduce weight; however, their principal purposes on most vessels are to make it easier to run cables and pipes and to improve access. A rigorous program of extensive lightening holes is required to make a significant impact on total structural weight. This can be done, but is only worth the expense on very lightweight high-performance vessels.

FORMULA 18-7

Lightening Holes

Lightening-Hole Closest Distance to Edge of Web

Hull and Deck: 22.5%

Superstructure: 20%

Upper Superstructure (e.g., flybridge): 17.5%

Lightening-Hole Maximum Height

Hull and Deck: 55% of web

Superstructure: 60% of web

Upper Superstructure (e.g., flybridge): 65%

Lightening-Hole Minimum Distance Between Hole Edges

Hull and Deck: 85% of web

Superstructure: 60% of web

Upper Superstructure: 45% of web

Lightening-Hole Maximum Total Area Removed from Web

Hull and Deck: 55%

Superstructure: 65%

Upper Superstructure (e.g., flybridge): 70%

The length of any individual hole may not be more than the web height. On floors, the bottom outside edge of the lightening holes can't be closer to the shell plate than 85 percent of the frame web height, or the minimum specified previously, whichever is greater.

Lightening holes can be circles, ellipses, or round-end rectangles. They must not have sharp corners anywhere. Engine mounts and mast steps cannot have lightening holes.

We found the 35-knot *AlumaNaught* had bottom-girder webs 8¼ inches high. Thus, lightening holes through the girder web would be as follows:

No closer to the edge than 0.225 × 8.25 in. = 1.85; use 1⅞ in.

Maximum Height = 0.55 × 8.25 in. = 4.53; use 4.5 in.

Minimum Distance between Hole Edges = 0.85 × 8.25 in. = 7.01; use 7 in.

Maximum Length = 8¼ in.

The 35-knot *AlumaNaught*'s frame spacing is 36 inches, so the area of the web between frames is

36 in. × 8.25 in. = 297 sq. in.

Maximum Total Lightening-Hole Area = 0.55 × 297 sq. in. = 163.3 sq. in.

or

The 35-knot *AlumaNaught*'s bottom-girder webs were 210 mm high, so the lightening holes through the girder web would be

No closer to the edge than 0.225 × 210 mm = 47.25; use 46 mm

Maximum Height = 0.55 × 210 mm = 115.5; use 115 mm

Minimum Distance Between Hole Edges = 0.85 × 210 mm = 178 mm

Maximum Length = 210 mm

The 35-knot *AlumaNaught*'s frame spacing is 90 cm, so the area of the web between frames is

90 cm × 21 cm = 1,890 cm²

Maximum Total Lightening Hole Area = 0.55 × 1,890 cm² = 1,039 cm²

Riveting Aluminum

Welding is the fastest and strongest method of fastening metal hulls with sufficient plate thickness. Small boats—under 25 feet or so—only require very thin plate too thin to weld. Using heavier plate on such vessels just to be able to weld it effectively makes for an unnecessarily heavy hull. The answer—and it's a good one—is riveting. (Steel would rust too quickly and is too heavy for efficient small-boat work.)

It's a little odd that some people seem leery of riveted hulls; after all, welding is the new technology and riveted boats have been around nearly 100 years longer. Airplanes are made of aluminum, but—needing to be so light—even giant jumbo jets are fabricated from thin aluminum sheets riveted together. Clearly, these airframes don't leak or fail. Indeed, the Lund Boat Company has been manufacturing small aluminum production boats in Minnesota since 1948. In a recent conversation with its manager, he related that since he had been with the company, they had produced more than 200,000 boats and there hadn't been a single hull-seam failure.

Riveted joints are so tight that no caulking is required, except at joints that might not draw tight together readily, such as hull-to-deck joints in production boats, where 3M sealing tape about ⅛ inch thick may be employed. In the rare event that a rivet or two did loosen, they're either easily hammered back in tight, using a bucking iron inside, or replaced with a slightly fatter rivet.

Although the rivets in a properly designed joint take the load in sheer, the two joint surfaces are clamped so tightly together that they add considerably to the joint strength by resisting sliding from their friction.

Riveted joints on hull seams are usually simple lap joints. Edge-to-edge joints with single backing (doubler) plate on the inside are also acceptable. Where maximum strength is needed in a larger structure, double-backing (doubler) plates—one on each side—can be used. This would be the strongest way to attach a T engine-bed web to a vertical hull-bottom girder, for example.

Rivets must be of the correct diameter for the sheet or plate they are fastening. Use the thinnest of the two plates to be

TABLE 18-8 Rivet Diameter, Sheet or Plate

Thickness, in. (mm)		Diameter, in. (mm)
from	to	
0.025 (0.64)	0.036 (0.91)	1/16 (1.59)
0.036 (0.91)	0.048 (1.22)	3/32 (2.38)
0.048 (1.22)	0.064 (1.63)	1/8 (3.18)
0.064 (1.63)	0.080 (2.03)	5/32 (3.97)
0.080 (2.03)	0.104 (2.64)	3/16 (4.76)
0.104 (2.64)	0.128 (3.25)	1/4 (6.35)
0.128 (3.25)	0.188 (4.78)	5/16 (7.94)
0.188 (4.78)	0.200 (5.08)	3/8 (9.53)
0.200 (5.08)	0.250 (6.35)	7/16 (11.11)
0.250 (6.35)	0.300 (7.62)	1/2 (12.70)
0.300 (7.62)	0.350 (8.89)	9/16 (14.29)
0.350 (8.89)	0.400 (10.16)	5/8 (15.88)
0.400 (10.16)	0.550 (13.97)	3/4 (19.05)
0.550 (13.97)	0.700 (17.78)	7/8 (22.23)

NOTE: All these are solid (not hollow) rivets.

The old rule-of-thumb for rivet diameter is that the rivet should be between 2.5 and 3 times the plate thickness and never less than the thickness of the thinnest plate.

FORMULA 18-9
Rivet Pitch, Edge Distance, and Row Spacing

Edge Distance, Normal = 2 × diameter

Edge Distance, Minimum = 1.5 × diameter

Pitch, Minimum Allowable = 3 × diameter

Pitch for Watertight Seams, Maximum = 4 × diameter or 10 × the thinnest plate thickness, whichever is less

Pitch for Non-Watertight Joints = 5 to 8 × diameter (6 is average)

fastened. Pitch and edge distance are equally important for a proper joint.

Double rivet rows are recommended on watertight lap seams. The rows should be spaced two times the rivet diameter apart, with the rivets alternating centers between rows.

RIVETED ALUMINUM SUPERSTRUCTURES

In addition to riveting light sheet on small aluminum boats, riveting permits the use of lighter sheets on the superstructure of larger lightweight high-performance boats. For instance, for the lightweight 35-knot *Aluma-Naught*, we could refer to Table 16-4A and use $^1/_8$-inch (3.2 mm) cabin-roof plate. The best welders could weld this with pulse-arc equipment, but distortion is still likely. This would not be a problem with riveting.

Remember that *AlumaNaught* had a trunk cabin roof with a maximum span (beam) of 12.2 feet (3.71 m). Referring to Table 16-4A, we would use the following:

$^1/_8$-in. plate
beams 7.5-in. O.C.
3-in. web × 2-in. flange × $^1/_4$-in. thick
    beams

or

3.2 mm plate
beams 190 mm O.C.
75 mm web × 50 mm flange × 6.4 mm thick

The beams in this construction need a flange against the underside of the deck plate to accept the rivets. This flange should be four times the rivet diameter. Rivets attaching the $^1/_8$-inch (3.2 mm) plate to the $^1/_4$-inch (6.4 mm) flange would be

$^1/_4$-in. diameter (6.35 mm); the flange under the deck would be 1 in. wide

Because this is not a watertight seam, the rivets would be spaced 1.5 inches (38 mm) pitch. At the edge of the cabin roof, the rivets would fasten down into a $^1/_4$-inch (6.4 mm) boundary bar. This is a watertight seam and rivet pitch would be reduced to 1 inch (25 mm).

On a somewhat smaller *AlumaNaught*, the cabin side too could be reduced to less than $^3/_{16}$-inch (4.75 mm) plate. It could also then be of riveted construction.

NINETEEN

Small Aluminum Boats and Copper-Nickel Hulls

Small Aluminum Boats

Aluminum, unlike steel, is an ideal material for small aluminum hulls. It is light enough so that boats as small as 20 feet (6 m) can be fabricated using welded construction. Most small welded boats are constructed of $^3/_{16}$-inch (4.75 mm) plate for weldability, which makes them heavier than necessary, but—on beefier small craft—this isn't too much of a drawback. Plate as thin as $^1/_8$ inch (3 mm) is welded using pulse-arc equipment by some production builders. This approach yields fairly light small welded hulls. Nevertheless, the very thin sheet necessary to produce really light structure weights on hulls with Sns less than 0.50 (roughly under 20 feet [6 m]) is really not suited to welding. Riveted construction is the best approach.

ALUMINUM SHEET THICKNESS FOR SMALL BOATS

Table 19-1 is a simple guide to proper sheet thickness on small riveted aluminum hulls.

- Planing boats over 15 feet (4.5 m) should increase the bottom plate in the forward third of the hull to 0.90 inch (2.29 mm).
- Planing boats over 15 feet (4.5 m) should use the framing thickness sheet size from the next boat size up on the table.
- Planing boats with Sns under 0.50 should use hull-bottom girders with thicknesses and dimensions as described in chapter 16, except that single-engine and outboard boats require only one girder per side, not two. The deep floors used to support the cockpit sole usually extend over the top of the bottom girder, so the minimum height above floor dimensions does not apply.
- Topside longitudinals are not required on boats with Sns under 0.50. Deck longitudinals are only required for hulls with large walk-on decks. Bottom longitudinals, or stiffeners of some sort, are required on these small hulls only for planing craft.
- Longitudinal spacing is not determined

TABLE 19-1 Aluminum Small Riveted Boat Scantlings (English)

LOA, ft.	Bottom, in.	Topsides, in.	Transom, in.	Deck and Cabin, in.	Keel, in.	Thickness, in.
10	0.050	0.050	0.063	0.050	0.000	0.050
13	0.063	0.050	0.090	0.063	0.075	0.063
15	0.063	0.063	0.090	0.071	0.075	0.063
16	0.071	0.063	0.090	0.071	0.075	0.067
18	0.080	0.063	0.090	0.071	0.075	0.080
21	0.090	0.080	0.090	0.071	0.075	0.085

TABLE 19-1 Aluminum Small Riveted Boat Scantlings (Metric)

LOA, m	Bottom, mm	Topsides, mm	Transom, mm	Deck and Cabin, mm	Keel, mm	Thickness, mm
3.0	1.3	1.3	1.6	1.3	0.0	1.3
4.0	1.6	1.3	2.3	1.6	1.9	1.6
4.6	1.6	1.6	2.3	1.8	1.9	1.6
4.9	1.8	1.6	2.3	1.8	1.9	1.7
5.5	2.0	1.6	2.3	1.8	1.9	2.0
6.4	2.3	2.0	2.3	1.8	1.9	2.2

according to the formulas in chapters 15 and 16. Instead, arrange the combination of longitudinals and frames so that no hull-bottom panel (or walk-on deck) is larger than 3 square feet (0.278 m²). In other words, the area contained between any two frames and their two intersecting longitudinals must be less than 3 square feet (0.278 m²).

- Interior components such as thwarts, engine beds, cockpit sole supports, and cuddy bulkheads should be used in place of frames and longitudinals wherever possible.

Riveted aluminum outboard fishing runabout.
(Courtesy Lund Boat Company)

Riveted aluminum-boat assembly. Note the deep floors to support the cockpit sole. Foam flotation and "belly" fuel tank are installed. (Courtesy Lund Boat Company)

INCREASING SHEET STIFFNESS

On most of these small craft, you can increase panel stiffness by stamping in joggles in the plate, like imitation lapstrake, or as spray rails. Displacement vessels and small boats under 14 feet (4.2 m) benefit only slightly from this—although they do benefit. Planing hulls over this size should employ this technique as much as possible.

FRAMING FOR SMALL ALUMINUM BOATS

The Sn can be used to determine the frame dimensions and longitudinal height for riveted aluminum craft under 21 feet (6.4 mm); however, use the sheet thickness from Table 19-1.

Let's say we wanted to build a riveted aluminum open-cockpit outboard skiff. We'll call it *MiniAlloy*. *MiniAlloy*'s dimensions are

LOA	19.22 ft.	5.85 m
WL	17.62 ft.	5.37 m
Beam	6.83 ft.	2.08 m
Chine Beam	6.00 ft.	1.82 m
Depth of Hull	3.22 ft.	0.98 m

This makes *MiniAlloy*'s Sn 0.41 (see Formula 1-1). Using the formulas in chapters 15 and 16 for a longitudinally framed aluminum hull and using Table 19-1, we would find our riveted *MiniAlloy*'s scantlings to be as follows:

Bottom Sheet = 0.090 in. (2.3 mm)

Topsides Sheet = 0.080 in. (2 mm)

Transom Sheet = 0.090 in. (2.3 mm)

Deck Sheet = 0.071 in. (1.8 mm)

Keel CVK = 0.075 in. (1.9 mm)

Note that the keel is often an external extrusion riveted to the plate, port and starboard, along the centerline.

Keel CVK Height – 1.81; use $1\frac{7}{8}$ in. (48 mm)

Framing Thickness (Webs, Flanges, and Longitudinals) = 0.085 in. (2.2 mm)

Frame Spacing O.C. = 28.8; use 29 in. (735 mm)

Bottom-Frame-Web Height = 1.62 in. (41.1 mm)

Riveted aluminum runabouts going together. (Courtesy Lund Boat Company)

If we say *MiniAlloy* is a 28-knot boat, we would increase web height by 1 percent for every knot over 20 knots:

1.62 in. × 1.08 = 1.74; use 1¾ in.

or

41.0 mm × 1.08 = 44.3; use 44 mm

Note that since the floors will be used to support the cockpit sole, they will probably greatly exceed this height.

Topsides-Frame-Web Height = 1 ⅜ in. (35 mm)

Bottom-Frame-Flange Width = 1.21; use 30.7 mm

MiniAlloy is a 28-knot boat, so increase flange width by 1 percent for every knot over 15 knots.

1.21 in. × 1.13 = 1.36; use 1⅜ in.

or

30.7 mm × 1.13 = 34.6; use 35 mm

Topsides-Frame-Flange Width = 1.21; use 1¼ in. (30 mm)

Deck-Beam-Web Height = 1.45; use 1 ½ in. (38 mm)

Deck-Beam-Flange Width = 1.09; use 1 in. (25 mm)

Few if any bottom longitudinals would be required if three deep stamped-in spray rails were formed into the bottom sheet. No longitudinals are required elsewhere; however, stamped-in lapstrake on the topsides will look handsome and make it stiffer.

MINIALLOY'S BOTTOM LONGITUDINALS

Without stamped-in spray rails, bottom longitudinals from angle should be installed on *MiniAlloy*'s planing hull as follows:

Longitudinal Spacing:

Frames are spaced 29 in. or 2.416 ft., so 3 sq. ft. ÷ 2.416 ft. = 1.24 ft., or 14.88; use 15 in.

Frames are spaced 735 mm, so 0.278 m² ÷ 0.735 m = 0.378 m, or 378 mm; use 380 mm

Longitudinal Dimensions:

Height from Formula 15-7A = 0.731 in.

MiniAlloy is a 28-knot boat, so increase height by 1 percent for every knot over 20 knots.

0.731 in. × 1.08 = 0.789; use ⅞ in.

or

Height from Formula 15-7A = 18.56 mm

18.56 mm × 1.08 = 20 mm

Because the longitudinals are riveted to the hull shell inside, they require a flange against the shell that is at least four times the rivet diameter wide.

The bottom sheet is 0.090 inch (2.3 mm) and the framing is 0.085 inch (2.2 mm); 0.085 inch (2.2 mm) is thinner. Thus, from Table 18-8, the rivets for the flange should be ³/₁₆ inch (4.76 mm) in diameter.

The flange to the hull should then be 4 × 0.1875 in. = 0.75 in. wide

(4 × 4.76 mm = 19 mm wide)

This is not a watertight seam in the hull plating, so average pitch is six times the diameter, accordingly,

pitch = 6 × 0.1875 in. = 1⅛ in. rivet O.C.

or

pitch = 6 × 4.76 mm = 28.5 mm rivet O.C.

If we used stamped-in spray rails on *MiniAlloy*'s bottom, we would make them about ⁷/₈ inch (20 mm) deep throughout most of the boat's length.

SMALL-BOAT ALUMINUM FRAMING DETAILS

Usually, the bottom frames are rather deep and straight across the top in small boats like *MiniAlloy*. In this way, the bottom frame is floor, frame, and cockpit sole beam all in one. Standard practice is to fabricate all the components from sheet, cutting them to shape and bending in flanges on a press brake. Cockpit soles, decks, and many joiner components (interior and exterior) are frequently made of marine plywood.

Aluminum thwarts, boxes, bulkheads, and engine wells are normally the same thickness as the topsides sheet. The press brake is used extensively to bend flanges into these components for stiffening.

Keep in mind that the thin plate on these hulls is very sensitive to hard spots. The framing needs to be thought out so that structural loads are dissipated into the structure at floors, frames, and stringers. Components like diagonal braces under thwarts cannot land on the plate; they must land on some framing member.

Copper-Nickel Hulls

There is one very different alloy that offers some significant advantages—at least on larger vessels over 45 feet (14 m) or so: copper-nickel. Copper-nickel is similar in strength to marine aluminum; however, at 530 lb./cu. ft. (8,490 kg./m³), it weighs somewhat more than steel. Therefore, it is not as light a construction material as aluminum, but—unlike steel and like aluminum—copper-nickel doesn't rust at all.

The really remarkable thing about copper-nickel is it requires no bottom paint ever. It's almost completely and totally non-fouling—forever! In fact, if you didn't want to, you wouldn't have to paint *any* part of an all copper-nickel boat. Of course, there must be some reason that you aren't completely surrounded by copper-nickel boats; there is one: they cost dearly. Copper-nickel is expensive, considerably more expensive than almost any other form of construction. Even so, a few commercial vessels—primarily fishing boats and tugboats—have been built of

TABLE 19-2 Copper-Nickel Boatbuilding Alloy Physical Properties, psi (mPa)			
Alloy	**Copper-Nickel %**	**UTS, psi (mPa)**	**Yield, psi (mPa)**
CA-706	90-10 cu-ni	40,000 (276)	15,000 (103)
CA-706 (¼ Hard)	90-10 cu-ni	55,000 (379)	30,000 (207)
CA-715	70-30 cu-ni	45,000 (310)	18,000 (124)

Modulus of elasticity E = 18,000,000 psi (124,050 mPa)

UTS = Ultimate Tensile Strength

copper-nickel because the savings in fuel and bottom-cleaning charges, as a result of having a clean bottom all the time, can make it worth their while.

COPPER-NICKEL SCANTLINGS

You can see from Table 19-2 that CA-706 and CA-715 alloys are very close in physical properties to marine aluminum. CA-706 ($1/4$-hard), on the other hand, is closer to steel. Copper-nickel's modulus of elasticity, however, is 80 percent greater than aluminum (it is 80 percent stiffer), while it is only 62 percent of that steel (38 percent bendier). Based on these factors, the following formula can be used to determine the scantlings for copper-nickel hulls.

FORMULA 19-3
Copper-Nickel Scantling Conversions

For CA-706 and CA-715:

Use the aluminum rule to calculate all scantlings.

- *Multiply the plate thickness found by 0.60 for copper-nickel.*

- *Use the same frame-web and flange dimensions and longitudinal heights, but multiply the thickness by 0.88 for copper-nickel.*

- *Because of the tremendous corrosion resistance of copper-nickel, even the lightweight aluminum rule can be used and converted to copper-nickel.*

- *Use the longitudinal spacing according to the aluminum rule based on the actual final copper-nickel plate thickness installed.*

For CA-706 ($1/4$-hard):

Use the steel rule to calculate all scantlings.

- *Use the steel longitudinal spacing rule and multiply the plate thickness by 1.4 to get the copper-nickel plate thickness.*

- *Or use the aluminum longitudinal spacing rule and multiply the plate thickness by 0.60 for copper-nickel.*

WELDING STEEL TO COPPER NICKEL

Note that several copper-nickel vessels have been constructed with copper-nickel hulls and all-steel framing. The goal of this approach is to get the nonfouling and nonrusting/nonwasting benefits of copper-nickel while keeping cost down. On several such commercial vessels, the galvanic corrosion was found to be minimal (although it was present) after more than four years of operation in tropical waters.

These hulls were sandblasted inside and the copper-nickel in the bilge was painted with epoxy paint. The steel (sandblasted as well) was painted throughout the boat. In the bilge—where water can collect from an interior electrolyte—internal zinc anodes were installed on portions of the steel framing.

Although this system of steel framing and copper-nickel plating has worked and is acceptable, it seems counterproductive to me. After all, copper-nickel's big advantage is its total lack of corrosion combined with total nonfouling. Even with a good paint system and anodes, the steel framing will eventually corrode (if slowly). On most craft, much of this corrosion would be difficult to get at to inspect or repair. If at all possible, I would stick to all copper-nickel: framing and hull.

This is how *Miss Rivere* was built. A 45-foot (13.7 m) motor yacht, *Revere* was launched in 1938 and served in the coastal patrol of the U.S. Coast Guard during World War II. Built of CA-715 copper-nickel (hull shell and all framing), its plating was just 0.080 inch (2 mm) thick, yet the boat gave reliable service even in ice conditions.

Conclusion

Not too long ago I received an interesting e-mail from one of my clients. Cruising his *Belle Marie* along the Intracoastal Waterway, he had . . . well, a minor adventure:

I've finally run the boat aground hard! Before, [when I've run aground] I've known that the water was shallow and was drifting or moving at idle speed. We were running down the Intercoastal Waterway, in South Carolina, Saturday, in one of the long ditch-like sections of the ICW. I moved over to the edge of the cut to let a faster boat go by but failed to notice the stream that crossed into the ditch. It had evidently built up a sand shoal out into the channel at the edge. The stern sank suddenly and as I reached to pull power off and turn back into deeper water, we hit the bar at about nine knots. Wham!! As our stern wave caught up to us, the transom lifted and we went over the bar into deeper water again. Although it threw us around inside, nothing flexed, nothing even rattled! I'm sure that it scuffed a couple of feet of bottom paint off the bottom plate. It also scuffed a couple of square inches of skin off Marie, and I haven't heard the end of it yet.

This is what *The Elements of Boat Strength* is all about—fabricating vessels that can take punishment and keep their crews safe. There was some good-natured banter at this boat's builder about "overbuilding." Certainly, *Belle Marie*'s shoal bottom was designed extra strong. After all, she was specifically drawn up to take ground at will. Still—heavily constructed or not—she floats on her lines and makes proper speed. *Belle Marie* has proven a fine seaboat too.

If *Belle Marie* were "overbuilt," she would have been too heavy, or too tender, or too slow, or all of the above. In the final analysis, what can be said for sure is that she is plenty rugged. As a result, we all sleep well at night—designer, builder, and owner. That's what *Boat Strength* is all about.

APPENDIX 1: PHOTO GALLERY

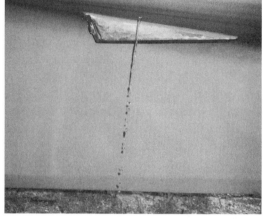

Above right: *No we didn't drill into a tank! This 34-foot (10.4 m) foam core hull was ruined by improper core bedding. All this water was forced in through improperly bedded fasteners for spray strips. More than 20 holes all over the bottom "leaked" like this (see p. 14).*

Above: *Bottom stringers and floors in a 40-foot (12.2 m) planing hull. The well-tabbed-in ply floors are acceptable. The thicker-cored FRP floors called for in the rule are better still (see p.16).*
Right: *A chopper gun in use. This fellow should at least be wearing a facemask and goggles (see p. 11). (Courtesy Owens-Corning Fiberglass Corporation)*

Right: This secondary bond failed when yanked on with one hand. The builder didn't pay attention to getting a good bond and didn't fillet the corners before tabbing (see p. 18). **Below:** Numerous bulkheads in the Cape Dory 40 motor yacht. All are well tabbed in and sealed (see p. 45). **Bottom:** Proper treatment of interior wood. Note that all structural members—bulkheads, furring strips, and the like—have been sprayed with gelcoat and sealed. This is a Cape Dory 40 motor yacht (see p. 18).

Left: Clear view of the robust continuous bulkhead tabbing on the Cape Dory 40 (see p. 45). **Below:** Engine-bed stringers and transverse hat-hection ring frame on the Gerr "Westbourne 44" (see p. 48). (Courtesy Westbourne Custom Yachts.) **Bottom:** A well-made elastometric foam spacer at a bulkhead joint (see p. 48).

Above: *The Gerr-designed 44-foot (13.4 m) catamaran* Slipstream *is built of vacuum-bagged balsa core with bi-axial E-glass laid in vinylester resin. All joiner panels, soles, and joiner bulkheads are Decolite (balsa core) and Nida core (plastic honeycomb) panels. The boat's displacement/length ratio is just 70 (see p. 75).* (Courtesy Z Sails). **Right:** *Interior of* Slipstream*'s bridge-deck cabin. Every joiner panel is balsa core or Nida core to reduce weight (see p. 75).*

The Gerr 34-foot (10.4 m) Sportfisherman is of
standard cored FRP construction. It is entirely
balsa core with stitch-mat and combi-mat style
glass. Scantlings and details follow the FRP
scantling rule. The boat does a steady 30 knots in
Force Six conditions and has proven very rugged
(see p. 64). (Courtesy Off Soundings Yachts)

Deck of the Sutherland Runabout (see p. 80).
(Courtesy Sutherland Boat and Coach)

Top: Sawn frames with plywood gussets for the hard-chine Sutherland Runabout (see p. 110). **Middle:** View of interior framing of Madrigal. Floors, frames, plank laps, sheer clamp, stem, and plank keel are all plainly visible (see p. 110). **Bottom:** The author's canoe-stern lapstrake sloop design Madrigal gleaming as she leaves her builder, North River Boatworks, on launching day (see p. 102).

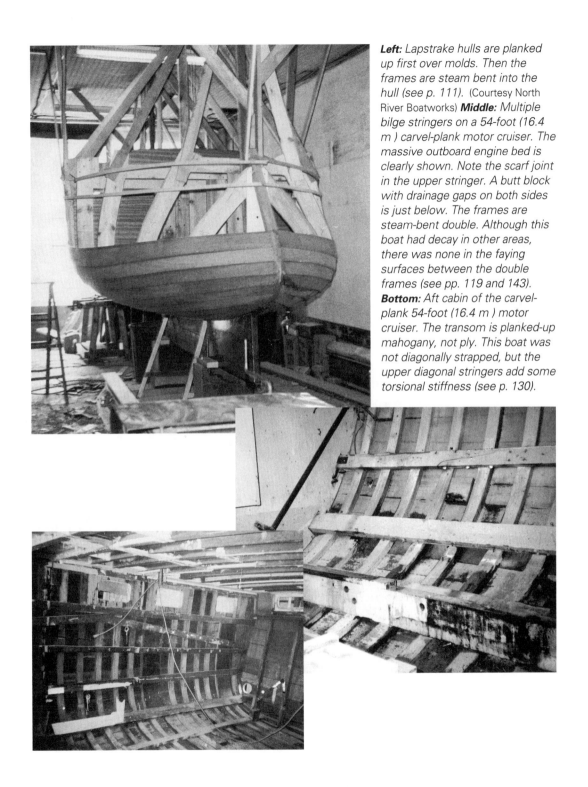

Left: Lapstrake hulls are planked up first over molds. Then the frames are steam bent into the hull (see p. 111). (Courtesy North River Boatworks) **Middle:** Multiple bilge stringers on a 54-foot (16.4 m) carvel-plank motor cruiser. The massive outboard engine bed is clearly shown. Note the scarf joint in the upper stringer. A butt block with drainage gaps on both sides is just below. The frames are steam-bent double. Although this boat had decay in other areas, there was none in the faying surfaces between the double frames (see pp. 119 and 143). **Bottom:** Aft cabin of the carvel-plank 54-foot (16.4 m) motor cruiser. The transom is planked-up mahogany, not ply. This boat was not diagonally strapped, but the upper diagonal stringers add some torsional stiffness (see p. 130).

Above: *Notching a double lodging knee for a half-deck beam (see p. 152).* (Courtesy Kortchmar & Willner)

Right: *Proper bulkhead/ring frames well tabbed in place in a sheathed wood-epoxy strip-plank hull (see p. 155).* (Courtesy Alan Salisch)

Top: *The author's 60-foot (18.2 m) Class 1 BOC racer* Holger Danske. *Wood-epoxy strip-plank construction sheathed with bi-axial S-glass allowed an extremely light but tough hull. D/L ratio is just 40 (see p. 156).* (Courtesy Onne van der Wal)

Middle: *A beautifully finished Gerr-designed 28-foot (8.5 m) tape-seam plywood Offshore Skiff built by Hill's Marine (see p. 166).* (Courtesy Hill's Marine)

Bottom: *Diagonal-veneer cold-molded V-bottom powerboat hull. The closely spaced longitudinal stringers and chine log are clearly visible. Note the treatment of the bottom stringers on the V-bottom (see p. 171).* (Courtesy Alan Salisch)

Top: Photograph of the first all-aluminum boat, a leeboard spritsail sloop built in 1890 (see p. 182). Middle: Photograph of Mignon, *the first aluminum powerboat (a naphtha launch) (see p. 182).* (Courtesy Kaiser Aluminum) *Bottom:* Imagine, *built by Kanter Yachts. This Gerr-designed 57-foot (17.3 m) aluminum voyaging motor cruiser has a range of more than 3,500 nautical miles and a top speed of 12 knots at light load (see p. 187).* (Courtesy Kanter Yachts)

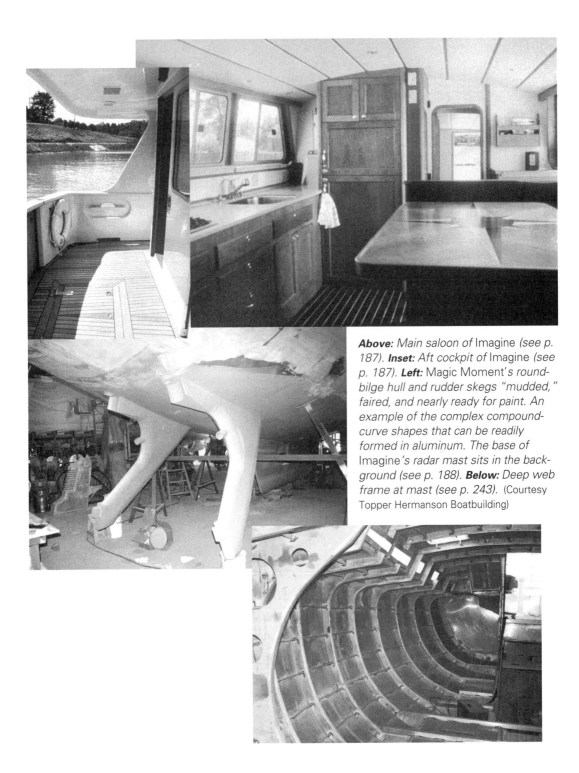

Above: Main saloon of Imagine *(see p. 187).* **Inset:** *Aft cockpit of* Imagine *(see p. 187).* **Left:** *Magic Moment's round-bilge hull and rudder skegs "mudded," faired, and nearly ready for paint. An example of the complex compound-curve shapes that can be readily formed in aluminum. The base of* Imagine*'s radar mast sits in the background (see p. 188).* **Below:** *Deep web frame at mast (see p. 243).* (Courtesy Topper Hermanson Boatbuilding)

APPENDIX 2: PIPE SIZES AND PROPERTIES TABLE

Nominal pipe size, in	Schedule no.	OD, in	ID, in	Wall thickness, in	Weight per linear foot, lb, plain ends†	Cross-sectional wall area, in²	Inside cross-sectional area, in²	Moment of inertia, in⁴	Section modulus, in³	Radius of gyration, in
⅛	40‡	0.405	0.269	0.068	0.085	0.0720	0.0568	0.0011	0.0053	0.1215
	80§	0.405	0.215	0.095	0.109	0.0925	0.0363	0.0012	0.0060	0.1146
¼	40‡	0.540	0.364	0.088	0.147	0.1250	0.1041	0.0033	0.0123	0.1628
	80§	0.540	0.302	0.119	0.185	0.1574	0.0716	0.0038	0.0139	0.1547
⅜	40‡	0.675	0.493	0.091	0.196	0.1670	0.1909	0.0073	0.0216	0.2090
	80§	0.675	0.423	0.126	0.256	0.2173	0.1405	0.0086	0.0255	0.1991
½	40‡	0.840	0.622	0.109	0.294	0.2503	0.3039	0.0171	0.0407	0.2613
	80§	0.840	0.546	0.147	0.376	0.3200	0.2341	0.0201	0.0478	0.2505
¾	10	1.050	0.884	0.083	0.297	0.2521	0.6138	0.0297	0.0566	0.3432
	40‡	1.050	0.824	0.113	0.391	0.3326	0.5333	0.0370	0.0705	0.3337
	80§	1.050	0.742	0.154	0.510	0.4335	0.4324	0.0448	0.0853	0.3214
1	5	1.315	1.185	0.065	0.300	0.2553	1.103	0.0500	0.0760	0.4425
	10	1.315	1.097	0.109	0.486	0.4130	0.9452	0.0757	0.1151	0.4382
	40‡	1.315	1.049	0.133	0.581	0.4939	0.8643	0.0873	0.1328	0.4205
	80§	1.315	0.957	0.179	0.751	0.6388	0.7193	0.1056	0.1606	0.4066
1¼	5	1.660	1.530	0.065	0.383	0.3257	1.839	0.1037	0.1250	0.5644
	10	1.660	1.442	0.109	0.625	0.5311	1.633	0.1605	0.1934	0.5497
	40‡	1.660	1.380	0.140	0.786	0.6685	1.496	0.1947	0.2346	0.5397
	80§	1.660	1.278	0.191	1.037	0.8815	1.283	0.2418	0.2913	0.5238
1½	5	1.900	1.770	0.065	0.441	0.3747	2.461	0.1579	0.1662	0.6492
	10	1.900	1.682	0.109	0.721	0.6133	2.222	0.2468	0.2598	0.6344
	40‡	1.900	1.610	0.145	0.940	0.7995	2.036	0.3099	0.3262	0.6226
	80§	1.900	1.500	0.200	1.256	1.068	1.767	0.3912	0.4118	0.6052
2	5	2.375	2.245	0.065	0.555	0.4717	3.958	0.3149	0.2652	0.8170
	10	2.375	2.157	0.109	0.913	0.7760	3.654	0.4992	0.4204	0.8021
	40‡	2.375	2.067	0.154	1.264	1.074	3.356	0.6657	0.5606	0.7871
	80§	2.375	1.939	0.218	1.737	1.477	2.953	0.8679	0.7309	0.7665
2½	5	2.875	2.709	0.083	0.856	0.7280	5.764	0.7100	0.4939	0.9876
	10	2.875	2.635	0.120	1.221	1.039	5.453	0.9873	0.6868	0.9750
	40‡	2.875	2.469	0.203	2.004	1.704	4.788	1.530	1.064	0.9474
	80§	2.875	2.323	0.276	2.650	2.254	4.238	1.924	1.339	0.9241
3	5	3.500	3.334	0.083	1.048	0.8910	8.730	1.301	0.7435	1.208
	10	3.500	3.260	0.120	1.498	1.274	8.346	1.822	1.041	1.196
	40‡	3.500	3.068	0.216	2.621	2.228	7.393	3.017	1.724	1.164
	80§	3.500	2.900	0.300	3.547	3.016	6.605	3.894	2.225	1.136
3½	5	4.000	3.834	0.083	1.201	1.021	11.55	1.960	0.9799	1.385
	10	4.000	3.760	0.120	1.720	1.463	11.10	2.755	1.378	1.372
	40‡	4.000	3.548	0.226	3.151	2.680	9.887	4.788	2.394	1.337
	80§	4.000	3.364	0.318	4.326	3.678	8.888	6.281	3.140	1.307
4	5	4.500	4.334	0.083	1.354	1.152	14.75	2.810	1.249	1.562
	10	4.500	4.260	0.120	1.942	1.651	14.25	3.963	1.761	1.549
	40‡	4.500	4.026	0.237	3.733	3.174	12.73	7.232	3.214	1.510
	80§	4.500	3.826	0.337	5.183	4.407	11.50	9.611	4.272	1.477
5	40‡	5.563	5.047	0.258	5.057	4.300	20.01	15.16	5.451	1.878
	80§	5.563	4.813	0.375	7.188	6.112	18.19	20.67	7.432	1.839
6	40‡	6.625	6.065	0.280	6.564	5.581	28.89	28.14	8.496	2.246
	80§	6.625	5.761	0.432	9.884	8.405	26.07	40.49	12.22	2.195
8	30	8.625	8.071	0.277	8.543	7.265	51.16	63.35	14.69	2.953
	40‡	8.625	7.981	0.322	9.878	8.399	50.03	72.49	16.81	2.938
	80§	8.625	7.625	0.500	15.01	12.76	45.66	105.7	24.51	2.878
10		10.750	10.192	0.279	10.79	9.178	81.59	125.9	23.42	3.704
	30	10.750	10.136	0.307	11.84	10.07	80.69	137.4	25.57	3.694
	40‡	10.750	10.020	0.365	14.00	11.91	78.85	160.7	29.90	3.674
	80§	10.750	9.750	0.500	18.93	16.10	74.66	211.9	39.43	3.628
12	30	12.750	12.090	0.330	15.14	12.88	114.8	248.5	38.97	4.393
	‡	12.750	12.000	0.375	17.14	14.58	113.1	279.3	43.81	4.377
	§	12.750	11.750	0.500	22.63	19.24	108.4	361.5	56.71	4.335
Construction pipe										
		2.00	1.900	0.050	0.3602	0.3063	2.835	0.1457	0.1457	0.6897
		3.00	2.900	0.050	0.5449	0.4634	6.605	0.5042	0.3361	1.043
		4.00	3.900	0.050	0.7297	0.6205	11.95	1.210	0.6051	1.397
		5.00	4.896	0.052	0.9506	0.8083	18.83	2.474	0.9896	1.749
		6.00	5.876	0.062	1.360	1.157	2.712	5.098	1.699	2.100
		7.00	6.856	0.072	1.843	1.567	36.92	9.403	2.687	2.450
		8.00	7.812	0.094	2.745	2.335	47.93	18.24	4.561	2.795

* Aluminum Co. of America.
† Weights calculated for 6061 and 6063. For 3003 multiply by 1.010.
‡ Also designated as standard pipe.
§ Also designated as extra-heavy or extra-strong pipe. All calculations based on nominal dimensions.

APPENDIX 3: BOLT-STRENGTH TABLES

Bolt Breaking Strength in Pounds: In Tension

No. or Inches	Decimal Inches	Millimeters	Threads/Inch UNC*	Threads/Inch UNF†	Stainless 85,000 psi UNC*	Stainless 85,000 psi UNF†	Bronze 60,000 psi UNC*	Bronze 60,000 psi UNF†
No. 4	0.112	2.84	40	48	513	561	362	396
No. 6	0.138	3.51	32	40	772	862	545	609
No. 8	0.164	4.17	32	36	1,191	1,252	841	884
No. 10	0.190	4.83	24	32	1,490	1,699	1,052	1,200
No. 12	0.216	5.49	24	28	2,054	2,192	1,450	1,547
1/4	0.250	6.35	20	28	2,705	3,092	1,909	2,182
5/16	0.313	7.94	18	24	4,457	4,936	3,146	3,484
3/8	0.375	9.53	16	24	6,587	7,465	4,649	5,270
7/16	0.438	11.11	14	20	9,036	10,091	6,379	7,123
1/2	0.500	12.70	13	20	12,061	13,596	8,514	9,597
9/16	0.563	14.29	12	18	15,465	17,253	10,917	12,179
5/8	0.625	15.88	11	18	19,210	21,756	13,560	15,357
3/4	0.750	19.05	10	16	28,429	31,702	20,068	22,378
7/8	0.875	22.23	9	14	39,247	43,305	27,704	30,568
1	1.000	25.40	8	12	51,488	56,359	36,345	39,782
1 1/8	1.125	28.58	7	12	64,878	72,736	45,797	51,343
1 1/4	1.250	31.75	7	12	82,374	91,200	58,147	64,377
1 3/8	1.375	34.93	6	12	98,165	111,751	69,293	78,883
1 1/2	1.500	38.10	6	12	119,446	134,387	84,315	94,861
1 3/4	1.750	44.45	5		161,454		113,968	
2	2.000	50.80	4 1/2		212,349		149,894	
2 1/4	2.250	57.15	4 1/2		276,054		194,861	
2 1/2	2.500	63.50	4		339,900		239,930	
2 3/4	2.750	69.85	4		419,391		296,041	
3	3.000	76.20	4		507,227		358,042	
3 1/4	3.250	82.55	4		603,407		425,935	
3 1/2	3.500	88.90	4		707,933		499,717	
3 3/4	3.750	95.25	4		820,803		579,390	
4	4.000	101.60	4		942,018		664,954	

Formula

$P = S \times At$

At = Net effective tensile area

$At = 0.7854(D - [0.9743/n])^2$

n = Number of threads per inch

S = Ultimate fiber tensile strength

P = Ultimate breaking load in pounds

D = Nominal screw diameter in inches

*UNC = Unified coarse

†UNF = Unified fine

Bolt Breaking Strength in Kilograms: In Tension

No. or Inches	Diameter Decimal Inches	Millimeters	Threads/Inch UNC*	UNF†	Stainless 585.8 mPa UNC*	UNF†	Bronze 413.5 mPa UNC*	UNF†
No. 4	0.112	2.84	40	48	233	255	164	180
No. 6	0.138	3.51	32	40	350	391	247	276
No. 8	0.164	4.17	32	36	540	568	381	401
No. 10	0.190	4.83	24	32	676	771	477	544
No. 12	0.216	5.49	24	28	932	994	658	702
¼	0.250	6.35	20	28	1,227	1,402	866	990
⁵⁄₁₆	0.313	7.94	18	24	2,021	2,239	1,427	1,580
⅜	0.375	9.53	16	24	2,988	3,386	2,109	2,390
⁷⁄₁₆	0.438	11.11	14	20	4,099	4,577	2,893	3,231
½	0.500	12.70	13	20	5,471	6,167	3,862	4,353
⁹⁄₁₆	0.563	14.29	12	18	7,015	7,826	4,952	5,524
⅝	0.625	15.88	11	18	8,714	9,869	6,151	6,966
¾	0.750	19.05	10	16	12,895	14,380	9,103	10,150
⅞	0.875	22.23	9	14	17,803	19,643	12,566	13,866
1	1.000	25.40	8	12	23,355	25,564	16,486	18,045
1⅛	1.125	28.58	7	12	29,429	32,993	20,773	23,289
1¼	1.250	31.75	7	12	37,365	41,368	26,375	29,201
1⅜	1.375	34.93	6	12	44,527	50,690	31,431	35,781
1½	1.500	38.10	6	12	54,181	60,958	38,245	43,029
1¾	1.750	44.45	5		73,235		51,695	
2	2.000	50.80	4½		96,321		67,991	
2¼	2.250	57.15	4½		125,217		88,389	
2½	2.500	63.50	4		154,178		108,831	
2¾	2.750	69.85	4		190,235		134,283	
3	3.000	76.20	4		230,077		162,407	
3¼	3.250	82.55	4		273,704		193,203	
3½	3.500	88.90	4		321,116		226,670	
3¾	3.750	95.25	4		372,314		262,810	
4	4.000	101.60	4		427,297		301,621	

Formula

$P = S \times At$

At = Net effective tensile area

$At = 0.7854(D - [0.9743/n])^2$

n = Number of threads per inch

S = Ultimate fiber tensile strength

P = Ultimate breaking load in pounds

D = Nominal screw diameter in inches

*UNC = Unified coarse

†UNF = Unified fine

Bolt Breaking Strength in Pounds: In Shear

No. or Inches	Diameter Decimal Inches	Millimeters	Area Sq. In. at Root of Thread, UNC*	Stainless Steel and Bronze 45,000 psi At Thread	Unthreaded
No. 4	0.112	2.84	0.00496	190	443
No. 6	0.138	3.51	0.00745	285	673
No. 8	0.164	4.17	0.01196	457	950
No. 10	0.190	4.83	0.01450	555	1,275
No. 12	0.216	5.49	0.02060	788	1,648
¼	0.250	6.35	0.02690	1,029	2,208
⁵⁄₁₆	0.313	7.94	0.04540	1,737	3,450
⅜	0.375	9.53	0.06780	2,593	4,968
⁷⁄₁₆	0.438	11.11	0.09330	3,569	6,761
½	0.500	12.70	0.12570	4,808	8,831
⁹⁄₁₆	0.563	14.29	0.16200	6,197	11,177
⅝	0.625	15.88	0.20200	7,727	13,799
¾	0.750	19.05	0.30200	11,552	19,870
⅞	0.875	22.23	0.41900	16,027	27,046
1	1.000	25.40	0.55100	21,076	35,325
1⅛	1.125	28.58	0.69300	26,507	44,708
1¼	1.250	31.75	0.89000	34,043	55,195
1⅜	1.375	34.93	1.05400	40,316	66,786
1½	1.500	38.10	1.29400	49,496	79,481
1¾	1.750	44.45	1.74000	66,555	108,183
2	2.000	50.80	2.30000	87,975	141,300
2¼	2.250	57.15	3.02000	115,515	178,833
2½	2.500	63.50	3.72000	142,290	220,781
2¾	2.750	69.85	4.62000	176,715	267,145
3	3.000	76.20	5.62000	214,965	317,925
3¼	3.250	82.55	6.72000	257,040	373,120
3½	3.500	88.90	7.92000	302,940	432,731
3¾	3.750	95.25	9.21000	352,283	496,758
4	4.000	101.60	10.61000	405,833	565,200

Formula

P = Area at root of thread × Shear stress x 0.85 (for thread stress riser) or

P = Area at full nominal diameter × Shear stress

*UNC = Unified coarse

Bolt Breaking Strength in Kilograms: In Shear

No. or Inches	Diameter Decimal Inches	Millimeters	Area mm² at Root of Thread, UNC*	Stainless Steel and Bronze 310.1 mPa At Thread	Unthreaded
No. 4	0.112	2.84	3.20	86	201
No. 6	0.138	3.51	4.81	129	305
No. 8	0.164	4.17	7.72	208	431
No. 10	0.190	4.83	9.35	252	578
No. 12	0.216	5.49	13.29	357	748
¼	0.250	6.35	17.35	467	1,001
⁵⁄₁₆	0.313	7.94	29.29	788	1,565
⅜	0.375	9.53	43.74	1,176	2,253
⁷⁄₁₆	0.438	11.11	60.19	1,619	3,067
½	0.500	12.70	81.10	2,181	4,006
⁹⁄₁₆	0.563	14.29	104.52	2,811	5,070
⅝	0.625	15.88	130.32	3,505	6,259
¾	0.750	19.05	194.84	5,240	9,013
⅞	0.875	22.23	270.32	7,270	12,268
1	1.000	25.40	355.48	9,560	16,023
1⅛	1.125	28.58	447.10	12,024	20,280
1¼	1.250	31.75	574.19	15,442	25,036
1⅜	1.375	34.93	680.00	18,287	30,294
1½	1.500	38.10	834.84	22,451	36,052
1¾	1.750	44.45	1122.58	30,189	49,071
2	2.000	50.80	1483.87	39,905	64,093
2¼	2.250	57.15	1948.38	52,397	81,118
2½	2.500	63.50	2400.00	64,542	100,146
2¾	2.750	69.85	2980.64	80,157	121,176
3	3.000	76.20	3625.80	97,507	144,210
3¼	3.250	82.55	4335.48	116,593	169,246
3½	3.500	88.90	5109.67	137,413	196,286
3¾	3.750	95.25	5941.92	159,794	225,328
4	4.000	101.60	6845.15	184,084	256,373

Formula

P = Area at root of thread × Shear stress x 0.85 (for thread stress riser) or

P = Area at full nominal diameter × Shear stress

*UNC = Unified coarse

APPENDIX 4: FINDING SPECIFIC GRAVITY

The Standard Specific Gravity Measurement

Specific gravity (SG) is the difference between the weight of an object and the weight of fresh water that occupies an equal volume

or

SG = weight of sample ÷ weight of displaced water

Where

the weight of displaced water = the weight of water filling a volume equal to the sample's volume

To find the SG of an FRP test piece, for example, you need an accurate scale and two containers open at the top. One container should fit inside the other (open end up) with plenty of room to spare. You also need a supply of clean fresh water (salt water would throw off the results).

- Weigh the sample and record the results.
- Weigh the larger container, empty and dry, and record the results.
- Place the smaller container inside the larger container and set them both on the scale.
- Fill the smaller container carefully all the way to the brim with fresh water, without spilling a drop.
- Gently ease the FRP sample into the water in the smaller container.
- Water will spill out into the surrounding larger container.
- Use a straw to lower the level of water in the smaller container until you can lift it out without spilling any additional water.
- Remove the smaller container and note the total weight of the larger container with the spilled water in it.
- Subtract the weight of the empty larger container from the total weight to find the weight of the displaced water.
- Divide the sample weight by the weight of the displaced water; the result is the SG.

Example:

Say your FRP sample weighed 3.72 oz. After following the procedure, you find that the water it displaced weighed 2.38 oz. The sample's SG is 1.56 (3.72 oz. ÷ 2.38 oz. = 1.56 SG).

The density of the sample is simply the density of fresh water times the SG, or 97.3 lb./cu. ft. (1.56 SG × 62.4 lb./cu. ft. fresh water = 97 lb./cu. ft.).

or

Say your FRP sample weighed 105.5 g. After following the procedure, you find that the water it displaced weighed 67.5 g. The sample's SG is 1.56 (105.5 g ÷ 67.5 g = 1.56 SG).

The density of the sample is simply the density of fresh water times the SG, or 1,560 kg/m³ (1.56 SG × 1,000 kg/m³ fresh water = 1,560 kg/m³).

Measuring Specific Gravity of Wood

You can determine the SG of materials that float (e.g., balsa or foam) the same way, but the quantity of displaced water is very small and will require either a large sample or many highly accurate measurements tabulated and averaged.

Structural woods are a little easier; they float roughly half in and half out of the water.

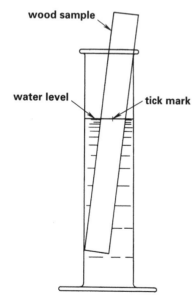

Measuring wood specific gravity

There is a simple method for determining a timber sample's SG. It doesn't even require a scale.

- Cut a sample from a board. Make it long, thin, narrow, and straight, and perfectly square and regular in dimensions; for example, 5 inches long by ¼ inch thick and ½ inch wide (125 mm long by 5 mm thick and 12 mm wide).
- Sand the edges lightly to remove roughness or saw-cut strands that can hold air bubbles; wipe clean.
- Float the sample in a tall, narrow, clear-plastic container—filled about half full—so the sample is held more or less vertical by the sides of the container.
- Lift out the sample and make a tick mark in the center of the waterline.
- Measure the distance from the bottom up to the waterline.
- Measure the distance from the bottom to the top.
- To find the SG, divide the distance to the waterline by the distance to the top.

Example:

Say you floated a wood sample 5 inches long and the tick mark at the waterline measured 3 inches up from the bottom. This sample's SG is 0.6 (3 inches ÷ 5 inches = 0.6 SG).

The density of the sample is 0.6 SG × 62.4 lb./cu. ft. fresh water = 37.4 lb./cu. ft.

or

Say you floated a wood sample 125 mm long and the tick mark at the waterline measured 75 mm up from the bottom. This sample's SG is 0.6 (75 mm ÷ 125 mm = 0.6 SG). This is a good average structural wood, say, Douglas fir.

APPENDIX 5: MEASURE AND UNIT CONVERSION TABLES

Linear Measure Conversions

	inches	feet	yards	mm	cm	m	
inches	1	0.08333	0.02778	25.4	2.54	0.0254	inches
feet	12	1	0.33333	304.8	30.48	0.3048	feet
yards	36	3.00000	1	914.4	91.44	0.9144	yards
mm	0.03937	0.00328	0.00109	1	0.1	0.001	mm
cm	0.3937	0.03281	0.01094	10	1	0.01	cm
m	39.37008	3.28084	1.09361	1,000	100	1	m

Square Measure (Area) Conversions

	sq. in.	sq. ft.	sq. yd.	sq. mm	sq. cm	sq. m	
sq. in.	1	0.00694	0.00077	645.16	6.4516	0.000645	sq. in.
sq. ft.	144	1	0.11111	92,903.04	929.0304	0.092903	sq. ft.
sq. yd.	1,296	9.00000	1	836,127.36	8,361.27	0.836127	sq. yd.
sq. mm	0.00155	0.0000108	0.0000012	1	0.01	0.000001	sq. mm
sq. cm	0.155	0.00108	0.00012	100	1	0.0001	sq. cm
sq. m	1,550.00	10.76391	1.19599	1,000,000	10,000	1	sq. m

Units of Density Conversions

	lb./cu. in.	lb./cu. ft.	g/cu. cm	kg/cu. m	
lb./cu. in.	1	1,728	27.6799	27679.9	lb./cu. in.
lb./cu. ft.	0.0005787	1	0.016018461	16.01846	lb./cu. ft.
g/cu. cm	0.0361273	62.42797	1	1,000	g/cu. cm
kg/cu. m	0.000036127	0.06243	0.001	1	kg/cu. m

Cubic Measure (Volume) Conversions

	cu. in.	cu. ft.	cu. yd.	cu. mm	cu. cm (ml)	cu. m
cu. in.	1	0.00058	0.00002	16,387.10	16.3871	0.0000164
cu. ft.	1,728	1	0.03704	28,316,846.60	28,316.85	0.028317
cu. yd.	46,656	27	1	764,554,858	764,554.86	0.764555
cu. mm	0.000061	0.000000035	0.000000013	1	0.001	0.000000001
cu. cm (ml)	0.061024	0.0000353	0.00000131	1,000	1	0.000001
cu. m	61,023.74	35.31467	1.30795	1,000,000,000	1,000,000	1
U.S. gal.	231	0.13368	0.00495	3,785,411.784	3,785.41178	0.00379
U.S. oz.	1.80469	0.00104	0.0000387	29,573.5296	29.57353	0.0000296
Imp. gal.	277.41943	0.16054	0.005946	4,546,090	4,546.09	0.00455
Imp. oz.	1.73387	0.001	0.0000372	28,413.0625	28.41306	0.0000284
Liters (l)	61.02374	0.03531	0.00131	1,000,000	1,000	0.001
ml (cu. cm)	0.06102	0.0000353	0.000001308	1,000	1	0.000001

	U.S. gal.	U.S. oz.	Imp. Gal.	Imp. oz.	Liters (l)	ml (cu. cm)
cu. in.	0.00433	0.0554126	0.003605	0.57674	0.01639	16.3871
cu. ft.	7.48052	957.50649	6.228835	996.61367	28.31685	28316.848
cu. yd.	201.97403	25852.67532	168.178557	26908.5692	764.55486	764554.858
cu. mm	0.0000002642	0.000033814	0.00000021997	0.0000351951	0.000001	0.001
cu. cm (ml)	0.000264172	0.03381	0.00021997	0.03520	0.001	1
cu. m	264.17205	33814.0227	219.96925	35,195.0797	1000	1000000
U.S. gal.	1	128	0.83267	133.22787	3.78541	3785.4118
U.S. oz.	0.007813	1	0.00651	1.04084	0.02957	29.5735
Imp. gal.	1.200950	153.7216	1	160	4.54609	4546.09
Imp. oz.	0.007506	0.96076	0.00625	1	0.02841	28.41306
Liters (l)	0.264172	33.81402	0.21997	35.1951	1	1000
ml (cu. cm)	0.000264	0.033814	0.00021997	0.0351951	0.001	1

NOTE: cubic centimeters (cu. cm) are the same as milliliters (ml)

Units of Force and Mass Conversions

	oz.	lb.	long ton	short ton	metric ton
oz.	1	0.0625	0.000027902	0.00003125	0.0000283495
lb.	16	1	0.000446429	0.0005	0.000453592
long ton	35,840	2,240	1	1.12	1.01605
short ton	32,000	2,000	0.89286	1	0.90718
metric ton	35,273.96	2,204.623	0.98421	1.10231	1
g	0.03527	0.0022046	0.0000009842	0.0000011023	0.000001
Kg	35.27396	2.20462	0.000984207	0.0011023	0.001
N	3.59643	0.22481	0.000100361	0.0001124	0.000101971
kN	3596.43	224.81	0.100361	0.112405	0.101971
mN	3596430	224810	100.361	112.405	101.971

	g	Kg	N	kN	mN
oz.	28.34952	0.02835	0.27801	0.000278	0.000000278
lb.	453.59237	0.45359	4.448221	0.004448	0.0000044482
long ton	1,016,046.909	1016.04691	9964.0146	9.964015	0.009964015
short ton	907,184.74	907.18474	8896.4416	8.896442	0.008896442
metric ton	1,000,000	1000	9806.64820	9.806648	0.009806648
g	1	0.001	0.00980665	0.0000098067	0.0000000098
Kg	1000	1	9.80665	0.0098067	0.0000098067
N	101.97	0.10197	1	0.001	0.000001
kN	101971	101.971	1000	1	0.001
mN	101971000	101971	1000000	1000	1

NOTE: Newtons are units of force only. Killograms, pounds, or ounces of MASS cannot be converted to newtons. Only killograms, pounds, or ounces of FORCE can be converted to newtons

Units of Pressure and Stress Conversions

	psi	lb./sq. ft.	g/sq. cm (cm water fresh)	kg/sq. cm	kg/sq. m	Pa (N/sq. m)	kPa
psi	1	144	70.307	0.070307	703.0695	6,894.76	6.894757
lb./sq. ft.	0.00694	1	0.4882	0.0004882	4.8824	47.88026	0.04788
g/sq. cm	0.01422	2.0482	1	0.001	10	98.0665	0.0980665
kg/sq. cm	14.22334	2,048.16	1,000	1	10,000	98,066.5	98.0665
kg/sq. m	0.00142	0.2048	0.1	0.0001	1	9.80665	0.009807
Pa (N/sq. m)	0.000145	0.0208854	0.010197	0.000010197	0.10197	1	0.001
kPa	0.14504	20.88543	10.197	0.010197	101.97	1,000	1
mPa (N/sq. mm)	145.03774	20,885.43	10,197	10.197	101,970	1,000,000	1,000
atmosphere	14.69600	2,116.2124	1,033.227	1.033227	10,332.27	101,325	101.325
in. water (fresh)	0.03613	5.2023	2.54	0.00254	25.4	249.079	0.24909
ft. water (fresh)	0.43350	0.0361	30.48	0.03048	304.8	2,989.067	2.98907
m water (fresh)	1.42233	204.8161	100	0.1	1,000	9,806.65	9.80665
hg in.	0.49115	70.7262	34.53155	0.034531	345.3155	3,386.38	3.38638
hg mm	0.01934	2.78446	1.35951	0.00136	13.5951	133.32205	0.13334

Units of Pressure and Stress Conversions

	mPa (N/sq. mm)	atmosphere	in. water (fresh)	ft. water (fresh)	m water (fresh)	hg in.	hg mm
psi	0.006895	0.068046	27.679910	2.30666	0.7031	2.0360	51.7149
lb./sq. ft.	0.00004788	0.00047254	0.192221	0.01602	0.0049	0.0141	0.3591
g/sq. cm	0.0000980665	0.00096784	0.393708	0.03281	0.01	0.02896	0.7356
kg/sq. cm	0.0980665	0.967841	393.700790	32.80839	10	28.9591	735.5592
kg/sq. m	0.0000098067	0.0000967841	0.03937	0.00328	0.001	0.002896	0.0736
Pa (N/sq. m)	0.000001	0.000009869	0.004015	0.00033	0.000102	0.0002945	0.00748
kPa	0.001	0.009869	4.014631	0.33455	0.1020	0.294523	7.4809
mPa (N/sq. mm)	1	9.869	4,014.631	334.5526	101.9718	294.523	7,480.88
atmosphere	0.101325	1	406.782	33.8985	10.3323	29.9213	760
in. water (fresh)	0.00024909	0.002458	1	0.08333	0.0254	0.186832	4.4755
ft. water (fresh)	0.002981	0.0294998	12.00000	1	0.3048	0.88267	22.4198
m water (fresh)	0.00981	0.096784	39.37007	3.28084	1	2.8959	73.2229
hg in.	0.00339	13.594	1.132925	0.345323	535.25364	1	25.4
hg mm	0.000133	0.001316	0.53524	0.044603	0.013595	0.03937	1

NOTE: cm water (fresh) is the same as g/sq. cm

BIBLIOGRAPHY

The Elements of Boat Strength required wide-ranging, intensive research. In addition to my own notes, observations, calculations, and data from my files, copious use was made of numerous references. The principal sources are listed here:

Adams, Jeannette T. *Arco's Complete Woodworking Handbook.* New York: Arco, 1981.

ALCOA Aluminum. *Aluminum Afloat.* New York: ALCOA Aluminum, 1964.

Aluminum Association. *Aluminum Construction Manual: Engineering Data for Aluminum Structures.* New York: Aluminum Association, 1969.

American Boat and Yacht Council (ABYC). *Standards and Recommended Practices for Small Craft.* ABYC, 1998.

American Bureau of Shipping (ABS). *Guide for Building and Classing High-Speed Craft.* Paramus NJ: ABS, 1991.

———. *Guide for Building and Classing Motor Pleasure Yachts.* Paramus NJ: ABS, 1991.

———. *Guide for Building and Classing Offshore Racing Yachts.* Paramus NJ: ABS, 1986.

American Institute of Steel Construction. *Manual of Steel Construction.* 7th ed. New York: American Institute of Steel Construction, 1970.

Attwood, E. L., and Longmans Pengelly. *Theoretical Naval Architecture.* 19th printing. London: Green & Co.

Baltek Corporation. *Care and Use of Contourkore.* Data File #115.

Barnaby, Kenneth C. *Basic Naval Architecture.* 5th ed. London: Hutchinson, 1967.

Breneman, John W. *Strength of Materials.* 3d ed. New York: McGraw-Hill, 1965.

Brockenbrough, R. L., and B. G. Johnston. *USS Steel Design Manual.* Pittsburgh PA: U.S. Steel Corporation, 1968.

Brown, David G. *Boatbuilding with Baltek DuraKore.* Camden ME: International Marine, 1995.

Carrick, Robert W., and Richard Henderson. *John G. Alden and His Yacht Designs.* Camden ME: International Marine, 1983.

Chapelle, Howard I. *The American Fishing Schooners: 1825–1935.* New York: Norton, 1973.

———. *Boatbuilding: A Complete Handbook of Wooden Boat Construction.* New York: Norton, 1941.

———. *Yacht Designing and Planning for Yachtsmen, Students & Amateurs.* Rev. and enl. ed. New York: Norton, 1971.

Cohen, Ghsoh, and Shepard. *Design and Construction of the U.S. Coast Guard's 47-Foot Self-Righting, Heavy Weather Rescue Craft.* Vol. 98. SNAME Transactions, 1990.

Colvin, Thomas E. *Steel Boatbuilding*. Vol. 1: *From Plans to Bare Hull*. Vol. 2: *From Bare Hull to Launching*. Camden ME: International Marine, 1985.

Cooley, R. H. *Complete Metalworking Manual*. New York: Arco, 1967.

Culler, R. D. *Skiffs and Schooners*. Camden ME: International Marine, 1974.

D'Arcangelo, Amelio M. *A Guide to Sound Ship Structure*. Cambridge MD: Cornell Maritime Press, 1964.

Devlin, Samual. *Devlin's Boatbuilding: How to Build Any Boat the Stitch and Glue Way*. Camden ME: International Marine, 1996.

Donaldson, Sven. *Understanding the New Sailing Technology: A Basic Guide for Sailors*. New York: Putnam's, 1990.

DuCane, Peter. *High-Speed Small Craft*. 4th ed., rev. Tuckahoe NY: J. de Graff, 1973.

Du Plessis, Hugo. *Fiberglass Boats*. 3d ed. Camden ME: International Marine, 1996.

Estep, Cole H. *How Wooden Ships Are Built: A Practical Treatise on Modern American Wooden Ship Construction with a Supplement on Laying Off Wooden Vessels*. Ohio: Penton Publishing, 1918.

Faherty, Keith F., and Thomas G. Williamson, eds. *Wood Engineering and Construction Handbook*. 3d ed. New York: McGraw-Hill, 1989.

Farmer, Weston. *From My Old Boat Shop: One-Lung Engines, Fantail Launches & Other Marine Delights*. Camden ME: International Marine, 1979.

Fock, Harald. *Fast Fighting Boats 1870–1945: Their Design, Construction, and Use*. Annapolis: Naval Institute Press, 1978.

Fox, Uffa. *Seamanlike Sense in Power Craft*. London: Peter Davies, 1968.

Friedman, Norman. *U.S. Small Combatants, Including PT-Boats, Subchasers, and the Brown-Water Navy: An Illustrated Design*. Annapolis: Naval Institute Press, 1987.

Garden, William. *Yacht Designs*. Camden ME: International Marine, 1977.

———. *Yacht Designs II*. Mystic CT: Mystic Seaport Museum, 1992.

Gerr, Dave. *The Baltek DuraKore Scantling Handbook*. Northvale NJ: Baltek Corporation, 1995.

———. *The Nature of Boats: Insights and Esoterica for the Nautically Obsessed*. Camden ME: International Marine, 1992.

———. *Propeller Handbook: The Complete Reference for Choosing, Installing, and Understanding Boat Propellers*. Camden ME: International Marine, 1989.

———. *Pocket Cruisers for the Backyard Builder: Thirty Small Sailboats You Can Build for Less than $12,000*. Camden ME: International Marine, 1987.

Gibbs & Cox, Inc. *Marine Design Manual for Fiberglass Reinforced Plastics*. New York: McGraw-Hill, 1960.

Gordon, J. E. *Science of Structures*. New York: Scientific American Library, 1988.

———. *The New Science of Strong Materials or Why You Don't Fall Through the Floor*. Princeton: Princeton University Press, 1984.

———. *Structures, or Why Things Don't Fall Down*. New York: Da Capo Press, 1978.

Gougeon, Meade. *The Gougeon Brothers on Boat Construction: Wood & WEST SYSTEM Materials*. Bay City MI: Gougeon Brothers, 1985.

Graul, Timothy. *Aluminum Planing Boats*. Monograph.

Griffiths, Maurice. *Little Ships and Shoal Waters: Designing, Building and Sailing Shoal Draught Cruising Yachts—With a Cruise or Two in Both Blue and Sandy Waters*. London: Conway Maritime Press, 1972.

Guarino, Salvadore, J. *The PCF, A Patrol Craft Standard*. Vol. 106. Naval Engineers Journal (ASNE), May 1994.

Henderson, Richard. *Philip L. Rhodes and His Yacht Designs*. Camden ME: International Marine, 1981.

Henry, Robert J., and Richards T. Miller. *Sailing Yacht Design: An Appreciation of a Fine Art*. Cambridge MD: Cornell Maritime Press, 1965.

———. *Sailing Yacht Design: A New Appreciation of a Fine Art*. Vol. 98. SNAME Transactions, 1990.

Herreshoff, L. Francis. *Common Sense of Yacht Design*. Jamaica NY: Caravan-Maritime Books, 1974.

———. *Sensible Cruising Designs*. Camden ME: International Marine, 1973.

International Maritime Organization. *SOLAS Consolidated Edition*. International Maritime Organization (U.K.), 1997.

James W. Brown, Inc. *Searunner Construction Manual*. Santa Cruz CA: James W. Brown, 1971.

Kaiser Aluminum. *Aluminum Boats*. Kaiser Aluminum, 1964.

Klingel, Gilbert C. *Boatbuilding with Steel*. Camden ME: International Marine, 1973.

Lambert, John, and Al Ross. *Allied Coastal Forces of World War II*. 2 vols. Annapolis: Naval Institute Press, 1994.

Larsson, Lars, and Rolf E. Eliasson. *Principles of Yacht Design*. Camden ME: International Marine, 1994.

Lincoln Electric Co. *The Design of Welded Structures*. Cleveland: Lincoln Electric Co., 1982.

———. *The Procedure Handbook of Arc Welding*. Lincoln Electric Co., 1973.

Lloyds Register of Shipping. *Rules and Regulations for the Classification of Yachts and Small Craft*. London: Lloyds Register of Shipping, 1983.

Lord, Lindsay. *Naval Architecture of Planing Hulls*. Cambridge MD: Cornell Maritime Press, 1963.

Manzolillo, J. L., Thiele, E. W., and Tuthill, A. H. *CA-706 Copper Nickel Alloy Hulls: The "Copper Mariner's" Experience and Economics*. Vol. 84. SNAME Transactions, 1976.

Marks, Lionel S. *Marks' Standard Handbook for Mechanical Engineers*. 8th ed. Eugene A. Avallone and Theodore Baumeister III, eds. New York: McGraw-Hill, 1978.

Muckle, W. *The Design of Aluminum Alloy Ships' Structures*. London: Hutchinson, 1963.

Najeder, K. W. *Machine Designers' Guide*. 2d ed.

Nicholson, Ian. *Boat Data Book*. Lymington, Hampshire, England: Nautical Publishing, 1978.

———. *Small Steel Craft*. Frogmore, St. Albans, England: Granada Publishing/Adlard Coles, 1978.

Oberg, Jones, Horton, and Ryffel. *Machinery's Handbook*. 24th ed. New York: Industrial Press, 1992.

Parker, Reuel B. *The New Cold-Molded Boatbuilding: From Lofting to Launching*. Camden ME: International Marine, 1992.

Phillips-Brit, Douglas. *Sailing Yacht Design*. Frogmore, St. Albans, England: Adlard Coles, 1971.

———. *Motor Yacht and Boat Design*. 2d ed. Frogmore, St. Albans, England: Adlard Coles, 1966.

———. *The Naval Architecture of Small Craft*. Philosophical Library, 1957.

Pretzer, Roger. *Marine Metals Manual: A Handbook for Boatmen, Builders, and Dealers*. Camden ME: International Marine, 1975.

Rabl, S. S. *Practical Principles of Naval Architecture*. Cambridge MD: Cornell Maritime Press, 1942.

Roark, Raymond J., and Warren C. Young. *Formulas for Stress and Strain*. 5th ed. New York: McGraw-Hill, 1975.

Rogers, Howard T. *The Marine Corrosion Handbook*. Toronto: McGraw-Hill Canada: 1960.

Rossell, Henry E., and Lawrence B. Chapman. *Principles of Naval Architecture*. Vols. 1 and 2. New York: Society of Naval Architects and Marine Engineers, 1942.

Scott, Robert J. *Fiberglass Boat Design and Construction*. 2d ed. Jersey City NJ: Society of Naval Architects and Marine Engineers, 1996.

Shenoi, R. A., and J. F. Wellicome, eds. *Composite Materials in Maritime Structures*. Vols. 1 and 2. New York: Cambridge University Press, 1993.

Sims, Ernest H. *Aluminum Boatbuilding*. 2d ed. Dobbs Ferry NY: Sheridan House, 1993.

Skene, Norman L. *Elements of Yacht Design*. New York: Kennedy Bros., 1938.

———. *Skene's Elements of Yacht Design*. 8th ed. Completely rev. and updated by Francis S. Kinney. New York: Dodd, Mead, 1973.

Smith, Carroll. *Carroll Smith's Nuts, Bolts, Fasteners, and Plumbing Handbook*. Osceola WI: Motorbooks International, 1990.

Steward, Robert M. *Boatbuilding Manual*. 4th ed. Camden ME: International Marine, 1994.

Sucher, Harry V. *Simplified Boatbuilding: The Flat-Bottom Boat*. New York: Norton, 1973.

———. *Simplified Boatbuilding: The V-Bottom Boat*. New York: Norton, 1974.

Traung, Jan-Olan. *Fishing Boats of the World*. Fishing News, 1955.

———. *Fishing Boats of the World*. Vol. 2. Fishing News, 1960.

———. *Fishing Boats of the World*. Vol. 3. Fishing News, 1967.

Union Carbide Corporation. *Oxy-Acetylene Handbook*. 2d ed. New York: Union Carbide, Linde Division, 1960.

U.S. Coast Guard NVIC 7-95. *Guidance on Inspection, Repair, and Maintenance of Wooden Hulls*. Navigation and Vessel Inspection Circular (NVIC), 1995.

U.S. Coast Guard NVIC 8-87. *Notes on Design, Construction, Inspection and Repair of Fiber Reinforced Plastic (FRP) Vessels*. Navigation and Vessel Inspection Circular (NVIC), 1987.

U.S. Coast Guard NVIC 11-80. *Structural Plan Review Guidelines for Aluminum Small-Passenger Vessels*. Navigation and Vessel Inspection Circular (NVIC), 1980.

U.S. Coast Guard NVIC 7-68. *Notes on Inspection and Repair of Steel Hulls*. Navigation and Vessel Inspection Circular (NVIC), 1968.

U.S. Code of Federal Regulations. *Shipping— 46*. Washington DC: U.S. Government (GPO).

U.S. Department of the Navy. *Wood: A Manual for Its Use as a Shipbuilding Material*. Vols. 1–4. U.S. Department of the Navy, Bureau of Ships, 1957.

Vaitses, Allan H. *Boatbuilding One-Off in Fiberglass*. Camden ME: International Marine, 1984.

Walton, Keith R. *Designing and Building with Cored Composites*. Northvale NJ: Baltek Corporation.

Warren, Nigel. *Metal Corrosion in Boats*. Camden ME: International Marine, 1980.

White, Gerald Taylor, ed. *Problems in Small Boat Design*. Dobbs Ferry NY: Sheridan House/Society of Small Craft Designers, 1972.

INDEX